The dynamic characteristics of Christian churches in Nigeria present, in many ways, an ecclesiological model for the entire continent. Dr. Sunday Komolafe has produced a much needed publication for his own context which, while located in Nigeria, is actually much broader than Nigeria. This is because the story of mission history, cultural expressions of African church and the more contemporary "Pentecostal"- type movements in Nigeria all have great implications for West Africa and Africa as a whole. This precedent work shows the author's ability to synthesize historical, cultural and theological dimensions in the Nigerian church. I commend this book highly as a product of excellence and integrity.

Prof. Dean S. Gilliland
Professor Emeritus of Contextualized Theology and African Studies
Fuller Theological Seminary, School of Intercultural Studies
Pasadena, California, USA

The story of Christianity in Nigeria remains one of the most remarkable of modern times. In this detailed study, Komolafe examines major factors that have shaped the church in Nigeria from the beginning and provides a meaningful appraisal of contemporary transformations from a biblical perspective. The treatment is insightful and the analysis is fresh. A welcome addition to the growing body of African scholarship.

Prof. Jehu J. Hanciles
Brooks Chair of World Christianity, Candler School of Theology
Emory University, Atlanta-Georgia, USA

This is an impressive account of mission history, of the role of African culture and agency in the historical transmission of the Christian faith, of the understanding of the nature of the church, and of the different ecclesiastical paradigms that have emerged from different experiences, practices, and theological thinking. The book has made its mark as an important interpretative account of Christianity in Nigeria. It deserves to be read by scholars of African Christianity, Christian missions, and those interested in religious change in Africa.

Prof. Matthews A. Ojo
Department of Religious Studies
Obafemi Awolowo University, Ile-Ife, Nigeria

The Transformation of African Christianity

Development and Change in the Nigerian Church

Sunday Jide Komolafe

MONOGRAPHS

© 2013 by Sunday Jide Komolafe

Published 2013 by Langham Monographs
an imprint of Langham Creative Projects

Langham Partnership
PO Box 296, Carlisle, Cumbria CA3 9WZ, UK
www.langham.org

ISBNs:
978-1-907713-59-0 print
978-1-907713-60-6 Mobi
978-1-907713-61-3 ePub

Sunday Jide Komolafe has asserted his right under the Copyright, Designs and Patents Act, 1988 to be identified as the Author of this work.

All rights reserved. No part of this publication may be reproduced, stored in a retrieval system or transmitted, in any form or by any means, electronic, mechanical, photocopying, recording or otherwise, without the prior written permission of the publisher or the Copyright Licensing Agency.

All Scripture quotations, unless otherwise indicated, are from the HOLY BIBLE, NEW INTERNATIONAL VERSION®. Copyright © 1973, 1978, 1984 Biblica. Used by permission. All rights reserved worldwide.

British Library Cataloguing in Publication Data
Komolafe, Sunday.
The transformation of African Christianity : development and change in the Nigerian church.
1. Nigeria--Church history. 2. Church growth--Nigeria.
3. Mission of the church--Nigeria.
I. Title
276.6'9-dc23
ISBN-13: 9781907713590

Cover & Book Design: projectluz.com

Langham Partnership actively supports theological dialogue and a scholars right to publish but does not necessarily endorse the views and opinions set forth, and works referenced within this publication or guarantee its technical and grammatical correctness. Langham Partnership does not accept any responsibility or liability to persons or property as a consequence of the reading, use or interpretation of its published content.

For

Tobi, Tomi, and Toni

and

Jennifer (for her life-giving sacrifices)

Contents

Acknowledgments xv

Foreword xix

Introduction 1

PART I: PAST AS PROLOGUE: REASSESSING NIGERIA'S PRE-CHRISTIAN CULTURAL PAST 7

Chapter 1 9
   The Ferment of Nigeria's Pre-Christian Cultural Past
      Social Organization and Political System 9
         The Igbo Socio-Political Structure 9
         The Yoruba Socio-Political Structure 11
      The Roles of Secret Societies within the Socio-Political System 13
         The Ekpe Society 13
         The Ogboni Fraternity 14
      Polygamy, Marriage, and Family Life 16
      Socio-Political Economy 18
         Agriculture and Commodity Trade 18
         Domestic Slavery: The Anatomy of a Socio-Political Economy 20
         European Commercial Presence and its Effects on the
         Local Context 23
      Religious System 24
         Theology, Cosmology, and Anthropology: The Supreme God
         and Other Agencies 25
         Islamic Contact and the Process of Religious Change 28
      Summary 29

PART II: TRANSFORMING THE CONTEXT: THE PROTESTANT MISSIONS ERA IN NIGERIAN CHRISTIAN HISTORY, 1841-1918 31

Chapter 2 33
   The Early Christianization of Nigeria
      The Evangelical Revival and the Appeal of Foreign Missions 34
         The CMS of Great Britain 34
         The Southern Baptist Mission of North America 36
      Protestant Missionary Presence in Nigeria: Motives and Prospects 39
      Missions Along New Frontiers: The Yoruba and the Niger Missions 42

    The CMS Yoruba Mission..43
    The Southern Baptist Yoruba Mission 45
    The Niger Mission 47
  Missionary Encounter with a Non-Christian Context 51
  From Mission to Church: The Evolution of a Movement 53

Chapter 3 57
The Formation of an African Ministry
  Henry Venn and the Ideal of a Native Ministry as a Working Objective.....57
    Indigenizing the Episcopacy: The Bishopric Controversy 61
    Bishop Samuel Crowther: "The Symbol of a Race on Trial" 63
  The Hijacking of the Episcopacy and the Rise of Nigerian Nationalism...66
  The Southern Baptist Mission, its Ecclesiology and Structures of Ministry..70
  The Emerging Theology of the Church 74
    Evangelical Theology and the General Hermeneusis of the Gospel 74
    Personal and Social Transformation..76
  Protestant Missions, Ecclesiastical Colonialism, and Respectability 84
  Summary 89

PART III: RECLAIMING THE CONTEXT: THE RISE OF NIGERIAN INDIGENOUS CHURCH MOVEMENTS, 1918-1980S 91

Chapter 4 93
Nigerian Ecclesiastical Independency
  The Starting Point of Independency 94
    Missionary Ideologies and Activities 94
    From Ethiopianism to Independentism 95
  Prophetic Aladura Churches 100
  The Origins of the Aladura Churches..102
    The Precious Stone Society and Foreign Alliances 103
    The Great Revival of the 1930s 105
  The Context of Aladura Christianity 111
  The Ministry of the Aladura 114
    Worship 115
    Aladura Worship: Gateway of Paganism? 120
  The Theology of the Aladura 123
  Vernacularization, Interpretation, and Appropriation......................124
    Prayer 127
    Spiritual Power 129
  Summary 131

PART IV: MODERNIZING THE CONTEXT: THE
RECONSTRUCTIONIST CHRISTIANITY OF THE CHARISMATIC/
PENTECOSTAL MOVEMENTS, 1980S-2000S 133

Chapter 5 135
  Charismatic/Pentecostal Movements
    Charismatics and Pentecostals: A Historical Perspective 135
    The Making of Nigerian Pentecostalism: Sketching the Connections... 137
      Classical Pentecostals, 1918-1941 137
      The Charismatic Movement, 1944-1980s 139
      Neocharismatics, 1980s-2000s 143
    The Context of the Neocharismatic Churches 147
      The Cultural Dimension 147
      The Religious Dimension 148
      The Socio-Political Dimension 150
      The Economic Dimension 152
    The Ministry of the Neocharismatic Churches 154
      Koinonia: The Community of the Saved 154
      Evangelism: Propagating the Word 156
      Socio-Political Activism 157
    The Theology of the Neocharismatic Churches 160
      The Theme of Salvation 161
      Power Theology 167
    Summary 170

PART V: FROM THE MARGINS TO THE CENTER: THE POLITICAL
ORIGINS OF UNITY IN NIGERIAN CHRISTIANITY, 1960-1993 171

Chapter 6 173
  Reluctant Ecumenism: Historical Legacies of Christian Political Thoughts
    The Politicization of Religion in Modern Nigeria 174
      Fulani Hegemony and Ethnic Politicking: The Legacy of
      Usman Dan Fodio's Jihad 175
      The Colonial Factor in the Hausa-Fulani/Northern Hegemony... 177
    Self-Government and Political Imagination:
    The Religious Dimension 179
      The First Republic: The Religious Politics of
      Sir Ahmadu Bello, 1960-1966 180
      The Political Dimension of Christian Ecumenism:
      The Christian Association of Nigeria Since 1976 185
    Toward a Religio-Political Synthesis: The Constitutional Debates of
    1978 and 1988 190

  Toward the Second Republic: The First Constitutional Crisis of
  1978-1979..191
  Toward the Third Republic: The Babangida Era, 1985-1993 197
 Violent Faces of Religion: The Christian-Muslim Clashes 202

Chapter 7 211
 The Past in the Present: Toward Authentic Christian Ecumenism
  Early Attempts at Christian Unity in Nigeria 214
   The Formulation of Church Union: Impulses from the
   Missionaries...214
   African Agents: Their Roles and Contributions.........................218
   Interdenominational Cooperation 222
  Toward Authentic Christian Ecumenism..227
  Summary 229

PART VI: WHAT ON EARTH IS THE CHURCH?: AN EXPLORATION IN BIBLICAL UNDERSTANDING..231

Chapter 8 233
 The Relevance of a Biblical Starting Point
  Etymological Analysis of Biblical Presuppositions 234
   Ekklēsia in the Old Testament 235
   Ekklēsia in the New Testament 236
  Paul, Israel, and the Church 240
  Luke-Acts: The Primitive Church in Jerusalem................................241
   The Context of the Church..241
   Contextual Issues in the Jerusalem Church 245
  The Ministry of the Jerusalem Church 246
   Liturgical Life and Worship 247
   Harmony and Community Sharing...248
  The Theology of the Jerusalem Church 250
   The Jerusalem Church Council...250
   Facilitating Social Unity between Two Factions........................253

Chapter 9 255
 The Apostolic Churches as Models for Appropriate Ecclesiology
  Christianity in Rome 255
  The Church in Rome 256
   The Context of the Church..257
   Contextual Issues in the Roman Church....................................259
  The Ministry of the Roman Church...262
   Sacrificial Living as a Mark of Christian Ministry 263

Complementarity of Charismatic Ministry 263
The Theology of the Church 264
    Dynamics of a Coherent Christian Relationship 264
    Christ: The Point of Convergence 265
Christianity in Corinth 266
The Church in Corinth 267
    The Context of the Church: "A Tale of Two Cities" 267
    The Establishment and Composition of the Corinthian Church .. 269
    Contextual Issues in the Corinthian Church 271
    The Ministry of the Church 275
    The Theology of the Church 278
The Church in the Epistle to the Ephesians 281
Composition of the Church 283
    The Context of the Church 284
    The Ministry of the Church 286
    The Theology of the Church 292
Summary 299

PART VII: FOUNDATIONS FOR ORTHODOXY IN THE POST-APOSTOLIC CHURCH 301

Chapter 10 303
The Early Church and Hellenism
The Context of the Early Church 303
    The Religious Trends 304
    The Intellectual-Literary Trends 310
    The Socio-Political Trend 315
The Ministry of the Early Church 319
    Ecclesiastical Office as Ministry 319
    The Ideal of Martyrdom 325
    Missionary Orientation as Ministry 328
    Reasoned Defense as Ministry 331
The Theology of the Early Church 334
    Early Christian Worship 335
    The Development of the Liturgy 336
    Theological Developments in the Early Church 342
Summary 350

PART VIII: BETWEEN PAST AND FUTURE: TRANSFORMING
ECCLESIOLOGY IN TWENTY-FIRST CENTURY NIGERIA.................351

Chapter 11 353
   Toward a Biblical, Contextual, and Missional Ecclessiology in Nigeria
        The Hermeneutical Obligation to Context and Scripture...................356
            New Testament Ecclesiology as "Hermeneutical Key" to
            Biblical and Contextual Ecclesiology...357
            The Challenge of Hellenism as "Hermeneutical Key" to
            Biblical and Contextual Ecclesiology...360
        Theological-Hermenutical Framework for a Biblical and
        Contextual Ecclesiology in Nigeria..362
        Toward a Responsible and Missional Ecclesiology in Nigeria.............366
            Doxological Challenge 367
            Leadership Challenge..371
            Discipleship Challenge 374
            Intellectual/Theological Challenge 380
            Ethical Challenge..383
        Conclusion 389

Bibliography...393

Index...441

List of Figures

Figure 1 Transforming Ecclesiology: Three Epochs of Nigerian Christianity 5

Figure 2 Christian Transformational Change 355

Figure 3 The Contextualixation Continuum 363

Figure 4 The Hermeneutical Spiral of Contextual Ecclesiology 365

Figure 5 The Four Reference Points of a Missional Church 370

Figure 6 A Continuum of Faithful Discipleship 377

List of Tables

Table 1   Churches Attacked in the Kano Riots of
          October 30, 1982 206

Table 2   The Maitatsine Uprisings of 1980-1985 206

Table 3   Students and Religious Clashes of 1987-1988 207

Table 4   Ethno-Religious Clashes in Northern Nigeria,
          1980-1996 207

Table 5   Attacks Attributed to Boko Haram from
          2009 – December 2011 208

Acknowledgments

He is not wise who takes sole credit for a collaborative project. This work is certainly no exception and many thanks are due to more people than I could possibly mention by name. Some of them, however, have to be singled out. I am especially indebted to my mentor, Prof. Dean S. Gilliland, for theoretical insight and ongoing instruction and for sharing generously of his encyclopedic knowledge of missionary work in Nigeria. I am equally grateful to him for painstakingly reading through the entire manuscript and for transforming my "flowery language" into language that is understandable. Sir, you were diligent beyond measure. It is my prayer that I would be the type of mentor that you have been to me.

I am grateful to my doctoral committee members, Prof. Wilbert R. Shenk and Prof. Roberta R. King, and the late Prof. Ogbu Kalu, not only for stimulating my thinking but for being the theological think-tank from which I could bounce off my own ideas. Coming to Fuller Theological Seminary was God's answer to a desperate prayer of three years. I am most delighted that I was not disappointed. I studied under and was enriched by professors who continue in the legacy of world-class scholarship and intellectual discipline: Prof. Jehu Hanciles, Prof. Charles Van Engen, Prof. Charles Kraft, Prof. Dudley Woodberry, Prof. Dan Shaw, and Prof. Eddie Gibbs deserve special mention. I would like especially to thank Prof. Matthews A. Ojo for his careful reading, as well as his suggestions in upholding the integrity of this work.

Financial backing for my doctoral research came initially from the Foundation for Advanced Christian Training (FACT) and, subsequently, from the merger with John Stott Ministries (JSM). I am eternally grateful to the founder of FACT, Meritt Sawyer, for her missionary zeal and enthusiasm about my work. I have been exceptionally privileged to meet with Christian leaders who embody Christ-likeness and resolute commitment to the kingdom agenda for all peoples. Such was my encounter with The Revd (Dr.) John Stott of blessed memory. Affectionately called "Uncle John," he was God's General in every literal sense of the expression, yet he was a man who exuded uncommon grace and simplicity both in words and deeds. I am grateful to him and the board of JSM, for believing my research to be strategic enough for funding.

Projects of this nature would hardly see the light of day without the selfless assistance of research librarians and archivists. I am indebted to staff at the McAlister Library (Fuller Theological Seminary), CMS Archives (Birmingham University Library), and Archie van der Byl, academic computing coordinator (Fuller Theological Seminary), for his help with complex diagrams. I would also like to express my appreciation to Judi Brodeen and Gari-Anne Patzwald, research librarians (School of Intercultural Studies, Fuller Theological Seminary), and the staff and director of the Doctoral Studies Program (School of Intercultural Studies, Fuller Theological Seminary).

I am grateful to Dr. Dean Smith, the founding pastor of High Way Community at Palo Alto in San Jose. I am especially indebted for his unstinting support of my future teaching ministry in Nigeria through generous donations of books and other resources. I would also like to express my appreciation to the leadership and the members of Moraga Valley Presbyterian Church at Moraga Valley, San Francisco, for providing care and warmth in the last year of this project. Other people in New Zealand, my beloved adopted home, deserve to be mentioned. Pastors Les and Lynne Denton stand out as my family's staunchest encouragers and spiritual support. Pastor Luke Iwunze and his wife, Caroline, believed in this project right from the beginning and never ceased to pray for its successful completion. I am also proud and thankful that my quest for theological pursuit began at New Covenant International Bible College and Seminary in Auckland, New Zealand, under the combined leadership of Dr. Kevin Dyson and Pastor Bryan Johnson. I pray for the grace to serve God faithfully and selflessly as these men continue to do.

I am ever grateful to my family for their love and support. My aunt and her husband, Overseer and Deaconess J.O.K. Ajayi, sowed the seeds of my love for teaching when they encouraged me to enroll in teacher's college back in 1979. Little did they realize at the time that they were orchestrating the divine plan for my life. What I owe them is beyond measure. I have benefited immensely from the fervent and unrelenting prayer support of my mother, Deaconess F.M. Komolafe. I cannot express in words the sacrifice she has endured as a young widow. In her simple, yet profound theology, she chose to "remarry" Jesus, believing he would be much more than a stepfather to her children. I owe this blessing to her numerous intercessions.

This writing project was updated and completed during a moment of intense personal situation. I cannot but single out the following: Pastors Charles and Francesca Fajinmi of DIOS International Missionary Church in Los Angeles, for being my family's strongest supporters, for their continued prayer support, love, and generosity; Pastor Deji Oseni and his wife, Bose; Rotimi Ojo, Lai Olomola, Monisola Komolafe, and Banjo Ayeni for their unwavering friendship and support. I thank my siblings, Abayo, for his understanding and prayers; Esther (Bukky) and her husband, Femi, for their unparallel support and enthusiastic egging on. As a couple they provided a year-long of free accommodation, food, and emotional support during my time of sabbatical in Sydney, Australia. What I owe them is eternal.

I am most grateful to my three saving graces and cheerleaders, Tobi, Tomi, and Toni, for enduring my academic eccentricity and for creating an atmosphere conducive for writing. Most of all, like other missionary kids, they've been moved back and forth a few times but not once did they complain but instead exuded the most cheerful forbearance in their own way of "doing God's work." Therefore, I could not imagine coming to this moment of achievement without them. You rock guys!

Foreword

Sunday Komolafe's book, *The Transformation of African Christianity*, provides lucid missiological and historical interpretations of the nature of Christianity in Nigeria and the cultural and socio-political contexts it operated from the 1840s to the first decade of twenty-first century. The first half of the book made up of the first seven chapters examined the historical, socio-cultural, and ecclesiastical factors that have shaped Christianity in Nigeria, while the second half is a theological examination of the concept and nature of the church.

In the first half, by focusing on three ecclesiastical traditions, the mainline Protestant churches, the Aladura churches, and the Pentecostal/Charismatic movements, the author has excellently shown how the church, gospel, and culture have interacted over the past 170 years to shape Nigerian Christianity. Indeed, the transformation has occurred as Christianity re-ordered African traditional worldviews and as the doctrinal emphases and practices of the three ecclesiastical traditions influenced one another; all together producing continuous transformation of the faith, the structure of the church, and the contexts in which the faith operate. This transformation, according to the author, has not come to an end; it will definitely shape the future Nigerian church.

The second half reflects the ministerial interest of the author. In this regard, one finds that the book possesses both the theoretical contents for scholars as well as the practical perspectives for ministers of the gospel. The author is also sensitive and sympathetic to challenges the gospel has faced under changing circumstances in Nigeria. In fact, this sensitivity to the practical perspectives has largely informed the examination of the history of the early church as well as the biblical understanding of the church.

Indeed, the book explored the biblical understanding of the church by looking at the Christian church in the apostolic era, the contextual challenges it contended with in defining and maintaining orthodoxy, and the theological responses to these challenges. According to the author, this exploration is important because whatever the church means to Christians in the contemporary period cannot be separated from historical events that began in the primitive or earliest church. In this regard, the author deserves commendation for developing a transforming ecclesiology that is biblical, missional, and contextual for the church in contemporary Nigeria.

Certainly, this is an impressive account of mission history, of the role of African culture and agency in the historical transmission of the Christian faith, of the understanding of the nature of the church, and of the different ecclesiastical paradigms that have emerged from different experiences, practices, and theological thinking. The book has made its mark as an important interpretative account of Christianity in Nigeria. It deserves to be read by scholars of African Christianity, Christian missions and those interested in religious change in Africa.

Professor Matthews A. Ojo
Department of Religious Studies,
Obafemi Awolowo University,
Ile-Ife, Nigeria

Introduction

The story of Christianity in Nigeria reveals a tightly woven narrative of the process of beginnings, growth, and change. First, there were, and still are, the denominational churches of the Protestant mission era with their deep roots in Western forms and theology. Then arose the so-called African Indigenous Churches (AICs) that gave witness to religious independency and a more authentic kind of African thinking. And lastly, there have come the more eclectic Charismatic/Pentecostal churches, revealing both Western and contemporary African expressions. These can be described as a "continuum," where the past, with its older traditions, flows together with the present, epitomizing religious innovation in twenty-first century Nigeria.

These ecclesiastical variations have not been particularly helpful in suggesting a corresponding awareness of the essence of the church. A casual reader of Nigerian church history, for example, may sometimes puzzle over the reasons that theological platitudes of an earlier era could have gotten people so excited only to lose their effect later and, by so doing, lay the groundwork for new expressions with their particular values, beliefs, shapes, and forms.

In a context like Nigeria where religion has traditionally been associated with everyday needs and realities, it is appropriate to hypothesize that the context sets the boundaries within which the church has to function. Yet, regardless of what the church feels prompted to do more specifically within the context, her responsibility to address the ethos and the cultural values must be guided by the supra-cultural nature of Scripture. The complex task, therefore, is about engaging in a systematic ecclesiological reflection with responsibility to the dynamic interplay of church, gospel, and culture. The problem of where and how to begin the investigation is exquisitely problematic. This, however, is not a question of epistemology. Rather, it has much to do with understanding the ecclesiological task of what it means to be church in radically different contexts.

To begin the investigation from experience and then describe the church in Nigeria phenomenologically is to have a picture of the church in the framework of the context in which it lives. On the contrary, to examine the church from the perspective of historical theology is to benefit from insights into historical movements, agents that shaped the church, and the various changes through which it has passed. The latter seems to be the more probable approach given the fact that the theoretical concern of this book is about new insights in biblical, missional, and contextual ecclesiology for Nigeria.

Consequently, this work is an investigation of the historical, sociocultural, and ecclesiastical factors that have shaped Christianity in Nigeria. The title reflects the central issue quite accurately. With the aid of the word "transformation," the work is a systematic ecclesiological reflection on the extent to which the understanding and practice of "church" have changed during one and half centuries of Christianity in Nigeria. The transformation of theological paradigms, formed by three variations of ecclesiastical development, reveals the dynamic interplay of church, gospel, and culture from early mission history to the present African expressions.

Its method is as much provocative as narrative. It presents a chronological and relatively comprehensive history, ministry, and theology of the Nigerian church by highlighting certain peaks, valleys, and paradoxes in its evolution, while trying at the same time to situate these developments within an overarching biblical and historical framework of global Christianity. To facilitate this, two representative churches were selected from each of the three streams that make up Nigerian Protestant Christianity:

Protestant Missions:	Anglican Church Missionary Society (CMS)
	Southern Baptist Mission
African Independent:	Christ Apostolic Church (CAC)
	The Church of the Lord (Aladura)
Charismatic/Pentecostal:	Deeper Christian Life Ministry
	The Redeemed Christian Church of God

Selecting the above churches as representatives of their particular ecclesiastical tradition is not to overlook the fact that each stream can still be further expanded to include typologies of various kinds through a bogus church-by-church analysis. Instead the discussions on these selected *representative* churches have been synthetic both in form and character. This is because churches within a particular tradition generally demonstrate certain traits that are unique and specific to that ecclesiastical tradition.

The book is, however, not just an analysis of the process of beginnings, growth and change, but also suggests that this transformation has not yet come to an end. It demonstrates that the Nigerian church is poised at a "strategic inflection point" where discernible strengths and limitations are juxtaposed with a fresh articulation of the task and role of the church in twenty-first century Africa. To this end, "transformation" carries a double meaning. It depicts an essential feature of the Nigerian church, while also revealing genuine aspirations toward a renewed vision of the church that is contextual, biblical, and missional.

Divided into eight parts, part 1 begins with a reassessment of Nigeria's pre-Christian cultural past and the challenges this posed to the process of Christianization. Parts 2 to 4 take into account pertinent ecclesiological developments. These include the Western missionary paradigm that provided the theological framework for the emerging biblical, liturgical, and denominational structures, to the threshold of indigenous agitations for ecclesiastical independency and the reconstructionist agenda of Nigerian Neo-Pentecostals. Part 5 is different in orientation. It examines the fundamental aspects of Christian ecumenism that was set in motion in the markedly anti-Islamic rhetoric and the new political activism of the Christian Association of Nigeria (CAN).

Believing that one can understand what the church should be in contemporary times only when one has a thorough understanding of what the church has been or ought to be, parts 6 and 7 look to the past in the effort to draw inferences that might inform the contemporary in Christian thought and practice. Part 6 explores the biblical understanding of the church by looking at the apostolic churches of the first century as models for appropriate ecclesiology, while part 7 takes the quest for a biblical and contextualized ecclesiology further by drawing insights from the struggle for orthodoxy in the post apostolic era of the second and third centuries. Part 8 provides a synthesis of the evolution of the Nigerian church and a reflection on the future of the church and its ecclesiology. It considers the question, "where do we go from here?" as the church continues into the twenty-first century with a challenge to articulate a renewed vision of the nature, mission, and ministry of the church.

Constructed under the rubric of a textbook for use by pastors and in seminaries and universities, the book has both practical and theoretical sides. On one hand, it challenges the practitioner on the need to constantly engage in thought processes that provide interpretive framework for a contextual yet biblical way of doing church. On the other hand, the book provides the theorist with a missiological and theological compass to guide the work of theorizing, giving symmetry of understanding and interpretation in the ongoing appraisal of non-Western and global Christianities. In both cases, the approach throughout is intentionally inclusive rather than exclusive, while inviting reflection and dialogue rather than confrontation and conflict.

On the whole, the book is an evangelical, denominational ecclesiology done ecumenically and with sensitivity to the three ecclesiastical strands that make up Nigerian Protestant Christianity. An important missiological dimension of this book is that it is perhaps the first investigation of Protestant Christian history in Nigeria with the aim of providing interpretive framework for the way of doing church as Nigeria moves into the future. By calling attention to the role of Scripture in the task of the church, the value of past theological constructs for the twenty-first century, and the effect of Nigeria's pluralistic context on the contemporary mission of the church, the book shows that transformation is what "being the church" is truly about.

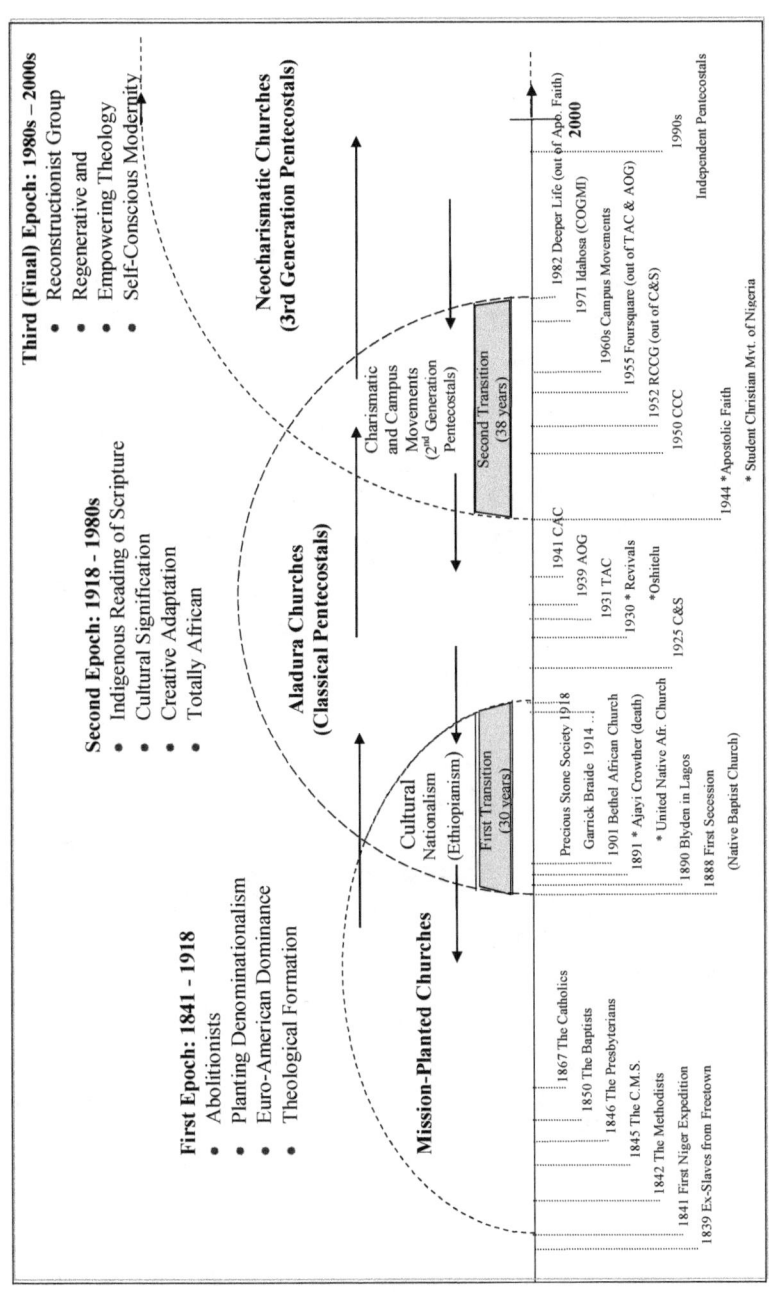

Figure 1
Transforming Ecclesiology:
Three Epochs of Nigerian Christianity

PART I

Past as Prologue: Reassessing Nigeria's Pre-Christian Cultural Past

The history of Christianity in Africa has usually been written within the context of missionary encounter with the indigenous culture and the subsequent influence of European cultural ideals. It is understandable, then, that several studies on Christian missions have emphasized the activities of Western-oriented missions and their policies. By contrast, however, little emphasis has been placed on how strongly the receiving culture can put its stamp on the invading religious system. This has been the limitation in previous studies of missions in Africa. Just how freely an imported structure can evolve "like some island isolate with no ecological interaction with other species" is an issue that is beginning to be taken seriously in African church history.[1]

We embark on this intellectual quest with the assumption that the church, by her calling and nature, exists at the center of the continuum between Scripture and context so that she functions as the subject examining the culture as well as being the object of that examination. Undergirding this section of this ecclesiological journey, therefore, is a simple thesis: namely, the construction and expression of faith in the present is contingent upon a synchronic link with Nigeria's pre-Christian cultural past. What I hope to do is to offer a broad reassessment of this cultural past and the challenges it posed to the missionary process of Christianization.

---

1. Michael Kearney, *World View* (1984:6).

CHAPTER 1

The Ferment of Nigeria's Pre-Christian Cultural Past

Projecting a normative view of Nigeria's cultural past is fraught with the danger of over-generalization. Nigeria, like most African nations, is a collection of different ethnicities fundamentally different in history, language, and even identity. Nevertheless, it is still possible to highlight some common features that form the template for understanding Nigeria's cultural past. As I do this, my aim is to point to those aspects of the pre-Christian context that posed the most significant challenges to the process of Christianization and tempered missionary penetration.

Social Organization and Political System

The following section examines briefly the socio-political structures of the two regional blocs that later came to be direct recipients of Protestant Christian Missions (the Igbo and the Yoruba) with a view to understanding how these structures shaped both individual and collective responsibilities.

The Igbo Socio-Political Structure
The absence of reliable written records makes it difficult to explore the history and ascertain the origins of the cultural values and political system of the Igbo people. The Igbo were not sufficiently numerous to be regarded an empire since they were a heterogeneous people divided into a very

large number of small village groups.¹ Each village was a small face-to-face society of lineages and clans. These village groups then formed the building blocks of the society and were arranged in a variety of ways to create varying degrees of autonomy in the loosely organized village democracies.

Characterized by these interrelations of different levels of kinship, territoriality, and allegiance, the Igbo concept of *Oha* represented the idea of the group and their way of life. *Oha* was far-reaching and extended to both the dead and the unborn. Although a "communal political culture" with emphasis on community life, the system recognized the individual as a unit whose identity and importance found full expression and strength in the common *umunna* (clan or larger family). The *umunna*, therefore, constituted a unifying autonomous and democratic body with the rights to its own government and decision-making. This system of Igbo democracy was closest to that of classical Greek city-states in which every adult male was entitled to direct and equal participation in the task of political decision making.²

The *ndi oha* (council of elders) exercised leadership and judicial authority within the *umunna*. This council was usually made up of the oldest members of individual families and villages. Its leadership and judicial power was a moral one and was self-regulatory with respect to group interest. In a pursuit of fairness and justice, an aggrieved person could appeal to a higher council representing a larger administrative unit of the village or a neutral village. In all cases, leadership at all levels of the social-political structure was based on general consensus of members and of the individuals concerned.

In the final analysis, the Igbo had no centralized political authority or unified hierarchies of political functionaries. What were observable in traditional Igbo society (which one still finds to some degree at the present time) were "pressure points of political power and authority rather than a

---

1. Although the socio-political structure was peculiar to the Igbo race and was much more prominent within the Igbo hinterland, my concern here is more on the political culture of the Igbo countries of east Niger (Efik, Ibibio, and the Ijo city-states). This region constituted the first contact with the Protestant Mission in the southeastern part of Nigeria.

2. For more information on the Igbo and their traditional political structure, see Michael Olisa, "Political Culture and Political Stability in Traditional Igbo Society" (1971:25).

recognizable center of such power and authority."³ As the bulwark of the Igbo social-political system, the *umunna* acted as the agency of socialization as well as the regulator of private and public life.

The Yoruba Socio-Political Structure

The Yoruba, unlike the Igbo, possessed considerable cultural homogeneity both in language and in the accounts of their origin. Their country occupied a wider zone that merged into non-Yoruba areas such as the kingdom of Benin to the east, Nupe and Borgu to the north, and the polities of the Ewe-Aja-Fon cluster (including Dahomey) to the west.⁴ Tracing their ancestry to a common progenitor in Oduduwa who set up his sons in the first Yoruba kingdoms, the Yoruba believe that later kingdoms were offshoots of the original families and as such were not wholly independent and autonomous regional systems.⁵

The Yoruba were organized in patrilineal descent groups that occupied village communities. However, these village groups were not an all-pervasive basis of Yoruba residential organization since the "Yoruba have long been known as an 'urban' people, living in large nucleated settlements."⁶ Rather, the term *ilu* (town or community) was the foundational concept of Yoruba political sociology. In view of their urbanized nature and because the political design of an *ilu* depended on the strength of its *oba* (king), allegiance to a paramount chieftain often replaced traditional loyalties to the clan.

The *oba* symbolized the unity of the *ilu* with a considerable centralization of authority placed on him. The *oba's aafin* (king's palace) was the *ilu's* distinct headquarters and its large resident population demonstrated the scope and dimensions of the king's political power. Among this large

---

3. Michael Olisa, "Political Culture and Political Stability in Traditional Igbo Society" (1971:23).
4. J.D.Y. Peel, *Religious Encounter and the Making of the Yoruba* (2000:28). For an early attempt at placing the Yoruba in a "wider-than-Yoruba zone," see I.A. Akinjogbin, *Dahomey and Its Neighbours, 1708-1818* (1967).
5. For further details on the history of the Yoruba, see Samuel Johnson, *The History of the Yoruba* (1921).
6. Here I am indebted to J.D.Y. Peel's excellent description of the Yoruba. For details, see his recent work *Religious Encounter and the Making of the Yoruba* (2000).

residential population were royal wives, slaves, messengers, priests, eunuchs, functionaries, and other dependents.[7] Some of these people were required to die with the *oba* so as to attend to his needs in the afterlife.

The *oba* combined his political and spiritual leadership in an inseparable fashion. As the spiritual and political head of the *ilu*, the *oba* was a quasi-divine personage (*ekeji orisa*, "companion of the deities") who had the primary responsibility of mediating with the *orisa* (deities) on behalf of his people. Although the town's *babalawo* (chief diviner) also functioned as a mediator between the gods and the people, his office was subordinate to the *oba's*. His duty was simply functionary, and he could only perform the necessary divination, sacrifices, and rituals to the gods on behalf of the *ilu* at the *oba's* orders.

Despite this expansive political and spiritual authority, the *oba* did not rule in isolation but was surrounded by a council of advisors, the chiefs or titleholders (*ijoye* or *oloye*, from *oye*, "title"). These were men or leaders who had been drawn from districts, villages, occupational groups or homesteads with some political relationships to the central government. The *ijoyes* (chiefs or titleholders) would perform the stabilizing functions of preventing imperial rule from becoming despotic while ensuring at the same time that royal subjects did not become insubordinate.

The Igbo and the Yoruba, including the various peoples of Nigeria, had at least one thing in common, namely secret societies. These societies exercised an overriding influence that was feared by the people because of the belief that they incorporated or embodied the spirits of the dead. The most important influence being the mystical quality they gave to secular leadership.

---

7. For details, see G.J.A. Ojo, *Yoruba Palaces* (1966).

The Roles of Secret Societies within the Socio-Political System

Secret societies were a valuable instrument of social control within the political system. Although they did not function as a central institution of government, they possessed clearly defined obligations of formalizing and enforcing community authority. They represented a political channel through which supernatural powers operated within the human space ("canalizing supernatural power"),[8] and their influence was reinforced by the strong religious and mystical sanctions they provoked.

The Ekpe Society

In a number of ethnic groups of southeastern Nigeria, *Egbo*, or more correctly the *Ekpe*, was the most important institution of government. Among the Efik of Calabar and the eastern and northern central Ibibio, the *Ekpe* society was the primary traditional cult and a rallying point for the people on social and religious issues. As Kannan Nair has observed, "unless the king was head of *Ekpe*, or at least an important member of it, he had no greater authority in the society than other titled members."[9] In other words, the king's authority was vested in his membership and position within the *Ekpe* cult.

The cult wielded so much political power such that early independent observers described it as the "legislature and police establishment of Old Calabar."[10] Instead of the traditional council of town heads exercising political authority, "the upper grades of *Ekpe* formed the nucleus of what became known as the king's council or cabinet."[11] This *Ekpe* elite group was the "cosmopolitan little republic" that exerted imperial rule over many of the markets in the hinterland and in other Delta city-states.

---

8. This was K.L. Little's way of describing the incursion of gods in the affairs of humans. For details, especially as it relates to his account of the working of Mende secret societies among the peoples of Liberia, Sierra Leone, and other related countries, see his work "The Role of the Secret Society in Cultural Specialization" (1960:199-213).
9. See his work, *Politics and Society in South Eastern Nigeria: 1841-1906* (1972:19).
10. Beecroft's letter to Palmerston, October 27, 1851. CMS, F. O. 84/858. CMS Archives.
11. Kannan Nair, *Politics and Society* (1972:19).

Most of these secret societies were dominated by male membership. Yet even when membership was composed mainly of women, the same political influence was exerted. A good example was the *Ebre* secret society among Ibibio women. The society represented the ideology of symbolic identification, democratic equality, and juridical accountability among its members. West of the Niger, the *Mo* among the people of Onitsha, was equally so powerful that it exercised control over the government of the region.

The Ogboni Fraternity

One of Nigeria's most prominent traditional societies, without doubt, was the *Ogboni* fraternity among the Yoruba. Although it generally represented principles of paramount authority throughout Yoruba country, it was most prominent among the Egba and the Ijebu.[12] The Ogboni was a conclave of old and influential men, and, in exceptional cases, a few old women who could be trusted to keep the secrets of the society. The material symbols of their authority were small brass figures, *edan*, one male and the other female. These had symbolic and instructive meanings and could invoke a fearful effect when sent to summon an offender.

The cult held wide political and judicial power, with major capacity of a governmental organ for preserving and executing law and order. For example, the cult acted as an advisory council and provided checks to royal powers. It also prevented royal power from becoming repressive while ensuring that citizens or royal subjects did not become insubordinate. As Biobaku has observed, the Ogboni "constituted at once the civic court, the town council, and electoral college for the selection of *Oba* [king] from candidates nominated by the ruling houses."[13] As part of its juridical

---

12. The most detailed account of the *Ogboni* cult, especially among the Egba and Ijebu, has been recorded in the works of O. Saburi Biobaku: *The Egba and their Neighbours: 1842-1872* (1957); and "An Historical Sketch of Egba Traditional Authorities" (1952). See also Peter Morton-Williams' work, "The Yoruba Ogboni Cult in Ọyọ" (1960); J.F. Ade Ajayi, *Christians Missions in Nigeria* (1965); E.A. Ayandele, *The Missionary Impact on Modern Nigeria* (1966); and Geoffrey Parrinder, *Religion in an African City* (1953).

13. O. Saburi Biobaku, *The Egba and Their Neighbours: 1842-1872* (1957:6).

influence within the political system, the Ogboni house was a school of jurisprudence as well as a court and a prison for convicted criminals.

The members of the Ogboni constituted a strong fraternity. Its operations were shrouded in impenetrable secrecy and members swore blood oaths to ensure solidarity and allegiance to collective decisions. *Oro*, the cult society of the ancestors symbolized by the bull-roarer, was the executive arm of the Ogboni. The *Oro* was used to proclaim curfews and confine women and nonmembers indoors when there was business to carry out.

Despite the political and juridical functions of the Ogboni as perceived by the natives, early European observers had mixed reactions to the actual role of the cult within the socio-political system. A good example was Samuel Ajayi Crowther. Also of Yoruba descent, Crowther was a freed slave-boy who later became one of the most prominent African agents and ministers of the Church Missionary Society (CMS).[14] He observed that the Ogboni cult was "an established religion of government, which is the worship of the dead or their deceased ancestors."[15] In 1859 when concerns were raised by some CMS missionaries about converts taking up Ogboni membership, several of them, including some African agents who had been initiated, gave moral weight to the civic virtue of the cult. The result was the Parent Committee's minute:

> as the system of Ogboni is of the nature of a political institution and has existed from remote antiquity as a recognized power in the state, it is entitled to some degree of public respect even from those who separate themselves from it. It will be right, therefore, to avoid open opposition to the system.[16]

Reconceptualizing the moral and political benefits of the Ogboni was not particularly a convincing one. There were still disturbing concerns about its political autonomy. An attempt to resolve this ambivalence was

---

14. A British society founded in 1799 by Anglican laymen.
15. Samuel Ajayi Crowther to T.J. Hutchinson, September 10, 1856. CMS Archives.
16. Minutes of the Parent Committee on the Ogboni System, November 23, 1861. CMS, CA2/L3. CMS Archives.

made in 1865 when Chichester Fortescue of the Select Committee asked C.A. Gollmer what the Ogboni Society was really about. Gollmer did not deny that the Ogboni Society had "great political power," and that the judicial system successfully answered the people's purpose. His conviction, however, was that "they are the counterpart of freemasonry; they are a secret society; no one knows what they are except those who are initiated."[17]

As it later turned out, this confusion beclouded these early Europeans in their respective policies and responses towards indigenous people. But the most difficult practice for them to comprehend was the traditional marriage and family system and its distinctively polygamous nature.

Polygamy, Marriage, and Family Life

An important feature of traditional Nigerian marriage was its communal aspect.[18] Marriage provided the mechanism whereby alliance between groups, and the kinship groups for which they were part, were drawn into relations with each other. It was this group relationship that regularized sexual unions and only in a limited aspect as a union between two individuals. It was also fundamental to the social construction of family life that marriage was potentially polygamous, so that men were free to enter into plural marriages without legal restriction.

This polygamous system of marriage, which seems to have become subservient to Western marriage ideal, was a distinctive characteristic of pre-Christian Nigeria. Its general recognition provided sufficient grounds for marital and societal stability. It was not a moral problem as early European observers portrayed it to be. Rather, it was an honorable system

---

17. Report of the Select Committee on the State of British Settlement in West Africa, *Parliamentary Paper* (1865), vol. 1. See the evidence of C.A. Gollmer on pages 241-242. See especially questions 5944, 5954, and 5955, and their respective answers.

18. Arthur Phillips has edited a useful historical account of African marriage and family life and of the attitude of the Christian Church to its salient features. See his work, *Survey of African Marriage and Family Life* (1953). See especially part 3 by Lyndon Harries on "Christian Marriage in African Society," pp. 329-456.

that provided a degree of social absorption into a respectable class with certain amount of privileges.

As the preferred form of marriage, polygamy provided certain social significance. The multiple possessions of mates provided the framework by which a man's wealth or influence was socially recognized. In order words, by identifying himself as head of households, the polygamist validated his right of access into social elderhood. Consequently, it was not uncommon for ordinary men to have two wives while the aristocrats and warlords had numerous women.

Women, for their part, were usually cooperative. Encouraged by the set system of ranking in order of marriage, the first wife usually persuaded or gave moral solidarity to the husband for additional marriages. To her, plural marriages were not an invitation to bickering or rivalry. Rather they provided the opportunity to earn a position of honor and prestige as the chief wife and "mother of the house." This privileged position of responsibility meant that she enjoyed the husband's confidence in a particular way.

In its economic aspect the home served as the primary unit of production and property. Consequently, polygamy was a socially recognized way to increase the work force. An increase in the number of wives meant an increase in the strength of adult labor. Similarly, multiple wives ensured the promise of additional children whose primary future roles would be to increase the family's productivity and acquisition of property. Thus the social anatomy of the institution of polygamy held the symbolic key to admission into the hierarchical polity of the rich and powerful.

Conversely, the monogamist was disadvantaged in the social order since his sphere of authority remained on the periphery of a single household. For the average Nigerian man, therefore, monogamy received little honor. It implied an inability to afford more than one wife. This provided powerful incentive to the aspirations of the average Nigerian man who wanted to measure up to social recognition.

Unfamiliar with the dynamics of such a marriage system, early European observers (especially the missionaries) found it difficult to distinguish between regularized polygamy and individual promiscuity. In their opinion, a polygamist was a sinner who had little or no control over his sexual impulses. And the pervasiveness of the institution meant it was considered the greatest obstacle to the acceptance of the Christian faith. The insistence on monogamy by these European missionaries, and its repudiation by Nigerians as an unacceptable Western imposition, set the stage for an enduring cultural conflict.

Socio-Political Economy

Much of the emphasis on African economic history has been on the trade with Europeans. Although this encounter was of great historical importance, European economic contact with West Africa, at least before 1880, was essentially peripheral to local economic activities. As Flint has observed, "it was the local economy which dominated the lives of the people, created the surpluses needed to provide for traders and craftsmen, the maintenance of kingship, ruling oligarchies and the state."[19] For the purpose of this discussion, however, I will focus on the economic system of Nigeria and the socio-political implications of European economic contact.

Agriculture and Commodity Trade

Consistent with the culture of social recognition and respect, each family or society was expected to be economically self-sufficient and able to feed its members. The first consideration in this respect is the agricultural economy which provided the much-needed surpluses for population growth, accumulation of wealth, and the development of large-scale social and political institutions. Even when farming was not the primary economic activity, most Nigerian societies supplemented their primary economy with a secondary one, such as farming, with the purpose of providing for what was not available locally. These were intercommunity commodity exchanges that were not to be thought of as simple barter, but as organized trading economy with considerable complexity.

---

19. J.E. Flint, "Economic Change in West Africa in the Nineteenth Century" (1974:390). Flint's work is a call for an engagement with the economic history of West Africa, an aspect that has received little attention.

The pre-Christian Yoruba country represented a good example of what may be regarded as primarily an agricultural economy. The real basis of their life was farming and nearly all Yoruba were engaged in farming of some kind. Although known to be city-dwellers, Yoruba cities were not really non-farm areas since there were always pockets of farmlands around them. Those with farms in more distant districts maintained temporary residence in farm huts during the height of the agricultural season, returning to their permanent dwellings in the city once harvesting was over. Specialized craft production and intercommunity trading provided the necessary supplement to the agricultural economy. This provided the interdependence necessary for economic and social stability.[20]

Unlike the Yoruba, the economy of the Igbo, especially those of the Niger Delta, was primarily a trading economy. Subsistence farming was practiced only to the degree that the environment made this possible. The Igbo, for example, cultivated yams as their staple crop. Due to the poor quality of their soil, and also the overpopulation that stretched available resources, the Igbo developed handicrafts and commercial skills that turned them into a prominent trading community. The Ijo and Efik areas of the Niger Delta, on their part, traded in palm oil, the most lucrative commodity to be obtained along the West Coast. In addition to trading in palm oil, many Ijo communities also engaged in fishing and salt-processing. The result was that surpluses were such that the people would export salt and fish to the hinterland in return for agricultural produce.[21]

The wealth and power that had been experienced in the Delta, however, had been at the expense of their neighbors, the densely populated Igbo hinterland. And with European commercial presence in the region, it was only a matter of time before this local economy went through revolutionary changes with respect to the article of trade. Although the first European visitors came in the late fifteenth century, the eighteenth century became a turning point in the economic activities of the Niger Delta.

---

20. For a good examination of Yoruba city life and their economy, see William Bascom's "Urbanization Among the Yoruba" (1960:255-267).

21. For further discussions on the trade and pattern of political change among the coastal peoples of the Niger Delta, see K.O. Dike, *Trade and Politics in the Niger Delta, 1830-1885* (1956); and G.I. Jones, *The Trading States of the Oil Rivers* (1963).

The European traders were not so much interested in fish and salt but in importing labor for the Americas. Since slave trade was the only kind of foreign trade open to the peoples of Niger Delta during this era, exporting slave labor became the economic response to the unusual growth that was already stretching the productivity of the land. Many people migrated to the coast to take advantage of the growing European trade. In a similar way, old fishing villages developed into the trading city-states of the Delta.[22] Not only did the population and wealth of these states depend on the new trade, it dominated their lives to the extent that the region became West Africa's largest slave exporting area.

As it later turned out in all of southern Nigeria (East and West), slavery became the most crucial element in domestic economy both for local labor and for export. These changes in local economy also brought with it revolutionary changes in the political sphere. These were socio-political changes that would later become a turning point in the history of West Africa, and indeed Nigeria.

Domestic Slavery: The Anatomy of a Socio-Political Economy

Modern arguments about the conceptual approaches to the study of slavery in African history are as problematic as the debates besetting the very nature of African slavery itself. Yet current syntheses reflect the different schools of thought that influence individual opinions. J.D. Fage has summarized the three views that were widely held, at least until the late 1960s: (1) that the institution of slavery was endemic in, and a natural feature of, indigenous West African society, providing an immediate market for foreign demands, (2) that it was the external demands for labor which led to a great growth of the institution of slavery thus corrupting its indigenous society, (3) that the external demand for slaves became so considerable that that there was a disastrous effect on its population.[23]

---

22. J.F. Ade Ajayi, *Christian Missions in Nigeria, 1841-1891: The Making of a New Élite* (1965:5).
23. See his work, "Slavery and the Slave Trade in the Context of West African History" (1969).

Frederick Cooper has also ably summarized the different approaches to the problems of African slavery in the 1970s. He has identified (1) the "absorptionist analysis" expounded by social anthropologists Suzanne Miers and Igor Kopytoff, (2) the "economic analysis" of A.G. Hopkins, and (3) the "Marxist analysis" of Claude Meillassoux. In his own addition, Cooper observes the polarities that exist between Africanists and Americanists who he claims "are studying slavery in isolation from one another."[24]

In a later study that focuses on the servile systems of Asia and Africa, Martin Klein argues that the two continents have much in common with the American experience, particularly in the efforts to control labor and family life.[25] In light of all these, my intention is not to add to the ongoing debates. Rather, what I hope to do is to present a descriptive sketch of domestic slavery in Nigeria as part of the historical processes of the local context before the contact with the Europeans, particularly in the overall efforts to Christianize Nigeria.

Although it is difficult to describe or define with certainty the origins of slavery among the different peoples of Nigeria, it was, nevertheless, an institution of pervasive importance. In its economic and cultural dimensions, slavery was not mainly a servile institution, but one that fed on the need to enlarge one's kinship group, and the desire to have servants and dependents. In 1860, for example, Consul Brand described slavery as a peculiar part of the people's ideas of social system. According to him, "the principal chiefs round the king are the king's slaves, the subordinate chiefs are the slaves of the superior and so on down to the lowest grade of society so that with the single exception of the king every Lagos man or woman has some one to look up to as master."[26]

---

24. Frederick Cooper, "The Problem of Slavery in African Studies" (1979:120). For the works of Suzanne Mier and Igor Kopytoff, see *Slavery in Africa: Historical and Anthropological Perspectives* (1977). For A.G. Hopkins, see *An Economic History of West Africa* (1973); and for Claude Meillassoux, see *The Development of Indigenous Trade and Markets in West Africa* (1971).

25. Martin Klein, *Breaking the Chains: Slavery, Bondage, and Emancipation in Modern Africa and Asia* (1993).

26. Percy A. Talbot, *The Peoples of Southern Nigeria* (1969:699).

To a large extent, therefore, the object in buying a slave was more often for prestige than for wealth. Slave owing was a privilege usually enjoyed by the rich and powerful. In the case of a chief or king whose problem of control required obtaining a large personal following, slave-owning conferred such social prestige and political influence.

People fell into slavery in various ways. One way was through the result of a judicial procedure. In situations where there were no police forces or prisons in which to isolate offenders who were likely to imperil the community, slavery was a ready answer. A good example was a case in point at Ijaye where "*Are* Kurunmi once enslaved a boy for putting the town in danger by insulting a mask of Egungun, the ancestral cult which he took very seriously."[27] Perhaps a more common way was through coercive acts of war. Prisoners of wars automatically became slaves and served a great variety of needs. Unless ransomed, a slave remained in servitude or was sold.

Seen from the perspective of their economic and socio-political value, slaves served a great variety of needs. They provided the major source of labor for the family units. In most cases, slaves were not set to do any one particular thing. Instead, their functions were diversified according to the career of their owners and by the prevailing occupation within a particular region. In the Niger Delta, for example, slaves conducted most of the trade, whereas the slaves in Yorubaland worked on plantations, or as domestic help and courtiers to royals and warlords.

Despite their servile roles, an important feature of domestic slavery uncongenial to the chattel slavery operated by westerners was its apparent liberality. In some regions, slaves were generally well treated. The Ijaw, especially the Kalabari, were known to treat their slaves extremely well. The same was the case with the neighboring Igbo. A slave who "proved himself industrious was not only allowed to marry a daughter of the house but was often chosen to succeed him as chief, in preference to the former's sons, when these were esteemed less capable of looking after and bettering the fortunes of the clan."[28] A good example of such rise to prominence was the

---

27. J.D.Y. Peel, *Religious Encounter and the Making of the Yoruba* (2000:63).
28. Percy A. Talbot, *The Peoples of Southern Nigeria* (1969:700-701).

well-known Jaja of Opobo, a one-time slave who rose in status to become the king of Opobo.

Overall, slaves could be integrated into the respective family units they served and, on a broader scale, could be integrated into the larger society and be allowed to contribute to political debates. Female slaves, for example, could obtain their freedom and be integrated into the social polity by marrying free men. Their male counterparts were allowed to work simultaneously for their own benefit as well as for their masters. As such, a well-placed and hardworking slave could earn enough to buy his own freedom. The most influential, however, were those taken into the personal retinues of royals and warlords. These were slaves with special privileges and influences far above the mass of the free population in the socio-political hierarchy.

In a letter to the CMS, Crowther wrote to stress how different the African was from the Euro-American slavery. According to him, "the slaves and masters in this (Africa) country live together as a family; they eat out of the same bowl, use the same dress in common and in many instances are intimate companions, so much so that, entering a family circle, a slave can scarcely be distinguished from a free man unless one is told."[29] As such, domestic slavery had not always been an intolerable condition. With the presence of European commercial interests, however, there also emerged revolutionary changes in local socio-economic patterns.

European Commercial Presence and its Effects on the Local Context

As I have already mentioned, European merchants were not simply interested in trading their goods for local produce. More important to them was acquiring African labor for their plantations. As European demand for labor for the Americas increased, so also came changes to indigenous features. The Delta hinterland, which by this time was witnessing an

---

29. Crowther to Venn. CMS, CA2/031, March 4, 1857. CMS Archives.

increasing Igbo population, thought it economically expedient to export slave labor to decongest the already overstretched land.

The Benin also began exchanging their slaves for European firearms in a bid to exert political control around the region. Likewise the Yoruba found the trading of slaves for firearms and other European goods to be economically and politically rewarding. Patterns of economic relationships with Europeans changed to the extent that by the nineteenth century the overseas slave trade had virtually taken over other legitimate trade in palm-oil, cocoa, rubber, cotton, and other agricultural produce.

The impingement of external trade on the local context changed the socio-political and economic activities of the different regions in no small measure. Bitter internecine warfare and increased internal social polarization resulted from the scramble for slaves for the lucrative human market. Local chiefs and kings captured and sold slaves for the express purpose of personal enrichment and for consolidating their power by building large empires. The Ashanti, Oyo, and Dahomeans were three examples of communities that thrived on this new economy.

It is obvious from the foregoing sketch that commercial slavery, which evolved under the influence of European demand for labor, was not a natural feature of domestic slave system. Rather, African involvement was an economic response and used to "strengthen streams of economic and political development that were already current before the Atlantic slave trade began."[30]

Religious System

It goes without saying that African societies had their respective religious systems that pre-dated Western theological encounter. However, unlike Western religious systems that have been reduced to a set of systematized doctrines, the Nigerian religious system was inextricably linked to its culture. Embedded deeply within the socio-cultural and ritual fabric of the

---

30. J.D. Fage, "Slavery and the Slave Trade in the Context of West African History" (1969:404).

people, this religious system presented the visible expression of Nigerians' underlying values and general beliefs about metaphysical order and temporal realities.

Although it is difficult to make generalized statements about the fundamental philosophy underlying the religious manifestations of the different Nigerian people groups, certain intellectual expressions of religious thought can be identified. These included, among others, three important aspects—theology (God), cosmology (world), and anthropology (humanity).[31] These three formed concentric circles that harmonized to give understanding to the indigenous spirituality.

Theology, Cosmology, and Anthropology: The Supreme God and Other Agencies

Several unfortunate distortions have attended scholarly enquiries about this aspect of Nigerian religious system. This confusion has arisen as a result of different presuppositions of the relation of the deities to the world. That is, between the one Creator God and the pantheon of other lesser gods and spirits. The conception of the existence of God among Nigerian peoples was not a European construction. Rather, it constituted an undeniable part of the people's understanding and interpretation of the cosmos. Among the Igbo, for example, God was and remains *Chukwu* or *Chineke* (the Creator). Commenting on the religious ideas of the Igbo in his report on the 1841 Niger Expedition, Ajayi Crowther observed:

> The Ibos are in their way a religious people, the word "Tshuku" [Chukwu] God, is continually heard. Tshuku is supposed to do everything. . . . Their notions of some of the attributes of the Supreme Being are in many respects correct and their manner of expressing them striking. "God made everything. He made both white and black," is continually on their lips. It is their common belief that there is a certain place or town where

---

31. I have found Joachim Wach's designations to be quite helpful in summarizing religious experiences and expressions in most societies (God, world, and humanity). In this regard I have borrowed and adapted his line of thinking. See his work *Sociology of Religion* (1944).

Tshuk dwells, and where he delivers his oracles and answers inquiries. Any matter of importance is left to his decision, and people travel to the place from every part of the country.[32]

The Yoruba were no less realistic about God. He was and is still believed to be the Creator of the universe (*Eleda*). God is also associated with heaven or the sky (*Ọrun*) from which the name *Ọlorun* ("Lord of Heaven," or "Owner of the sky") was derived. His attributes and conceptions among the locals were theologically comparable to those of biblical Christianity.[33]

Lesser gods, spirits, and the ancestral cults also occupied their respective spaces within the Nigerian religious universe. On one hand, these lesser divinities were spiritual agencies of the Supreme God. As part of their functional roles, they were considered to be more involved in everyday religious experience of the people and as such received direct worship. Nevertheless, Nigerians never mistook their place for a subordinate one. On the other hand, the ancestors were the progenitors, who, although physically dead, continue to live on in the spirit world. They are believed to visit the earth regularly, taking on the form of the Egungun[34] and Oro spirits, or as reborn in the persons of their descendants.[35]

These ancestors were thought not to be far away but watching over their families. And because of the relationship between the living and the dead, continuing mutual exchanges were maintained at all times. The pattern of this relationship varied considerably from region to region. However, its main characteristic usually involved the erection of ancestral shrines where sacrifices and acts of invocation were substantial provisos for exploiting the ancestors' continued solidarity and adjudication with the Supreme Being.

---

32. Journals of Schön and Crowther, pp. 50-53.

33. A dominant and relevant literature in this regard is Bolaji Idowu, *Olódùmarè: God in Yorùbá Belief* (1962). Idowu's work is an attempt at maximizing the area of possible agreement between Christianity and Yoruba culture.

34. The Egungun, among the Yoruba, are known as *ara ọrun*, "denizens of heaven." For a detailed account of the ancestral spirituality among the Igbo, see Ogbu Kalu, "Ancestral Spirituality and Society in Africa" (2000:54-84).

35. J.D.Y. Peel, *Religious Encounter and the Making of the Yoruba* (2000:174).

Although the boundary between the Supreme God and these other intermediaries was undoubtedly a blurry one, in the categorical distinction of divine hierarchy, the Supreme God remained in a class all by himself. T.J. Bowen, the pioneer missionary of the Southern Baptist expressed his observation in the distinction between the indigenous conception of God and the pantheon of native idols and other agencies in no ambiguous terms,

> Polytheism has no existence in Sudan [Nigeria], nor yet in Guinea. The objects which they worship are not regarded as God; they are not even called gods, but by other names to distinguish them from God. In Yoruba many of the notions which the people entertain of God are remarkably correct. They make him the efficient, though not always the instrumental, Creator. They have some notion of his justice and holiness and they talk much of his goodness, knowledge, power and providence. . . . They may extol the power and defend the worship of their idols, whom they regard as mighty beings, but they will not compare the greatest idol to God.[36]

A converging point for the worship of the Supreme God and his many intermediaries was in the sacramental system. For this reason, there was a wide range of symbolisms that acted as an index finger to both the material and metaphysical realities. These symbols were not merely shorthand descriptions of what reality is, "but they also shape the world to conform with this reality."[37] In this respect, the symbols acted as a form of social control by which the collective consciousness of the individual was awakened. These mythical symbols and their ritual acts were believed to have harmonizing effects, mediating peace between the individual, the society, and ultimately with the mysterious-metaphysical realm.

---

36. T.J. Bowen, *Adventures and Missionary Labours in Several Countries in the Interior of Africa from 1849-1856* (1968:310).
37. For a detailed discussion of symbolism in African religions, see Benjamin C. Ray's excellent work, *African Religions: Symbol, Ritual, and Community* (1976).

Despite this categorical distinction, a large percentage of early European missionaries in Nigeria insisted that the African mind was incapable of constructing theological discourse about God. Instead, they held the contradictory opinion that theistic trace identifiable in the fabric of the African culture was a mere illusionary concept with no substantive position in the people's religious experience and spirituality. Whether or not the culture was illusionary, the basic pattern of indigenous religious system was well established. For any invading religion to attempt to disrupt or uproot it, such a religion was bound to test the strength of its own forces or adaptability. It is from this perspective that Islam, the first alien religion to have contact with the ancient religions of Nigeria, must be examined.

Islamic Contact and the Process of Religious Change

This is not an attempt to write the history of Islam in Nigeria nor is it concerned with highlighting the scope of conversion to Islam. In the context of the overall interest of this book to describe the pre-Christian past of Nigeria, my discussion on Islam is only to the extent of outlining those aspects that made the adoption of Islam less problematic than Christianity. In other words, what were the psychological aspects of "dialogue" that made the accommodation of Islam less complicated than those of Christianity?[38]

The spread and assimilation of Islam into Nigeria is believed to have been in two phases. The first phase was its introduction to Bornu and Hausa states in the fourteenth and fifteenth centuries. Influenced by learned clerics and the widely-traveled Muslim traders, the Hausa-Borno contacts with Arab-Muslim culture predated the part of Northern Nigeria called the "middle belt" by some 200-400 years.[39] The second phase, however, was a secondary development, arising from internal *jihad* led by Uthman Dan Fodio in 1804 as well as by Fulani clerics and Hausa traders.

---

38. For historical studies on the development of Islam in Africa, and of early contact with African religion, see the works of Dean S. Gilliland, *African Religion Meets Islam* (1986); J. Spencer Trimingham, *Islam in West Africa* (1959); and *The Influence of Islam Upon Africa* (1968). See also I.M. Lewis, *Islam in Tropical Africa* (1966); J. Greenberg, *The Influence of Islam on a Sudanese Religion* (1946); and Peter B. Clarke, *West Africa and Islam* (1982).

39. Dean Gilliland, *African Religion Meets Islam* (1986:4).

Although an alien religion, Islamic elements were harmonized with indigenous socio-religious systems such that the possibility of its voluntary acceptance was increased. Following what Spencer Trimingham refers to as the processes of *germination, crisis,* and gradual *reorientation,* Islam made no far-reaching demands either in change of outlook or mode of life.[40] Its method of worship was simple and free. In a way parallel with indigenous material culture, Islamic teachers allowed such elements as the wearing of amulets and ornaments even though these practices were not specifically Islamic. Perhaps the greatest psychological aspect in the voluntary acceptance of Islam was in its adoption of key institutions such as polygamy and bride-price.

It should be mentioned, however, that while the Muslim malams stressed features parallel to indigenous system, Islamic educators counterbalanced this pragmatic adaptability with doctrinal teachings and legal foundations.[41] As the two religious systems existed side-by-side, overtime local religious features became weakened, giving way to almost total assimilation of Islamic elements. The implication was that Islam forged a synthesis that gave it a new status as an African religion.

Summary

I have explored briefly those aspects of the pre-Christian cultural past that formed the worldview of Nigerian peoples. If the role of the context is as important as I say it is, it must follow that the process of Christianization must be cognizant not only of the reordering of a non-Christian worldview but, more importantly, of identifying those cultural bridges that make the work of mission more effective and almost non-alien in outlook. This was, without doubt, the approach adopted by Islamic preachers.

---

40. With respect to the process of religious and culture change, Trimingham's analysis is a classic to which I am greatly indebted. See his works, *Islam in West Africa* (1959); and *The Influence of Islam upon Africa* (1968). For an analysis of the interaction between Hausa traditional religion and Islam, and the developmental stages of Islam in Hausaland, see Gilliland, *African Religion Meets Islam* (1986).
41. Jeff Haynes, *Religion and Politics in Africa* (1996:33).

To simply say that Christianity came into a context where the totality of life was already fixed, therefore, is to minimize the complexity of the ecclesiological task. It was one thing for the Christian church to repeatedly claim to have clear and compelling hermeneutical insights about God, life, salvation, and afterlife. It was another thing to fit these insights into the contours of Nigerian religious and cultural mentality. This tension provides the intellectual starting point in the examination of the Christianization of Nigeria.

PART II

Transforming the Context: The Protestant Missions Era in Nigerian Christian History, 1841-1918

Recent statistics and writings have confirmed Africa's strategic place in the shift of Christianity's center of gravity from the northern continents to the south.[42] Yet scholarly opinions differ as to whether the historical experience of African Christianity has received a legitimate attention in the overall analysis of global Christian history. On one hand are those who approach African church history by adopting the hegemonic view that Christianity is a product of imperialist expansion. Such a view sees the African as a passive recipient of the ecclesiastical construct of the enlightened Western mind. On the other hand, there are those who point to the North African Church of the early centuries, the Coptic Church of Egypt, and the Ethiopian Orthodox Church as manifestations of the on-going history of Christianity in Africa.

Another perspective to African historiography has dismissed the former approach as one which deprives African church historiography its rightful place in the real origins of African Christianity. This new approach considers

---

42. The reality of this phenomenon is not confined only to academic or religious literature. Even the secular press, which is sometimes impervious to religious matters, has embraced the phenomenal explosion of Christianity in developing nations. For a recent example, see Kenneth L. Woodward, "The Changing Face of the Church" (2000:146-152).

African agency to be more essential in the historical transmission of the Christian faith than had been previously thought.[43]

There are also scholars who have addressed themselves to a critical examination of missionary heritage and historical events at regional levels, such as J.F.A. Ajayi and E.A. Ayandele of Nigeria. Ajayi presents a large-scale synthesis on the socio-political evolution of Nigeria and the role played by Christian missions in the emergence of the new Nigerian elite.[44] For his part, Ayandele focuses on earliest missionary activity and the resistance of Nigerian potentates.[45]

The focus of this section is the missionary era in Nigerian Christian history. Although some of the issues to be discussed overlap with certain aspects in previous studies, my assumptions and objectives are clear. The overall purpose is to engage in systematic ecclesiological reflection in order to understand the socio-cultural and ecclesiastical factors that provided the framework and the general conditions in the formation and development of the church in Nigeria.

---

43. Lamin Sanneh is one African voice who continues to challenge the standard historiography by emphasizing the significance of indigenous contributions to the whole Christian expansion. See some of his works, *Encountering the West* (1993); *Translating the Message: The Missionary Impact on Culture* (1989); and *West African Christianity: The Religious Impact* (1983).

44. J.F. Ade Ajayi, *Christian Missions in Nigeria, 1841-1891: The Making of a New Élite* (1965).

45. E.A. Ayandele, *The Missionary Impact on Modern Nigeria, 1842-1914: A Political and Social Analysis* (1966).

CHAPTER 2

The Early Christianization of Nigeria

A total of five mission agencies were active in the period under review: the Wesleyan Methodist Missionary Society (Badagry, 1842); the Anglican Church Missionary Society (Badagry, 1845); the Foreign Mission Committee of the United Presbyterian Church of Scotland (Calabar, 1846); the Foreign Mission Board of the Southern Baptist Convention, USA (Badagry, 1850); and the Roman Catholic Society of African Missions of France (Lagos, 1867). For the purpose of this book, however, I have selected two representative churches as case studies: the Anglican Church Missionary Society (CMS), and the Southern Baptist Convention of the United States.

Two reasons account for these choices. First, the choice of CMS, with its roots in the British ecclesiastical heritage, and the Southern Baptist Convention of the United States, provides us with an Anglo-American perspective in our examination of the missionary endeavor during this period in Nigerian Christian history. The second reason, perhaps the more important, is to make it possible to find a balance between an investigation of the different approaches to ecclesiastical practice and the theological presuppositions that shaped this earliest form of the Christian church in Nigeria.

I must state initially that the story of Christianity in Nigeria did not begin with Protestant missions but rather with Catholic missions in Benin and Warri during the last quarter of the fifteenth century. By the beginning of Protestant missions in the 1840s, however, only a few vestiges and memories enshrined in oral narratives attested to this earlier missionary enterprise.[1] Protestant missions pushed further the boundaries of Christianity and realized in pragmatic ways the territorial conception of the faith as a universal religion. Sustained Christian presence in Nigeria, and indeed of the whole global missionary movement, therefore, was in every way an evangelical undertaking.[2]

The Evangelical Revival and the Appeal of Foreign Missions

Protestant Missions owed their cause to the Evangelical Revival in England. The revival clarified the urgency of rescuing both England and its most prominent symbol, the established Church, from spiritual apathy. It also provided the rationale for the formation of the voluntary societies for the promotion of Christian activities beyond England.

The CMS of Great Britain

Beset by ecclesiastical status quo, the Established Church of England had a disconcerted view of missionary work. There was much vested interest in the church as institution and religion was more formal than life-giving. Bishop Butler lamented apologetically the depressing situation in England and within the Anglican Church in particular:

> It is come, I know not how, to be taken for granted by many persons that Christianity is not so much as a subject for inquiry; but that is, now at length, discovered to be fictitious. And accordingly they treat it, as if, in the present age, this were an agreed point, among people of discernment and nothing remained but to set it up as a principal object of mirth and

---

[1]. For a detailed discussion of this earlier attempt, see J.F. Ade Ajayi, *Christian Missions in Nigeria* (1965); E.A. Ayandele, *The Missionary Impact on Modern Nigeria* (1966). See also A.F.C. Ryder's works, "The Benin Missions" (1961:231-259); and "Missionary Activity in the Kingdom of Warri to the Early Nineteenth Century" (1960:1-20).

[2]. For an insightful account of the evangelical initiatives in global Christian expansion, see Andrew Walls, *The Missionary Movement in Christian History* (1996).

ridicule, as it were by way of reprisals for its having so long interrupted the pleasures of the world.[3]

However, while the established church was caught up in its apathy, a spiritual reawakening was already shaping the consciousness of certain individuals within it. These were new generation of Anglican Evangelicals who "could not so readily divorce the interests of the gospel from the discipline of the church."[4] Borne out of the Evangelical Revival that was highlighted by the ministry of John Wesley, this new crop became convinced of the twin dimensions of restoring Anglican piety and fidelity to foreign missions. For their purpose, the pre-existing Society for the Propagation of the Gospel, (SPG); the quasi-official organ of the Church of England overseas was neither appropriate nor committed to the gospel. In fact, many CMS subscribers maintained their membership (an annual fee) in SPG out of loyalty to the Church. But SPG was not dynamic and growing.

Toward the end of the eighteenth century, these men who were composed of a small group of clergy and influential laymen (popularly know as the Clapham Sect), began to meet regularly for fellowship. Membership included such men as John Venn (who presided over the fellowship meetings), William Wilberforce (a foremost anti-slavery campaigner), Lord Teignmouth (a former governor-general of India), James Stephen (the lawyer of the group), Thomas Clarkson and Zachary Macaulay (both of the Sierra-Leone Company), and Charles Grant (of the East India Company).[5]

With such an amalgam of experiences and interests, "The Society for Missions to Africa and the East" was formed on April 12, 1799. Thirteen years later it became "The Church Missionary Society for Africa and the East" (hereafter CMS). The CMS surpassed the SPG in purpose and vision. Unlike the latter, it possessed a world consciousness that transcended the

---

3. See Eugene Stock, *The History of the Church Missionary Society*, vol. 1 (1899:32).
4. Andrew Walls, "Missionary Vocation and the Ministry: The First Generation" (1980:25).
5. See E.M. Howse, *Saints in Politics: The "Clapham Sect" and the Growth of Freedom* (1952). See also J.F. Ade Ajayi, "From Mission to Church: The Heritage of the Church Mission Society" (1999:53); and C.P. Groves, *The Planting of Christianity in Africa*, vol. 1 (1948:180-184).

confines of missionary activity to the British Empire. As it was clearly stated in their purpose statement, the fundamental goal of the CMS was to convert the "heathen" and save their unregenerate soul from eternal damnation: "the one object of the Church Missionary Society is to provide for the preaching of the Gospel of Christ to those who have not yet received it; and to train up the Christian Converts in the doctrine and discipline of the Church of England."[6]

The Southern Baptist Mission of North America

It should be pointed out that the new religious spirit, with its corresponding proliferation of missionary societies, was not limited to Great Britain. As a matter of fact, the American Protestant missionary conscience of the Second Great Awakening had undeniable connections with the pioneering endeavors of the British revival. However, unlike British missions that were directed primarily towards the conversion of "heathens" in other nations, the breadth of American missionary conscience was initially directed towards evangelizing uncharted local frontiers among the American Indians.[7]

Although I must add that lack of American missionary presence in other nations was not an oversight but a result of circumstance. While Puritan missions to the Indians have been a part of the American church since since 1640, things had wound down by 1775. The proposal to extend the boundaries of Americam Christian mission beyond the Indians to other places like Africa was proposed by Samuel Hopkins, but this idea was overtaken by the Revolutionary War of 1776-1780, and was not to be realized until 1810.

---

6. William Knight, *Memoir of the Rev. Henry Venn* (1880:468).
7. Earl R. MacCormac has observed that missions to the American Indians were considered as "foreign mission" and that despite this inclusion, "home missions occupied the greater part of the missionary effort in America." For details, see his work, "The Transition from Voluntary Missionary Society to the Church as a Missionary Organization among the American Congregationalists, Presbyterians, and Methodists" (1960). For other accounts of Protestant missionary awakening in America, see Charles R. Keller, *The Second Great Awakening in Connecticut* (1942); Oliver W. Elsbree, "The Rise of the Missionary Spirit in America, 1790-1815" (1928); and Colin B. Goodykoonthz, *Home Missions on the American Frontier* (1939).

In the meantime, "home" missions among the Indians were multiplying. It was for the purpose of establishing a plausible connection with the American Indians that the American Society for propagating the gospel among the Indians and others in North America was given legal status in 1787. However, no missionary work was undertaken among the Indians until 1816 when the American Board of Commissioners for Foreign Missions undertook this distinctly Christian obligation.

The frontier did more than merely portray a picture of religious needs. More importantly, it became the necessary precondition for the absorbing passion to spread the gospel. These voluntary lay-initiated missionary societies were a hallmark of the Evangelical revival. In the words of Kenneth Latourette:

> Protestants were bringing into being new instruments for propagating the Christian faith. The societies which they were forming were without exact precedent in the expansion of Christianity, or, indeed, in the spread of any religious faith. They were organizations, not purely of the clergy, but in which laity and clergy joined. Moreover, several of them did not draw their financial support from the state or from merely a few wealthy donors, as did most of the Roman Catholic missions of the period. They appealed to a large number of donors.[8]

Among the earliest American denominations to become involved in this compelling missionary responsibility were the Baptists, although their involvement in the wider Christian philanthropy did not begin until 1814. Before this time, Baptist missionary activities had been largely sporadic and incidental. The first indication of missionary awareness is found in the formation of the Massachusetts Baptist Missionary Society in 1802. Its object, according to its constitution, was "to furnish occasional preaching and to promote the knowledge of evangelical truth in the new settlements

---

8. Kenneth Latourette, *A History of the Expansion of Christianity: Three Centuries of Advance, A.D. 1500-A.D. 1800* vol. 3. (1939:50).

within these United States, or further if circumstances should render it proper."⁹

The formation in 1814 of the "General Missionary Convention of the Baptist Denomination in the United States of America for Foreign Missions" was, therefore, a substantial convergence aimed at annexing the energies of the different and isolated missionary societies within the Baptist denomination towards common missionary goals. According to the constitution of the Convention which was adopted by a unanimous vote,

> We, the delegates from Missionary Societies, and other religious of the Baptist denomination, in various parts of the United States, met in Convention, in the City of Philadelphia, for the purpose of carrying into effect the benevolent intentions of our constituents, by organizing a plan for eliciting, combining, and directing the energies of the whole denomination in one sacred effort for sending the glad tidings of Salvation to the heathen, and to nations destitute of pure Gospel light.[10]

Also known as the Triennial Convention, the unification jointly formed by northern and southern Baptists in the course of benevolent enterprise suffered a setback in 1844. The controversies over the moral justification of appointing a slaveholder as minister and missionary came to an irreconcilable point, leading to the sectional division between northern and southern Baptists. Convinced that it was not inconsistent with Christian ideals and benevolent providence to engage the services of a slaveholder, the Southern Baptist Convention was born in 1845.

The newly-constituted independent Convention gave voice to its mission purpose with the decision to "increase the fervency of our progress for the conversion of the world" by immediately constituting the Foreign Mission Board of the Southern Baptist Convention.[11] And by the time of its first

---

9. See William Gammell, *A History of American Baptist Missions in Asia, Africa, Europe and North America* (1849:3).

10. William Gammell, *A History of American Baptist Missions* (1849:19-20).

11. For accounts of the controversies between the northern and southern Baptists, see the

annual report the board had already made preferences of its prospective mission fields: "China is open. Africa is accessible. God has gone before us and prepared the way, inviting us to follow."[12]

Encouraged by this indication, and since the board already had a missionary presence in China, Thomas Jefferson Bowen volunteered himself to go to the country in "Sudan" or "Central Africa."[13] His appointment on February 22, 1849, made him the pioneer emissary of the Southern Baptist Convention in Nigeria. Bowen set sail from America with the instructions to penetrate into "the Sudan" or some adjacent country, and to remain there until his party has become acquainted with the climate and the people. Bowen landed in Badagry on August 5, 1850, and so was founded the Southern Baptist Mission in Nigeria.

On the whole, the missionary movement epitomized a new beginning that helped to address the concern to bring the non-Christian world into mainstream evangelicalism as well as into the cultural development of civilization.

Protestant Missionary Presence in Nigeria: Motives and Prospects

Sustained missionary enterprise in Nigeria dates to the 1841 Niger expedition. The logic behind the expedition was simple. It was envisioned as the most effective way to end the trans-Atlantic slave trade and to make amends for what was then considered the "blackest stain on civilized

---

work of Robert A. Baker, *The Southern Baptist Convention and its People* (1974).
12. Routh Eugene, "Foreign Mission Board of the Southern Baptist Convention" (1958:461).
13. In the context of Bowen's recorded account, "Central Africa" refers loosely to what is today Northern Nigeria. The term "Sudan" also sometimes refers to the interior as contrasted with the coastal region known as "Guinea." See Bowen's work, *Adventures and Missionary Labors in Several Countries in the Interior of Africa, from 1849-1856* (1968, original 1857). For a biographical account of Bowen and his activities in Nigeria, see Edgar Burks' *Planting the Redeemer's Standard* (1994). See also Baker James Cauthen, *Advance: A History of Southern Baptist Foreign Mission* (1970).

Europe," the trade in human beings.[14] Earlier British abolition of slavery (1834) coupled with the treaties with other European nations, and the activities of the British squadron in West Africa, had not brought a quick end to the slave trade as anticipated. It became obvious that a new approach to the problem was needed. On the account of these exigencies, Thomas Fowell Buxton, the leader of the abolitionists in the British parliament, published his book, *The African Slave Trade and its Remedy* (1839) in which he resurrected the original policy that had led to the foundation of Sierra Leone in 1787 as a settlement for freed slaves.[15]

Buxton contended that the slave trade was an illegitimate economic institution that must be combated through legitimate economic means. As a way of achieving this objective, his suggested plan involved the strategic cultivation of Africa through local labor with equivalent "legitimate commerce" on the part of the Europeans. And in order to give the moral consciousness of the expedition some spiritual expressive forms, Christian missions were to advance into the interior territories with the government-sponsored exploratory mission. According to him, "the Bible and the Plough" is the combination for civilizing the "Dark Continent" and for securing the eternal fate of unregenerate Africa:

> Whatever methods may be attempted for ameliorating the condition of untutored man, this [Christianity] alone can penetrate the root of evil. We must elevate the minds of her people and call forth the resources of her Soil. . . . Let missionaries and schoolmasters, the plough and the spade, go together and agriculture will flourish; the avenues to legitimate commerce will be opened; confidence between man and man will be inspired; whilst civilization will advance as the natural

---

14. For a detailed account of the carefully prepared expedition, see C.C. Ifemesia, "The 'Civilizing' Mission of 1841" (1962:291-310). See also J.F. Ade Ajayi *Christian Missions in Nigeria* (1965:12).

15. For the relation of Buxton's proposal to existing colonial policy, see J. Gallagher's "Fowell Buxton and the New African Policy, 1838-1842" (1958:36-58). For an insightful study on the first missionary endeavor of the CMS in Africa, see Jehu J. Hanciles, *Euthanasia of a Mission: African Church Autonomy in a Colonial Context* (2002).

effect and Christianity operate as the proximate cause of this happy change.[16]

It should be mentioned that Buxton's plan was in many respects similar to an earlier proposal made by James MacQueen in 1822. MacQueen, who having foreseen the Lander brothers' discovery had proposed a plan involving both Fernando Po (an almost indispensable base for the growing trade with the Niger Delta) and another station under the British flag at the Niger-Benue confluence.[17] The difference, this time around, was that Buxton's proposal had met with the approval of the British government. Encouraged by this new development, the CMS supplied two missionaries, James Frederick Schön (the able German linguist who had already spent ten years in Sierra Leone studying African languages) and Samuel Ajayi Crowther (a young catechist who himself had once been a slave but was "recaptured" and freed by the British squadron).

The expedition turned out to be a dismal failure with regards to its objectives. Out of 120 Europeans, 42 died within three months while the rest went down with malaria. Among the 158 Africans on the expedition, there was no death from illness and only eleven cases of fever.[18] The result was that the land that had been acquired at Lokoja for a model farm was abandoned, and the treaties signed with African chiefs left unimplemented.

Any sense of heroic history was lost as a consequence and the humanists were subjected to vigorous attacks in both literary and commercial reviews. Ajayi records that "philanthropy was laughed to scorn as the wishy-washy

---

16. Thomas F. Buxton, *The African Slave Trade and its Remedy* (1968:510-511, original 1839).
17. See his work, *A Geographical and Commercial View of Northern Central Africa* (1822). See also W.L. Mathieson's *Great Britain and the Slave Trade, 1839-1865* (1929:31). For other views, especially those relating to the earlier commercial expedition of 1832, see Macgregor Laird, *Narrative of an Expedition into the Interior of Africa* (1837). For detailed descriptions of the Niger expeditions of the years between 1832 and 1857, see A.F. Mockler-Ferryman, *British West Africa* (1900); and Norton A. Cook, *British Enterprise in Nigeria* (1943).
18. A similar high European mortality was suffered in an earlier commercial expedition. Out of forty-eight Europeans, only nine survived. See Alan. C. Burns' *History of Nigeria* (1969:101-102).

dreams of old women not fit to guide the actions of governments."[19] Although the expedition turned out a tragic failure with regards to the heavy European mortality, lack of African casualties, however, made a possible case for adopting a different mode of penetrating Africa.

James Frederick Schön, who had represented the CMS on the expedition, was very blunt in his report. He argued that European missionaries were physically unfit for the evangelization of inland Africa. Instead, the CMS should use the liberated Africans who would be trained in Sierra Leone (Fourah Bay Institution). He then gave this suggestion a practical shape by drawing attention to Crowther's intellectual qualities, and by recommending that the CMS invite Crowther to England for further training and ordination.[20]

This suggestion appealed to Henry Venn (CMS Honorary Clerical Secretary from 1841-72) who at this time was reshaping the policy of the Society. Himself a strong believer in African potential, he sought to the implementation of Schön's recommendation. Subsequently, Crowther was invited to England for further training, and upon completion in 1843, was given both deacon and priest's orders. This was not only a radical re-orientation in CMS's missionary enterprise; it was a step that would launch the Society further into a horizontal expansion in the efforts to Christianize Nigeria.

Missions Along New Frontiers: The Yoruba and the Niger Missions

There are various interwoven narratives in the events that led Protestant missions to Nigeria. The starting point, as I have sketched, falls within Buxton's scheme that "the Bible and the Plough" is the combination for civilizing Africa and for securing the eternal fate of the unregenerate soul.

---

19. J.F. Ade Ajayi, *Christian Missions in Nigeria* (1965:13).
20. This conclusion and recommendation was contained in a letter to the CMS lay secretary, *Journals of the Rev. James Frederick Schön and Mr. Samuel Crowther* (1970:151, 182-183, 365-366, original 1842). See also Jesse Page, *The Black Bishop: Samuel Adjai Crowther* (1908:68-72).

Although the scheme met with abysmal failure, it succeeded in raising a new awareness about "legitimate commerce." The spate of economic activities from Sierra Leone down the coast by some of the recaptives could be attributed to this new awareness. As it later turned out, the "plough" (commerce) became the precursor and the catalytic force to the subsequent introduction of Christianity to Yorubaland.

The CMS Yoruba Mission

The mission to Yorubaland, which was as much by providence as by design, came through African initiative. It was pressure from some liberated slaves, particularly those of Yoruba extraction (known as the Aku) that brought the first Protestant missionaries to Yorubaland. Earlier in 1838, these recaptives serving on a trading ship reached Badagry. Recognizing it as the slave port from which they had been shipped, they decided to settle there and to put their new talents to use by trading European and Sierra Leonean goods for palm oil and other local products. Still, others were compelled to move inland to the newly founded Abeokuta, their hometown.

The news of the success of the first Akus in settling in Badagry and Abeokuta gave impetus to a more regular stream of emigrants into Yorubaland. It was estimated that between 1839 and 1842, more than 500 Akus had returned home to Abeokuta.[21] Although initial motivation for the movement was economic, the wish to find and be reunited with families became increasingly strong and irrepressible.

The substantial convergence of Aku population in Yorubaland and their overarching concern for pastoral aid played important parts in later ecclesiastical presence in Nigeria. The returnees wanted a smooth continuum of the spiritual ethos and fervor they had been exposed to in Sierra Leone. Subsequently, the emigrants sent to the missionary bodies in Sierra Leone requesting "one of the Messengers of God to teach us more about the way of salvation." The request was more than a personal one. It was also for the purpose of "bring[ing] our fellow Citizens in the way which

---

21. See C.P. Groves, *The Planting of Christianity in Africa*, vol. 2 (1948:46).

is right and to tell them the goodness of Jehovah what he had done for us; and by so doing . . . broke that stony heart from them."[22]

The missionaries responded with skepticism. To them, the emigrants were forsaking a Christian settlement for "a land of darkness." In fact, Henry Townsend, the CMS missionary who was later assigned the responsibility of an exploratory mission to Yorubaland, felt that the emigrants were leaving "the country where God was known for this where God was not known."[23] The Wesleyans, to whom the letter for missionary presence had been sent, acted first. Thomas Birch Freeman, superintendent of the Methodist Mission at Cape Coast, was instructed to start a station in Badagry.

His arrival in Badagry on September 24, 1842, in the company of his wife and William de Graft, an African from Cape Coast, marked the beginning of sustained missionary enterprise in Nigeria. Concerned about being outdone by their Wesleyan counterparts, the CMS sent Henry Townsend to Nigeria. Even then, his trip to Abeokuta was only a "mission of research" to collect information about the Yoruba country, the emigrants, and the possibilities of missionary work.[24]

Townsend landed in Badagry on December 19, 1842, having been given free passage on the trading vessel *Wilberforce*, owned by an African trader, Harry Johnson. He reached his final destination of Abeokuta on January 4, 1843, into the warm and generous embrace of the town's paramount ruler, Chief Sodeke, in appreciation of the British efforts in securing freedom for the slaves.

Townsend's report back to the CMS on his "mission of research" could not have been otherwise. The friendly reaction of Chief Sodeke, the request of the emigrants for missionary presence, and the apparent willingness of the emigrants to promote the cause of Christianity themselves, were positive signals to the missionary parties in Sierra Leone. For the CMS, therefore, the establishment of the Yoruba Mission, with Abeokuta as its first station

---

22. James Fergusson's letter to Thomas Dove, Badagry, March 2, 1841. NRO:ECC 2/1096. CMS Archives.
23. Henry Townsend, "Journal on a Mission of Research," January 5, 1843. CMS, CA1/0215. CMS Archives.
24. J. Warburton, "Instructions of Local Committee," November 9, 1842. CMS, CA1/0218. CMS Archives.

was a strategic move. A subsequent CMS mission team arrived in Badagry on January 17, 1845, with the instruction to make straight for Abeokuta.[25]

As a result of the unexpected death of Chief Sodeke, compounded by the missionaries' fear of the slaving chiefs of the coast, the team was delayed in Badagry for eight months. However, the team turned the waiting period into a fruitful venture by proceeding at once to establish a mission station in Badagry. The proposed mission to Abeokuta, however, became a reality when Townsend and Crowther arrived there in August 1846, leaving Gollmer behind in Badagry to take charge of that station.

The CMS made a considerable progress despite the internecine wars between Yoruba and Dahomey which were compounded greatly by internal dissensions among the different Yoruba towns. Two important factors can be identified in this respect. First, the early congregations of the first missionary team were from among the well-disposed Sierra Leonean returnees who were making a confident re-entry into their native land. Secondly, a favorable disposition to religious liberty by the Abeokuta elders ensured that protection was granted to Christian converts.

With these developments, the place of Abeokuta as "sunrise within the tropics" was firmly established. Along with the establishment of other missions in Lagos and Ibadan by 1852, it is fair and historically accurate to say that the role of the CMS, and the Anglican Yoruba in particular, provided the starting point for approaching the history of Protestant Christianity in Nigeria.

The Southern Baptist Yoruba Mission

In another respect, the opening of the Yoruba Mission by T.J. Bowen under the auspices of the Southern Baptists added a new impulse to the widening Anglo-American missionary enterprise in Nigeria. Bowen landed in Badagry on August 5, 1850, and proceeded overland until he reached Abeokuta on August 18. His settlement in Abeokuta was in a way providential. He settled temporarily here when he was unable to secure permission to proceed to Igboho, the place thought to be suitable for the first station.

---

25. J. Warburton, "Instructions of Local Committee." October 25, 1844. CMS, CA2/11. CMS Archives.

He soon found himself attracted to the Yoruba country, declaring that "[a] more lovely country than this can scarcely be found on the globe . . . a very pleasant country [which] abounds in the good things of life."[26] As a result of his love for the Yoruba country, Bowen committed himself to the study of the local language.

In 1852, he proceeded to Ijaye, a town north of Abeokuta in the direction of Igboho, at the invitation of Kurumi, the paramount chief. There he decided to make his first permanent station. Unfortunately, Bowen's missionary zeal and the general work of the Southern Baptist Mission were hampered by frustrating circumstances taking place back home in America. The board had come under attack from an anti-missionary movement and also suffered from harsh economic conditions.[27] This was to have a negative effect on Bowen's missionary effort in Nigeria. Incapacitated by lack of funds and depleting physical strength, Bowen returned to America on furlough in February 1853.

He returned to Nigeria in August of the same year with a wife and two other missionaries, Dennard and Lacy, and their wives. This reinforcement was, however, short-lived. While some returned home due to sickness, those who chose to remain behind did not live long. In the end, it was left to Thomas Bowen and his wife to proceed to Ijaye. He labored at Ijaye until he transferred to Ogbomosho where he opened a new station on September 23, 1855. Early in 1856 the Bowens returned home with no further opportunity to return to Nigeria.

This first phase of the Baptist Yoruba Mission suffered further setback due to the civil wars of 1861 to 1865 which destroyed the first station at Ijaye and the work at Abeokuta. And from 1858 to 1874, the Foreign Mission Board appointed no missionaries to Nigeria. The flickering light of hope that was left behind was thus sustained by Africans such as J.C. Vaughn, Moses Ladejo Stone, a refugee boy from Ijaye, and Sarah Harden, widow of J.M. Harden, an African missionary who died in 1864. It was not until 1875, during the second phase, highlighted by the work of W.J.

---

26. See T.J. Bowen, *Adventures and Missionary Labours in Several Countries in the Interior of Africa from 1849-1856* (1968:xvii, original 1857).
27. See Routh Eugene, "Foreign Mission Board" (1958:459-460).

David and W.W. Colley, that the work of the Southern Baptist in Nigeria became more stable and concentrated.

The Niger Mission

The path of Christianity into Niger Delta was not a smooth one. The failure of the 1841 expedition was one grim reminder and, compounding this, was the assumption that the river afforded no easy accessibility. Despite this, there was still the compelling conviction that the "Niger could and must be opened to the influence of Christian civilization."[28] For the CMS, the lack of regular steamers beyond Delta made any independent exploration an almost impossible enterprise.

However, another opportunity to penetrate the Niger came in 1854 when the British government, in conjunction with merchant Macgregor Laird, launched another exploratory mission. The expedition went up the Niger under William Baikie, with Samuel Crowther on board the *Pleiad* as the CMS representative. The outcome was a happier one. Not only were there no deaths, but additionally Crowther's report of a warm reception and the prospects it held for Christianity induced optimism and reinforced new aspirations.

Following the success of the 1854 expedition, the government projected another mission for 1857, extending another invitation to CMS. The Society accepted the offer and selected Samuel A. Crowther and J.C. Taylor, an Ibo who was to be Crowther's lieutenant on the expedition, as its two representatives. Both were charged with the responsibility of establishing a Niger Mission.[29] As it was in the Christianization of Yorubaland, Sierra Leone was once again to provide the labor force for evangelizing inland Africa. In the words of the editor of *The Church Missionary Intelligencer*:

> we expect to hear a great movement in Sierra Leone towards the Niger, and we trust there will be no restraint put upon

---

28. This was the opinion of Macgregor Laird, the enterprising London merchant who had commanded the first expedition to ascend the Niger (1832-1833), when the mortality rate was very intimidating. See C.P. Groves, *The Planting of Christianity in Africa*, vol. 2 (1953:74); and F. Deaville Walker, *The Romance of the Black River* (1930:79).
29. "Proceedings of the CMS" (1857:49-50). Cited in C.P. Groves, vol. 2 (1953:74).

it, no narrow feeling permitted, which would leave the Niger unoccupied.[30]

The above statement showed the high expectation the Society placed on the 1857 Niger Mission. Even more was the bold plan that Samuel Crowther, the head of the Niger Mission, put into his careful preparations for the expedition. As it was with the Yoruba Mission, the spread of Christianity along the banks of the Niger and in the Delta was wholly an African enterprise. Included in Crowther's party were twenty-five other liberated Africans who would function as schoolmasters and evangelists in major stations that were to be opened along the Niger River.

Crowther did not only intend to establish stations along the Niger River, but also included in his bold plan the establishment of stations in the Muslim areas of Northern Nigeria, particularly Sudan, Rabba, Bida, Kano, and Sokoto. In order to actualize his elaborate plan along this line, Crowther included in his team a liberated Yoruba Muslim, Kosomo, who was to be his interpreter in Muslim-dominated Northern Nigeria. In his opinion, "such a man will do a vast deal in softening the bigotry and prejudice of men by his persuasion."

The expedition started in the *Dayspring* from Liverpool on May 7, 1857, for Fernando Po where Crowther and Taylor joined in. The expedition arrived at Onitsha on July 25, 1857, where the first permanent station was eventually established. J.C. Taylor was left in charge of the Onitsha station and worked there for twenty months. More stations were established at Igbede and Rabba. Crowther considered Rabba to be a particularly strategic "connecting link between the Yoruba and Hausa, and a stride into Mohammedan country, under a direct Mohammedan government."[31] Although Rabba had seemed a promising station, the vested religious interest of the Muslim mallams and their suspicion toward missionary propaganda caused the work there to lapse.

---

30. *The Church Missionary Intelligencer* (1858:93).

31. The CMS published Crowther and Taylor's Journals under the title, *The Gospel on the Banks of the Niger: Journals and Notices of the Native Missionaries Accompanying the Niger Expedition of 1857-1859*, henceforth cited as *Journal*. For reference to this particular citation, see *Journal* (1968:210).

Despite the initial obstacle at Rabba, Crowther was never deterred in his resolve to make further contacts with the Muslims. A strategic move in this regard was his policy of friendliness and the determination that "the beginnings of our missionary operations under Mohammedan government should not be disputes about the truth or falsehood of one religion or another, but . . . [to] aim at toleration, to be permitted to teach their heathen subjects the religion we profess."[32] Through his patience, dialogue, and tactful engagement with traditional rulers, Crowther overcame the suspicion that he was an agent of alien rule. His personal friendship with the Etsu of Nupe, for example, led to the establishment of mission stations at Lokoja and Egga.

Crowther pursued his course of least resistance in dealing with Muslim rulers of Nupe country, always pointing to the benefits of Christian-Muslim cooperation. He gave presents frequently and occasionally offered political advice. One such piece of political advice was in acquitting the emir of Bida with the possibility of adopting European technology "and the advisability of prospecting for minerals in his territory."[33] He also succeeded in persuading the emirs of Bida, Ilorin, and Gwandu and the sultan of Sokoto to receive Arabic Bibles from the Church Missionary Society.[34] So favorably disposed was the emir of Bida to Crowther that he considered his missionary program for the Nupe kingdom. Ayandele records that Crowther became "the most powerful external influence on the Muslim rulers of the Nupe country between 1869 and 1888."[35]

---

32. Jesse Page, *The Black Bishop: Samuel Adjai Crowther* (1908:149).
33. "Annual Reports, 1869 to 1880." CMS, CA3/04(b). CMS Archives. Cited in E.A. Ayandele, "The Missionary Factor in Northern Nigeria" (1980:136). Other examples used by Crowther in his pursuit of cooperation with Muslims were the references to Britain (a Christian country) working with Turkey and Egypt (both Muslim countries) over the Suez Canal. Another one was the request of the Shah of Iran to Britain to help build railway in Iran to facilitate communications and commerce. For details, see Peter B. Clarke, *West Africa and Christianity* (1986:62-66). See also Gabriel Okafor, *Development of Christianity and Islam in Modern Nigeria* (1992:73-74).
34. S.A. Crowther, "Annual Report" for 1873. CMS, CA3/04 (b). CMS Archives. See also E.A. Ayandele, *The Missionary Impact on Modern Nigeria* (1966:117-118).
35. I have borrowed largely from Ayandele's extensive account on Crowther's effort to push the missionary frontier northwards on the Niger. For details see his work, "The Missionary Factor in Northern Nigeria, 1870-1918" (1980:133-158).

Having gained the confidence of the emir of Bida, Crowther's activities in pushing further into the Islamic frontier of Northern Nigeria were unprecedented. In 1861 he occupied Akassa, in the Delta, at the Nun entrance of the Niger. In 1864, the year of his ordination as Bishop, he established stations at Idah and Bonny, the latter at the invitation of King Pepple. He moved into Brass in 1868 and established stations at Tuwon in that year and in Nembe the following year. Between 1874-1875, he founded more stations among the Kalabari and at Kipo Hill.

Kipo Hill was especially a strategic point for Crowther because of its being on the direct route of the Hausa ivory traders from the north and north-east, with connections with Keffi, Zaria, and Yakoba. Another strategic move was his occupation of Shonga in 1876. Shonga, like Kipo Hill, was on the caravan route to Sokoto and Salaga. Other stations were opened in Bida, Ilorin, Loko, Yimaha, and Kotangora, all at the personal invitation of their respective emirs.[36] In this way, Crowther's Niger Mission came to stretch from the Nupe country to all the Delta States in the South.

Any evaluation of the historical record of Christian missions, especially one that attempts to chronicle sustained missionary engagement with African Islam, therefore, must appreciate these pioneering efforts of Samuel Ajayi Crowther.[37] The hope that was almost extinguished with the first expedition of 1841 had been restored. And from 1878 onwards, both the Yoruba and Niger Missions experienced unprecedented extension from the coast to the hinterland. In this respect, the valiant efforts of African agency, under the leadership of Samuel Ajayi Crowther, were complementary to the Society's missionary expansion.

The Baptists were not as successful. In fact, their work was still largely confined to the Yoruba country. An extension into the interior of Nigeria was still a function of the imagination, articulated and confined to the thinking of Bowen, its pioneer missionary in Nigeria. In his appeal to get the Foreign Board to fulfill its obligations by sending enough personnel so

---

36. See Crowther's own account, "A Brief History of the Niger Mission Since 1857." CMS, G3/A3/O2, October 8, 1885. CMS Archives.

37. This view has been expressed by no less a figure in Christian mission history than Andrew F. Walls. See his article, "The Legacy of Samuel Ajayi Crowther" (1992).

the mission could advance as far as the Niger and beyond, Bowen writes, "the Nufi [Nupe], Hausa and Kanike, whom I met are more intelligent and civilized than I expected. Most of them desire missionaries though they know our doctrine and designs."[38]

Bowen attempted to found a station in the Muslim town of Ilorin in order to "speak freely of salvation through Christ." As we have already noted, Bowen could not do much during this first phase of Baptist presence in Nigeria; a phase of uneven development, dogged by a particular ambivalence of progression and regression.

Missionary Encounter with a Non-Christian Context

I have shown the evangelical revival as a major contributory factor in the drive behind foreign missions. Added to this was the central theological motive that the missionaries gave in support of their enterprise; the priceless value of the human soul. And since the missionaries were overwhelmed with the idealistic vision of the number of perishing "heathen," the work of converting non-Christians became an extremely urgent one. Yet this zeal was not without a low and depreciatory view of the very people the missionaries were out to convert. In the words of an Evangelical hymn:

> The heathen are foolish and brutish and blind. They are mortals in body but demons in mind. Yet their souls we must seek though their sins be abhorred; for our labor shall not be in vain in the Lord.[39]

With such an understanding of the task ahead of them, it was not a mistaken assumption, then, that the missionaries construed Nigeria as being on the path of heathendom. The reason for this is not a complicated one.

---

38. See T.J. Bowen, *Adventures and Missionary Labours in Several Countries in the Interior of Africa from 1849-1856* (1968:1).
39. Elizabeth Isichei, *History of West Africa Since 1800* (1977:155).

Up until this time, the image the Christianized world held about the non-Christian world, especially Africa, was one of a primitive and barbarous continent; a benighted people, lost in the darkest shadow of paganism. In one Missions publication, Nigeria was described as:

> A land formless, mysterious, terrible, ruled by witchcraft and the terrorism of secret; where the skull was worshipped and blood sacrifices were offered to *jujus*; where guilt was decided by ordeal of prison and burning oil; where scores of people were murdered when a chief died, and his wives decked themselves in finery and were strangled to keep him company in spirit land, where men and women were satiated with feeding on human flesh; where twins were done to death and the mother banished to bush; where semi-nakedness was compulsory; and girls were sent to the farms to be fattened for marriage.[40]

With this type of description, the missionaries brought proofs to situate Nigeria within the ideological matrix of Christian philanthropy. Nigeria, as it were, held a beckoning prospect for the benevolent purveyor of truth and light. As it later became apparent, Protestant missions were set on their way to the Niger.

The zeal of Christian philanthropy in Nigeria, notwithstanding, the missionaries had forgotten that they were coming into a context already dominated by traditional religions and Islam. A striking feature of the establishment of Islam in Nigeria, unlike Christianity, was its willingness to "wait for its turn." Islamic preachers did not straightforwardly attempt to overrun indigenous religions but presented their faith in a way that was apprehensible and with little disturbance to the pre-existing religious practices and ways of life. It was after this initial natural affinity that Islam began to "apply more stringent aspects of its own code."[41]

---

40. Kofi Agbeti, *West African Church History, Christian Missions and Church Foundations: 1482-1919* (1986:160).
41. Lamin Sanneh, *Piety and Power: Muslims and Christians in West Africa* (1996:13).

Driven by their evangelical assumption that divine truths could not be perceived in other religions other than the Christian faith, the missionaries were not willing to make any concessions to the indigenous religions. Similarly, cultural forms and institutions, because of their incompatibility to the already known Western forms and ideals, were almost totally rejected or labeled as pagan, immoral, and idolatrous. In the words of Ayandele, "the new wine of European Christianity had to be put into new bottles. They sought the creation of a completely new social order which would wipe away most of the customs and institutions of the old society."[42] Achebe captures this antithetical stance of Protestant missionaries well:

> The white man [Christianity] came quietly and peaceably with his religion. We were amused at his foolishness and allowed him to stay. Now he has won our brothers and our clan [society], we can no longer act like one. He has put a knife on things that held us together and we have fallen apart.[43]

The missionaries, unlike their Islamic counterparts, could not be bothered by a methodology of compromise. Instead, they apologetically defended their position claiming that Islam made more rapid progress because it "tolerated a lax morality and was therefore regarded by Africans as an easier option than Christianity."[44] Undeterred by their slow progress, but fired by the idealism of the faith to which they ascribed, Christian missionaries attempted expanding their influence into new frontiers.

From Mission to Church: The Evolution of a Movement

A fundamental problem of missionary enterprise has been how to initiate a conceptual scheme that enhances the natural movement from mission to

---

42. E.A. Ayandele, *The Missionary Impact on Modern Nigeria* (1966:4-5).
43. Chinua Achebe, *Things Fall Apart* (1958:124-125).
44. J.F. Ade Ajayi, *Christian Missions in Nigeria* (1965:107).

church without the latter being irredeemably dependent on the external agency that fostered it. In the case of the CMS, Henry Venn, the man who was responsible for formulating the mission strategy as the Society's general secretary from 1841 to 1872, emerged as a man of wide vision and insight far ahead of his time. He saw the missionary as a temporary agent of the gospel whose aim must be to create "self-supporting, self-propagating, and self-governing" churches.

Venn described such churches as *Native Pastorates* because he anticipated that a native pastor, supported by local congregations, was a necessary step towards ecclesiastical independence. By this time the role of the missionary, in his view, would have been complete and the natural *euthanasia of a mission* would have taken place.[45]

His approach was informed by his understanding of the dual nature of the objectives of a foreign mission: to preach the gospel to the heathen and to gather the converts into a native Christian church. In a metaphorical allusion to the processes similar to those observable in the construction of a building, Venn regarded the indigenous church as the holy temple, and the missionary as the master builder:

> The Mission is the scaffolding; the Native Church is the edifice. The removal of the scaffolding is the proof that the building is completed. You will have achieved the greatest success when you have taught your converts to do without you, and can leave them for fresh inroads into the "regions beyond."[46]

Venn's secretariat gave this theoretical construct a practical shape in the encouragement he gave Samuel Ajayi Crowther. The elevation of the latter

---

45. For major studies on the missionary philosophy and policy of Henry Venn, see Wilbert Shenk, *Henry Venn—Missionary Statesman* (1983); and Jehu Hanciles, *Euthanasia of a Mission: African Church Autonomy in a Colonial Context* (2002).

46. Wilbert Shenk, *Bibliography of Henry Venn's Printed Writings with Index* (1975, 134:112). Citations form Shenk's bibliographic compilation of Venn's printed writings will henceforth be referred to as "VB." The second compilation of Venn's writings, also by Shenk, appears in another work, *Henry Venn—Missionary Statesman* (1983:138-157).

to the position of a Bishop in 1864 had the full signature of Henry Venn, thus epitomizing his idea of the indigenization of the episcopate.[47]

For their part, the Baptists were less preoccupied with institutionalization. In fact, their involvement in the missionary enterprise was conceptualized in terms of dynamic organizations of action devoted solely to the promotion of the gospel and the furtherance of the kingdom. The genius of Baptist heritage, therefore, was its emphasis on the decentralization of ecclesiastical authority. Each local congregation was, in some respect, an autonomous body of believers where the missionary or the pastor is no more than a servant. In the case of the Southern Baptist in Nigeria, this was expected to be the *modus operandi* since its Foreign Mission Board was in no way immune to the overriding Baptist polity of individual freedom.[48]

It is appropriate to conclude, therefore, that the Christianization of Nigeria is one of various interwoven narratives. It is a history that, despite external initiatives and good will, rests substantially on African agents and their contributions to the whole Christianizing process.

---

47. For a detailed chronicle of the life and activities of the Anglican Church since coming to Nigeria, see J. Akinyele Omoyajowo, *The Anglican Church in Nigeria: 1842-1992* (1994).

48. For other accounts of the Southern Baptist Convention missionary work in Nigeria, see the works of: Louis M. Duval, *Baptist Missions in Nigeria* (1928); Travis M. Collins, *The Baptist Mission of Nigeria, 1850-1993* (1993). For works dealing directly with the various Baptist churches in Nigeria, see J.A. Atanda, *Baptist Churches in Nigeria, 1850-1950* (1988); Thomas O'Connor, *Outlined Notes on the Expansion of Baptist Work in Nigeria, 1850-1939* (1970); and T.O. Ogundare, *A Christian Church on the March: A History of the First Baptist Church, Isokun, Oyo: 1858-1992* (1993).

CHAPTER 3

The Formation of an African Ministry

The eternal fate of the unregenerate African souls, coupled with the evangelical obligation to rescue them on their road to divine wrath, formed a powerful missiological motif in the Christianization of Africa. In this Christianizing mission, the missionaries played a special role although without much functional distinction between "evangelizing heathen" and "ministering to the Native Church."

Conditioned by their institutionalized ecclesiastical structures, the missionaries conceived of ministry in terms of particular functions performed by titled persons and exercising some formal authority. As we have already indicated, in the case of the CMS, for example, what was to become the "elementary organization" that would give direction to the "corporate life" of native congregations evolved in the context of vigorous ideological and theological arguments of Henry Venn, the CMS secretary (1841-1872).

Henry Venn and the Ideal of a Native Ministry as a Working Objective

Henry Venn was not a man of small stature in matters of principle. In all ecclesiastical and missionary matters, his unique gifts of visionary administration and imposing intellectual ability were somewhat intimidating to lesser men. The period of his secretariat embodied the very nature of a frontier, engaging uncharted territories on the maps of missionary ideologies. His single-minded pursuit of a policy of indigenization constituted an important theoretical ingredient for a new model of mission.[1]

Venn's vision of an indigenous church and a native episcopate developed and progressed over a number of years as can be seen from his papers of 1851, 1861, and 1866.[2] Fundamental to Venn's conviction was that a distinction must be made between "the office of a *missionary*, who preaches to the heathen, and instructs inquirers or recent converts—and the office of a *pastor*, who ministers in holy things to a congregation of Native Christians." As Knight puts it, "the one was the means, the other the end; the one the scaffolding, the other the building it leaves behind when the scaffolding is removed."[3]

The whole tenor of Venn's thinking extended beyond merely achieving independence for the native church, but also included an attempt to solve "the great missionary problem of the day," the relationship of native ministry to European missionaries. He envisioned the establishment of the native church upon a self-supporting system and under native pastors which would free the missionaries to get on with the work of evangelism. His descriptive concept for this principle was the "three-self" formula. A concept by which a native ministry would become "self-supporting, self-governing, and self-propagating."[4]

---

1. Accounts of Henry Venn's missionary strategies and theories are well documented. I will only reference them here in so far as has become necessary in understanding missionary activities during this period in Nigerian Christianity. Among works that have detailed the missionary policies of Henry Venn and the Society he represented, see Wilbert Shenk, *Henry Venn—Missionary Statesman* (1983); C. Peter Williams, *The Ideal of the Self-Governing Church: A Study in Victorian Missionary Strategy* (1990), William Knight, *Memoir of the Rev. Henry Venn: The Missionary Secretariat of Henry Venn* (1880); Max Warren, *To Apply the Gospel: Selections from the Writings of Henry Venn* (1971); and Timothy E. Yates, *Venn and Victorian Bishops Abroad: The Missionary Policies of Henry Venn and Their Repercussion upon the Anglican Episcopate of the Colonial Period, 1841-1872* (1978).

2. On the three papers constituting his memorandum on "The Native Pastorate and Organization of Native Churches," see Wilbert Shenk, *Henry Venn—Missionary Statesman* (1983:118-129).

3. William Knight, *Memoir of the Rev. Henry Venn*, (1880:277).

4. This concept has also been attributed to Rufus Anderson, foreign secretary of the American Board of Commissioners for Foreign Missions, 1832-1866. Shenk has argued that it was Venn who first employed the concept in conjunction with each other in 1851 to define aspects of his indigenous church principles. For details, see Wilbert Shenk, *Henry*

In currency with this principle, Venn saw as wholly desirable the need to expand the slogans, "Native agency under European superintendence" and "Native ministry the crown of the Native agency," into another slogan that sufficiently indicated missionary thinking of the day. His new maxim, "Native Church the soul of a Mission," emphasized the absolute urgency and priority of the "euthanasia" in the passing phase of the missionary endeavor, the phase in which a mission became progressively indigenous and independent. This "euthanasia of a mission" takes place "where the Missionary, surrounded by well-trained native congregations under native pastors . . . gradually and wisely abridges his own labors, and relaxes his superintendence over the pastors, till . . . the District ceases to be a Missionary field, and passes into Christian parishes under the constituted Ecclesiastical Authorities."[5]

Modern commentators on the implementation of Venn's policy of "euthanasia" have been overtly critical. The earliest of these modern critics was Stephen Neill in his work of 1957. Neill comments about Venn's policy with regard to Sierra Leone thus:

> Sierra Leone suffered from one of those premature and ill-considered attempts to create an independent church. . . . As early as 1860 the Church Missionary Society brought into existence the native church council, placing responsibility for the congregations in the hands of African clergy, and reducing the missionary staff almost to vanishing point. The theory, of course, was that the Christians of the Colony area would gradually spread out into the interior and bring the gospel to their African brethren. What happened, as ought to have been foreseen, was exactly the opposite.[6]

Venn—Missionary Statesman (1983:16-66).
5. "Minute upon the Employment and Ordination of Native Teachers." First paper issued in 1851. CMS, G/AZ1/1, no. 71. CMS Archives.
6. See his work, *The Unfinished Task* (1957:166). R.S. Foster substantially embraced this contention in his work, *The Sierra Leone Church* (1961:23-45).

Commenting later in 1986, Stephen Neill remains unsparing in his bitter criticisms of Venn's policy of the "euthanasia":

> Later experience has placed many question marks against Henry Venn's formulation. Any such sharp separation between church and mission as is implied in Venn's solution seems to lack theological foundation in the New Testament. And the first attempts to carry out the principles of Venn's dictum proved almost wholly disastrous. The establishment of the "Native Pastorate" in Sierra Leone in 1860, with the complete withdrawal of the missionaries from participation in the affairs of the pastorate, inflicted on the church a paralysis from which a whole century has not availed to deliver it.[7]

It is not my primary concern to respond to these criticisms, but to examine briefly some of the factors that have been advanced as influencing Venn's advocacy of a native ministry.[8] Some of these factors have been attributed partly to personnel and partly to financial problems. The personnel problem was considered to have been occasioned by the heavy missionary mortality rate of the Niger Expedition of 1841 and the lack of a substantial reservoir of missionaries from which the Society could draw. The financial problem centered on the acute financial crisis the Society was going through in 1841. Another important factor has been attributed to Venn's confidence in the social and intellectual capabilities of the native races.[9]

---

7. See his later work where he continues his unrelenting criticisms of Venn's policy, *A History of Christian Missions* (1986:260).

8. For a direct response to Stephen Neill's criticism of Venn's policy, see Timothy Yates' work, *Venn and Victorian Bishops Abroad* (1978). For more recent examination of Venn's policy, especially relating to its practical application, see Jehu Hanciles' works, *Euthanasia of a Mission: African Church Autonomy in a Colonial Context* (2002); and "Anatomy of an Experiment: The Sierra Leone Native Pastorate" (2001). Finally, for a study of Venn's policy with regards to its importance in contextual ecclesiology, see C. Peter Williams, "'Not Transplanting': Henry Venn's Strategic Vision" (2000).

9. Henry Venn, *The Missionary Life and Labours of Francis Xavier* (1862:252).

While these factors remained the most persuasive ideological premise for understanding Venn's motivation, the last one undoubtedly bore the imprint of his policy more as a virtue in itself than as an economic measure. Known for his profound faith in native ability, Venn believed that the Parliamentary Committee's Resolution of 1865 had vindicated his policy:

> The positive Resolution that the natives are to be trained for ultimate self-government is an important principle on our side . . . and seems to have set at rest the senseless outcry against the [financial] support of the colonies and against the capacity of the Negro.[10]

Considering Venn's theory of "euthanasia," the three-self formula of missionary strategy, and his faith in the intellectual capacity of native people, it is no exaggeration, therefore, to suggest that the considerable churches of West Africa and elsewhere came into being on the principles advocated by his secretariat.

Indigenizing the Episcopacy: The Bishopric Controversy

Venn's strategy of indigenous episcopacy did not lend itself to an easy implementation but occurred amidst crossfire of ideological polemics. For as he was carefully developing the complex formulations of his theories, so was Henry Townsend in championing an opposition of comparable persuasion. Although a man of undisguised ambition, Townsend's racial rhetoric revealed his inherent prejudice and skepticism about the intrinsic capacity of the native to lead.

As early as 1851, in reaction to the proposed ordination of T.B. Macaulay and Theophilus King, Townsend wrote to oppose the proposal: "I have a great doubt of young black clergymen. They want years of experience to give stability to their characters; we would rather have them as schoolmasters and catechists."[11] This perception was nothing compared to the venom he unleashed in order to stop the consecration of the man he looked upon as

---

10. Venn to Townsend, September 22, 1865. CMS, CA2/L3. CMS Archives.
11. Townsend to Venn, October 21, 1851. CMS, CA2/085. CMS Archives.

his rival to the bishopric, Samuel Ajayi Crowther. Although a man of great credentials himself, Townsend staked his claims to the bishopric on his being a white man. In his 1851 petition, he declared:

> Native teachers of whatever grade have been received and respected by the chiefs and people only as being the agents or servants of white men . . . not because they are worthy. . . . Our esteemed brother Mr. Crowther was often treated as the white man's inferior and more frequently called so, notwithstanding our frequent assertions to the contrary. . . . This state of things is not the result of white men's teaching but has existed for ages past. The superiority of the white over the black man, the Negro has been forward to acknowledge. The correctness of this belief no white man can deny. . . . There is one other view that we must not lose sight of . . . that as the Negro feels a great respect for a white man, that God kindly gives a great talent to the white man in trust to be used for the Negro's good. Shall we shift the responsibility? Can we do it without sin?[12]

Townsend carried his theme of the African's unfitness for leadership well into the 1860s. Although it is not my intention to provide great detail of his bigoted missionary paternalism, another example of his formal objections to Crowther's consecration would suffice. When in 1855 Crowther's name was mentioned as successor to Weeks as Bishop of Sierra Leone, Townsend objected:

> We are anxiously expecting to hear of a new Bishop of Sierra Leone. Crowther will not be acceptable to us as such, and whatsoever opinion one may form of his personal worth, it will not do to make him a Bishop (except in or over a diocese in England).[13]

---

12. Townsend, David Hinderer, C.A. Gollmer, and Isaac Smith to Major Straight, October 29, 1851. CMS, CA2/016. CMS Archives.
13. Townsend to Venn, July 21, 1857. CMS, CA2/085. CMS Archives.

Crowther's sensitivity and response to the whole bishopric controversies was in the most positive terms. In the modesty proper to Christian conduct, he wrote Venn declaring that, "[t]he European missionaries who have sacrificed everything to come out to Africa, taking their lives in their hands, have a greater right to this claim. . . . As a man I know something of the feelings of men."[14] As it became apparent, neither Townsend's objections nor Crowther's lack of ambition for higher ecclesiastical office were to shake Venn's intention. For in Crowther, Venn had seen sufficiently recognizable leadership qualities that would justify his theory of indigenous leadership. In a letter to Crowther in 1858, Venn remarked on the "honour which you have long had of promoting harmony and brotherly love in the mission by your wise and humble spirit."[15]

Bishop Samuel Crowther: "The Symbol of a Race on Trial"

In spite of European opposition, Crowther was consecrated a bishop under the Jerusalem Act on June 19, 1864.[16] The consecration of Crowther under this Act was understandably something of a compromise in the face of strong European missionary opposition. Perhaps this would explain why the terms of Crowther's episcopal jurisdiction were less than the inauguration of a native diocesan episcopate. The Royal Licence authorizing his consecration declared:

> We authorize and empower you, the said Reverend Samuel Adjai Crowther, to be bishop of the United Church of England and Ireland, in the said countries of Western Africa beyond the limits of our dominions.[17]

---

14. Crowther to Venn, April 4, 1860; CMS, CA3/04. CMS Archives.
15. Venn to Crowther, July 22, 1858. CMS CA3/L2. CMS Archives.
16. "Bishops in Foreign Countries Act," sometimes called the Jerusalem Bishoprics Act, 5 Vict. c6 1841. CMS Archives.
17. Church Missionary Society, "Minute on the Constitution of the Anglican Native Bishopric on the West African Coast" (1864). Cited in J.F. Ade Ajayi, *Christian Mission in Nigeria* (1965:274-277).

The implication of this licence was that Crowther had no definite diocese, but was merely authorized to exercise episcopal functions over an undefined territory. Although a Yoruba man, with the added responsibilities of Yoruba translation and orthography, Crowther was not bishop over the Yoruba towns of Lagos, Abeokuta, or Ibadan, places where European missionaries happened to be. The only Yoruba town under his jurisdiction was Otta (midway between Lagos and Abeokuta) and this was so because European missionaries had not yet occupied the place. Instead, his diocesan episcopacy covered largely the Niger, a vast territory whose language and culture were foreign to him.

Despite this obvious contradiction, Venn saw Crowther's consecration as a special event that justified his theory of the "euthanasia of a mission." On the one hand, the new church, even if not totally self-supporting, realized a measure of self-government by having an indigenous bishop. On the other hand, the involvement of the bishop in missionary work in another part of the country also meant that the church was also becoming self-propagating.[18]

A few observations are necessary here. First, Venn interpreted the consecration of Crowther as the "full development of the native African church."[19] Yet a closer look shows that the "euthanasia" was merely a partial one. The reason for this is because Crowther was expected to organize the churches established into a "national institution" that will be answerable to England:

> The church in Western Africa over which he presides will be a branch of the United Church of England and Ireland and will be identical with the mother Church in doctrine and worship and assimilated in discipline and government as far as the same may be consistent with the peculiar circumstances of the countries in which the congregations are formed.[20]

---

18. J.F. Ade Ajayi, *Christian Missions in Nigeria*, (1965:207).
19. Venn to Lamb, January 23, 1864. CMS, CA2/L3. CMS Archives.
20. Church Missionary Society, "Minute on the Constitution of the Anglican Native Bishopric on the West African Coast" (1864). Cited in J.F. Ade Ajayi, *Christian Mission in*

Second, Venn indicated in his letter to the Yoruba Mission that the terms of Crowther's episcopacy "can only be regarded as temporary."[21] The temporality of this arrangement meant that Venn's scheme could scarcely be regarded as a move toward the full establishment of an indigenous church. As I have noted, Crowther's jurisdiction did not have a precise definition. Equally important was the fact that he was placed at the mercy of European missionaries who would have to decide whether or not to submit to his episcopal superintendence.

The above not withstanding, fairness to Henry Venn posits that he may have had to walk on a tight rope between his appreciation for the labors of the European missionaries and the delicate execution of his own missionary strategies. Equally important is the fact that Venn was in failing health. He wanted to retire in 1867, but no successor was named. He died in January 1873 at 77 years of age and an invalid.

Nevertheless, that he vacillated over the area of Crowther's jurisdiction, that he never pressed for Crowther to be appointed as bishop in the Yoruba country, that he gave a relatively lukewarm support to Crowther once he had taken up his episcopal duties are issues of great importance in understanding the potency of metropolitan policy-making and the complexities of its implementation on the mission field.[22]

Modeled quite self-consciously on European opposition to African leadership, therefore, the installation of Bishop Samuel Ajayi Crowther over an ambiguously defined jurisdiction placed him in an impossible situation. First, the long distances that he had to travel and the dependence on traders for passage made supervision rather inadequate and periodic. There was also the psychologically destabilizing effect of overseeing a wide variety of tribes foreign to him both in language and custom.

Perhaps the greatest challenge was finding sufficient and qualified "natives." Crowther had to work the area with Yoruba and Sierra Leonean immigrants who, much like the Europeans, had to learn the local language

---

Nigeria (1965:274-277).
21. Venn to missionaries in the Yoruba Mission, July 23, 1864. CMS, CA2/L3. CMS Archives.
22. Max Warren, *To Apply the Gospel: Selections From the Writings of Henry Venn* (1971:30).

and custom. That Crowther had to employ a person like William John, a man who was once accused of seducing the daughter of a leading Christian, was because he could not find suitable and credible agents. William John's 1882 conviction of beating a slave-girl to death was to become ammunition in the hands of Crowther's opponents who would accuse the bishop of over-indulgent episcopacy.

It was not surprising that disquieting reports reached Salisbury Square that things were not in a satisfactory condition in the Niger. Of particular importance were rumors about the spiritual laxity of the African agents as an affront to the Society's ideal of Christian conduct. These rumors had become so persistent and so disturbing that in 1878, T.J. Hutchinson, the new secretary of the CMS, introduced a temporary measure of joint control arrangement in which a European lay agent, J.A. Ashcroft, was assigned to relieve Crowther of the temporal affairs of the mission.

This arrangement, Hutchinson hoped, would leave Crowther's "mind free for the more solemn and important spiritual duties."[23] The arrangement, apart from introducing European supervision to the Niger without necessarily displacing Crowther, also orchestrated sustained distrust among the Society's European and African agents.

The Hijacking of the Episcopacy and the Rise of Nigerian Nationalism

As criticisms of Crowther and his African assistants grew steadily, so also was Hutchinson's subtle strategy to hijack the Niger. In 1879, he appointed a finance committee based in Lagos and vested it with the management of the Niger Mission. This was followed in 1880 with the appointment of a Commission of Inquiry headed by Jonathan (J.B.) Wood, an experienced missionary in the Yoruba Mission.[24] The commission was to make a tour

---

23. E. Hutchinson to Bishop Crowther, April 26, 1878. For details of the new arrangement, see E. Stock, *The History of the Church Missionary Society*, vol. 3 (1899:83, 383-844).

24. Committee of Correspondence, Minutes on the Niger Mission, October 21, 1879. CMS, CA3/L1. CMS Archives.

and report on the Niger situation. With the exception of Brass and Bonny of the Delta section, Wood's 136-page report was so shattering and so damaging to Crowther and the Niger Mission that it was secreted to the CMS in London "under a self-protective cloak of confidentiality."[25]

In his remarks to Crowther about the report, Hutchinson declared, "The report sent to us by Wood reveals such a state of moral delinquency ... that at first the disposition is to sit down in despair and pronounce the mission an entire failure."[26] The general feeling amongst the rank and file of the Society was further expressed by its clerical secretary, R. Lang. In his remark to Wood regarding the report, Lang declared rather regretfully that "the absolute need of European supervision," and the lack of which "has been the occasion of the grave offences in the Niger and of the generally low tone of Christianity there."[27] With this post-Venn outlook in Salisbury Square, it leaves little to the imagination that the policy of re-Europeanization would become an alternative pathway to episcopal superintendence.

If the Wood report was deployed to justify a complete handing over of the Niger Mission to the Europeans, Venn's plan could begin to appear visionary and vulnerable. And because the committee was not united in its perception of the Niger Mission and of its African agents, the Society opted for a deputation to meet with Crowther and hold full discussion on new arrangements for the Niger. The conference that took place at Madeira in March 1881 did little to reconcile the conflicting parties and the situation deteriorated. Between 1887 and 1890, the Society attempted a series of half-measures to ameliorate the Niger situation by sending a number of Europeans.

The story of the young and zealous European recruit that came to the Niger during this time has been well documented.[28] The enlisting of this

---

25. Lamin Sanneh, *West African Christianity* (1983:171).
26. E. Hutchinson to Bishop Crowther, November 20, 1880. CMS, CA3/L1. CMS Archives.
27. R. Lang to J.B. Wood, March 17, 1882. CMS, G3A3/12. CMS Archives.
28. For full treatments, see J.F. Ade Ajayi, *Christian Missions in Nigeria* (1965); E.A. Ayandele, *The Missionary Impact on Modern Nigeria* (1966); J.B. Webster, *The African Churches among the Yoruba* (1964); G.O.M. Tasie, *Christian Missionary Enterprise in the Niger Delta, 1864-1918* (1978); and Andrew Porter, "Evangelical Enthusiasm, Missionary Motivation and West Africa in the Late Nineteenth Century: The Career of G.W. Brooke" (1976:23-46). See also the works of C. Peter Williams, "From Church to Mission: An

reforming group, headed by J.A. Robinson, the CMS secretary on the Niger in 1887, was markedly a turning point. Any effort to improve Crowther's administration was certainly undermined by the Society's decision to include a figure like G.W. Brooke in the reforming group. Brooke was one of the young Cambridge graduates who "wanted to scrap the traditional theology in favor of Keswick theology as well as the whole mission method that the older theology entailed."[29] Not only did the Society consider his radicalism to be deeply dangerous, but that the Society went against its judgment to appoint a man who was not of Anglican background and who was likely to challenge its own *raison d'être* leaves much to be desired.[30]

Brooke was to be instrumental in the purge that later proved so disastrous to the entire Niger Mission. He was convinced right from the beginning that the whole missionary approach to the heathen was wrong and that "there is no hope of success until we have first taken down the whole of the past work so that not one stone remains upon another."[31] This was not an empty threat. The meeting of the finance committee at Onitsha in August 1890 had the characteristic signature of a carefully planned agenda.[32] Not only was the ecclesiastical authority of Bishop Crowther challenged and overruled, the suspension of his archdeacon son, along with several other African clergy, was an added insult. The Society itself was not spared in its attempt to remain committed to Venn's policy. It was condemned for "allow[ing] zeal to outrun discretion and sentiment to have greater weight than sober facts."

Crowther could not bear to see the most outstanding of his labors torn down. He was determined "that the pulling down should not extend to the Delta Mission."[33] He announced his resignation from the committee, and planned a native pastorate in the Delta. The purpose was to make it

---

Examination of the Official Missionary Strategy of the Church Missionary Society on the Niger, 1887-93" (1986); and *The Ideal of the Self-Governing Church: A Study in Victorian Missionary Strategy* (1990).
29. Wilbert Shenk, *Henry Venn—Missionary Statesman* (1983:112).
30. *The Intelligencer* (1889:123-124); and CMS Register, no. 1148.
31. G.W. Brooke to J. Touch, June 5, 1890. CMS, G3/A3/93. CMS Archives.
32. J.A. Robinson to Lang, August 5, 1890. CMS, G3/A3/122. CMS Archives.
33. Crowther to Lang, December 1, 1891. CMS, G3 A3/O, no. 15. CMS Archives.

possible for the people and clergy to control the affairs of the Delta with minimum interference from outside. He died on the 31st December 1891, four months before the launching of his Niger Delta pastorate.

In a climate dominated by sustained racial feelings and mistrust, the CMS appointed European successor to Crowther, appointing an African as assistant bishop only as a matter of conciliation to the agitations of Nigerians. It was not surprising, therefore, that Nigerians reacted strongly in "Ethiopian" terms. Dandeson Crowther, in recognition of what he regarded as his father's legacy, organized the Delta congregations into a pastorate on April 29, 1892.

This was significant in many ways. First, his Niger Delta pastorate was independent of the CMS mission thus constituting a transitional stage in the eventual emergence of an indigenous church under native ministry. Second, perhaps more importantly, it was a palpable triumph of African initiative intended to stifle European doubts about African administrative and organizational abilities. The eventual result was the wave of counter-assertion in schisms and secessions that led to the formation of the United Native African Church in 1891 and the African Church Bethel in 1901.

The impact of the hijacking and re-Europeanization of the Niger left the whole mission in danger of disintegration. Henry H. Dobinson, the secretary of the mission, and the only European on the Niger, came to a rude awakening. Without sufficient natives to work with, he belatedly realized the value of the African agents. He discredited his enthusiastic support of Brooke's "great purge" as being "hurried along in unknown depths of fierce-flowing river."[34] The most remarkable feature of this transformation was Dobinson's open apology in Freetown and Lagos in 1896:

> I greatly long to see an African Diocese formed. . . . May God forgive us the bitter slanderous and lying thoughts we had . . . in those dark days of 1890. . . . We condemned others, and we ourselves have done less than they did.[35]

---

34. Dobinson to Baylis, March 29, 1894. CMS, G3 A3/O, nos. 47 and 60. CMS Archives.
35. Dobinson to Baylis. CMS, G3 A3/O, nos. 47 and 60. CMS Archives.

As he later realized, the work on the Niger had been largely due to the policy of Crowther and the efforts of his men. Although Europeans may have supervised the work, it was principally sustained by Africans and was to a surprising extent the result of African initiatives. This wholehearted recognition of African agents occasioned his appeal for educated Africans to work on the Niger. Europeans, in his estimation, lacked the necessary features of working among the natives and were as such a nuisance.[36]

The Southern Baptist Mission, its Ecclesiology and Structures of Ministry

I have demonstrated that the paternalistic elements concealed within the ideology of post-Venn CMS in its handling of the Niger Mission crisis provided a powerful incentive for the trail to independency of the United Native African Church and the African Church Bethel respectively. Yet, the Anglican experience was not an isolated incident. In fact, it had its antecedence in the pattern set by the revolt that split the Baptists in 1888. It is ironical, however, that the independency that was in the CMS "the result of a conscious design of the statesmanship of Venn was, in the Baptist church, the consequence of an historical accident."[37]

Although an argument could be made that the Baptists took a more "congregational" view of church structures by according greater freedom and independence to local congregations, it is impossible to say rather straightforwardly if this was more of a denominational polity or by a hermeneutic of New Testament ecclesiastical concept. As Henry Cook has conceded, "there is no such thing as 'Baptist church polity,' because Baptists by their own fundamental principle are committed to accepting the church polity of the New Testament, and no one can really say with positive certainty what that actually is."[38]

---

36. Dobinson to Baylis. CMS, G3 A3/O, nos. 47 and 60. CMS Archives..
37. Lamin Sanneh, *West African Christianity* (1983:174).
38. See his work, *What Baptists Stand For* (1947:10, 66).

Whether or not one can say with positive certainty what aspects of the New Testament church polity have remained fundamental to Baptist ecclesiology, what is undeniable is that "Baptists would prefer to speak of the New Testament principle of the church rather than of a doctrine of the church."[39] In other words, a church is accredited on the basis of being composed of individuals who understand their relationship with one another under the Lordship of Christ, and not as an ascending series of ecclesiastical institutionalism. In Baptist belief, therefore, the local congregation is the fellowship of individual believers, whose collective experience and action provide the premise for developing their own structures of ministry and government.

This ecclesiological concept of the New Testament inscribed itself into the very fabric of Baptist missionary practice and ideology. As E.C. Routh has observed regarding one of the earliest directives of the Southern Baptist Foreign Mission Board regarding the board's operations in their different mission fields:

> A Mission consists of all regularly appointed missionaries who are in active service within specified territorial limits defined and agreed upon by the Mission and the Foreign Mission Board.... The Mission is the agency through which the Foreign Mission Board functions on the field, and through which the members of the Mission conduct a co-operative program of work.... It must have powers of self-government and freedom of action on the field in harmony with the Board's responsibility to the Southern Baptist Convention. Provision should be made, just as rapidly as possible, for the national Baptist constituency to assume full financial and administrative responsibility in the work.[40]

---

39. Han W. Florin, "The Southern Baptist Foreign Mission Enterprise in Western Nigeria: An Analysis" (1960:69).
40. Eugene Routh, "Foreign Mission Board of the Southern Baptist Convention" (1958:471).

The Southern Baptist pioneer missionary in Nigeria, T.J. Bowen, was convinced from the beginning that the Christianization of Africa should be left mainly to the hands of Africans. In his correspondence with the board, he never failed to stress the value of African agency, insisting that, "native agents are of the highest importance to our operations. In a word we cannot do without them."[41]

It is, however, possible to infer that rather than be seen as a faithful adherence to Baptist ecclesiastical polity, Bowen may have arrived at this conviction based on two reasons.[42] First, this logic may have been triggered as a result of a careful analysis of historical evidence that the Anglicans and Wesleyans owed their success to their African agents. Second, and perhaps the more expedient, was that the climate had proved fatal even to the most resolute European missionary constitution. As he reported to the board on the climatic condition of Yorubaland, "I am really afraid that our African missions will stand on a sandy foundation until we have more colored laborers. What if the brethren now in Yoruba should unexpectedly return or die, the Mission itself might be lost."[43]

The substance in Bowen's apprehension came in 1869 when the Foreign Mission Board had to withdraw entirely from Nigeria as a result of the financial bankruptcy that the American Civil War had caused the board's mission enterprise. During this time, 1869-1875, Baptist work continued and was sustained through the efforts of the American Negro J.C. Vaughan, and two Africans, M.L. Stone and Sarah Harden. As it turned out later, the roots of the schism in the Baptist church and the clamor for independency can be traced to this period.

According to Mọjọla Agbẹbi, a nationalist of Baptist denomination, "it is worthy of observation that they (the Negroes) were liberated on the ground of political expediency by the same civil war which gave self-support to the Liberian churches and subsequently to the Yoruba churches.[44]

---

41. Bowen Letter to Taylor, July 10, 1851. See also T.J. Bowen, *Adventures and Missionary Labours* (1968:xxxvi).

42. T.J. Bowen (1968:xxxvi-xxxviii).

43. Bowen Letter to Taylor, November 23, 1857.

44. For details, see J.B. Webster, *The African Churches Among the Yoruba* (1964:50).

The return of the American missionaries to Nigeria in 1875 brought strains which were contributory causes of the schism that led to the African Church Movement. During the years of missionary absence, Africans had assumed such a measure of self-reliance and leadership that they were not willing to abdicate to the returning missionary team led by the white American, W.J. David. As Lamin Sanneh has aptly described it, "Africans were unwilling to turn back the clock, and missionary insistence that this be done produced all the classic signs of a separatist scenario."[45]

The insistence of African agency led by M.L. Stone that the Nigerian church had passed the phase of white supervision conflicted sharply with David's contention that Africans must remain in a subordinate position. While Stone's point of reference was that Baptist polity bestowed legitimacy on self-support and the accompanying independence, David largely neglected this aspect of ecclesiastical stipulation, emphasizing instead that the church and its African agency must remain "under the superintendence of *white man*."[46]

The result of these irreconcilable differences was the expulsion by the missionaries of Stone and his supporters. Actual separation followed in March 1888, thus initiating a trail to independency of dissatisfied Africans both within the Baptist church and in other mission-planted churches.

There are other versions that have attempted to define the reasons behind the schism. One account held that Stone was engaged in trading activities to supplement his salary. The missionary, W.J. David advised him to stop, Stone then asked for salary increase and upon being refused, resigned his ministerial appointment with the Baptist church. Another version held that Stone asked for salary increase and upon being refused took to trading and was dismissed. Yet another version traced the beginning of the discord to David's refusal to use his influence to secure finances for Stone's further training in America just as he had previously done for S.M. Harden.[47]

---

45. Lamin Sanneh, *West African Christianity* (1983:174).
46. E.A. Ayandele, *The Missionary Impact on Modern Nigeria* (1966:199).
47. For accounts of these different versions, see J.F. Ade Ajayi *Christian Missions in Nigeria* (1965); and J.B. Webster *The African Churches Among the Yoruba* (1964).

Whatever the true story may be, what must be put into perspective is that the divisive outcome of ecclesiastical affiliation was shaped by the response of the missionaries and their insensitivity to domestic clamor for indigenous leadership. However, unlike the Anglicans who set out with a resolve on the desirability of re-Europeanization, the Baptists surrendered to African leadership. As it later turned out, the Anglicans "reaped a major schism in 1901; the Baptists enjoyed a reunion in 1914."[48]

The Emerging Theology of the Church

Evangelical concern to create Christian communities, as we have noted, took the gospel message to the African hinterland. To this extent, it is fair to say that the concern for evangelism was undoubtedly the primary motivation of missionary attempts to transform aspects of their host societies. It must be added, however, that such an orientation could not avoid a clash of African cosmologies and the dogma of missionary theology. It was difficult to lay out a hermeneutical pathway in the complex task of evangelization. What I intend to do, therefore, is to attempt to display the lines of continuity connecting the theology of the missionaries in its Western cultural orientation, and indicating, at the same time, its spiritual ethos in directing the personal and social lives of the new Christian communities.[49]

Evangelical Theology and the General Hermeneusis of the Gospel

The internal conviction of nineteenth-century evangelical theology, which constituted its comprehensive interpretive scheme, was its commitment to the message of the work of Christ. Evangelicals not only preached the atoning death of Christ as a vicarious propitiatory sacrifice for the human

---

48. J.B. Webster (1964:60).
49. I do not intend to infer that the missionaries had a "theology of mission" as it has come to be perceived in contemporary missiology. Rather, I refer to the theological views that constituted the organizing principle for missionary activities and responses to cultural questions.

race, but the overarching feature of their message was its interpretation as a "salvific economy," as God's plan of redemption. Consequently, topics such as sin, death, and eternal perdition, as important as they were, became subordinate to Christ's messianic dignity as the fulfillment of the universal hope of salvation.[50]

This Christocentric perspective of the gospel was understood to be the objective of the missionary enterprise and the central focus of responsible evangelization. Baptist Noel, an Anglican Evangelical who became a Baptist declared:

> Whatever may be the results of mission, or whatever the apparent impracticability of the work, God has said that missionaries must be sent, and Christians send them. To these efforts they are no less prompted by the world's necessities. Millions are now perishing in ungodliness and immorality because they know not Christ, who might be saved by the preaching of the Gospel. They are now miserable and the Gospel would instantly ameliorate their lot; they are exposed to the curse of God, and the Gospel would bring them under his blessing: how can Christians believe this and leave them to perish?[51]

For its part, the CMS General Committee did not fail to emphasize the centrality of Christ, and of the message of the gospel in its written instructions to missionaries:

> The Saviour of sinners will be the theme of your preaching, teaching, and private meditation, and pervade your entire

---

50. On the question of the final state of the "heathen," the CMS took no official party line. Henry Venn declared himself in 1850 unable to come to "any firm conclusion in my own judgment either from scripture or reason." Instead, he turned to "all enlightened writers upon the question," particularly first-generation CMS leader Thomas Scott, in arguing that the divine love demonstrated in the vicarious death of Christ was motive enough to go to the "heathen." See Wilbert Shenk, *Henry Venn—Missionary Statesman* (1983:27); and Brian Stanley, *The Bible and the Flag* (1990:66).

51. Baptist W. Noel, *Christian Missions to Heathen Nations* (1842:346-347).

life—Christ in the pulpit, Christ in the bazaar, Christ in the school, Christ in the household, Christ in the closet; for Christ is in the heart.[52]

This cognitive dimension to the gospel became the finer points of missionary preaching on authentic transformation at both personal and social levels.

Personal and Social Transformation

The Christian message preached by the missionaries did not deviate from its traditional content of calling people to leave the old ways and make a radical turn to Jesus Christ. And with Western perception of Africa as a "dark continent" and its people as "perishing heathen," the purveyors of the gospel of truth and light came to see Nigeria as a soteriological necessity; a place and people that needed to be changed. As a result, native customs and ways of life such as polygamy, domestic slavery, and politico-religious systems became theological issues of highest priority in the missionary imperative.

Polygamy

I have already identified the form of moralism and rational abstraction that constituted the Nigerian worldview regarding marriage custom and family life. However, the thought-world of mid-nineteenth-century evangelical theology and Protestant biblicism was not one that would accept African marital ideals. Despite instructions to missionaries that they should respect native customs and to avoid judging them by "Anglo-Saxon ideas," polygamy was considered a pagan practice fundamentally incompatible with Christian doctrine.[53] For their part, native agents rebutted the missionary claim, arguing that such orthodox and rigorist emphasis on monogamy undermine the "minimum qualifications necessary for salvation":

---

52. Wilbert Shenk, *Venn Bibliography* (1975, 78:522). For details on CMS General Committee's instructions to missionaries, see further Shenk, "Henry Venn's Instructions to Missionaries" (1977:467-485).
53. See Henry Venn, *Retrospect and Prospect of the Operations of the Church Missionary Society* (1865:17).

> We use our discretion that such practices which the laws of the country allow, but not being among those in immediate requirements necessary for salvation, but which Christianity after a time will abolish, are not directly interfered with.[54]

For Crowther, the Society's approach to local culture should be sensitive and sympathetic. Convinced that "Christianity does not undertake to destroy national assimilation," he advised that reform should be introduced with suavity and tact.[55] On the contrary, Henry Venn was not persuaded that there was any saving clause in the system of polygamy. He embarked on an intensive Bible study that resulted in the issuance of a memorandum of guidance for CMS missions in 1857.[56] Venn's memorandum, described as "a review of the Scriptural argument against polygamy," confirmed earlier position of the mission:

> While the wives of a polygamist, if believed to be true converts, might be received to baptism, since they were usually the involuntary victims of the custom, no man could be admitted who retained more than one wife.[57]

Venn held unshakably to the biblical conviction that Christ equated polygamy with adultery; supporting his theological argument with the written exhortation of 1 Corinthians, "Let every man have his own wife, and let every woman have her own husband" (7:2-4). He held further "that persons living in polygamy be not admitted to baptism until such time as they shall be in a position to accept the law of Christ."[58] Consequently, the rejection of polygamy became the most sensitive element in the essential

---

54. Crowther to Venn, January 3, 1875. CMS, CA2/031. CMS Archives.
55. Crowther to Venn, January 3, 1875. CMS, CA2/031. CMS Archives.
56. For an account of Henry Venn's scriptural examination and conclusion, see William Knight's *Memoir of the Rev. Henry Venn: The Missionary Secretariat of Henry Venn* (1880:345-357). See also Max Warren's *To Apply the Gospel* (1971:79-82).
57. See Eugene Stock, *History of the Church Missionary Society*, vol. 3 (1899:646).
58. Secretaries to missionaries in Yoruba, February 17, 1857. CMS, CA2/L2. CMS Archives.

dogma of mid-nineteenth-century missionary theology, contrasting sharply to a rather sanguine attitude to domestic slavery:

> The Committee think there'll be no hesitation to refuse baptism to a kidnapper of slaves unless he has repented and left his evil way, because the practice is directly contrary to Scripture. But the Committee would not interfere with the discretion of a missionary in admitting a slave-holder to baptism. The Word of God has not forbidden the holding of slaves, though it has forbidden the oppression and injustice of various other evils which too often, though not necessarily, cleave to the character of the slave-holder. Christianity will ameliorate the relationship between master and slave; polygamy is an offence against the law of God, and therefore is incapable of amelioration.[59]

Once the undesirability of polygamy was established by an appeal to Christian orthodoxy, the stage was set to implement an individualistic direction of missions. For the missionaries it was the individual conversion to God and to better moral conduct that mattered. In some cases, new converts were gathered into mission houses that functioned as the nucleus of "civilization" and the centre of a new way of life. These converts had become "new creatures in Christ" and must be insulated from the harmful influences of the national moral depravity around them.

As strategic as the emphasis on individual conversion was, it created another grievous situation diametrically opposed to the monolithic structure of the Nigerian society. It marked the beginning of a gradual disintegration of communal solidarity eminently represented in family social units. Similarly, the Anglican church's rigid stand on monogamy raised other moral and theological issues. To simply "put away" all wives except the first was a legalistic answer that gave little thought to the welfare of those wives who were put away. At best it was an awkward solution to questionable

---

59. Secretaries to missionaries in Yoruba, 1857. CMS, CA2/L2. CMS Archives.

alternatives of remedying the offence of polygamy with the resultant sin of divorce, prostitution, and abdication of conjugal responsibility.

The Lambeth Conference of 1888 did little to help the Nigerian cause. Instead, it sealed the Anglican position by placing the authority of the Church firmly behind Venn's memorandum. The Anglican Church leadership believed that converts who gave themselves to Christ in other ways and did not abandon polygamy have not entered into full commitment either to Christ or to full Christian fellowship.[60] The conference did not resolve the tension but instead created other problems. It led to other urgent issues relating to conditions of church membership, baptism, and Holy Communion.

The theological significance of such practices as baptism and Holy Communion is that they demonstrate the highest expression of the love of Christ and participating in them are a means of grace rather than a reward for righteousness. One of the strongest voices in pointing out the theological implications of the Anglican position was Bishop Sumitra, the first moderator of the Church of South India. Commenting on polygamy during his extensive tour of Nigeria in 1955, Bishop Sumitra argued:

> The practice of prohibiting from the Holy Communion those who have more than one wife deprives them of "spiritual food" which is necessary for the growth in the spirit. There can be no church life in a community in which about 70 or 80 or 90 percent of members never approach the Lord's Table. I am not advocating polygamy, but I want the church in Nigeria to understand the direct effect of its policy. Polygamy must be stopped. It can be stopped only by African Christians who by the Grace of God have been converted to monogamy. Instruction, persuasion, sympathy and love on the one hand, and prayer, united worship and witness on the other hand, can effect changes.[61]

---

60. For a full discussion of the Lambeth Conference, see Arthur Phillips, *Survey of African Marriage and Family Life* (1953:351-354).
61. Bishop Sumitra as quoted in Michael Marioghae and John Ferguson, *Nigeria Under*

Unfortunately, as with other indigenous voices, Sumitra's went unheeded.

Domestic Slavery

It was one thing for evangelical humanitarianism to be drawn into the Niger by the strategic lobbies of British abolitionism, it was quite another thing to exterminate native interests and the prominence attached to domestic slavery. As I have already pointed out, unlike the chattel slavery perpetrated by the West, the economic interest in domestic slave-dealing and the apparent leniency and gentleness of its operations, made any missionary anti-domestic slavery policy a particularly difficult one.

In Yorubaland where the practice was most prevalent, for example, the Southern Baptist Mission did not make any fuss about the institution. This cannot be too surprising since woven into the fabric of Southern Baptist thought and life was the conviction that engaging the services of a slaveholder was not inconsistent with Christian ideals and benevolence. What was to constitute missionary involvement was occasioned in 1877 with the appointment of James Johnson, a native agent of the CMS, as the new superintendent of Abeokuta and Ibadan.

"Holy Johnson," as he was nicknamed in Lagos for his zealous and puritanical fervor, did not mince words on what he felt about domestic slavery after traveling through the areas of his superintendence. In his characteristic opposition to the holding of slaves by agents of the CMS Yoruba Mission, he declared, "[t]here is no Christian government to stamp out this accursed institution with the stroke of a pen. We must [work] it out through the church and educate our people to it."[62] Out of consideration to Johnson's denunciation, the CMS took necessary steps between 1879 and 1890. Even then, their response did not constitute a sufficient condition for total eradication. Instead, they drew up a minute on domestic slavery and sent a copy to Johnson:

---

the Cross (1965:65).

62. Report from James Johnson on Ibadan, August, 1877. CMS, CA2/056. CMS Archives. For a useful account on the prevalence of this practice in Yorubaland, see E.A. Oroge, "The Institution of Slavery in Yorubaland, with Particular Reference to the Nineteenth Century" (1971).

> With members generally of the Christian church in Africa, the committee do no more than appeal in loving remembrance . . . . but no one in the employment of the Society shall hold man, woman or child, or have personally any connection with the practice.[63]

Perhaps the only theological interpretation on the practice was the pronouncement in the Society's *Intelligencer*,

> We venture to maintain that slavery in any shape or form, as distinguished from voluntary hiring and service, is thoroughly alien from the spirit of the Gospel. . . . As the law of gravitation determines the descent of heavy bodies, so, as its necessary result, the spirit of the Word of God has eliminated slavery from Christianity.[64]

The Society's adherents remained undeterred but rebutted with an alternative theological position deduced from Pauline advice for slave-owners to exemplify kindly and peaceable conduct towards their slaves. This apparent theological crossfire, and the threat of "a wholesale slaughter of the Native Christians . . . and a total extirpation of Christianity,"[65] drew the CMS into a position of compromise.

In order to forestall anticipated attacks on their anti-slavery propaganda, the Society did not only renege from excommunicating slave-owing members, it also set up a Court of Redemption in Abeokuta in 1881. Through this court the Society was able to redeem some of the slaves along the traditional lines of redemption and gave them freedom and Christian training. After 1890 the Society made no more reference to domestic slavery but left it to the formidable battery of colonial gunfire.

---

63. "Minutes of the Parent Committee on Domestic Slavery in the Yoruba Mission." CMS, CA2/L4. CMS Archives.
64. *The Church Missionary Intelligencer* (1880:399). Quoted in E.A. Ayandele, *The Missionary Impact on Modern Nigeria* (1966:332).
65. CMS Agents: Letter to the CMS Secretariat, June 14, 1889. CMS, G3/A2/05. CMS Archives.

Politico-Religious Systems

We have indicated what the missionary theological response was to polygamy and slave-owning. The negative positions of missionaries did not account for the fact that Africans saw both institutions as indicators of respect and social status. These two spheres, intersecting with a third, the politico-religious sphere, presented what the missionaries understood to constitute another problematic dimension in their attempts to transform all areas of the Nigerian life and culture.

Pressured by local traditions, the missionaries felt they must advise converts if their new faith could be integrated with traditional practices of the culture. In fact, the missionaries found themselves caught up in the infinite complexities of native customs which they did not understand or accept. A case in point was the secret cults with the conflicting interpretations attached to them. On one hand, treating the Ogboni cult of the Yoruba people as a religious institution, for example, would require holding it up as an idolatrous practice and, as such, it was incompatible with Christianity. On the other hand, to look upon the Ogboni as a part of the civil or community structure would require giving it the degree of public respect it deserves.

Beclouded by such confusion, the parent committee of the CMS took to a middle ground, advising its missionaries and African agents not to abandon Christian ideals and principles for nationalistic sentiment:

> That whilst there is a wide difference of opinion amongst those equally well informed respecting the connexion of the Ogboni system with idolatry, yet as all agree that it is inconsistent with the principles of the Christian religion, and must fall when these principles prevail in the country; it is necessary that the Native Christian church should maintain its high position of witnessing for the truth by a broad separation from this and all other questionable country fashion.... That as the system is believed by many Christians to be essentially idolatrous, those who take a different view of the case and who may regard themselves as "stronger" than their brethren, should

nevertheless abstain from all connexion with the system upon the principles laid down by St. Paul in the 8th and 10th Chapters of the First Epistle to the Corinthians lest a "weaker" brother be offended.[66]

Instead of disappearing in the conflict with the establishment of Christian principles, the Ogboni cult received considerable attention from both native and European mission agencies. First, there was the "Christianization" of the old Ogboni cult through what was given the specious name, "Christian Ogboni Society." Perhaps the bolder attempt was the "heathenization" of Christianity which came about through the adoption of Ogboni symbols and titles into Christian rituals and the insistence that the "Christian Ogboni Society" was the best expression of Yoruba Christianity.[67] Membership in Ogboni and other secret societies acquired certain notoriety, leading Peel to say that this "has continued to be a vexatious issue among Christians and Muslims down to the Nigerian present."[68]

Although the missionaries were unavoidably driven into a compromising position about freemasonry due to ambiguous interpretations as to what it really was. Nevertheless, there was no question in their minds about native religious system. Considered an idolatrous system that was overtly rebellious to the governance of God and the lordship of Christ, missionary reaction to the indigenous religious system was one extremely negative. Anna Hinderer declared after seventeen years of work in Yorubaland, that their "religion is a system of idolatry in which a multitude of Orishas, or idols, above all, Ifa, the god of divinations, who is represented and consulted by means

---

66. Minutes of the Parent Committee on the Ogboni System, November 23, 1861. CMS, CA2/L3. CMS Archives.
67. For some useful discussions on the Christian Ogboni Society/Reformed Ogboni Fraternity, see E.A. Ayandele, *The Missionary Impact on Modern Nigeria* (1966:270-8); Bolaji Idowu, *Olódùmarè: God in Yorùbá Belief* (1962:228-231); Geoffrey Parrinder *Religion In an African City* (1953:174-184); and Gordon Hewitt *The Problems of Success: A History of the Church Missionary Society, 1910-1942* (1971:64-65).
68. J.D.Y. Peel, *Religious Encounter and the Making of the Yoruba* (2000:270).

of palm-nuts, are worshipped as mediators between the people and the Supreme God whom they acknowledge."[69]

Natives who were attached to the missions also shared this perception. Samuel Crowther, for example, could not emphasize enough the darkness and degradation of idolatrous system and peoples. He thought of his Yoruba countrymen as gross idolaters because while they "acknowledge the worship of the only true God as superior to any other," they could not give up their gods whom they believed to be "created by the great God for the good of mankind," and who, therefore, "ought to be worshipped." To him, these divinities were devices of Satan to keep people away from God and in a state of darkness and superstition.[70]

The belief in the existence of many gods as mediators between the people and God was considered an affront to the sovereignty and rule of God. More importantly, it struck at the very heart of missionary Christocentric theology. Driven into this situation of contestation and problematic theology, the missionaries assumed that the baneful influence of idolatry extended to all aspects of the native culture. Consequently, the missionary conscience was further influenced to emphasize a salvation-gospel for the misguided African soul who needs to be redirected to the truth that is in Jesus.

Protestant Missions, Ecclesiastical Colonialism, and Respectability

Presently, as Africans evaluate the Protestant missionary enterprise, a characteristic theme is vehement denunciation of the missionary movement for its complicity with exploitation during the colonial era. While an exhaustive documentation of the force of this negativism can dangerously distract from the main focus of this book, a typical example of

---

69. Anna Hinderer, *Seventeen Years in the Yoruba Country: Memorials of Anna Hinderer, Wife of the Rev. David Hinderer, Church Missionary Society Missionary in West Africa* (1872:19).
70. For details, see P.R. McKenzie, *Inter-religious Encounters in West Africa* (1976:17).

the condemnatory rhetoric will suffice. When attempting to define "Black Consciousness" in the early 1970s, for example, Pityana writes of Protestant missions in this way:

> It has been alleged with truth that the trader and the settler followed the missionary, who was the agent of European imperialism, working hand in hand with the colonial powers for the subjugation of the black people and the territorial extension of the imperialist power.[71]

Perhaps in no other area have the missionaries been so much maligned for imposing Anglo-American values and consciousness over indigenous traditions in the name of expanding the worldwide Christiandom. Biobaku charges them with "undermining native custom,"[72] while in the opinion of Ade Ajayi, the missionaries were not merely bearers of Protestant evangelicalism but were vehicles of the ideological thrust of Western hegemony and civilization.[73] Even more devastating is the summary by Ayandele:

> Missionary activity was a disruptive force, rocking traditional society to its very foundations, denouncing ordered polygamy in favour of disordered monogamy, producing disrespectful, presumptuous and detribalized children through the mission schools, destroying the high moral principles and orderliness of indigenous society through denunciation of traditional religion, without an adequate substitute, and transforming the mental outlook of Nigerians in a way that made them imitate European values slavishly, whilst holding in irrational contempt valuable features of traditional culture.[74]

---

71. N. Pityana, "What is Black Consciousness?" (1973:59).
72. O. Saburi Biobaku, *The Egba and Their Neighbours* (1957:35).
73. J.F. Ade Ajayi, *Christian Missions in Nigeria* (1965:14).
74. See especially chapter 5 of his work, *Missionary Impact on Modern Nigeria* (1966). For an examination of other African criticisms of the missionary enterprise, see Harris Mobley, *The Ghanaian's Image of the Missionary* (1970); and Ram Desai, *Christianity in Africa as*

Although education, medicine, agriculture, and other civilizing efforts were considered by the missionaries to be legitimate social correlates of evangelism, these activities should not be disparaged or looked upon as contradictory to the gospel. Afterall, care for the whole person was a hallmark of Jesus' own earthly ministry. Consequently, fairness and objectivity require an appreciation of the motivation, commitment, and endurance of the early mission work.

No matter the ideological point of view of the missionaries, there is no denying the fact that the primary motivation was the numerical vision of saving perishing souls, propelled by the divine mandate to "go ye into all the world." If the motivation had been otherwise, we can assume that the missionaries would have withdrawn at the very points where death and tropical diseases diverted and nearly overwhelmed them. How are we to reconcile the following words of Baptist pioneer missionary T.J. Bowen with the accusations that the missionary purpose was to plant the cultural forms of bourgeois America in Nigerian soil?

> Let me be poor and forgotten but let me not violate that impulse of heart which has almost dragged me to this land and still continues unabated. . . . When I look round on these thousands of people ever ready to listen to the gospel, who can wonder if I should feel that tribulation, nor distress, nor persecution, nor famine, nor peril, nor sword, nor any other cause must be allowed to lead or drive me from this work.[75]

Mrs. David, wife of Baptist missionary W.J. David, mustered her last words to her husband. With her almost lifeless lips she said, "never give up Africa."[76] This was after the couple had lost two of their four children to missionary work in Nigeria:

Seen by Africans (1962).
75. For details, see Edgar H. Burks, *Planting the Redeemer's Standard: A Life of Thomas J. Bowen, First Baptist Missionary to Nigeria* (1994:42).
76. George W. Sadler, *A Century in Nigeria* (1950:89).

> With sad and aching hearts we turned away, leaving our little Nettie, to whom we cling, as we thought of our first-born beneath the palms of Africa and our only son in the deep, deep sea.[77]

Yet these examples are incomparable to the totality of suffering for the sake of the gospel. To reckon these fatalities as divine retribution as some have claimed can only be attributed to persons with no sense of human decency. We do well to heed the words of Lamin Sanneh who argues that:

> To view missionaries as perennial historical villains is too one sided to be useful for any dynamic understanding of change, and that to view Africans as a victimized projection of Western ill will is to leave them with too little initiative to be arbiters of their destiny and meaningful players on the historical stage.[78]

If our assault on missions is now driven by simply questioning all types of foreign domination—cultural, political, and religious—we would also do well to remember that by reducing our languages to writing, missionaries gave us the most treasured possession of our cultures and a sense of national pride. Perhaps this was what Andrew Walls infers when he states, "if missionaries are associated with the rise of imperialism, they are equally associated with the factors which brought about its destruction."[79]

The argument that the missionaries were a collective colonizing consciousness of imperialism is loaded with contradictions. Mission historians have shown clearly that senior colonial officials not only rejected people connected to the church but actively combated them with administrative measures.[80] Although there were some complex political maneuvers on the part of the missionaries, these were only complementary

---

77. Louis M. Duval, *Baptist Missions in Nigeria* (1928:109).
78. Lamin Sanneh, "The Yogi and the Commissar: Christian Missions and the African Response" (1991:2-11). See also his earlier work, *West African Christianity* (1987).
79. Ruth Tucker, *From Jerusalem to Irian Jaya* (1983:111).
80. Lamin Sanneh, *Encountering the West* (1993:206).

to the intertribal wars and other local conflicts that threatened to snuff out the gospel light that many of their colleagues had died for.

Writing particularly about Nigeria, Yusufu Turaki did not see Protestant missions as an imperial project, declaring instead, "Colonialism is quite distinct from missions even though both were products of the same society, sharing the same socio-political roots, worldview and ethos but each differs from the other in its primary motif, goals, objectives and interests."[81] Commenting also about the strain on missionary-colonial relationships, Turaki stresses:

> Colonial control and regulations of missions were also transferred to their converts. . . . Northerners who became Christians were subjected to much ridicule and contemptuous treatment by some of the British political officers. . . . Ayandele and Crampton listed some of the cruel treatment of African converts by the British political officers.[82]

What may be associated respectively with ideology and hegemony in the missionary enterprise were the "imperial" demands of the gospel. The missionaries had a clear and compelling grasp of the "absolutist element in Christian theology" and understood that the "gospel of Christ has reference to all areas of human life [without] exclusions from his claims to sovereignty."[83] It was inevitable, then, that in becoming Christians, both the natives and certain elements of indigenous culture must undergo a transformation, that is, some sort of conversion that accepts new elements while purging itself of others.

The missionaries may have over-idealized their convictions, they may have displayed paternalistic attitudes in their lack of trust in the indigenous capacity to discharge ecclesiastical responsibilities, they may also have

---

81. Yusufu Turaki, "The Socio-Political Context of Christian-Muslim Encounter in Northern Nigeria" (1995:123). See also Frances F. Hiebert, "Beyond a Post-Modern Critique of Modern Missions: The Nineteenth Century Revisited" (1997:259-275).
82. Yusufu Turaki, "The Socio-Political Context of Christian-Muslim Encounter in Northern Nigeria" (1995:130).
83. Brian Stanley, *The Bible and the Flag* (1990:184, 172).

protected their own biases and failed to recognize the values of culture, still fairness demands that we must not assume the judgments of character or purpose without taking into consideration the inevitability of simple human fallibility.[84]

In the final analysis, we do well to succumb to the fact that "[t]he history of the Christian mission in the colonial period must in the end be left to the judgment of God, who alone knows all the facts. . . . One thing, however, may be said. . . . As a result of the Christian mission in the colonial period, the Christian church exists in every corner of the earth."[85]

Summary

Thus far I have explored the contours and the policy decisions which governed missionary operations in Nigeria. After one hundred and seventy plus years since sustained missionary activities began in Nigeria, it is the consensus presently that the Christian influence has been deep, effective, and growing. The paradox of the whole Protestant missions, as I have highlighted, is the indigenous nationalism that has produced critics of the entire missionary enterprise. Even the fact that many of these critics owe their education and literary reputation to the benefits that the missions provided has not invoked much sympathy. How then are we to reconcile these differences?

Words such as inculturation, and more recently, contextualization, have become common currency in missiological anthropology. Unfortunately, what we have overlooked is the inherent difficulty the missionaries faced in reconciling the absolutist elements of the Christian faith with the religious and cultural assumptions of the local people at a time when the fields of missiology or applied anthropology were non-existent.

The unwarranted generalizations of the whole mission enterprise as "ethnocentric," "oppressive," "colonialist," and "imperialist," certainly are not conducive to better understanding. What we need is an appreciation of

---

84. C.G. Baëta, *Christianity in Tropical Africa* (1968:14).
85. Stephen Neill, *Colonialism and Christian Missions* (1966:424-425).

the missionary labors and perhaps a re-interpretation of historical events so as to heal the pains of the past and move towards a creative future for the Nigerian church. The self-deception and myopia inherent in the campaign to remake the Nigerian world by negatively interpreting highlights of the missionary enterprise is an attempt to replace one hegemony with another. The period of independency in Nigeria Christianity demonstrates this clearly and it is to this aspect of our inquiry that I now turn.

PART III

Reclaiming the Context: The Rise of Nigerian Indigenous Church Movements, 1918-1980s

The Nigerian Christian experience is formed around a great story. Initially set within the ecclesiastical construct of the Western mind and its idealistic vision of the number of perishing "heathen," the Nigerian experience provided the occasion for Christian philanthropy. It was no labor loss because the Nigerian context was shown to be conducive to the message of the gospel. The result was the establishment of mainline denominations with deep roots in Western forms and theology.

But this story is one of change. Since the inception of Protestant Christianity dating back to the mid-nineteenth century (1841), the expressions of church in Nigeria have been revised in the context of changing cultural and ecclesiastical transitions. The first of such changes was orchestrated by the indigenous church movements with their emphasis on authentic African expression of Christianity.

In what follows, I will explore these movements by identifying the intellectual starting point of their theme of ecclesiastical independence. I will also examine and analyze their attempts to contextualize Christianity to local aspirations.

CHAPTER 4

Nigerian Ecclesiastical Independency

In discussing independency in Nigerian Christianity, one cannot dismiss the initial response epitomized by the Ethiopian movement.[1] Ethiopianism, which had been embryonic during the second half of the nineteenth century, is a phenomenon of momentous significance, comparable in many ways to the sixteenth-century Reformation in Europe.[2]

Rooted in cultural nationalism, the point about Ethiopianism is that it retained characteristics of the mission churches while making African culture visible. In other words, Ethiopianism provided an outlet to assert a new kind of Africanness that focused on racial equality and ecclesiastical independence. This dual nature of Ethiopianism, the religious and the political aspects, are not fully appreciated in studies on independent church movements.[3]

---

1. The term "Ethiopianism" was coined from Ps. 68:31: "Ethiopia shall soon stretch out her hands unto God" (KJV). The term is symbolic of all Africa and was motivated by the conviction that the day of Africa's liberation had arrived. It should be mentioned, however, that West African Ethiopianism differs from the one associated with Central and Southern Africa. For studies on the South and Central Africa brand of Ethiopianism, see Bengt Sundkler, *Bantu Prophets in South Africa* (1961); and George Shepperson and Thomas Price, *Independent Africa* (1958).
2. For arguments in this regard, see David Barrett, *Schism and Renewal in Africa: An Analysis of Six Thousand Contemporary Religious Movements* (1968); and Allan Anderson, *African Reformation: African Initiated Christianity in the 20th Century* (2001).
3. J. Mutero Chirenje's *Ethiopianism and Afro-Americans in Southern Africa, 1883-1916* (1987) was one of the earliest works to highlight this dual nature of Ethiopianism at a time when most scholars were concerned with securing precision of terminology.

The Starting Point of Independency

The waves of dissent and schism that I have mentioned as sweeping across Protestant missions in Nigeria towards the end of the nineteenth century did not emerge in a vacuum. Rather, we can gain insight into the nascent stage of independency by looking further at the missionary activities that prompted a critical response among early advocates of the Ethiopian ideology.

Missionary Ideologies and Activities

The consecration of Ajayi Crowther as bishop was to Africans a symbol of racial self-respect as well as the groundswell of indigenous confidence in ecclesiastical and national leadership. Unfortunately, the gains of Venn's missionary strategy were diminished by the bitter criticisms of overzealous iconoclasts in the Niger Mission who arrived between 1887 and 1890. These Cambridge-trained, young, and industrious English "reformers" were disposed toward paternalism. To them, Venn's ideas were sentimental and premature. Led by G.W. Brooke and J.A. Robinson, the general secretary of the mission during this time (1887-1890), their mission was to keep intact the paternalistic expression of the church.

In their undisguised disapproval of Venn's scheme for the native pastorate, Robinson said with much contempt that "[t]he Negro race shows almost no signs of 'ruling' power."[4] Their natural objective, therefore, was to dismantle the building-up of African nationalism for a European-led, missionary-controlled ecclesiastical structure. As G.W. Brooke unequivocally puts it, "there is no hope of success until we have first taken down the whole of the past work so that not one stone remains upon another."[5]

The dismantling of the Niger Mission and the collapse of Bishop Crowther's episcopate hardly need be rehearsed.[6] However, it is necessary

---

4. Robinson to Lang, June 20, 1889. CMS, G3/A3/04. CMS Archives.
5. Brooke to J. Touch, June 5, 1890. CMS, G3/A3/93. CMS Archives.
6. The Niger crisis continues to inspire varied reactions and interpretations. Of note is Ogbu Kalu's argument that these young European missionaries were "the true indigenizers." For details, see his work, "Beyond Nationalist Historiography: White Indigenizers of the Igbo Church, 1876-1892" (1992).

to highlight that Africans saw the ignominious treatment of Crowther as an insult upon the whole Negro race. It leaves little to the imagination, therefore, that even Muslim leaders, traditional chiefs, and the Nigerian newspapers were unanimous in their outburst of ill-treatment.[7]

Consequently, the controversy that ensued over the reassertion of white control by the CMS acquired racial overtones. It also generated a backlash of separatist sentiment. The nationalism of James Johnson and his followers called for "Africa for the Africans." The determination to establish an independent African church turned "Ethiopians" into "Independents," altering the basis of the Nigerian church in the process.

From Ethiopianism to Independentism

It is not surprising that the slighted labors of the Africans in the denationalization of the Niger Mission provided the context for increased agitation for ecclesiastical independency. It is important, therefore, to recognize that the crude manner in which paternalism was allowed to overwhelm ecclesiastical convention was not appropriate. Despite the argument that the clamor for an independent African church was premature and ill-fated, it should be noted that the clamor for independency was not so much about the innovation of doctrine.[8] This is evident in the fact that none of the torchbearers of independency stepped over into doctrinal schism.[9]

In their call for administrative autonomy, the important thing for the Africans was the compelling mandate to repair the torn fabric of African hope. In the words of James Johnson, the most learned and respected of the African Anglican clergy, "there are times when it is more helpful that

---

7. E.A. Ayandele, *The Missionary Impact on Modern Nigeria* (1966:217).

8. For perspectives that argue that the clamor for African ecclesiastical independency was ill-fated and premature, see Jehu J. Hanciles "The Legacy of James Johnson" (1997). See also Stephen Neill, *The Unfinished Task* (1957); and *Colonialism and Christian Missions* (1966).

9. It should be pointed out that Edward Blyden's call for the establishment of a quasi-political religious organization in what he called the West African Church was stifled at birth precisely for this purpose. For details, see J.B. Webster, *The African Churches Among the Yoruba* (1964); Lamin Sanneh, *Translating the Message* (1989); and *West African Christianity: The Religious Impact* (1983).

a people should be called upon to take up their responsibilities, struggle with and conquer their difficulty than that they should be in the position of vessels taken in tow, and that for West African Christianity, this is the time."[10]

With a declaration as clear as this, it is important that we distinguish between the religious factors and the quasi-political agitations of Edward Blyden, James Johnson, and Mọjọla Agbẹbi, who were the leading participants in the independence crusade.[11]

Edward Blyden, James Johnson, and Mọjọla Agbẹbi[12]

Animated by the spirit of the slogan, "Africa for the Africans," these three can best be described as the apostles of cultural nationalism. Although united in their policy of Africanization, each exerted a peculiar sphere of influence in the overall campaign for independence. Edward Blyden, for example, was an erudite Pan-Africanist from Liberia who was criticizing the church from without with his vitriolic pamphlets, books, lectures, and correspondence. His visit to Lagos in December 1890 fuelled the smoldering forces that had been gathering over the Niger Mission.[13]

His campaign was not merely to extol African identity. Equally important to him was the need to make church liturgy and canons culturally relevant to the African culture. According to him, Africa was "the first home of God," hence "the Christ we worship must be African . . . [for] the Christ revealed in the Bible is far more African than anything else."[14] Unfortunately,

---

10. J.B. Webster, *The African Churches Among the Yoruba* (1964:1).

11. For prior discussion concerning this perspective, see Lamin Sanneh, *West African Christianity: The Religious Impact* (1983:173-180); and *Translating the Message* (1989:139-141). See also J.D.Y. Peel, *Aladura: A Religious Movement Among the Yoruba* (1968:56).

12. Mojola Agbẹbi's name prior to 1894 was D.B. Vincent. He changed his name as a way of exemplifying his campaign for the retention of native names, customs, and habits.

13. Blyden's biographer, H.R. Lynch, speaks of him as "the most learned and articulate champion of Africa and the Negro race in his own time." For more on Lynch's work, see *Edward Wilmot Blyden: Pan Negro Patriot, 1832-1912* (1967).

14. See Edward Blyden's works, "West Africa before Europe" (1903:361-365); and *The Three Needs of Liberia* (1908:32).

Blyden's vision of a West African church was seriously hampered by hints of doctrinal schism.[15]

Johnson and Agbẹbi, on the other hand, were "reformers" within the CMS Anglican and the Southern Baptist Mission respectively. Considered to be the "pioneer of African nationalism" and "the leading figure in the agitation for ecclesiastical independence,"[16] Johnson was no less equivocal in his claims. In a declaration characteristic of his grievances with the Niger Mission he declares:

> [t]he desire to have an independent church closely follows the knowledge that we are a distinct race, existing under peculiar circumstances and possessing peculiar characteristics . . . and that the arrangement of foreign churches made to suit their own local circumstances can hardly be expected to suit our own in all their details.[17]

Compelling as he was in the wave of African counter-assertion, James Johnson's Ethiopian rhetoric remained ambiguous and his clamor for ecclesiastical independence was hindered by an unwavering loyalty to the CMS.

Spiked on the twin prongs of Blyden's numerous writings and the sensational speeches of Johnson, Mọjọla Agbẹbi, for his part, embodied a sharpened articulation of the spirit of cultural nationalism. "To render Christianity indigenous to Africa," he declared, "it must be watered by native hands, pruned with the native hatchet, and tended with native earth. . . . It is a curse if we intend for ever to hold at the apron strings of foreign teachers, doing the baby for aye."[18]

---

15. Lamin Sanneh, *Translating the Message* (1989:140).
16. For biographical studies on James Johnson, see E.A. Ayandele, *Holy Johnson: Pioneer of African Nationalism, 1836-1917* (1970); and Jehu Hanciles, "The Legacy of James Johnson" (1997).
17. James Johnson to M. Taylor and others, April 19, 1873. CMS, CA1/0123. CMS Archives.
18. E.A. Ayandele, *The Missionary Impact on Modern Nigeria* (1967:200).

Agbẹbi advised his contemporaries to distinguish between the "essentials" and "non-essentials" of Christianity. "Among the great essentials" of Christianity, he claimed, "are that the lame walk, the lepers are cleansed, the deaf hear, the dead are raised up and the poor have the Gospel preached to them."[19] The "non-essentials" of Christianity are the white man's names and dress, pew constructions, surpliced choir, and so on.

Herein lies the importance of Agbẹbi's brand of independency that is appreciated in Nigerian church history. He is not only to be recognized as merely taking the decisions which the other nationalists advocated.[20] More importantly, he extended the issue beyond a narrow call for ecclesiastical independence into a much larger "question of the appropriation of Christianity by indigenous criteria."[21] In an almost reckless zeal to indigenize worship forms, he declared, "to be successful [as missionaries] we have to study the names, designs, and influences of the stone and wooden gods of our fathers. . . . The lives and doings of our heathen sages, the origin of the several gods of whom our brethren worship will be useful instruments in the hands of the aggressive missionary."[22]

Here Mọjọla Agbẹbi demonstrated in practical ways his cultural nationalism. In 1894 he abandoned all his Western names, David Brown Vincent, and also rejected European dress. In both actions, "he was endeavoring to symbolize the underlying motivation of the African church movement, escape from the culturally Westernized model of Christianity."[23] His strongest achievement, without doubt, was made by fusing local (Yoruba) forms within his church to the extent that he became "recognized as the voice of the African churches in Lagos, in Britain, and in the United States."[24]

---

19. African Church Organization, *Report of Proceedings of the African Church Organizations for Lagos and Yorubaland, 1901-1908* (1910:91).

20. Adrian Hastings, *The Church in Africa, 1450-1950* (1994:494).

21. J.B. Webster, *The African Churches Among the Yoruba* (1964:68-69); and Lamin Sanneh, *Translating the Message* (1989:141), have attributed the significance of this awareness—the Africanization of Christianity through indigenous means—to the founding resolution of the United Native African Church (UNAC).

22. E.A. Ayandele, *The Missionary Impact on Modern Nigeria* (1966:264).

23. Adrian Hastings, *The Church in Africa, 1450-1950* (1994:494).

24. J.B. Webster, *The African Churches Among the Yoruba* (1964:52).

In a statement which can only be interpreted as complimentary, Webster compares him to "the Anglican converts of the Keswick revivals in Lagos in his enthusiasm for a national Yoruba Christianity."[25] We should not be too surprised, then, that he emerged as the leading figure in the 1888 secession from the Baptist mission that gave birth to the Native Baptist Church. This was a catalyzing event from which "independency was to gush forth in bursts of quick succession."[26]

Ethiopian/African Churches: Precursors of Independency

We are just beginning to understand that the complexity of African Christianity cannot be comprehended adequately through the categories and typologies per se.[27] This approach undermines the particularities of Africa's historical and cultural realities. Even well-used terms like "Ethiopian" and "African/Independent" do not describe adequately or share certain features commonly found in different parts of Africa.[28] In the midst of this complexity, perhaps it is best to follow Turner's advice to think of a typology of "tendencies and emphases rather than of individual religious bodies and movements." This way, we will be able to "construct an African typology based on the ways in which the phenomena tend to be grouped."[29]

The different expressions of church in Nigeria can fit into Turner's typology of "tendencies and emphases" without much complication. The Ethiopian/African churches in Nigeria, for example, can be understood as an anthropological rather than a theological classification. This is because

---

25. Webster (1964:52).
26. Lamin Sanneh, *West African Christianity* (1983:169).
27. See Bengt Sundkler, *Bantu Prophets in South Africa* (1961). Harold Turner's two-volume work on the Church of the Lord (Aladura) is a pioneering and sympathetic account yet published on any group of African Christians: *History of an African Independent Church, The Church of the Lord (Aladura)*, 2 vols. (1967).
28. Scholars who have devoted themselves to the study of the phenomenon of African Christianity began to highlight this problem as far back as the mid 1970s. See Martin West, *Bishop and Prophets in a Black City* (1975). See especially Harold Turner, *Religious Innovation in Africa: Collected Essays on Religious Movements* (1979).
29. Harold Turner, *Religious Innovation in Africa: Collected Essays on Religious Movements* (1979:52). See especially section B, "Methodological and Bibliographical." This approach has been adopted in a more recent study on African Christianity by Allan H. Anderson, *African Reformation: African Initiated Christianity in the 20th Century* (2001).

their Africanness is characterized by the interesting ambivalence formed by a secessionist sentiment on one hand and fidelity to a particular missionary tradition on the other. In other words, they are committed to their slogan "Africa for Africans" while upholding certain ecclesiastical and theological remains of an "older" missionary tradition.

The first of these Ethiopian-type churches in Nigeria was the Native Baptist Church established in Lagos in March 1888 by a group of disaffected Baptists who were unimpressed with missionary high-handedness.[30] Following this was the launching of the non-denominational United Native African Church. Established in August 1891 in response to the CMS's shabby handling of the Niger Mission, it had as its *raison d'être* the evangelization of Africa by Africans.[31] The sacking of James Johnson from his church in Lagos in July 1901 occasioned the third secession, the independent Bethel African Church.[32]

These Ethiopian-type "African" churches, without doubt, are abstractions from the "mainline" churches and are therefore indistinguishable in doctrine, rituals, and hierarchical structure. Their "newness" can only be described "in a historical and [not] in a qualitative sense."[33] Nevertheless, they demonstrate an insuppressible widening of the rift with the missionaries and an attempt to show an African response to European racial attitudes and ecclesiastical subjugation.

Prophetic Aladura Churches

What constituted the policy of Africanization in the first wave of indigenous reaction epitomized by the mission-derived Ethiopian/African churches found a fuller expression in the second, internal wave of Christian independency. The prophetic Christianity of the Aladura movement rose from the initiatives of Nigerians who found reasons to

---

30. Adrian Hastings, *The Church in Africa* (1994:493-497).
31. Lamin Sanneh, *West African Christianity* (1983:175-176).
32. See E.A. Ayandele, *Holy Johnson* (1970:318-325).
33. Andrew Walls, *The Missionary Movement in Christian History* (1996:114).

separate from older mission churches. Although linked in certain ways to the "Ethiopian" ideology, the Aladura group had a much wider focus on the reconceptualization of Christianity than on the more narrow issue of institutional and administrative reforms that beset their Ethiopian predecessors. When viewed as a common type, the important aspect of their ecclesiology is the retention of traditional African culture as the hermeneutical bridge for transmitting and deepening the Christian faith. This interface is most noticeable in the adoption of African symbols and rituals in matters of faith and worship.

The pioneer of this new spate of independency was the Prophet Garrick Braide, a man that was nurtured in the "tense and fraught atmosphere of the Niger Delta Pastorate."[34] Unfortunately, his ministry was hindered by the restrictions of officialdom, lasting only from 1914-1918. As a representative group of Aladura Christianity, however, I will examine the Christ Apostolic Church and the Church of the Lord (Aladura). The reason for this choice is clear. Unlike the short-lived work of Garrick Braide, these churches broke into the religious space of Nigeria with the intensity of a raging fire.

As I have already mentioned, the prophetic Christianity of the Aladura churches represents a demonstration model of a contextualized ecclesiology. Developed by Africans and shaped by the concerns and aspirations of Africans, Aladura Christianity is a complex confluence of cultural signification, ritual adaptation, and Christian self-confidence. For the church in Nigeria, the advent of these churches into the religious scene early in the twentieth century was a phenomenon with distinctive characteristics.

"Aladura," a Yoruba word standing for "praying people," was constructed on a model that arose from an indigenous reading of the Scriptures. As it will become clear in the following historical sketch, Aladura, at first, meant no more than a number of small praying groups of committed Christians functioning on the fringes of mission churches. Their emphasis on the efficacy of prayers in matters of spiritual healing, and on the significance of dreams and visions for prophetic guidance, offered a special appeal to the priorities of many Nigerian people.

---

34. Lamin Sanneh, *West African Christianity* (1983:180-184).

It is not the concern of this book to rehearse the different stories of the Aladura churches. This has been done by other scholars whose works are standard for the early history and life of these churches. Our overall concern is to understand the transforming pattern of the church in Nigeria and the radical variations it has gone through since sustained Christian missions began in the country in 1841. In light of this, my approach to the investigation of the Aladura churches will be a synthetic one. Rather than a church-by-church approach, the two Aladura churches that I have selected as case study provide the opportunity to see issues and concerns that are common to the Aladura group. Overall, the book will focus primarily on the context within which the Aladura churches emerged and on what they understood their mission to be in the whole ecclesiastical mandate.[35]

The Origins of the Aladura Churches

While the Aladura churches comprise four main subtypes and many splinter groups, they still have similarities in their origin and belief.[36] Grouped under the typology of prophet-healing movements, they emerged out of informal prayer groups during the worldwide influenza epidemic of 1918.[37]

---

35. For major studies on the four main subtypes of Aladura churches and their splinter groups, see Harold W. Turner, *History of an African Independent Church: The Church of the Lord (Aladura)* 2 vols. (1967); J.D.Y. Peel, *Aladura: A Religious Movement Among the Yoruba* (1968); J. Akinyele Omoyajowo, *Cherubim and Seraphim: The History of an African Independent Church* (1982); C.O. Oshun, "Christ Apostolic Church of Nigeria: A Suggested Pentecostal Consideration of its Historical, Organizational and Theological Developments, 1918-1975" (1981); Lamin Sanneh, *West African Christianity* (1983); and Afeosemime U. Adogame, *Celestial Church of Christ* (1999).

36. The four main subtypes, all formed between 1918 and 1930 out of the existing Anglican churches, are The Apostolic Church (1931), Christ Apostolic Church (so-named in 1941)—both churches emerged out of the Precious Stone Society, a subgroup within the Anglican Church established in 1918. The group adopted the name of its foreign "sponsor," Faith Tabernacle, in 1922, the year it severed relationship with Anglicanism. The third, the Cherubim and Seraphim Society, became a separate church about 1925. The fourth, the Church of the Lord (Aladura), became an independent church in 1930, although its founder, Josiah Oshitelu, had lost his position in the Anglican Church in 1926.

37. It is estimated that 250,000 died from the disease in all of Southern Nigeria. For details, see J.D.Y. Peel, *Aladura: A Religious Movement Among the Yoruba* (1968:62).

The prayer groups were, in part, a response to the urgent need for healing at the height of the influenza epidemic. Among such groups, perhaps the most notable was the one organized and led by Joseph B. Shadare, a lay leader at St. Savior's Anglican Church, Ijebu-Ode, and Sophia Odunlami, a teacher in a nearby Anglican school.

They started the prayer group in response to the dreams they shared that the human devastation caused by the epidemic could be cured only through prayer and holy water. As a result, the group devoted itself to praying for the victims of the epidemic and applying sanctified rainwater as directed through divine revelation. The prayer group continued after the epidemic and was formally inaugurated in July 1920, as *Egbẹ Okuta Iyebiye* (Precious Stone or Diamond Society).[38] The Precious Stone Society was in effect a Pentecostal prayer and spiritual healing group organized around charismatic lay Christians of evangelical Anglican vintage.

The Precious Stone Society and Foreign Alliances

As people received healing through the faith-based and prayer-reliant Society, its fame became widespread within and outside the Anglican Church. As a result, other Christians became drawn to this small pietistic group and the enthused fashion by which they healed people. One such admirer was David Odubanjo who himself was an emphatic and confident believer in the effectiveness of prayer. Prior to his membership in the Society, Odubanjo had served as a clerk with the Nigerian police at Warri in 1917. It was during this time that he became acquainted with a religious paper, *The Sword of the Spirit*, published by a small faith-healing church in Philadelphia, called Faith Tabernacle.

An article in the paper, "The Seven Principles of Prevailing Prayer," particularly fascinated him. Equally impressive to Odubanjo was Faith Tabernacle's spontaneous rejection of all forms of medicine, traditional or western. This doctrinal stance fitted particularly well with the events in Nigeria at the time and it was not too long before Odubanjo got Shadare and the Society into accepting the formulations of Faith Tabernacle.

---

38. J.D.Y. Peel, *Aladura* (1968:62-63).

It should be pointed out, however, that the alliance with Faith Tabernacle did not so much influence the Precious Stone group except in clarifying the necessity of adult baptism and the rejection of infant baptism. It was this issue of baptism that created such serious conflict with the Anglican Church that by 1922 the Society detached itself from the Anglican Church and became affiliated to Faith Tabernacle.[39]

The adoption of "Faith Tabernacle" as their new name, notwithstanding, the movement was primarily a Nigerian initiative, led by Nigerians and nourished in the Nigerian context. It was essentially a union that was fostered through the "post office." What constituted a primary gain for the Nigerian Faith Tabernacle was the protection from persecution at the hands of the colonial government and the historic mission churches. For this reason, the American connection was a helpful and welcome relief.

In the meantime, the movement spread to other areas so that by mid-1920s there was a small network of Faith Tabernacle communities in Yorubaland: Ijebu-Ode (1920, led by Shadare); Lagos (1921, 1923, led by D.O. Odubanjo and S.G. Adegboyega); Ilesha (1924, led by J.A. Babatope); Ibadan (1924, led by Isaac Akinyele); Abeokuta, Oyan and Ile-Ife (all formed in 1927 and led by Onasinwo). Other commercial or government centers in other parts of Nigeria populated by the Yoruba also had small branches of Faith Tabernacle. Such places included Minna, Zaria, Onitsha, Benin, Jos, Kano, Kaduna, Port Harcourt, Makurdi, and Enugu.[40]

But the alliance with the Americans was on shaky ground. Other issues of irreconcilable doctrinal differences were too strong to sustain the semblance of unity. The two parties disagreed on such beliefs as the practical outworking of the gifts of the Holy Spirit. While glossolalic utterances were to the Africans a sign of Holy Ghost baptism, they were to the Americans delusional and satanic. The complete break came when the

---

39. Lamin Sanneh, *West African Christianity* (1983:184-185). See also Harold Turner, *History of an Independent African Church*, vol. 1 (1967:11).

40. For the whole concept of mission through the post office, and on the early history of Faith Tabernacle in Nigeria, see Ogbu Kalu, "Doing Mission through the Post Office: The Naked Faith People of Igboland, 1920-1960" (2000:263-280). See also J.A. Ademakinwa, *Iwe Itan Ijo Wa* (History of Our Church, 1945); Adeware Alokan, *The Christ Apostolic Church, 1928-1988* (1991); and Gbolahan Olukayode Akinsanya "'You Shall Receive Power': The Establishment of the Pentecostal Movement in the Nigerian Context" (2000).

Nigerians refused to take sides in the internal crisis that began to trouble the Philadelphia headquarters in 1925. Pastor Clarke, the presiding pastor, was alleged to have committed adultery and had refused disciplinary actions. The Nigerian Faith Tabernacle discontinued the collaboration, opting instead to become autonomous. An attempt to foster another alliance with the Canada-based Faith and Truth Temple of Toronto in the same year, 1928, was stifled even before it had taken roots.

Although the Faith Tabernacle churches were generally referred to as "Aladura," a different type of African response to missionary Christianity was also brewing. This movement fell outside the boundaries of the Faith Tabernacle. What came to be a significant incursion into the whole Aladura movement can be ascribed to the 1925 visionary experiences of two charismatic figures, Moses Orimolade and Abiodun Akinsowon.

These two individuals, like their Precious Stone counterparts, came out of the doctrinal backdrop of Anglicanism. The prayer meetings that were occasioned by their respective visionary experiences became regular and were soon organized into an interdenominational prayer society named Egbe Serafu (Seraphim Society). This took place in September 1925. The society was subsequently renamed the Eternal Sacred Order of Cherubim and Seraphim Society as a result of yet another vision. From 1927 onwards, the church embarked on major evangelistic outreaches that flowed into the pneumatic challenge of the Aladura movement. What was to represent a large-scale charismatic movement among the Faith Tabernacle network of churches took place under the impulse of the great 1930 revival led by its first prophetic leader, Joseph Ayodele Babalola.

The Great Revival of the 1930s

The revival of the 1930s was to have widespread consequences for the Faith Tabernacle network and for the whole Aladura movement in Nigeria. The revival was itself an answer to the "highly charged atmosphere of charismatic expectancy" orchestrated by a movement within the Faith Tabernacle. This subgroup had committed itself to a seven-year period of fasting and prayer for revival and miracles.⁴¹ Joseph Babalola, the charismatic prophet who was to become the nodal point of the revival and of the expansion of Aladura Christianity, was a relatively obscured, semi-skilled steamroller driver with the public works department. But in October 1928, he emerged with a call that was as dramatic and unusual as was the rest of his prophetic career.⁴²

Working on the road between Akure and Ilesha, he heard voices telling him to leave his secular job for a preaching life for which he had been born. He resisted the voices until the third day, when his roller stopped working. Interpreting the incident as a rebuke for his stubbornness, he yielded, returning to his hometown of Ilofa naked and covered with ashes. A number of important introductions followed this. Babalola was introduced to Babatope and in 1929 was invited to Ibadan and then to Lagos where he met other leaders of the Faith Tabernacle churches. It was in Lagos, precisely on December 19, 1929, that Babalola was baptized in the sea at Ebute-Metta. Almost at once he became Faith Tabernacle's leading evangelist.⁴³

In the next few months after his baptism, his activities were taken up with mostly itinerant preaching until he accompanied Faith Tabernacle leaders to a reconciliatory meeting at Ilesha. The meeting, which was attended by Shadare, Akinyele, and Odubanjo, had as its objective a reaffirmation of the church's position on monogamy and on complete opposition to all forms of medicine. These were two important doctrines on which some of the leaders in the Ilesha branch had disagreed.

But there were to be strange events much more than these leaders had expected. For there on the third day at the Oke Oye branch, Babalola prophesied and prayed for people with many of them receiving sudden and instantaneous healings. A particularly remarkable incident was his raising to life of a deceased boy who had been the only child of his parents. It is

---

41. For a primary account of the revival as recorded by one of its key participants, see S.G. Adegboyega, *Short History of the Apostolic Church of Nigeria* (1978).

42. For studies on the life and ministry of Joseph Babalola, see John Ojo, *The Life and Ministry of Apostle Joseph Babalola* (1988); O. Ige, "Joseph Babalola—A Twentieth Century Prophet" (1965); and J.A. Medaiyese, *Itan Igbedide, Woli Joseph Babalola Fun Iṣe Ihinrere* (A life of Babalola, n.d.).

43. Adrian Hastings, *The Church in Africa* (1994:515-516).

needless to say that much of the miracles spread swiftly, attracting large crowds from long distances to Ilesha. Here, in the most isolated and weakest area of the network of Faith Tabernacle churches, the revival had begun.[44]

The revival spread through the Ilesha and Ekiti districts east of Ibadan, transforming the small pietistic Faith Tabernacle into a large-scale movement in the process. It is against this background that the story of the whole Aladura movement, and in our cases, the Christ Apostolic Church and the Church of the Lord (Aladura) must be understood.

The Church of the Lord (Aladura)

Josiah Oshitelu, the man who was to be the founder and primate of Church of the Lord (Aladura) rose to prominence in the matrix of the spontaneous expansion of the 1930 revival. As with the other Aladura prophets, Oshitetu came out of the nurturing of Anglicanism. What was to set him on a different course, however, began on the night of May 17, 1925. For on this night, he began to have intense visionary experiences that signaled a call to ministry.[45]

The "mildly unorthodox practices" that followed these experiences resulted in his excommunication from the Anglican Church in 1926. For the following three years, Oshitelu devoted himself to developing his powers and studying under Somoye, a local Aladura prophet. The ministry that followed from this was largely that of itinerant preaching, healing and

---

44. Ilesha is a major town in the Yoruba kingdom of South Western Nigeria and is the hometown of the author. The town is not only unique for being the center and the "chosen" place for the revival, it continues even today to benefit from the "aftershock" of the 1930 revival. Presently, most of the principal players in Nigeria Pentecostalism are Ijeshas (a uniform title for those born in Ilesha and those with lineages from towns that were founded under Ilesha auspices). Among living Ijesha church leaders in Nigeria today are Pastor (Dr) Gabriel Oladele Olutola, the National President of The Apostolic Church, Nigeria and LAWNA Territorial Chairman, Prophets D.O. Obadare and S.K. Abiara (both leading significant movements within the Christ Apostolic Church); Pastors E.A. Adeboye of the Redeemed Christian Church of God and W.F. Kumuyi of the Deeper Life Ministries (both constituting the largest and fastest growing segment of the Neocharismatic Churches in Nigeria and Africa). Today, Ilesha is unarguably described as the "Jerusalem of Nigeria" because of the privileged role she continues to play in Nigerian Christianity. For an excellent study on the Ijeshas, see J.D.Y. Peel *Ijeshas and Nigerians: The Incorporation of a Yoruba Kingdom, 1890s-1970s* (1983).

45. For a detailed account of Oshitelu's visionary experiences, see M. Sam Wobo, *A Brief Résumé of Dr. J.O. Oshitelu* (1955).

prophecy until his acquaintance with the Faith Tabernacle leaders in 1930. The collaboration was initiated by the Faith Tabernacle leaders and was predicated on the understanding that such a cooperation would fuel the smoldering fire of revival in Yorubaland and beyond. The romance lasted just six months. This was because Oshitelu had a personal confidence and a claim to esoteric revelations that ran counter to the fundamental doctrines and style of Faith Tabernacle.

The problem was that Oshitelu was favorably disposed to issues that were at variance with the more sophisticated position of the Faith Tabernacle leaders. Among these were Oshitelu's cataclysmic and apocalyptic prophecies, witch-finding, toleration of polygamy, Masonic symbolism, and esoteric knowledge derived from the use of mysterious "holy names." The use of "holy names" was the most disagreeable and fiercely contested issue. The vindication for the Faith Tabernacle leaders came in a dream revelation to Akinyele. According to his testimony, "[t]hese names can bring no forgiveness, salvation, or benefit of any kind." He testified further "Christ came and showed us his real name and as we are promised everything in the name of Christ, all other names should be left aside."[46]

A meeting was called on January 23, 1931 to resolve the differences between the two parties. The doctrinal gap was too wide, defying any possible reconciliation. A total separation was inevitable. Oshitelu went his own way back to Ogere, his hometown, to found the Church of the Lord (Aladura). He eventually took seven wives for which he also claimed divine permission.

The Apostolic Church Movement

The 1930 revivalist meetings expanded uncontrollably into 1931, stretching the already volatile socio-political situation across Yorubaland and into other regions. For what had been God's work *par excellence* was soon taken over by a host of secondary prophets. While some were engaged in making apocalyptic prophecies, others were agitating against the poll tax. The colonial government became far less tolerant and it was not too long before

---

46. Harold Turner, *History of an African Independent Church*, vol. 1 (1967:23).

the revival ran afoul of administrative powers. In the aftermath of this post-charismatic disorder, Babalola was jailed for six months for calling a person a witch. The adversity and opposition forced Faith Tabernacle, for the third time within the decade, to look westward for help.[47]

Again the contact had been established through literature, this time from the British Apostolic Church with roots in the Welsh revival. The three British delegates who arrived in Nigeria in September 1931 recognized that a revival had been underway and signed an agreement of cooperation. It was, however, not a marriage of convenience as the Faith Tabernacle leaders asked the Apostolic pastors detailed questions about their doctrines.

Once a doctrinal pact was reached, the British Apostolic Church reordained (for some of them were already ordained by proxy under the Faith Tabernacle) seven Faith Tabernacle leaders as pastors: J.B. Shadare (Ijebu-Ode); D.O. Odubanjo (Lagos); I.B. Akinyele (Ibadan); J.A. Babatope (Ilesha); S.G. Adegboyega (Ebute Metta, Lagos); E.G.L. Macaulay (Zaria); and S.A. Mensah (Kaduna).[48]

The Apostolic Church of Nigeria

Consequent upon the affiliation with the British Apostolic Church, Faith Tabernacle changed its name to The Apostolic Church of Nigeria. In order to consolidate the arrangement, two British resident pastors, George Perfect and Idris Vaughan, arrived in Nigeria on July 22, 1932. Having now placed themselves under "adequate European supervision," the Nigerian Apostolic Church gained a semblance of respectability and the confidence of the colonial authorities.[49]

However, the gains of the affiliation were soon eclipsed by disagreement on the doctrine of divine healing. While the British pastors agreed in principle to this doctrine, in practice they were taking quinine as preventive medicine against malaria. Both parties found out that they could not

---

47. See especially the desperate and sobering reflection of S.G. Adegboyega, one of the principal players in the Aladura movement, *Short History of the Apostolic Church of Nigeria* (1978).
48. For details, see J.D.Y. Peel, *Aladura* (1968:105-106).
49. Idris Vaughan, *Nigeria: The Origins of Apostolic Church Pentecostalism, 1931-52* (1991).

quite agree about medicine. For people like Odubanjo and Akinyele, the renunciation of all forms of medicine had been for them the decisive issue in leaving the Anglican Church for Faith Tabernacle. Separation from the British Church was, therefore, inevitable.

In October 1939, Odubanjo, together with Akinyele and Babalola, severed relationships with both the British and Nigerian Apostolic leaders. In 1941 they chose to be called by a new name, known to this day as Christ Apostolic Church (CAC).[50] For their part, Adegboyega, Babatope, and the churches in Kaduna, Zaria, Funtua, and Jos under S.F. Odunaike, and the Calabar churches under J.U. Udom and E.O. Ene all supported the white missionaries. They remained as The Apostolic Church, thus continuing the affiliation in effect since 1931.[51]

Christ Apostolic Church (CAC)

The leadership of the newly founded CAC naturally fell on the three "secessionists"—Akinyele as the president, Odubanjo as the vice president and general superintendent, and Babalola as the general evangelist. An epoch came to an end in the Aladura Christianity with the death of Odubanjo and Babalola, both in 1959, and with the death of other pioneering leaders in the 1960s.[52]

Controversy and debate continue to surround the issue of whether CAC seceded from The Apostolic Church or vice versa. The CAC camp claims that Adegboyega and his associates betrayed the initial and fundamental doctrine of divine healing which was the original stance from their founding as Precious Stone Society. For their part, The Apostolic Church leadership claimed that CAC seceded by breaking away from the "mother church" (The Apostolic Church) to form a new church. These arguments and counter-arguments have since gone beyond any historical basis into sentiment and emotionalism.

---

50. The church used different names before finally adopting its present name, Christ Apostolic Church (CAC), see S.G. Adegboyega, *Short History of the Apostolic Church of Nigeria* (1978).
51. For details see, Akinsanya Olukayode, "'You Shall Receive Power': The Establishment of the Pentecostal Movement in the Nigerian Context" (2000:144-145).
52. See Matthews Ojo, "Christ Apostolic Church" (2001:85).

Currently, The Apostolic Church of Nigeria is an autonomous body. Yet it understands its continuity in history by recourse to its British affiliation. Nevertheless, it has not had the type of worldwide expansion that had been the case in the Christ Apostolic Church. Bureaucracy and administrative bottlenecks continue to stifle its growth. Ironically, the expansion of the Christ Apostolic Church has been a source of internal imbroglio since the early 1990s. Presently, its executive council is struggling with personality and administrative factors that is splitting the church even further.

It is within this wide and dynamic historical context, interlaced by complexity and varying characters, that the origins of the Aladura churches have to be understood. In spite of their differences, all the Aladura leaders share a common approach to issues of the religious life. Lamin Sanneh is, therefore, right when he observes: "If history and the common idiom of Yoruba culture had not united them, a significant overlap of religious perception and practice would have brought them together."[53] It is to this area of Aladura Christianity, the context of belief and practice, which I now turn.

The Context of Aladura Christianity

Conversion, or a local adaptation of foreign religious forms, takes place within a dynamic context. This context encompasses "a vast panorama of conflicting, confluent, and dialectical factors that both facilitate and repress the process of [adaptation]."[54] This realization, however true, is not enough. In constructing a sound basis for religious encounter, we have to account for aspects that bind the "new" religious experience to the "old" dispensation. For it is the presence of continuity, or the lack of it, that drives us to the very heart of how adequate a religion is for providing satisfactory responses to religious questions.

---

53. Sanneh, *West African Christianity* (1983:189).
54. Lewis Rambo, *Understanding Religious Conversion* (1993:20). For other insightful studies on the importance of cultural context, also cited by Rambo, see Hans Kasdorf, *Christian Conversion in Context* (1980) and Charles H. Kraft, *Christianity in Culture* (1979).

In the case of Africa, religious allegiance oscillates between meeting the intellectual and real-life needs. As Harold Turner notes, "In Africa the prime concern is with spiritual satisfaction and power."[55] The claim by the mission churches of possessing hermeneutical insights to issues of doctrine, life, and faith may be one thing, but the ability to make the application to and practice of these insights to personal needs and aspirations is something else. It is within the context of this experiential adequacy that Africans saw the advent of the Aladura churches as a welcome alternative to the mission churches.

"The major premise of all Yoruba religious practice" observes Peel, "was that the material, phenomenal world is continuously affected by unseen powers of various kinds and indefinite number."[56] The central and distinguishing element of Aladura Christianity, therefore, was in how embedded it was into Yoruba cosmology and worldview. It addressed the questions that deal with unseen powers, and responded in concrete ways to indigenous needs and aspirations. Aladura Christianity brought Christ into the very heart of Yoruba culture so that the Christ they preach is the Savior who gives hope to the future as well as meeting present needs.

The Aladura expression of religion permeates the entire traditional African way of life. African cosmology, for example, has a two-tier structure. The first tier is that of the lesser spirits and forces that underlay all events and processes in the microcosm of the local setting. The second tier is that of the Supreme Being with power over the wider world and the lesser spirits.[57]

---

55. Turner, *History of an African Independent Church*, vol. 2 (1967:70).
56. J.D.Y. Peel, *Religious Encounter and the Making of the Yoruba* (2000:93).
57. Robin Horton popularized the idea of a two-tier structure to African cosmology by identifying the context as catalyst for conversion. In supporting this thesis, he developed the "intellectualist theory" that attempts to account for the differential response to Christianity and Islam in sub-Saharan Africa. I recognize the volatility of Horton's "intellectualist theory" and have only adopted his line of thinking in so far as this helps to articulate this dimension of Aladura Christianity. For Horton's works on this thesis, see "African Conversion" (1971); "On the Rationality of Conversion, Part I" (1975a); and "On the Rationality of Conversion, Part II" (1975b). For the staunchest criticism of Horton's argument, see Humphrey J. Fisher's "Conversion Reconsidered: Some Historical Aspects of Religious Conversion in Black Africa" (1973); and "The Juggernaut's Apologia: Conversion to Islam in Black Africa" (1985). For a treatment of both perspectives and of other views on conversion, see Lewis R. Rambo, *Understanding Religious Conversion* (1993).

Aladura Christianity does not dismiss the reality of these two worlds and nor does it attempt to dichotomize between the sacred and the secular. Instead, it functions at the symbolic crossroads between the two worlds, offering a God who is powerful enough to deal with the lesser spirits and who meets the needs of everyday realities—security, fertility, good health, and protection from evil spirits.

Confidence shown in the effectiveness of prayer to deal with the influenza epidemic of 1918 testifies to the special nature of Aladura Christianity. In the African worldview, diseases and misfortunes are sometimes understood to be manifestations of evil agencies and must be confronted by spiritual means of higher powers. It is understandable, then, that the Aladura churches devoted themselves to prayers and to prophetic therapies in order to tap into the supreme power of the high God amidst human devastation and spiritual depression.

In a context where certain misfortunes automatically prompt people to ask the question "why?", recourse to human or spiritual agency for answers is inevitable. As a result, divination plays a crucial role in the African world so that religious rituals function primarily to act on the "other" world for the purpose of influencing "this" world. Therefore, as a spiritual agency of the Christian type, Aladura prophets fulfill functions similar to local diviners. This is probably why they are sometimes inaccurately identified with them.[58]

Traditional diviners are religious functionaries who perform ritual techniques to diagnose the cause of a particular misfortune. People take their prescriptions with all seriousness because it is deep in their worldview that these practitioners can remedy or reverse a situation. Among the Yoruba, for example, the *Ifa* oracle is credited with very special powers to explain, predict, and control space-time events.[59]

---

58. Allan Anderson, *African Reformation: African Initiated Christianity in the 20th Century* (2001:200).
59. Jacob Olupona, *African Spirituality: Forms, Meanings and Expressions* (2000:xvi). This is an important study on issues of Yoruba and African spirituality in general. For more on Yoruba *Ifa* divination, see Wande Abimbola, *Ifa: An Exposition of Ifa Corpus* (1976); and *Ifa Divination Poetry* (1973). For Yoruba spirituality and belief in general, see Bolaji Idowu, *Olódùmarè* (1962).

In many ways, the Aladura rituals and worship patterns are similar to the traditional. Both use rituals that are familiar to the people (Yoruba), but the method and means for accessing power are not the same. While the traditional diviner contacts the spirits through his own manipulative powers, the Aladura prophet anoints with oil, uses sanctified water, and proclaims special words in prayer to invoke the benevolent power of God to intervene, heal, and deliver. The Aladura prophet's prayers are also a call on God to repel the dark or malevolent spirits. Paul G. Hiebert, R. Daniel Shaw, and Tite Tiénou put it well, "The traditional diviner seeks remedies that placate the spirits, but the prophet affirms the power of the Christian God which surpasses all other powers."[60]

By adapting Christianity to African taste and sensibility, the Aladura churches continue to provide a theological framework that combines fundamental elements of Christianity and African culture in a way that did not devalue the distinctive elements of each. It is through this resilient and dynamic form of Christianity that the church gained its initial momentum and maintained its authenticity among the Nigerian people.

It needs to be mentioned, however, that because the Yoruba of Southwestern Nigeria provided the major initial impetus does not categorize the Aladura churches as an essentially Yoruba phenomenon or expression of Christianity. The rapid spread of these churches to other parts of Nigeria and Africa, and even overseas, disallows such narrowness. Rather, they provide features for a phenomenological description of independency in Nigeria. Such a vantage point reveals a unique synthesis of Christian liturgical forms and African religious and ritual concepts in shaping a new version of Christianity.

The Ministry of the Aladura

The New Testament provides charter documents that are important ministry principles for the contemporary church. The Jerusalem church and the church in Antioch, for example, functioned within certain cultural,

---

60. See their work, *Understanding Folk Religion* (1999:362).

social, and geographical contexts and each reflected ministry models that were appropriate to their respective memberships. Even so, we must bear in mind the extent to which the early Christians conceived of ministry in terms of "institutional offices," and the more nonofficial, need-based services (*diakonia*) performed by any believer.

The ministry of Jesus is particularly insightful in this regard. Jesus was just an itinerant prophet with no official title, yet he inspired a large following as he healed people, fellowshipped with the undesirable, and taught both in clear and parabolic forms about the kingdom of God.

This observation leads on to key hermeneutical insights in discussing the ministry of the Aladura churches. Their understanding of ministry oscillates between two poles—their ecclesiastical origins in Anglicanism and the cultural context which gives life and meaning to their beliefs and practices. Even though Aladura churches conceive of ministry in terms of particular functions performed by entitled persons, contextualization demands that they take seriously the thought-forms and mindset of the culture in which the ministry takes place. In unique ways, then, the ministry of the Aladura churches is a correlation between belief and practice, challenge and response, and proclamation and service.

Worship

I have already mentioned that the core of Nigerian traditional cosmology is a system of beliefs about the invisible worlds of the Supreme God and a pantheon of lesser gods. Yet in the categories of divine hierarchy, the Nigerian recognizes the position of these lesser gods as merely functional agencies of the Supreme God. And because of their roles as channels to the Supreme God, the lesser deities receive immediate attention in daily worship and ritual.

It is within the context of this pragmatic attitude towards the invisible world that the practice and rationale of Aladura worship must be understood. Aladura worship moves spontaneously in response to deeply held cultural factors and habits that prevent it from harmonizing into a single fixed pattern like that of the mission-type churches. To analyze this, I will construct a pattern of Aladura responses in worship along the following lines: vertical, ritual, and didactic types of worship.

Vertical Worship

We have shown that Nigerians have always had a deep sense of the reality of God that even the stylistic dogma of the missionaries could not dispute. Consequently, the primary contextual issue for the missionaries was in refocusing the indigenous concept of God in order to bring it in alignment with biblical Christianity. In the case of the Yoruba, for example, *Olodumare*, the supreme deity, was a *dues remotus et incertus,* who, after creating the world, concerned himself very little with it. Hence, *Olodumare* became a remote deity who was approached through the mediation of the *orişa* (lesser deities). The task of missionary preaching, therefore, was to reconceptualize God as a jealous God who forbids the worship of other gods. This meant that the jealousness of God drew out a fundamental differentiation that now identified the lesser deities as antagonistic to him. As a full measure of this conviction, God became the one source of salvation and sole object of worship.

Concomitantly, the hermeneutical principle in the Aladura worship of God is the new revelation of a transcendent and majestic God who desires exclusive reverent homage. It is only on the basis of this fundamental postulate of the awe-full holiness and majesty of God that we can understand worship in the Aladura churches. For God in the Aladura churches is an awe-inspiring, majestic King who is likened to the awesome *Ọba* (King). Moreover, the Aladura affirm that God is a transcendent and all-powerful God who is no longer remote but very personal. The dramatic celebration of God in his supreme majesty becomes the norm and inspiration of Aladura worship:

Kabiyesi Ọba Alaiyeluwa	Hail King, Majesty,
Mẹtalọkan Alagbara	Powerful Trinity,
Awamaridi Olodumare	Incomprehensible, Almighty
To nşe işẹ iyanu	Who does wondrous works.
Ọba mi de! Aşegun mi de!	My King comes, My Victor comes,
Ogo, Ọla at'Agbara at'Ipa	Glory, Honor, Power and Might
F'Ọdagutan to gunwa	To the Lamb who sits in Majesty.[61]

---

61. J.D.Y. Peel, *Aladura* (1967:163).

In both purpose and form the above Aladura hymn bears the deep imprint of the liturgical nature of Yoruba ritual worship. It is not so much that hymns occur in Yoruba communal worship. More important is the fact that in structure the praise-songs are connected with certain divinities and their cults. For in Yoruba worship, invocation of divine prowess and attributes is predicated on highly selective ritual words. The length of such praise chants also depend on how much there is to say about a particular divinity with regards to his origin, greatness, past deeds, ability, and capability.[62] For the Aladura, therefore, *Olodumare* (God) is *Kabiyesi Ọba Alaiyeluwa. Mẹtalọkan Alagbara, Awamaridi Olodumare to nṣe iṣẹ iyanu* (Hail King, Majesty. Powerful Trinity, Incomprehensible Almighty who does wondrous works).

The biblical writings offer insights as to what activities can serve as vehicles for the Christian worship. Perhaps no activity is more central to biblical worship than music. In the words of Roberta King, "music is not just singing; it is a channel of communicating a given message."[63] Aladura worship combines this biblical practice in a way that corresponds with and reflects the Yoruba culture. For the Yoruba, reverence for God by means of worship and moral practice is what constitutes religion. Hence, praise-songs, clapping, dancing, and African musical instruments are used freely and joyfully to authenticate the worship experience. For the Aladura, it is a celebration and worship of *Olodumare*, the "Incomprehensible Almighty who does wondrous works."

Ritual Worship

The two primary rituals of Christian worship are the eucharist and baptism, both of which still exhibit great varieties both in forms and meanings. Other rituals, usually involving physical movement such as symbolic gestures, postures and prayer are all important aspects of the worship experience.

---

62. For details, see Bolaji Idowu, *Olódùmarè: God in Yorùbá Belief* (1962:114).
63. For details, see her work, *A Time to Sing: A Manual for the African Church* (1999:vii). For her other insightful studies on the use of music as a guidepost to the communication of biblical truth within the African context, see "Pathways in Christian Music Communication: The Case of the Senufo of Cote d'Ivoire" (1989); and "The Role of Music in Theological Education" (1990).

Among the Aladura these rituals occur within a constellation of symbolic acts and objects that link the temporal order with the transcendent. In other words, these visible aspects function as vehicles for worship as well as formulas for invoking divine intervention. For example, prayers and rituals are not merely word utterances; they are intended to make things happen.[64] Hence, objects such as candles, water, staff of office, and incense, represent visible promise for the worshipper that personal help and change will occur.

For example, when the Aladura prays with a lighted candle, it is believed that the light will repel malevolent spirits while attracting benevolent ones. Water also has performative force. It can be made "holy" through consecration by the Aladura prophet who invokes the power of God while dipping his iron rod into it. Once sanctified, the uses for "holy water" are almost endless. It can cure various diseases, wash off evil spells, be ingested as purgative, disable the potency of charms, or be used as a sign of sanctification when sprinkled on the people.

As much as Aladura rituals are directed to God as forms of worship, they are also an effective way of annexing his powers. In a situation that is controlled by the powers of the invisible, the client-centered esoteric expertise of the Aladura prophet is a welcome service. As ministers of God, they occupy a central role as possessors of mediating powers and are, therefore, engaged in a very similar way as the *babalawo* (Ifa diviner) and other religious specialists. Strict conformity to their spiritual diagnosis and prescriptions guarantee divine sanctions and blessings.

This procedure resembles traditional patterns in which self-actualization is achieved by means of controlling the invisible. As in traditional religious life and practice, these rituals are based on performing "the right kind" of worship in order to achieve a desired end. This doctrinal and ritual innovation by the Aladura can be described as contextualization at its best. It explains why the Aladura churches continue to appeal to many Nigerians, especially the Yoruba.

Ritual worship continues to be an integral part of Aladura spirituality, especially in the Church of the Lord (Aladura). The CAC, for its part,

---

64. For an insightful perspective in this regard, see Benjamin C. Ray, "Aladura Christianity: A Yoruba Religion" (1993:266-291).

maintains a more careful balance between biblical and cultic practices. The church continues in the legacy of prayer and the use of holy water as demonstrated in the ministry of its first great prophetic leader, Joseph Ayodele Babalola.

Didactic Worship

Didactic worship denotes the instructional side of Aladura worship and covers all ministries in understandable form. Didactic worship may be traced to fall along several lines. The first is the ministry of the Word in preaching and liturgy. This is usually based on practical exposition of the text for the purpose of extracting doctrinal and ethical teachings for the congregation. The second aspect, the more prominent and the most controversial of Aladura spirituality, includes prophecy, dreams, and visions. These are understood as means to reveal and clarify the will of God. In both cases, the exercise of spiritual authority is almost an exclusive privilege of a select few from whom charismatic ministry could be expected.

The fundamental conviction that God does speak to his people is the centerpiece of Aladura ritual worship and preaching. Unlike the remote and theoretical liturgy of the mission churches, the clearest note in Aladura liturgy is the concern for intelligibility and proximity between the text and the human condition. Since the Bible is considered to be the source of God's will with its power and promise to navigate all of life, Aladura sermons are usually composed of practical and illustrative anecdotes aimed at helping and encouraging believers in their day-to-day affairs.[65]

Harold Turner's synopsis of the sermon texts of "the Church of the Lord (Aladura)" bears witness to this. Using texts as an index of Aladura preaching, Turner contends that the most favorite texts revolve around themes on the general components of a good life—deliverance, salvation, health, and success.[66] In this respect, human maturity and experience are as important as the degree of theological insights that the Aladura preacher brings to his or her sermons.

---

65. J.D.Y. Peel, *Aladura* (1968:161).
66. Harold Turner, *Profile through Preaching* (1965)

The second aspect, the hallmark of Aladura didactic worship, involves prophecies, visions, and dreams. Seen in the light of Joel 2:28-29, these practices place the Aladura churches within "the magnetic field of the Holy Spirit."[67] To the Aladura, pentecostal revelations in prophecy, dreams, and visions are a practical manifestation of the Holy Spirit. Therefore, messages received as a result of the outworking of any of the spiritual gifts function to reveal the will of God as well as reconcile the people to the pragmatic necessities of their cultural context. In other words, prophecy, visions, and dreams are taken to be both diagnostic and therapeutic since they reveal the cause(s) of a particular problem and divine prescriptions for solving that problem.

Aladura Worship: Gateway of Paganism?

Critics of Aladura worship patterns, especially the didactic type dealing with prophecies, visions, and dreams, have refused to accept this form of ministry as being authentically Christian. Instead, they have maintained that these practices are a mistaken application of Scripture. Two important reasons stand out among several others. The first borders on a very high degree of supernaturalism in which unrestricted revelations by the leaders carry almost equal authority with the Bible. Gilliland calls this type of Aladura church the "Revelational-Indigenous Type."[68]

The second compares Aladura revelations to the projective and manipulative system of African religious practice. There is some validity to the first claim, especially in the face of unrestricted visions that have become characteristic of some Aladura churches. Even then, care must be taken to avoid accusations that can be both subjective and patronizing. In the words of Gilliland, "superficial acceptance is as intolerable as unfair condemnation."[69]

---

67. W.C. Van Unnik, "Dominus Vobiscum: The Background of a Liturgical Formula" (1959:294).

68. See Dean Gilliland, "Limits of Contextualization and the African Independent Churches" (1999:2).

69. Dean Gilliland, *African Religion Meets Islam* (1986:271).

A distinction on the degree of reliance on revelations among the Aladura is of fundamental importance. While it may be correct to claim that the Church of the Lord (Aladura), for example, is typically inclined to unfounded and novel revelations, the same cannot be said of the Christ Apostolic Church. The Church of the Lord continues very much in the revelatory style that characterized its founder, Josiah Oshitelu. The CAC, by contrast, continues in its practice of weighing everything against the Scriptures. As it was during the church's formative years, the church still continues to apply the injunction to "try the spirits whether they are of God" (2 Pet. 1:20-21, 2:1; 1 Jn. 4:1). Equally important is the long-standing conviction of CAC leaders that "the Gift of the Spirit without the Word of God" leads to error.[70]

On the second charge, Bengt Sundkler was one of the earliest critics to compare the pentecostal revelations of prophet-healing churches to the phenomena of spirit-possession and to the projective system of African religious heritage. Drawing from his own experience among the Zulu of South Africa, Sundkler saw the prophet-healing churches as "the back doors through which African past enters the church" to paganize it.[71] It is one thing to claim that the prophet-healer became to the African Christian what the native diviner was to the non-believing traditionalist. But to claim that the prophet-healing churches were a gateway of paganism into the Christian church does not apply in the Nigerian situation, however true this may be among the Zulu churches. Even the Church of the Lord, despite its affinity to esoteric revelations, cannot be seen in terms of continuity with paganism. Regrettably, this observation continues with wide acceptance even in contemporary times. Perhaps the prophetic legacy of Israel may give us serious pause in this matter. In this, we are thankful for an insightful study of Walter Brueggemann.[72]

---

70. J.D.Y. Peel, *Aladura* (1968:284). See also D.H. Crumbley, "On Being First: Dogma, Disease and Domination in the Rise of an African Church" (2000:176-177); Adeware Alokan, *The Christ Apostolic Church* (1991:295-297).

71. Bengt Sundkler, *Bantu Prophets in South Africa* (1961:216). For Harold Turner's perspectives on this, see *African Independent Church*, vol. 2 (1967:137-140).

72. Walter Brueggemann, *The Prophetic Imagination* (1978).

Brueggemann has shown that "the task of prophetic ministry is to nurture, nourish, and evoke a consciousness and perception alternative to the consciousness and perception of the dominant culture around us."[73] Interpreting the covenantal tradition of Moses to support his thesis, Brueggemann challenges us to move beyond the insensitivity that has arisen as a result of our familiarity with the exodus narratives. Instead, he compels us to see the emergence of Moses as a radical break with the social reality of Pharaoh's Egypt. This way, we will be able to incline ourselves to the revolutionary *alternative community* that emerged in the process.

It is by being so sensitive that we can also understand that "Moses was mainly concerned with the formation of a counter-community with a counter-consciousness." This alternative consciousness, Brueggemann adds, "was exceedingly radical in its implications both for religion and for the social and political order."[74]

An interpretation of the prophetic ministry of Moses in this way requires an understanding of the social world of Israel and an appreciation of the *alternative community* that was birthed in the process. It is necessary to point to the fact that we have become so familiar with Aladura Christianity that we are no longer sensitive to the social world in which they emerged. The "social reality" that accounts for the rise of Aladura Christianity was one in which the power of the *orisha* cult took center stage. It was a context in which Nigerians who claimed to be Christians went to church on Sunday mornings and patronized the *Ifa* diviner at other times.

The emergence of Aladura prophetic ministry, like that of Moses, gave rise to the formation of an "alternative community." It was an applied Christianity intended to contradict the powerful hold of the orisha-world by meeting the deep spiritual needs of Nigerians through charismatic gifts of prayer, dreams, visions, and healing. Lamin Sanneh seems to be echoing Brueggemann when he refers to Aladura prophetic ministry as "the most fruitful source of doctrinal and ritual innovation, a revolutionary instrument bringing changes which might have been difficult or impossible

---

73. Brueggemann (1978:13).
74. Brueggemann (1978:28-29).

to introduce otherwise."⁷⁵ A similar analysis of several crucial components in Aladura Christianity will enable us to see more clearly the dynamics of their biblical hermeneutic.

The Theology of the Aladura

The evangelistic mandate of the church presupposes a theological reflection upon the gospel as it engages the cultural context in which it finds itself. As to this theological task, Wilbert Shenk reminds us that the New Testament provides us with examples *par excellence* in the sense that it "reflect[s] the historical, social, religious, and political context in which the missionary encounter of the Christian Gospel with Middle Eastern culture took place."⁷⁶

The same can be said for the culture of intellectualism that dominated the Hellenistic world of the second century. Engaged in a context that was largely shaped by Greek philosophical tradition, early Christian apologists formulated theological constructions that elevated Christianity as the true philosophy.⁷⁷ In fact, both Origen and Clement of Alexandria even went so far as to suggest that Christian theology is itself a kind of "divine philosophy" and that Greek philosophy merely served as a "schoolmaster" bringing the Greeks to Christ.⁷⁸ Unfortunately, from as early as the fourth century, this cultural engagement of theological reflections became largely introspective and intellectual.⁷⁹

Contemporary theological task in the West has become ahistorical and remains largely captive to the repetitious tradition of doctrinal formulations. Worse still, theological enterprise has become a somewhat

---

75. Lamin Sanneh, *West African Christianity* (1983:129).

76. Wilbert Shenk, "Recasting Theology of Mission: Impulses from the Non-Western World" (2001:98).

77. For details see Roger Olson, *The Story of Christian Theology: Twenty Centuries of Tradition and Reform* (1999).

78. Clement of Alexandria, *The Stromata*, I.5.; Origen, *Against Celsus*, 68.

79. Wilbert Shenk, "Recasting Theology of Mission: Impulses from the Non-Western World" (2001:98).

personal repository of privileged professionals; a paradigm which is itself a product of the intellectual foundation of the Enlightenment. In recent times, however, the call for an appropriate recontextualization of theology in response to changing cultural and historical conditions has won a hearing in the world of theologians.[80] Ironically, this new approach to theological construction "has its genesis not in theology itself but in missiology, [and] more particularly in the missiological question of 'gospel and culture.'"[81]

The missiologists' call for contextualization has, indeed, a precedent in the Aladura approach to theologizing. A critical issue that has been actively engaged in Aladura Christianity is the ability of African leaders to conceptualize theology in terms of the social-cultural context. Although the search for distinctiveness in Aladura theology can, at times, seem like an endless quest given its variety and dynamism, nevertheless, Aladura theology can be understood in terms of its indigenous reading and application of Scripture.

Vernacularization, Interpretation, and Appropriation

The wider issue on the extent to which Aladura Christianity developed a theology of its own cannot be discussed without recognizing the commitment of the missionaries to the translation enterprise. In Nigeria, as in many parts of Africa, the translation enterprise was the "centerpiece in the machinery of mission."[82] As Sanneh has pointed out, missionaries often acted as vernacular agents and by so doing, acted as a means of cultural renewal. In the case of Nigeria, for example, the vernacular exposition of the Scriptures heralded a new era for the Nigerian church with far-reaching consequences. It provided the platform for the natives to share

---

80. For a summary of the major approaches to contextualization in contemporary scholarship, see Stephen B. Bevans, *Models of Contextual Theology* (1992).
81. Stanley J. Grenz and John R. Franke, *Beyond Fundamentalism: Shaping Theology in a Postmodern Context* (2001:154).
82. Lamin Sanneh, *Translating the Message* (1989:147).

the missionaries' intellectual heritage by connecting them with the most important literature in the Christian faith, the Bible.

In Nigeria, the vernacularization process received its most rigorous affirmation through the indigenizing principles of Henry Venn, CMS secretary from 1842 to 1872. However, the African impetus came from Samuel Ajayi Crowther, the first African bishop and the able linguist who remained "the most important influence" in the production of the Bible in the Yoruba language.[83] Crowther was equally a pioneer in translating substantial literature into the Yoruba language. The significance of this vernacularization of Scripture for the Aladura of Nigeria has not always been appreciated.

The existence of a vernacular Scripture became a powerful factor for the African initiative in Christian expansion. On one hand, it provided a forum to evaluate and question certain theological ideas taught by the missionaries. On the other hand, and undoubtedly more important, it opened the way for a "Christian reaffirmation of some ancient aspects of African religion that were not part of missionary Christianity at all."[84]

These "ancient aspects of African religion" are the revelatory phenomena of dreams, visions, trance, and ecstatic utterances that have formed part of the "*effective* canon" of Aladura Christianity.[85] For Nigerians, and the Aladura in particular, "the missionary adoption of vernacular categories for the Scriptures was in effect a written sanction for the indigenous religious vocation."[86]

It is against this backdrop that Aladura theology has to be understood. The Aladura read Scripture in a certain way, so persistently, in fact, that this indigenous reading has become the template through which they view all of Scripture. Unlike the mission churches, the Aladura are not merely given to an intellectual systematization of Scripture. Rather, their reading and interpretations of Scripture are conditioned by presuppositions arising

---

83. Andrew F. Walls, *Cross-Cultural Process in Christian History* (2002:42).
84. Walls (2002:130).
85. Walls (2002:130).
86. Lamin Sanneh, *Translating the Message* (1989:159).

out of their cultural context and how it speaks into their life situation.[87] While we can claim that the Scripture is central to their beliefs and practices, it is nonetheless, a theological reflection largely influenced by their local situation.

Perhaps the criticisms of Aladura theology have to be put in perspective. The tendency to read the Scripture in a certain way is not peculiar to the Aladura but representative of the Christian community. David Kelsey's work on the use of the Bible in theology is most helpful in pointing out this critical component in scriptural interpretation. According to him, there is no single, standard interpretive scheme to which all must subscribe. Rather, every faith community brings its own hermeneutic to Scripture.

Arguing his case by analyzing the writings of seven Protestant theologians, Kelsey concludes that the art of theologizing is not based solely on a close study of biblical texts but on a prior decision in which we imaginatively try to authorize theological ideas. This "prior construal" of Scripture, Kelsey argues, determines which patterns or aspects of Scripture are more meaningful to us than others.[88]

There are historical precedents to justify Kelsey's claim. A case in point is to recall that the Anglican litany grew out of the particular situation and needs of England towards the middle of the sixteenth century. It was a theological enterprise that grew out of the need to address a succession of troubles, bad weather, diseases, and wars.[89] Be that as it may, then, it can be said at this point that the Aladura also see a pattern of Scripture to which they ascribe wholeness—all of life's problems. In a context where afflictions of various kinds are presumed to be caused by evil forces, it is not surprising that the *sine qua non* of Aladura theology is prayer and spiritual power. We need to look further at these domains of Aladura theology.

---

87. See also Allan Anderson's discussion on the hermeneutical perspectives of the AICs in his recent work, *African Reformation* (2001:220-224).

88. For Kelsey's treatment of this thesis, see *The Uses of Scripture in Recent Theology* (1975). For a very important study that adopts Kelsey's perspective in interpreting theological enterprise among African-American preachers, see Cleophus J. LaRue, *The Heart of Black Preaching* (2000).

89. Harold Turner, *History of an Independent African Church*, vol. 2 (1967:166).

Prayer

Aladura churches are well-named. The extensive practice of *adura* (prayer) and the belief in its efficacy for every eventuality is the keynote of all their doctrines and the one single factor which characterizes the whole movement. Prayer does not function merely as incidental reference to God, but establishes divine communion and a potent point of contact with the spiritual realm. It is the medium whereby the supernatural power of God most decisively meets human need to subdue evil, gain specific guidance, or infuse divine vitality into human life.

This pragmatic view of prayer is in direct contact with Yoruba spirituality. In Yoruba religious and cultural beliefs, prayer is central to all areas and seasons of life. There is no artificial boundary separating the sacred and the secular. The primary concern of Yoruba prayer is to obtain benefits from the *oriṣa*, the agents of *Olodumare*, in matters of spiritual guidance and self-actualization. To enlist the help of the *oriṣa* means a constant recourse to divination (*Ifa*) and sacrifice (*ẹbọ*).

Divination plays a crucial role as the medium through which hidden things and personal problems that are not easily perceptible are brought to light. The complement to divination is sacrifice (*ẹbọ*). This religious act is oriented toward changing the course of things to one's advantage. In this sense, ritual speech and action have performative force because for the Yoruba, "prayers and offerings not only say things, they are supposed to do things."[90]

The Aladura have adapted this element of Yoruba religious consciousness by giving it their own distinctive Christian interpretation. In this shift from traditional belief, divine intervention into daily life is not sought through intermediaries but by directly "talking with God" in prayer (*ibaọlọrunsọrọ*).[91] This is the conviction of most Aladura leaders. The explanation given by Emmanuel Adejobi, the late primate of the Church of the Lord (Aladura) bears witness to this:

---

90. For a study that has dealt most impressively with divination, sacrifice, and prayer in Yoruba religion, and for the distinctive Yoruba character of Aladura Christianity in particular, see Benjamin C. Ray "Aladura Christianity: A Yoruba Religion" (1993).

91. In Yoruba cosmology, prayer is central, forceful, and almost impromptu in nature. Peel mentions the centrality of prayer in the CMS journals, citing specifically David Hinderer's observation on the importance of prayer for the Yoruba converts, *Religious Encounter and the Making of the Yoruba* (2000:256ff.).

> It [prayer] is an act of praise and worship. It is the resort of the soul, a revitalization of spiritual strength. . . . Yea, it is a meeting place with God where the creature talks with the Creator, and communes as friend to friend . . . where all wants and poverty are laid bare for divine abundance and blessing. It is a meeting place of heaven with the earth. It is a place where the forces of darkness are put to flight and Satan's power disarmed. There a Christian perceives heavenly visions; eats and drinks of heavenly manna, and wine. . . . Prayer is the mighty power house of a believer.[92]

Construed in this way, prayer does not only greatly intensify the sense of the immediacy of the presence of God, it also represents an aspect of both communicating with and of eliciting a response from God. Granted this conceptual transformation, the solution to problems that would have otherwise been sought in a pseudo-scientific manner through Yoruba rituals is sought, instead, in the moral-religious milieu of Christianity.[93]

Eliciting a favorable response meant that the communication had to be done in the "right way." In Yoruba oratory discourse, praise-singing (*oríki*) is employed for just this purpose. These are evocative utterances which are believed to capture the essential qualities of their subjects and, by being uttered, motivate them to act.[94] This is why Aladura prayers are heavily punctuated with the element of adoration and praise epithets for God. These are a deliberate attempt to move the divine hands of God. It needs to be mentioned, however, that the instrumentality of evocative epithet is not what brings about an answer. The prospect of a favorable response is totally a divine prerogative. The most the Aladura can do is to "compel" God to act favorably on his or her behalf.

---

92. Benjamin C. Ray "Aladura Christianity: A Yoruba Religion" (1993:280-281).
93. J.D.Y. Peel, *Aladura* (1968:121).
94. For a detailed study of the nature and significance of praise-singing (*oríki*) among the Yoruba, see Karin Barber, *I Could Speak Until Tomorrow: Oriki, Women, and the Past in a Yoruba Town* (1991).

Spiritual Power

The approach of the Aladura had enough points of contact with local idioms to give their religious activity serious consideration by ordinary people. As Peel has noted, "the search for power, individual or collective, was the dominant orientation of the Yoruba toward all religions."[95] This is especially important when we consider that the Yoruba are given to cosmo-historical presuppositions where spiritual powers exist and tensions between good and evil are always in focus. These forces of evil are organized under the control of the enemy of God and of human welfare; the devil or Satan. To defeat him and his cronies, therefore, requires gaining access to a higher alternative, to the limitless powers of *Olodumare* whose very name denotes fullness or superlative greatness.

The response of the Aladura must be seen as taking on a strong local initiative in offering a greater power in the battle with evil. In fact, the Aladura consider themselves to be the special recipients of spiritual power (*agbara ẹmi*). Their God is the *Alagbara* (Dispenser of Power) through whose power (*l'agbara Ọlọrun*) things can be done.[96] The revival of the 1930s was a vindication of the charismatic claim of the Aladura. Joseph Ayodele Babalola, the most prominent of the revivalists, was reported to have ministered in such a great power that miraculous events were common sights in his meetings. Further demonstrations of the supremacy of the God of the Aladura were the numerous confessions of witches either in the Aladura revival meetings or as a result of drinking water that was sanctified by an Aladura prophet.[97]

The source of Aladura power is the God of the Scriptures whose power is identified with the Holy Spirit. The Holy Spirit is viewed as the all-embracing, pervasive power of God who, in turn, "fills people with power." To be "filled with power" requires one to earnestly seek after the baptism of the Holy Spirit. Most Christ Apostolic Churches organize "tarrying

---

95. J.D.Y. Peel, *Religious Encounter and the Making of the Yoruba* (2000:217).
96. Peel (2000:217-225. See also his earlier work, *Aladura* (1968:135-144).
97. For a detailed study on the life and ministry of Apostle Joseph Babalola, and on the revivals of the 1930s, see John Odunayo Ojo, *The Life and Ministry of Apostle Joseph Ayodele Babalola* (1988). See also Adeware Alokan, *The Christ Apostolic Church, 1928-1988* (1991).

meetings" for this purpose. The witness of baptism is validated by spiritual power; and demonstrated by the ability to prophesy, speak in tongues, heal, exorcize demons, have visions and dreams, and live holy lives. This promise of Holy Spirit power to meet existential needs and to provide protection from the devastation of evil forces is compelling reasons for Aladura membership. The Christ Apostolic Church knows this and does not fail to instruct new members on the importance of the Holy Spirit, "as the source of transforming power in the life of the Church."[98]

Therefore, to allege as Temples and Beyerhaus have done that Africans conceive of the "power" of the Holy Spirit as an impersonal and manipulative force is an argument that belongs in the 1960s.[99] We know enough about the pneumatology of African Pentecostalism than to unfairly represent their views and doctrines.[100] Similarly, we have to draw a line between the idea of power in a traditional pagan and an Aladura Christian setting. Peel has noted that "in the former the power was not inhibited by doctrine; in the latter, Christianity had unleashed the power, and the power became subject to doctrinal conditions."[101]

This is an important observation that is corroborated by the doctrinal stance of the general council of the Christ Apostolic Church. As early as 1955, the council was careful to review the practice of divine healing and to redirect members' attention from the prophet who has the gift of healing back to God, the author of the gift.[102]

The Christ Apostolic Church leadership, despite its recognition of the signs of the Holy Spirit through the gifts of healing, prophecy, and speaking in tongues, did not fail to maintain that these gifts were capable of being misused. In such instances, the Bible became the final source of testing legitimation. According to Sadare, one of the founders of Aladura Christianity in Nigeria, the indwelling of "the Holy Spirit is for those

---

98. Lamin Sanneh, *West African Christianity* (1983:195).
99. See P. Temples *Bantu Philosophy* (1959) and P. Beyerhaus, "An Approach to the African Independent Church Movement" (1969:73-77).
100. Allan Anderson also addresses this misrepresentation in *African Reformation* (2001:217-243).
101. J.D.Y. Peel, *Aladura* (1968:138).
102. Peel, *Aladura* (1968:139).

who have been purified by the Word of God and not for every Dick and Harry."[103] In the final analysis, we would do well to yield to the wise words of Andrew Walls when he argues:

> The Spiritual churches may offer the divine power mediated through holy water or some other substance, or demonstrate that power in exorcism by a blow on the afflicted head from the Bible; but again it is crucial to their identity that it is *God's* power that is mediated, *God's* book that is used in the mediation. All other objects of power are not only inferior . . . but also illegitimate.[104]

Summary

So far I have focused on the thought-world of Nigerian culture and on the reordering of worldview as a primary consequence of the indigenous reading of the Bible. We have also insisted that the wonders of Christianity must be attributed to its incarnate character, reflecting both time and specific contexts. This is the reorientation that has resulted in the Aladura model of Christianity.

Yet, the paradox is that the Aladura model, whose primary appeal was to offer a Christian faith that is contextually appropriate, has negatively impressed those who insist that it is "this worldly" in motivation. To these scholars, "the Aladura have transformed the other-worldly, spiritual, and ethical character of western Christianity into this-worldly ends of traditional Yoruba religion."[105]

Perhaps the hermeneutical key to appreciating Aladura Christianity is to come to a clearer and a more definitive idea of what is "this-worldly" or "other-worldly" in Yoruba spirituality. The Yoruba, and more generally

---

103. Peel, *Aladura* (1968:141).
104. See his latest work, *Cross-Cultural Process in Christian History* (2002:129).
105. Benjamin C. Ray addresses this issue further in his study, "Aladura Christianity: A Yoruba Religion" (1993:269).

Africans, conceive of time and space as cyclical and so is their concept of "this-worldly." In Yoruba cosmology, "this-worldly" does not mean simply the material-phenomenal universe, as is often the case in Western thinking. Rather, the two worlds function in a symbiotic way; the crossroads between life and death and also between the spirit and physical. In other words, the two worlds are in a constant state of interaction and influence.[106]

The unnecessary dichotomy that has been ascribed to Nigerian cultural beliefs, and indeed to Aladura Christianity, is alien to Yoruba sensibility. The Aladura are not inhibited with using terms and categories that espouse their understanding and practice of Christianity. In fact, their way of "doing church" bears witness to the incarnate character of Christianity and of the ministry of Jesus Christ.

Jesus was not simply interested in telling stories about the kingdom. He demonstrated in practical ways that the kingdom had entered human history by attending to the physical and spiritual needs of his listeners. At other times, he told his listeners that the kingdom of God has come upon them (Mt. 12:28; Lk. 10:9-11). Consequently, the Aladura preach a Christ who is also the healer, the protector, and the friend of those who live on the fringes of human society.

The false dichotomy and, indeed, the intra-ecclesiastical debates that continue to characterize Western theology can no longer be imposed on a context like Africa where gospel and culture have been brought into a creative and dynamic encounter. Modern day citizens and Nigerian Christians are inundated with many options to accept any one religion rather uncritically. What is in a religion that offers the promise of another world when it is inadequate to address the concerns and aspirations of this world? What the Aladura have done is to proclaim a holistic gospel and to offer a Savior, Jesus Christ, who is able to save both eternally and materially. As Ray has put it, "for the Aladura Christians the eschatological Kingdom of God, which they also call 'Heaven,' has come into the world. It is not only transcendent, it is also immanent."[107]

---

106. See E.A. Ayandele, "The Aladura Among the Yoruba: A Challenge to the 'Orthodox' Churches" (1978:384-390). See also Cyril Okorocha, *The Means of Religious Conversion in Africa: The Case of the Igbo of Nigeria* (1987).
107. Benjamin C. Ray, "Aladura Christianity: A Yoruba Religion" (1993:273).

PART IV

Modernizing the Context: The Reconstructionist Christianity of the Charismatic/Pentecostal Movements, 1980s-2000s

The place to begin consideration of the Charismatic/Pentecostal movement is taking note of the attention it continues to attract as the new religious force that is re-shaping the face of Christianity in Nigeria and, indeed, Africa. In an overall analysis of the history of the church in Nigeria, one important factor that characterizes the present phase is that the Pentecostal/Charismatic churches have brought change in the existing historic mission denominations as well as in the indigenous Aladura churches. Presently, the borders of Pentecostalism have become so broad that charting the full measure of its diversity is a formidable task.

The increasing concern with globalization and transatlantic connections further compound trying to grasp the outlines of Nigerian Pentecostalism. Yet, it is because of the elements of more indigenous practice that are so visible that Pentecostalism in Nigeria captures the local imagination. For example, the restructuring of reality, the construction of practical theology, and the ability to adopt idioms that assure the worshipper that he or she can strive for survival in a complex world are assets that make Nigerian Pentecostalism very attractive. In what follows I will focus my attention on Pentecostalism as yet another attempt to vigorously contextualize Christianity to local aspirations.

CHAPTER 5

Charismatic/Pentecostal Movements

Since the terms Pentecostals and Charismatics are used interchangeably, my starting point will be to nuance a distinction between the two.

Charismatics and Pentecostals: A Historical Perspective

The larger story of Pentecostalism is one of rapid numerical growth. Historians of Pentecostalism have charted the contours of the movement from Kansas to Texas and to Azusa Street, a nondescript neighborhood in downtown Los Angeles that facilitated the transformation of the movement into a global phenomenon. Today, more than one hundred years after it first emerged in January, 1901, Pentecostalism has moved from the margins to the very center of the church. This inward penetration, complemented by the movement's own establishment as a *type* of Christianity, is not a simple story.[1]

Even in North America, differentiating between Pentecostals and Charismatics had a long and complicated history. In the attempt to manage Pentecostals and Pentecostal-like groups as types, David Barrett uses the analogy of an ocean tide with three distinguishable "waves." The first wave (the Pentecostal renewal) began in 1901 and led to the formation of classical

---
1. For a good survey of the movement over the course of its one hundred years of existence, see Vinson Synan, *The Century of the Holy Spirit: 100 Years of Pentecostal and Charismatic Renewal, 1901-2001* (2001).

Pentecostal churches. The second wave (the charismatic renewal) began among mainline Protestants about 1960 and quickly spreading through the Roman Catholic Church in 1967. The third wave (the neo-charismatic renewal) emerged around 1980 and is a "catch-all" description of groups that cannot be classified as either Pentecostal or charismatic but share in common features of Pentecostal supernaturalism.[2]

David Barrett's statistics and periodization do help the historian to chart the development and demography of Pentecostalism as a global phenomenon. They show that these disparate groups share many features in common, especially the central focus on the person of the Holy Spirit. Even then, these innumerable groups do not all fit into a predictable doctrinal or stylistic profile. This ambiguity makes drawing boundaries and characteristics difficult.

To bring order to the fractured identities of Pentecostals and Charismatics, Stanley Burgess has suggested a pair of observations for conceptualizing the ecclesiastical constructs of the two. The criteria for approaching Pentecostals and Charismatics are "theological" and "ecclesiastical."[3] Theologically, the Pentecostals retain their churchly heritages of evangelical belief while adding a new cluster of beliefs centering on a post-conversion crisis experience (the "baptism of the Holy Spirit"). This baptism is evidenced by the glossolaic (speaking in tongues) experience as witnessed in Acts. In some cases, the baptism of the Spirit must follow or occur simultaneously with another act of grace, namely, sanctification. The Charismatics, on the other hand, "emphasize the present work of the Spirit through gifts in the life of the individual and the church" but with little or no emphasis on "the necessity of a second work of grace or the evidence of glossolalia."[4]

Ecclesiastical differentiation is based on denominational affiliation. The classical Pentecostals, according to Burgess, represent a secessionist

---

[2]. For David Barrett's most recent analyses of the Pentecostal renewals, see "The Worldwide Holy Spirit Renewal" (2001:381-414).

[3]. For details and penetrating insights, see his revised and expanded work, *The New International Dictionary of Pentecostal and Charismatic Movements* (2002). See also Russell Spittler, "Theological Style among Pentecostals and Charismatics" (1991).

[4]. Stanley Burgess, *The New International Dictionary of Pentecostal and Charismatic Movements* (2002:xxi).

groups that form ecclesiastical entities of their own. Charismatics, on the other hand, are individuals or groups for whom charismatic spirituality is a matter of adopting a pentecostalized spiritual lifestyle without necessarily leaving their own mainstream denominations.

Neocharismatics, the latest group, represent pentecostalized local congregations who found reasons to sever relations with their charismatic parent church and to startup independent charismatic churches.[5] Even with these broad differences, there is a consensus among scholars that the distinction between Pentecostals and Charismatics is a difficult line to draw.

The Making of Nigerian Pentecostalism: Sketching the Connections

Constant mobility of Nigerian churchgoers makes any demarcation between Pentecostals and Charismatics a difficult enterprise. A helpful approach may be to look at the Pentecostal phenomenon historically, and then survey the forms, nature, and extent of its influence in Nigerian Christianity. Because Pentecostalism in Nigeria is packaged in different varieties, I will use broad descriptive terms: classical Pentecostals, the charismatic movement, and Neocharismatics but with interpretations that are appropriate to the Nigerian situation.

Classical Pentecostals, 1918-1941

The origins of Pentecostalism in Nigeria and the pneumatic ethos found in churches that we shall broadly categorize as "classical" are neither an offshoot of nor an African reproduction of the Azusa Street phenomenon. Instead, early Pentecostalism in Nigerian Christianity was inspired by spontaneous manifestations of the Holy Spirit through various charismatic figures who emerged in the "pressure of primal religion and culture on the Christian message."[6]

---

5. Russell Spittler, "Theological Style among Pentecostals and Charismatics" (1991:292-293).
6. For details, see Ogbu Kalu, *Power, Poverty and Prayer: The Challenges of Poverty and*

Among events and personalities that are associated with the rise of classical Pentecostalism in Nigeria was the Prophet Garrick Braide. Initially an Anglican catechist, Braide launched a religious movement that became distinguished for its many Spirit revivals and healing. This was called the Christ Army, 1914-1918. Once the fire of Pentecostalism was ignited, it did not take long before this new Christian experience influenced and gathered momentum within the mission-planted churches.

As we have already mentioned, most active were the Aladura who were responsible for "bringing" the Faith Tabernacle of Philadelphia to Nigeria. The union with Faith Tabernacle was essentially a union that was fostered "through the post office," that is, accomplished by mail. The romance was short-lived, precipitating another foreign alliance that brought the British Apostolic Church to Nigeria in 1931. Today, The Apostolic Church of Nigeria (1931) and the Christ Apostolic Church (so-named in 1941) remain as the enduring legacies of this second alliance.

In similar manner, some young adherents of the Faith Tabernacle in Umuahia in the East were disowned by the established church for speaking in tongues and manifesting Spirit-baptism. They were forced to organize themselves into a church in 1934, which they called the Church of Jesus Christ. This group subsequently invited the American-based Assemblies of God to Nigeria in 1939.

Preoccupied by the drive for continuity, these indigenously-initiated movements sought overseas alliances and adopted foreign names mainly to avoid persecution at the hands of colonial authorities who wanted native-led churches to come under "adequate European supervision." These three Pentecostal groups (The Apostolic Church, Christ Apostolic Church, and the Assemblies of God) constitute the Nigerian brand of classical Pentecostalism.

Although indigenous in origins, character, and forms, the theological and ecclesiastical profiles of these churches are comparable with those of historical Pentecostalism in North America. Theologically, they all subscribe to formalized statements of beliefs and doctrines of the so-called

---

Pluralism in African Christianity, 1960-1996 (2000:111).

mainstream denominations. Points that are heavily emphasized or added have become Pentecostal distinctives—salvation by grace, divine healing, baptism of the Holy Spirit, glossolalia, and the second coming of Christ.[7] Ecclesiastically, these Nigerian Pentecostals all emerged out of the oldest established denomination, the Anglican Church, then, over time, became institutionalized and distinguishable ecclesiastical entities of their own.

The Charismatic Movement, 1944-1980s

Two significant layers in the development of the charismatic movement in Nigeria have often been overlooked. Both dating back precisely to 1944, the first layer, specifically denominational, took place within the existing first generation of classical Pentecostals and the historic mainline churches. The second, more trans-denominational, took the Pentecostal experience into the academic institutions and among the young and energetic student community. Although parallel in formal developments, both drew their inspirations from the desire for spiritual renewal and an increased interest in spiritual gifts, including glossolalia, prophecy, and physical healing.

The first formulation of charismatic renewal occurred within classical Pentecostalism and was responsible for initiating what might now be called African Pentecostals such as the Apostolic Faith Mission, the Redeemed Christian Church of God, and the Foursquare Gospel Church. All three churches developed around charismatic figures who were initially members of the classical Pentecostal denominations but were compelled to establish new churches because of their quest for more demonstrable and unmediated experience of the Holy Spirit.

The Apostolic Faith Mission, for example, was established in 1944 by Timothy Gbadebo Oshokoya (an evangelist with the CAC).[8] The Redeemed Christian Church of God was established in 1952 by Josiah Olufemi Akindayomi (a prophet of the Cherubim and Seraphim),[9] and

---

7. For a helpful study on the basic doctrinal beliefs of Pentecostalism, see Donald Dayton *Theological Roots of Pentecostalism* (1987).

8. For a fuller historical account of the Apostolic Faith in Nigeria, see the church's publication, *The Man with a Vision: The Biography of Timothy Gbadebo Oshokoya* (n.d.).

9. For the sake of brevity, the Redeemed Christian Church of God will henceforth be referred to simply as RCCG. For studies on this church, see Moses Akinwumi Adekola,

the Foursquare Gospel Church, established in 1955 by James Abayomi Boyejo, Samuel Olusegun Odunaike (both former members of The Apostolic Church), and Friday Chinyere Osuwa (an ordained minister of the Assemblies of God).[10]

These Pentecostal denominations retain traditional Christian beliefs and so are equally theologically conservative. However, in the interests of maintaining the cohesion of their charismatic experiences, they also showed the desire for the doctrines and practices of holiness and a tangible expression of evangelistic Christianity. Because of their ecclesiastical legacies, all three denominations can be described as second generation Pentecostals.

The most influential agency for charismatic renewal was the second layer, the transdenominational movement among university students. It was precisely the Pentecostalization of campus Christian groups that blew the winds of charismatic Christianity all over Nigeria. The student-led renewal movement was first established in Eastern Nigeria with the founding of Student Christian Movement (SCM) in 1937 by Akanu Ibiam. However, the movement existed on the margins of public visibility until its first entry into a Nigerian academic institution in Western Nigeria in 1940, Yaba Higher College, Lagos, through the pioneering efforts of Theophilus Ejiwumi.

The Eastern and Western segments of the SCM brought their work together in 1944 to form the Student Christian Movement of Nigeria.[11] Two important events in 1944 seem to indicate a providential design. It was in this year that the first second-generation Pentecostal church (Apostolic Faith Mission) was established. It was also in this year, 1944, that the

---

"The Redeemed Christian Church of God" (1989); Olusola Ajayi, *Warrior of Righteousness: The Life and Ministry of Rev. J.O. Akindayomi* (1997); and Olusegun Bankole, *The Trees Clap Their Hands* (1999).

10. For more history, see Tunde Ojo, "Forty and Forceful: The Story of Foursquare in Nigeria" (1995); and S.G. Adegboyega, *Short History of the Apostolic Church of Nigeria* (1978).

11. Ogbu Kalu sees this charismatic renewal on university campuses as "providential" and categorizes the vertical expansion of Pentecostalism in Africa in "three models": the "cultural-historical model," the "providential model," and the "functionalist model." See his work, *Power, Poverty and Prayer* (2000:110-117).

Student Christian Movement of Nigeria was established, thus orchestrating large-scale trends in campus spirituality.

The SCM was introduced into the University College, Ibadan in 1948 (renamed the University of Ibadan). The Ibadan branch was to become the pivot of SCM in Nigeria. From there and onward, charismatic renewal took center stage in Nigerian academic institutions through other interdenominational Christian student organizations such as Christian Union (CU) and Scripture Union (SU). The Scripture Union was especially strong among secondary school students. In the Southeast, for example, it was the secondary school student members of the Scripture Union that brought the charismatic fervor into public consciousness by miraculously raising a dead person to life at a rally in Onitsha, the sprawling commercial center of the East.[12]

Equally, the impact of the charismatic revival moved into Northern Nigeria through zealous evangelistic activity of students, especially graduates of tertiary institutions. Although taking place at a much later period (the mid 1970s), there was a similar charismatic renewal in the Catholic Church brought about by the establishment of the Catholic Charismatic Renewal (CCR). The group initiated a vibrant renewal movement among Catholic students in the higher institutions, from where it continues to influence the mainstream Catholic Church in Nigeria. On the whole, the main emphases of the various charismatic renewal movements among the students were on personal salvation and baptism of the Holy Spirit, evidenced by a pentecostalized style of speaking in tongues, physical healing, holiness, and spiritual gifts.[13]

The general characteristics of these renewal movements were from indigenous causes. External influences, especially before the 1970s, were almost non-existent. It was not until early 1970s that foreign influence in forms of theological direction and funding for ministry opened a door

---

12. Kalu (2000:113).
13. For a comprehensive history on the development of these transdenominational Christian movements on Nigerian academic campuses, see Matthews A. Ojo, "The Contextual Significance of the Charismatic Movements in Independent Nigeria" (1988:175-192).

to the American connection. Even then, the American influence was incidental and limited.

In some important ways, therefore, the name of. S.G. Elton, a veteran missionary of the British Apostolic Church, is an important one. He was responsible for linking the university-student pioneers of the charismatic movements with foreign organizations and individuals for theological and financial assistance. An example of this was the linking of Benson Idahosa with Gordon Lindsay and his wife and other independent Pentecostals like T.L. Osborne and Jim Baker in the United States. Together, they assisted in the training and funding of Idahosa's Church of God Mission International.[14]

The charismatic movements among students and university graduates were loosely structured at first, operating on the periphery of established churches as Bible study and prayer groups. The compulsion to evangelize gained its momentum towards the mid-1970s, transforming the students' renewal movements into independent charismatic organizations. Matthews Ojo records that by 1974, "more than ten Charismatic organizations had been established by graduates already influenced by the revival."[15]

By late 1970s through early 1980s, the charismatic renewal experienced a phenomenal explosion. It was during this period that these transdenominational charismatic organizations began to take on institutional characteristics. The charismatic denominations that emerged in the early 1980s, such as William Kumuyi's Deeper Life Ministry (1982) and Enoch Adeboye's take-over of the Redeemed Christian Church of God (1980), became ecclesiastical juggernauts, in large part because of their educational background and self-conscious modernity. This leads the way into a third category in the development of Nigerian Pentecostalism, namely, the Neocharismatics.

---

14. For details on the life and ministry of Benson Idahosa, see Ruthanne Garlock, *Benson Idahosa: Fire in His Bones* (1981).

15. Matthews Ojo, "The Church in the African State: The Charismatic/Pentecostal Experience in Nigeria" (1998:28).

Neocharismatics, 1980s-2000s

The transformation of charismatic organizations of the young and educated into formal ecclesiastical structures eventually climaxed into what today constitutes the third-generation Pentecostals in Nigeria, the Neocharismatics. This group represents pentecostalized congregations who found reasons to sever relations with their charismatic ecclesial connections to start independent denominations.

Composed initially of the educated, young, and mobile, this group can be described as a movement within Nigerian Pentecostalism because they bridge across and into mainline, classical, and charismatic churches and then move beyond the constraints of denominationalism. Since its origin in the early 1980s, a period described by Matthews Ojo as "the second phase of [charismatic] growth," the Neocharismatic movement has matured and, to a large extent, established itself as a formidable Christian tradition.[16] Today, it acts as a pressure group within Nigerian Christianity.

Nigerian Neocharismatics come in at least two distinctive packages—the holiness and the prosperity groups. The characteristic feature of the holiness group is the search for deeper spirituality, expressed clearly in such phrases as "lay all on the altar," "become clay in the potter's hands," "experience a closer walk with Christ," and "live a new life." As its name implies, the Deeper Life Bible Church offers a compelling example of the holiness ethic and spirituality. In the words of the founder and general superintendent, Pastor William F. Kumuyi, "[t]he prop and hub of our ministry is holiness of life and conduct . . . the tripod on which the church rests is the Word, holiness, and evangelism."[17]

Those often inclined to the "prosperity gospel," on the other hand, attempt to be a model of religious adaptation or response to severe economic crisis and contemporary realities. Contrary to the economic boom that

---

16. Matthews Ojo, "Charismatic Movements in Africa" (1996:101).
17. William F. Kumuyi, "Deeper Christian Life Ministry" (1998:249). For the beginning and the spiritual ethic of Deeper Life Bible Church, see Alan Isaacson, *Deeper Life: The Extraordinary Growth of the Deeper Life Bible Church* (1990). See also Matthews A. Ojo's works, "Deeper Christian Life Ministry: A Case Study of the Charismatic Movements in Western Nigeria" (1988:141-162); and "Deeper Life Bible Church of Nigeria" (1992:135-156).

sustained earlier charismatic renewal of the 1970s, "prosperity gospel" came into public visibility in the mid-1980s, a period coincident with the government's introduction of the austerity and economic restructuring, the Structural Adjustment Programme (SAP).[18] Prominent among this group are Zoe Ministry, Church of God Mission, and David Oyedepo's Winner's Chapel, an arm of the Living Faith World Outreach Centre where he is "presiding bishop."

The contours of "prosperity gospel" portray an attempt to project a collective perception of victorious living in an age of socio-economic and political decline. These contours include the spiritual economic principle of prosperity and a self-conscious modernity appropriated in a westernized lifestyle. The accelerated speed of socio-economic decline called for urgent change and a shift in emphasis such that even the idealistic ethic of the holiness group had to be reconceptualized. Thus, the collapse of the ecosystem and the popular "doctrine of prosperity" provided the symbolic platform for adapting the Christian message to the contemporary situation.

Prosperity and miracles, therefore, become incentives for a holy living and an evidence of the indwelling of the Holy Spirit. As a result of this adaptation, Neocharismatics have created communities of discontinuity and transformation, offering the people a new identity and values in dealing concretely with matters of spiritual and socio-economic problems. This orientation raises a fundamental issue about the expression of faith in the secular space. In this area, then, both the Redeemed Christian Church of God (RCCG) and Deeper Life Bible Church offer us important perspectives.

The Redeemed Christian Church of God (RCCG) Since 1980

The Redeemed Christian Church of God was established in 1952 by the late Josiah Akindayomi. The founding of the church was the result of conflicting attitudes toward ritual and ceremonial activities that characterized the Cherubim and Seraphim Church of which Akindayomi was a member. Reforming the existing churches to appreciate orthodox discourse on

---

18. It is modeled on the American "word of faith," "name-it-and-claim-it" prosperity gospel. For details on the Structural Adjustment Programme (SAP), see T. Olagunju, A. Jinadu and S. Oyovbaire, *Transition to Democracy in Nigeria, 1985-1993* (1993).

spiritual regeneration, righteousness, and holiness was a major part of his agenda.[19] Although the social and ecclesiastical influence of the new church was not large in its early years, the teachings of Josiah Akindayomi continue to be a major legacy in the life and practices of RCCG even today.

The installation of E.A. Adeboye in 1980 as Akindayomi's successor bridges the church into the third-generation strand of Nigerian Pentecostalism. A successful university professor with a Ph.D. in mathematics, Adeboye's leadership and the subsequent transformation of RCCG furnishes compelling testimony of how personal transformation and affiliation with a new experience of faith can influence and shape even an established organization. I have identified this trend as a characteristic feature of Neocharismatic ecclesiology.

Adeboye does not differ significantly from his predecessor's holiness ethic. Instead, he has expanded his ecclesiastical agenda taking seriously the socio-economic and political trends within contemporary Nigeria. He continues to emphasize strongly the need for holiness in the midst of a wrong-headed materiality that has infiltrated the church and the nation. Today, RCCG has pushed its boundaries to more than one hundred other countries, and it continues to experience a dizzying growth that is projecting it as one of Nigeria's fastest-growing Pentecostal denominations.[20]

Deeper Life Bible Church Since 1982

Deeper Life Bible Church is an autumnal child of a Bible study group begun in 1973 in the campus residence of the University of Lagos mathematics professor, William Folorunso Kumuyi. Nine years separate the humble beginnings of this Bible study group (later named Deeper Christian Life Ministry) and its transformation into a denominational church in 1982. Yet, without this initial focus on Bible teaching and the enthusiasm for evangelism, Deeper Life Bible Church would not have been possible.

---

19. For insightful studies on RCCG, see Olusola Ajayi, *Warrior of Righteousness: The Life and Ministry of Rev. J.O. Akindayomi* (1997); and Moses A. Adekola, "The Redeemed Christian Church of God" (1989).
20. Obong Akpaekong, "The Miracle Man" (1999:10).

Today, the church functions as an arm of the ministry although outsiders often refer to both as one and the same calling them simply, "Deeper Life." William F. Kumuyi, the founder and general superintendent of Deeper Christian Life Ministry, was initially an Anglican who became converted to the holiness-pentecostalism of the Apostolic Faith Mission in April 1964. His experiential orientation to pietism has been the driving force in the holiness revivalism for which Deeper Life is renowned.

Kumuyi's original intention was to function on the fringes of established churches as a Bible study group. The vision was to supply sound exegetical teaching of the Bible which he felt was missing in the charismatic revival in educational institutions and established churches. However, he ran afoul of the leadership of the Apostolic Faith Mission on matters of healing and evangelism. His excommunication from the Apostolic Faith Mission in 1977, coupled with intense harassment of his followers from the established churches, led him to introduce Sunday services in November 1982.[21]

What is important for Kumuyi and Deeper Life is not merely the founding of another denomination. Rather, the church occupies a unique position in the development of a new paradigm that is faithful to the biblical witness. Today, over twenty years after its institutionalization as a church, Deeper Life Bible Church is still engaged in a ministry of responsibility to the Word, holiness, and evangelism. Like RCCG, the boundaries of Deeper Life continue to extend far beyond Nigeria into other countries.

I must add that my attempt to nuance Pentecostals and Charismatics, notwithstanding, it is appropriate to say that both are so much alike that it is impossible to make clear lines between them. Unless we acknowledge this problem, we run the risk of taking the Pentecostal phenomenon at face value.

---

21. For details, see Allan Isaacson, *Deeper Life: The Extraordinary Growth of the Deeper Life Bible Church* (1990:123-143).

The Context of the Neocharismatic Churches

> A boundary is not that at which something stops but, as the Greeks recognized, the boundary is that from which something begins its presencing[22]

These words of Martin Heidegger articulate, quite accurately, the transmission and adaptations of the Christian faith in Nigeria. I have shown that three different strands—the historic mainline churches, the AICs and the Neocharismatic churches—conceptualize influences of the church in Nigeria. This means, then, that the wider significance of the present life of the church in Nigeria lies in the awareness that the "limits" of early mission church traditions mark out normative boundaries in the new expressions of church.

Thus the recent Neocharismatic churches represent a continuum where the past flows together with the contemporary in a variety of combinations. Consequently, I will analyze the context of the Neocharismatics through multidimensional factors that include culture, religion, socio-political, and economic issues.

The Cultural Dimension

I have said that the Neocharismatic churches represent a "continuum" where the past, with its older traditions, flows together with the contemporary as the older forms are modified by current trends. The implication of this is that the cultural dimension of the Neocharismatics must be understood against the old forms as a contextualized version of the continuing quest to explain the mysteries of life. It is appropriate, therefore, to say that Neocharismatic expressions about supernaturalism are not that different from their predecessors except that they go further to clarify what these predecessors did not confront or left vague.

Nigerian worldview assumptions highlight the centrality of the spiritual realm and the forces that are behind events in the physical world. Human

---

22. Martin Heidegger, *Poetry, Language, Thought* (1971:91).

beings are engaged in a desperate struggle for survival in a world dominated by forces over which they have no control. The African world is dominated by dark forces and by agents of chaos and destruction that force humans to act in hostility, one against another, and against everything that is good. Neocharismatics, therefore, attempt to correlate the Christian message with the human situation in order to show the concrete effectiveness of Christianity within the cultural milieu.

Neocharismatic conceptual framework confronts the cosmic hostility between Christ and Satan as the basis for order and power in a chaotic world. The victorious death and resurrection of Christ is witness to God's cosmic superiority over Satan and his evil cronies that have enslaved men and women. Hence, salvation takes on a new meaning. The presence and power of Christ guarantees victory to believers over demonic forces. Neocharismatics view themselves as witnesses to the continued presence and universal Lordship of Christ over the cosmos. This enables them to create a community of the redeemed and liberated on a new ideological and institutional base. Thus, the approach of Neocharismatics to problems raised by culture is not "through a wholesale *rejection* of the past, but through an engagement with it; refashioning history and domesticating it at the same time."[23]

The Religious Dimension

Traditionally, the Nigerian religious field is characterized by its plurality, and to some degree, its flexibility. However, the arrival of the Neocharismatics unto a field already dominated by other forms of religious expressions has provoked controversy. Neocharismatics understand the religious context and see other religious players in starkly antagonistic terms. Hence their ecclesiastical polity tends to project a christocentric exclusivism that devalues or demonizes everything not "born-again."

Neocharismatics set themselves up in strong opposition even to some Christian denominations. For example, historic churches, especially the

---

23. Ruth Marshall-Fratani is, in my judgement, the foremost scholar on Pentecostalism in Africa. I am thankful for the opportunity to refer her work quite judiciously in this work. For reference to this particular quotation, see her work, "Mediating the Global and Local in Nigerian Pentecostalism" (1998:291).

Catholic Church, are perceived to be "nominal" or "powerless." Their dissatisfaction with these older historic churches comes from the watering-down or lack of power, allowing people to have their feet in both traditional religion and biblical Christianity.

Neocharismatics are merciless toward indigenous religious practices. These are bluntly referred to as "demonic" or "satanic." Consequently, they express profound reaction against any Christian church which has connections with these traditional practices such as might be found in the Aladura churches. A corollary is that traditional religion seems to be losing ground to the Neocharismatics as the latter continue to expand through their promise of "modernity," prosperity, healing, miracles, and eternal life.

In Neocharismatics' hierarchy of religious stereotyping, Muslims occupy the distinction as unparalleled agents of Satan. This demonization of Muslims provides Neocharismatics with the platform from which to blame the succession of Muslim-led governments for the severe socio-economic decline. Neocharismatics point especially to 1985, the year the fraudulent government of the military junta and unrepentant dictator, Ibrahim Badamosi Babangida, secretly incorporated Nigeria into the Organization of Islamic Conference (OIC). The OIC constitutes a rallying ground for Islamic countries in political and economic matters. Since OIC is considered as part of Satan's empire, Neocharismatics see Muslims as objects of conversion and from whom the control of the state itself must be rescued.

This has had profound implication in Muslim-Christian relations in contemporary Nigeria. For one thing, such a demonization of Islam has generated very complex interreligious tension that has earned Nigeria the unenviable reputation as a major country of religious violence and aggression. For another thing, and perhaps more indicative of religious stress in Nigeria, Muslim-Christian verbal wrangling and demonstrations that began in the 1970s (beginning of the Neocharismatic movement) degenerated into full-blown violence and aggression in the 1980s and 1990s (the decades the Neocharismatics became institutionalized).[24]

---

24. For a comprehensive study on religious violence and aggression in Nigeria, see Toyin Falola, *Violence in Nigeria: The Crisis of Religious Politics and Secular Ideologies* (1998). See also Jan H. Boer, *Nigeria's Decades of Blood, 1980–2002* (2003).

On the whole, the high visibility of the Neocharismatics and their continuing expansion make them one of Nigeria's most dynamic realities. Ironically, their Christian competitors seem to be conceding to them by incorporating Pentecostal elements into their church services. For their part, the Muslims have responded by engaging in open-air "crusades" and occupying unwelcome spaces through television broadcasts. In the meantime, the religious tension in Nigeria continues to escalate and appears to be insoluble.

The Socio-Political Dimension

Neocharismatics came onto the religious field in a socio-political context that has its roots deeply entrenched in colonial history. As Falola has rightly observed, "some of the issues that generated crisis and violence in the 1970s and beyond [between Christians and Muslims] had their origins in the colonial period."[25] Nigeria was a British colonial creation resulting from an artificially constructed agglomeration of diverse groups with little regard to histories, cultural-linguistic differences, ethnopolitics, and demographic configurations. The decision to amalgamate the North and South on January 1, 1914 by Lord Frederick Luggard has come to be described in Nigerian post-independence politics as "the mistake of 1914."[26]

Although this is not an attempt to explain Nigeria's post-independence political problems in terms of a colonialist paradigm, the colonial period does help us to see the underlying structure and conditioned the political behavior of post-independence Nigeria. The disenchantment of Nigerians with their leaders began much earlier in the 1960s and continues to be reflected in the "high turnover of governments" that has become a feature of Nigerian politics.

Failed civilian governments, unpopular, longstanding military regimes, inconclusive and contested electoral outcomes, political violence and the crises related to legitimacy continue to bedevil the political situation of

---

25. Toyin Falola, *Violence in Nigeria* (1998:37-38).
26. Eghosa Osaghae, *Crippled Giant: Nigeria since Independence* (1998:1). Osaghae's work is an insightful study of post-independence political developments in Nigeria.

Nigeria.[27] Without counting the unsuccessful and unreported military coup attempts, Nigeria experienced four civilian governments and eight military regimes between 1960 and 2002.[28] Despite persuasive promises, each government has offered little more than a replay of personal financial enrichments, ethnic marginalization, denigration, and oppression.

The decades of the 1980s-1990s, incidentally the period the Neocharismatics became more *established*, have socially and politically been the most volatile in modern Nigeria. The regimes of Babangida (1985-1993) and Abacha (1993-1998) stand out as most insidious of all. On one hand, Babangida, the self-styled "evil genius," earned the moniker "Maradona" for his diabolical political trickery, shiftiness, deceit, and money-mongering.[29] On the other hand, Abacha, who succeeded Babangida, was a less than intelligent dictator who recklessly and brutally suppressed or killed his political opponents.

Overall, both "were powerful and unapologetic representatives of northern [Muslim] interests" and the most corrupt and repressive, even by African standards.[30] The deep economic crisis, political engineering, profound cynicism, and disaffection towards political leadership that became very much part of popular consciousness during their regimes continue to underlie the suspicion held for all Nigerian leaders and political orders.

Seen in this way, one can understand the political context to which the Neocharismatic churches had to respond and which, in fact, explains their civic activism. Neocharismatics set to work by attempting to reconfigure the moral order. They are speaking a "new political language" that is aimed at

---

27. Osaghae (1998:14).
28. Osaghae (1998:14). The civilian governments were those of Tafawa Balewa (First Republic, 1960-1966), Shehu Shagari (Second Republic, 1979-1983), Ernest Shonekan (Interim National Government, 1993), and Olusegun Obasanjo (Fourth Republic, 1999-2007). The military regimes were those of Generals Aguiyi Ironsi (1966), Yakubu Gowon (1966-1975), Murtala Mohammed (1975), Olusegun Obasanjo (1975-1979), Muhammadu Buhari (1983-1985), Ibrahim Babangida (1985-1993), Sanni Abacha (1993-1998) and Abdulsalami Abubakar (1998-1999).
29. The tag "Maradona" is a sarcastic salute to the devious dimensions of the Babangida saga, which, on sober reflection, does injustice to the soccer artistry of the Argentine soccer star, Diego Maradona.
30. Toyin Falola, *Violence in Nigeria* (1998:56). For other historical work on Nigeria by Falola, see *The History of Nigeria* (1999).

empowering the people to develop strategies for overcoming the oppression they continue to experience with successive bad governments. Here, the core idea of their theology of "rebirth" is readily applied at the level of the nation itself.

This presupposes a political strategy that hopes to create an alternate form of citizenship through "a community of individuals who feel capable of overcoming the world as they experience it, and changing it."[31] Thus, their new approach reflects the widespread sentiment that the older and corrupt establishments must be challenged with a new presence and even a new generation of political leadership.

The Economic Dimension

It is one thing to explain the greater part of Nigeria's socio-political instability in terms of the baneful effect of colonial legacies. It is, however, a completely different thing to blame Nigeria's economic woes totally on external factors. Although colonialism may not have bequeathed much to Nigeria, the economic boom of the 1970s, the decade after Nigeria's independence, weakens the externalist perspective in explaining the obstacle to economic growth in Nigeria.

The 1970s was a period of economic prosperity unprecedented in the history of modern Nigeria. The 1973 Arab-Israeli war worked in Nigeria's favor, making her oil a highly marketable commodity to the West. In the league of nations, Nigeria became a third world opportunity. The petro-naira, exchanging at $1.60 to N1.00, lured expatriates from around the world to Nigeria to "find markets for their knowledge."[32] Nigeria's problem, as Apter has described, "was the proverbial fate of all oil economies, which is not how to make money but how to spend it."[33]

Nigeria attempted to solve this "problem" by embarking on programs that emphasized the provision of basic human needs. On the international

---

31. Ruth Marshall, "'God is Not a Democrat': Pentecostalism and Democratisation in Nigeria" (1995:247-248).
32. Andrew Apter, "IBB = 419: Nigerian Democracy and the Politics of Illusion" (1999:268).
33. Apter (1999:268).

front, the country almost unilaterally hosted the second All-Africa Games in Lagos in 1973 and the Festival of Black Arts and Culture (FESTAC '77). Today, most Pentecostals view FESTAC '77 as a "demonic invasion of our dear country" and as "an insignificant show of nudeness and idolatry" that is responsible for the country's present economic woes.[34]

By contrast, the 1980s saw Nigeria in deep economic decline and as early as 1983, the oil economy had entered its downward spiral. Nigerians applauded the ouster of the corrupt civilian government of Shehu Shagari by the military coup of December 31, 1983. Buhari's team, the successor to Shagari, gained initial credibility by advancing primarily a program for economic recovery, citing electoral malpractices only as a secondary consideration.

When Babangida toppled the Buhari regime in the bloodless coup of August 27, 1985, his goal also "was to restore Nigeria's credibility by floating the naira to establish its 'free' market value."[35] But compared to Buhari who was "straightforward and sincere, Babangida was an evil genius—affable and cunning . . . a master of double-speak, deceit, and ambiguity."[36]

Babangida's economic policy of Structural Adjustment Program (SAP) brought with it massive inflation, devaluation of the naira, and a large-scale decline in the standard of living. His government proved to be more corrupt than any other that had preceded it. It institutionalized corruption on a massive scale, diverted state funds, and accentuated the problems of inequality by obliterating the middle-class. By the time he was disgraced out of office in 1993, income per head was one-tenth of what it had been when he came to power in 1985.[37]

Sanni Abacha, the dictator who ruled from 1993 until his welcomed death in 1996, was no intellectual match for Babangida's evil ingenuity. Although his regime inherited a most fragile economy, the economic indicators show that his mediocre regime took steps that were to consume

---

34. For details, see Lugard Ononyemu, "Stop the Delphic Games! Another Demonic Invasion Looms on Nigeria" (1993:40-41).
35. Andrew Apter, "IBB = 419" (1999:269).
36. Toyin Falola, *The History of Nigeria* (1999:183).
37. *The Economist*, August 21, (1993:14). See also Steve Brouwer, Paul Gifford, and Susan Rose in *Exporting the American Gospel: Global Christian Fundamentalism* (1996:152).

Nigeria for years. For example, the real GDP growth rate, which was 2.6 percent in 1993, fell to barely 1 percent in 1994.[38]

It is logical to conclude that the economic decline of the 1980s and 1990s was one of many factors that fueled discontent and the search for alternative means to socio-political and economic survival. It is in responding to these and other similar challenges that the Neocharismatics became a viable reconstructionist group. It is to this aspect of their ministry that I now turn.

The Ministry of the Neocharismatic Churches

The discussion so far has indicated that variety is the main characteristic of the churches in Nigeria. This variety helps us understand that each strand has been an attempt to bring the Christian message in line with the specific socio-cultural and historical context. This contextual adaptation of the gospel and Christian ministry account for the populist character of the church, giving the image of one that is vigorously attempting to both reflect and respond to the deepest longings of common people. Admittedly, responding to a more *modern* context and with all it offers, the Neocharismatics clearly outperform their predecessors by providing a dizzying array of massages in idioms and techniques that are popular in chaotic urban culture.

Koinonia: The Community of the Saved

Theological reflection presupposes the church to be the fellowship of Christ's disciples. It is a unifying impulse that extends beyond the church itself and places its existence firmly "in Christ." The facilitator of this connection is the Holy Spirit, who is the agent of the new birth through which believers become co-heirs with Christ in the family of God (Rom. 8:14-17). This invitation to participate in the community of the triune God raises the church's awareness as God's eschatological redeemed community.

---

38. Eghosa Osaghae, *Crippled Giant: Nigeria since Independence* (1998:281).

It presupposes the church's fundamental calling to be the foretaste of the *imago dei*, determining its proclaiming, reconciling, sanctifying, and unifying in the world.

Neocharismatics see themselves in this perspective. Hence the desire to transform the religious landscape by constructing a "born-again" community springs from the willingness to be responsive to the higher calling of the Holy Spirit. It is in this light that we can articulate the separatism and exclusivist purity of a "holiness" church like Deeper Life. This church sees itself not as "new" but as a model of the New Testament church in a way that questions the ecclesiality of previously existing churches. To be a member of the Deeper Life, for example, is to recognize that one belongs to a community that sets strictly Christian standards and recognizes a higher call.

On the whole, the born-again community crosses regional, ethnic, cultural, and even national boundaries with extraordinary ease. This unprecedented transformational fluidity presupposes that one is first a "born-again person" before any ethnic particularity, whether Yoruba, Igbo, Edo, or Nigerian. The born-again community is characterized by a surprising degree of egalitarianism where the old form of kinship is replaced by a new one; that is, a "brother/sister in the Lord." Important decisions of life like marriage that would have otherwise been negotiated along ethnic lines now become subordinated to the higher biblical teaching that Christians should not be "unequally yoked with unbelievers." Marriage must be solemnized with a born-again brother or sister with little or no deference to ethnicity.

Neocharismatic communities also form conglomerate networks that extend beyond the local church to include other born-again churches. These networks, both spiritual and material, offer members the opportunity with which to reinvent themselves in an atmosphere of fraternal support. Members are provided with "material benefits such as employment opportunities, exchanges of goods and services, and even access to officialdom without the usual costly red tape and inevitable 'dash.'"[39]

---

39. See Ruth Marshall-Fratani, "Mediating the Global and Local in Nigerian Pentecostalism" (2000:85).

In other words, the born-again prefers domestic or office helps who are likewise born-agains. General clientele with privately-owned institutions such as hospitals, schools, and businesses are also within the born-again community. The overriding logic is that born-again institutions and companies are more reliable and trustworthy. By constructing communities that have developed a stronger sense of identity, these Neocharismatic churches are responding to and helping resolve the fear and uncertainty of chaotic urban life and social relations.

Evangelism: Propagating the Word

The fervor and harmony that bring the Neocharismatic churches into a visible spiritual unity also informs most of their activities. With the understanding that previously existing churches have practiced powerless Christianity, the rock on which the Neocharismatic churches are founded is evangelism. This central belief can be set in a wider framework. In terms of biblical mandate, Neocharismatics belief that the work of evangelism is in obedience to the express command of Christ as recorded in Matthew 28:19-20. In its wider context, the apocalyptic and millennialist beliefs of Neocharismatics add urgency to evangelism, requiring dynamic participation in the business of the kingdom.

Overall, evangelism is a religious preoccupation that is undoubtedly regarded as the most important work for the "born-again." In the words of William Kumuyi of the Deeper Life Bible Church, "soul-winning is the greatest work you can ever be involved in. It's the most rewarding enterprise you can undertake. It's a work that gives joy in this life and brings reward in the world to come. It is a work of the greatest consequence."[40] This significance of evangelism can also be weighed against other important facts. These include the understanding that the struggle for territory between the agents of God and those of Satan mean that evangelism be directed towards conversion. It also means that evangelism opens the way for men and women to be freed from the forces of evil.

Propagating the Word through multi-media is novel, effective, and breaks with past traditions by facilitating ministry in the modern urban

---

40. William F. Kumuyi, *Have Compassion on Them* (1975:7).

setting. This means the use of speech, print, audio-visuals, and open-air ministry. While providing the most effective approach to evangelism in Nigeria today, these modes of evangelism do provoke harsh criticism from those who are not favorable to born-again theology and who see the Neocharismatics as "invading unwelcome spaces."[41]

On the one hand, Neocharismatics are well known for recounting numerous testimonies to miracles in their open-air crusades. Claiming a close correlation between religious experience and "right doctrine" enables them to demonize or disparagingly label other religions, even other churches, as "dead" or "false." On the other hand, the use of the media also "allows for the multiplication of narrative forms and the delocalization of messages."[42] Even more important is the fact that the evangelical packaging of these messages "is designed to reach beyond the saved, to incorporate a theoretically unlimited group of potential converts."[43] As a result, conversion of those who are not born-again, especially of Muslims, is highly prized. For Neocharismatics, the advantage of using all technological facilities is to have the greatest capacity for evangelism. But for non believers, especially the Muslims, the proselytizing appeal of the Christians, directly offered and electronically mediated by Neocharimatic preachers into the privacy of one's own home, is threatening and intrusive.

Socio-Political Activism

The recent revival of pragmatism provides a timely intellectual background for understanding the role and value of the church in the public sphere. Controlling the space of the divine has always been the preoccupation of the church in Nigeria. Becoming entangled with the realm of Caesar was considered unchristian and worldly. The involvement of Christians in politics, therefore, is a fairly recent occurrence, going back only to the religious violence of the mid 1980s. Even then, the church's deep

---

41. For an insightful study on the use of the media in both Nigeria and Ghanaian Pentecostalism, see Rosalind I.J. Hackett, "Charismatic/Pentecostal Appropriation of Media Technologies in Nigeria and Ghana" (1998:258-277).
42. Ruth Marshall-Fratani, "Mediating the Global and Local in Nigerian Pentecostalism" (2000:94).
43. Marshall-Fratani (2000:92).

sense of evil and the need to see justice done were made even worse by the unsympathetic actions of successive Muslim-led governments. Today, this has changed. No other ecclesiastical tradition exhibits an attitude for reshaping the socio-political order as do the Neocharismatics.[44]

The socio-political ethos of engagement of the Neocharismatic churches is based on the hope they have to reorganize a morally chaotic world. This can be explained in two ways. First, they do not attempt to make excuse for previous absence of political opposition by simply critiquing or giving religious support to political systems. Second, they do not promise earthly salvation through the dawning of some kind of ideal republic. Rather, their engagement is a reflective kind of political consciousness, having one eye on socioeconomic and political morality while being simultaneously engaging in ideological criticism of the church's own beliefs and pronouncements.

This stance provides the Neocharismatics with the right to engage in prudent criticism of the state in order to foster a new state of mind and awaken Christians to citizenship. Responsible socio-political theologizing, therefore, becomes the central theme "in which the moral government of the self" becomes the symbolic realm in which the "failure of the nation" is manifested.[45] A good example is the fact that most "born-agains" do not give, take, or tolerate bribery, no matter how financially pressed they may be. This demonstrates the Neocharismatics' emphasis upon the individual's responsibility for the private, inner state of conscience and morality.

In its collective sense, this kind of personal accountability provides the moral basis for Neocharismatics to participate in popular discontent with institutionalized corruption. Matthews Ojo captures this well when he quotes from the publication of the Sword of the Spirit Ministries (a Neocharismatic church founded in Ibadan by Francis Wale Oke): "Corruption is our bane in this country. Pray that the people of God will stand up for truth, honesty, and integrity and stand together against corruption wherever they are."[46]

---

44. See Ruth Marshall, "'God is not a Democrat'" (1995:239-260).
45. Marshall (1995:247).
46. Matthews Ojo, "The Church in the African State: The Charismatic/Pentecostal Experience in Nigeria" (1998:27). For details on Francis Wale Oke's viewpoint, see *Sword*

This is confirmed by Ruth Marshall-Fratani's interview with Kehinde Osinowo, the founder of "Christians for the Regeneration of the Nation." Osinowo started his organization with the conviction that "the sin of the nation is based on the sin of the individual . . . we shall restore Nigeria to moral probity, godliness, and prosperity."[47] This new language of private moral probity, therefore, has as its premise to obliterate the dichotomy between individual morality and the established structures of evil.

Fortunately, this imperative is derived from the Pentecostal view of the world as an arena where "the powers" are constantly in competition, the good vis-à-vis the evil, and of God versus those of the devil. The following declaration by the Sword of the Spirit Ministries (an Ibadan based Ministry founded by Francis Wale Oke) articulates the thinking of most Neocharismatics:

> The plan of the devil is to ruin Nigeria's economy beyond repair. There is demonic confederacy to achieve this. His ultimate goal is to hinder Nigeria from fulfilling God's plan to carry the Gospel around the world, knowing that a buoyant economy as well as advancement in technology are boosters to the propagation of the Gospel Message.[48]

By linking the spiritual world with the physical, Neocharismatics are developing a theology that shows how events in the physical world are manifestations of power encounters between forces of good and evil. For Neocharismatics, therefore, the real issue is to cultivate a transformational faith that is powerful enough to redeem the nation from the clutches of demonic agents.

In the face of this challenge, Neocharismatics have to contend with "competing moral orders." With respect to other religions, the struggle is most obviously against Islam, "since it, like pentecostalism, provides a

---

of the Spirit November 15, (1986:35).
47. Ruth Marshall-Fratani, "Mediating the Global and Local in Nigerian Pentecostalism" (2000:100).
48. Sword of the Spirit Ministries, *Sword of the Spirit*, No. 27 (1986).

total vision for the moral redemption of the nation and the forms of its socio-political organization."[49] It was no mere coincidence that attempts to Islamize Nigeria by surreptitiously enrolling her in the Organization of Islamic Conference in 1985 (OIC) was and continues to be interpreted as a secret act of the devil. Such demonization of Islam provides a powerful incentive for Neocharismatics to present an alternative form of "governmentality" in which Nigeria is redeemed and its public sphere remoralized. For Neocharismatics, "the only legitimate form of power is that of the Holy Spirit, and only those who posses it can be saved, and can act as saviors at the social and political level."[50]

Affirming that the rule of saints is essential to the recovery of the nation also requires the presence and power of God for dynamic political activism. The subtle strategy to realize this moral vision, for Neocharismatics, is through the power of prayer. Consequently, it is not uncommon for them to pray fellow "born-agains" into public offices. The basis for political involvement becomes fundamentally connected to the biblical statement that "righteousness exalts a nation but sin is a reproach to any people" (Prov. 14:34).

Today, the Pentecostal Fellowship of Nigeria (PFN) and the Christian Association of Nigeria (CAN) continue to show great vitality and staying power. Their unambiguous solidarity and prayer support to the presidency of Olusegun Obasanjo, a self-confessed born-again Christian, is an indication that indeed the Pentecostals are determined not to be outplayed.

The Theology of the Neocharismatic Churches

The Neocharismatics, like their Pentecostal counterparts, have been understood primarily in terms of their most visible behavior, glossolalia, or "speaking in tongues." Even when attempts are made to understand deeper

---

49. I am indebted to Ruth Marshall whose interpretation has influenced the line of thinking adopted here. For details, see her work, Ruth Marshall, "'God is not a Democrat'" (1995:258).
50. Marshall (1995:259).

the issue of their theology, attention becomes focused, almost exclusively, on pneumatology, especially Spirit baptism and the gifts of the Spirit. It is only recently that the so-called "prosperity gospel" has become a popular theme of the Neocharismatics.

Even then, this has been influenced largely by the American televangelism scandals of the 1980s. After the flush of the oil boom of the 1970s, Nigerian people felt the economic decline of the 1980s. The popularity of prosperity preaching in Pentecostal circles in the USA caught on like wildfire in Nigeria, along with the extremes and scandals it was known for.[51]

The attempt to define the Neocharismatics, as well as the whole Pentecostal movement in Nigeria, has been done "in an operational rather than normative manner."[52] While this approach has its value, this approach does not do justice to the distinctive *gestalt* of Neocharismatic theology. While not ignoring their practice of glossolalia or their emphasis on Spirit baptism, we will focus on the underlying theological categories, namely, salvation and power theology.

The Theme of Salvation

Nigerian Neocharismatics teach the evangelical doctrine of fallen humanity in need of a Savior. Nevertheless, their understanding of the "good news" of salvation does not stop with the cross. Rather it emphasizes fuller aspects of the Christian life such as health, victory over demonic forces, and liberation from poverty. Salvation, in a word, is holistic. It is objectified as spiritual and material realism and is experienced on both the individual and social levels.

Salvation as "Good News" of the Kingdom

The Neocharismatics believe that the historical Jesus was the result of a divine plan to provide a Mediator between an offended God and a sinful humanity. The evangelicalism which undergirds their theology, therefore, is

---

51. For an insightful study on American televangelism, see Quentin J. Schultze's *Televangelism and American Culture: The Business of Popular Religion* (1991).
52. Ogbu Kalu, "The Third Response: Pentecostalism and the Reconstruction of Christian Experience in Africa, 1970-1995" (1998:8).

a simplified message of personal salvation through faith in Jesus Christ. To be "born-again" means the individual acknowledges his or her sinful nature and shows conviction through repentance and "self-surrender" or "giving your life to Christ." This is considered the essential feature for accessing divine pardon and developing a relationship with God.

To be "born-again" also means that the believer must reorder his or her life to demonstrate the "new life in Christ." In other words, true conversion requires the reforming of one's life to the image or likeness of Christ. Such conformity to the likeness of Christ requires a radical rejection of other forms of religious and social identification. It also implies abandoning old, unacceptable behavior such as lying, stealing, quarreling, bribery, drinking, smoking, and all forms of sexual immorality. Within the strictures of this personal renewal, converts must restitute by making amends for past sins or pay recompense where necessary. This is to ensure that the process of linear growth towards salvation is tempered with moral responsibility.

Such a close correlation between religious conversion and its ethical expression was a major emphasis in the life and ministry of the founder of the Redeemed Christian Church of God, the late Josiah Akindayomi. This has equally been a distinguishing characteristic of William Kumuyi, the founder and general superintendent of Deeper Life Bible church. With an interest in holiness and evangelical piety, both exemplified the practical implications of the new birth through public confessions and restitutions. Akindayomi restituted by divorcing his second wife and reconciled with his erstwhile detractors days before his death. Kumuyi, for his part, reinforced the practical need to sustain holiness with testimony of his own restitution to the West African Examinations Council (WAEC).[53]

The emphasis on personal salvation, notwithstanding, Neocharismatics reflect a duality of opinions on the pattern of salvation. There are those who reflect the Wesleyan Holiness tradition of a three-stage pattern of regeneration, sanctification, and Spirit baptism. The order and relationship of these three categories continue to represent points of tension with the vast majority who subscribe to the two-stage pattern of salvation. This

---

53. For accounts of Akindayomi's restitution, see Olusola Ajayi, *Warrior of Righteousness* (1997); and regarding Kumuyi's own testimony, see "The Good Old Days" (n.d.:2-3).

second group affirms that "conversion" is the *first* act of grace, which reconciles the "born-again" to God. This experience, according to them, must be followed by a *second* life-transforming event generally called "the baptism of the Spirit."

The two-stage pattern of salvation distinguishes between the "converted" ("the born-again") and those who have, in addition, been "sanctified" ("baptism of the Spirit"). The sanctification experience is understood as a process which continues throughout life and may be lost through breaches of conduct and moral compromises. William Kumuyi of the Deeper Life Bible Church, for example, encourages his followers to be separate from those who may not subscribe to the church's expositions of biblical teachings on sanctification:

> After God has told us what he will do, He tells us what we should do. We are to come out from among people who will defile us. We should be separate. It is some year since I came across this passage that instructs me to come out from among people that will defile me; from among habits that destroy and defile.[54]

In spite of the duality of voices on the pattern of salvation, Neocharismatics share a common conviction that "conversion is less an event than an ongoing process whose underlying structure is linear and teleological."[55] On the whole, to be saved requires a new perspective on life. It requires a complete transformation of life that does not conform to the pattern of this life (Rom. 12:2). As Gerard Roelofs has put it, "[t]he reinterpretation of the past, which forms an integral point of conversion, produces new starting points and prospects for the present and future."[56]

---

54. William Kumuyi, *Holiness Made Easy* (1983:16).
55. Ruth Marshall-Fratani, "Mediating the Global and Local in Nigerian Pentecostalism" (1998:285).
56. Gerard Roelofs, "Charismatic Christian Thought: Experience, Metonymy, and Routinization" (1994:219).

Salvation as "Good News" for Healthy Living

For much of Protestantism, the concern to maintain orthodoxy means that the "good news" of the gospel has been limited to a message of spiritual salvation for the individual. In Neocharismatic theology, however, the message of salvation stretches beyond this intellectual religious domain to include practical experiences of salvation in other areas of life. For them the "good news" also involves instances of divine healing as externalized forms of salvation. Such a theological position enables Neocharismatics to integrate God's salvific work in the spirit as well as in the body.

In Neocharismatic spirituality, the experiences of healing are very personal, dramatically intense, and are usually wide in scope. In its metaphorical and salvific application, healing encompasses the spiritual, physical, demonic, and emotional aspects. With copious scriptures such as those that "wish above all things that you may prosper and be in good health, even as your soul prospers" (3 Jn. 2), Neocharismatics operate on the divine desire for good health as a powerful theological motif for their numerous programs of action on healing. William Kumuyi of Deeper Life, for example, believes that "if you give your life to the Lord and become an overcomer, nothing—no sickness, no diseases, no evil power shall by any means hurt you."[57] It is little wonder that Kumuyi has devoted extensive teachings and crusades to witness to this physical benefit of being a born-again.

Neocharismatics operate through the implementation of healing sessions which promise to enhance the quality of the believer's life. Apart from the power of corporate prayer, the leader demonstrates his anointing as the "man of God" to heal with or without the laying on of hands. He also demonstrates his democratic access to the throne of God through an express command and expulsion of the indwelling demons from the believer's life. This is termed "deliverance." As Kumuyi once preached:

> If you are blind, sick, lame, barren, jobless, tired, and dead spiritually, hear and believe the word of God as it is coming forth from my mouth and the power of God will touch you.

---

57. William F. Kumuyi, *Deeper Life* (1989:32).

... If you are sick and I command the sickness to stop, the sickness will stop. The man of God is not just saying his own words. His pronouncements are from God above.[58]

Healings and miracles can be obtained by believing in the words and authority of the "man of God." When not physically present at a revival meeting or crusade, the same faith can be exercised through the mediatory role of the television set. All that is required is to simply follow the instructions of the preacher, for it is through him that the anointing which casts out demons and heals the sick is made active. As Marshal-Fratani has rightly put it, "in the hands of the 'annointed' electronic media can work its own special miracles."[59] For Neocharismatics, these divine healings authenticate the spoken message. They also serve as a sign for the Spirit's presence to the believer and a form of witness to the unbeliever.

Except for the fact that Neocharismatics rely on the "anointing of the Holy Spirit" rather than the use of objects such as candles and consecrated water, healing and "deliverance" in their theology have the same restorative goals as those of the Aladura. In the context of urban popular language, Neocharismatics have reformulated the theology of divine healing to create a new *opportunity* for those who are not able to neither afford expensive private medical care nor receive adequate medical services from the ill-equipped public health establishments.

Salvation as "Good News" for the Poor

The reinterpretation of the meaning and nature of salvation as expressed in Neocharismatic theology may represent a fundamental shift in traditional discourse. Yet, their understanding of salvation as "good news" to the poor lay firmly anchored in Jesus' ministry to the poor and marginalized. To them, Jesus brought the gospel in reality to what it is already in principle, the "good

---

58. Kumuyi (1989:8).
59. Ruth Marshall-Fratani, "Mediating the Global and the Local in Nigerian Pentecostalism" (1998:295). This is Marshall-Fratani's reference to a preached message by the Nigerian televangelist, Ayo Oritsejafor. For the full account, see Ayo Oritsejafor, "Jesus on the Offensive." Message preached at the Lagos National Theatre, May 13, 1993. Lagos, Nigeria.

news." In the context of the deep economic crisis of the 1980s in Nigeria, mistrust of political ideologies could no longer be merely assumed but needed to be demonstrated by turning to the religious realm. As a result, the radical perception of the gospel as "good news" became a theological innovation. It allowed Neocharismatics to provide alternative source for articulating and providing practical solutions for individual survival and success.

This alternative source of empowerment is not simply a case of false consciousness. Rather, it reconceptualizes the redemptive action of God in the lives of the poor. The liberating rule of God is understood as involving all parts of the created order—persons, human civilization, and even the nonhuman creation. Consequently, the reality of the reign of God in the world is the experience of its transforming power. Within this transformed cosmic order lays a corresponding divine destiny for the people of God. This destiny points towards fulfillment and anything that denies this to people—unemployment, sickness, and social and individual problems—is directly opposed to the will of God.

For the Neocharismatics, the gospel is the liberating word that frees people from the compulsion and control of evil powers and from the apathy of the empty life. It invites people to open themselves to the undisputed reign of God and to receive the enabling power of his Spirit to assail every form of contradiction, resistance, and antagonism to life's success. Responding to this invitation gives the believer a new sense of direction and a call to mission in life. Rather than feel guilty or engage in self-pity, the confidence in the divine power infuses practical steps toward risk-taking initiatives and the restructuring of life altogether. The born-again seizes the opportunity to improve his or her economic situation by moving from one realm of reality to another.

The new realm of reality conceives the born-again as being destined to have all that is necessary for a full and prosperous life. According to David Oyedepo of Living Faith Church, this prosperity "is a state of well being in your spirit and body. It is the ability to use God's power to meet every need. . . . In prosperity, you enjoy life of plenty and fulfillment. Prosperity is a state of being successful; it is life on a big scale."[60]

---

60. Matthews Ojo, "The Church in the African State: The Charismatic/Pentecostal

Thus, what the Neocharismatics have done is to set in motion a new thinking by which their members can confront and respond to contemporary situation. In the words of André Corten, this response is carried out in a set of contrasts: "from empty to full, from destroyed to prosperous, from humiliated to respected, from depressed to happy, from anguish to peace, and from loneliness to life in the community of the church."[61]

Power Theology

The high incidence of the word "power" in Neocharismatic theology brings together the traditional construct of a world imbued with ambivalent powers. This framework of thinking is diminished by the mainline churches as both defective and superstitious. But quite to the contrary, the distinguishing element of indigenous ecclesiology is its breadth of variety and crosscurrents on "power theology." On one hand, "power" in Aladura classical Pentecostalism offers a realistically obtainable freedom from poverty, witchcraft, sorcery, sickness, and death; although the techniques employed tend to render this Christian prophylaxis rather cultic. In the emerging Christianity of the Neocharismatics, on the other hand, "power" expresses the heart of their mission. It seeks to recover the theology of the Holy Spirit as well as cause to resurface the impact of the *charismata* in everyday Christian life.

Confronting the Powers: Neocharismatics and Supernatural Forces

Neocharismatics construct reality with binary opposites and image a tension-ridden world of the good versus the evil. In this way, misery and suffering can be explained, just as the means with which to neutralize abnormal experiences. At the most basic level, this rigid division of the world between the forces of God and those of Satan provides a ready-made ideological premise for explaining the struggle that is happening in the

---

Experience in Nigeria" (1998:30).
61. André Corten discusses this Pentecostal phenomenon in relation to Latin America, "Transnationalised Religious Needs and Political Delegitimisation in Latin America" (2000:106-123).

world. In Neocharismatic theology, the existence of Satan is responsible for the tragic and irreducible predicament of individuals who undergo despair, disease, and death. And on the social level it exposes institutional forms of oppression as the ongoing effort of the Devil to dehumanize people.

This confrontation of the good and the evil forces flourishes on a basis of traditional spiritual syntax. The traditional Nigerian culture nourishes the operations of the occult for the enhancement of human powers and personalities. The possessors of such powers are the human agents of Satan who can inflict pain and misery at whims. Neocharismatics accept the reality and power of the old gods. However, they look back to Christ's victory on the cross as a reassurance that God's power is greater and that the Devil will be ultimately overcome.

As a result, the old gods are demythologized, stripped of their powers and stereotypes, and are demonized as malignant elements that have to be exorcised. The consequence of the baptism in the Holy Spirit for Neocharismatics, therefore, equips and inspires the born-again to resist and fight the powers of Satan. This tragic struggle is not a confirmation of disorder but one that demonstrates moral courage and the inevitable presence and power of the Holy Spirit. By seeing themselves as God's unwavering soldiers, Neocharismatics are able to enlist collective insurgency to push forward the decisive termination of Satan and his cronies both in individual and collective experiences.

Power for Victorious Living

The above seems to define the Neocharismatics as "*turbo*-Christians" who constitute human arsenals of God on earth. This is rightly so. But beyond that, "power," for Neocharismatics, also serves to sum up the whole impact of a renewed Christian life. The conversion experience, and the subsequent experience of the Spirit, helps the born-again to embrace a rupture from a sinful past, bolstering the resolve to set off on a new path of moral vision and life goals.

In the words of Ogbu Kalu, the born-again religiosity "starts as an inner odyssey that brings the force of the transcendent into everyday life."[62] Ruth

---

62. Ogbu Kalu, "Pentecostal and Charismatic Reshaping of the African Religious

Marshall captures this as well, "[t]he 'infilling' of the Holy Spirit . . . must be accompanied by a new set of practices and moral attitudes. The disciplining of the body, its physical and emotional passions, is the principle means for avoiding sin, and being a fit temple for the Spirit to dwell in."[63]

It is not surprising, for example, that the "Deeper Life Bible Church," an arm of the "Deeper Christian Life Ministry," is so named. In the words of founding Pastor William Kumuyi, "[t]he prop and hub of our ministry is holiness of life and conduct."[64] He corroborates this when he stresses further that "the gospel . . . needs to change our lifestyle deeply and impressively in whatever ways may be appropriate to our context."[65]

The other side of this "inner odyssey" is its characteristic power to enable the born-again live an abundant life in spite of the precarious socio-economic and political situations. The experience and power of the Holy Spirit become the believer's source of life and hope, giving him or her the power to make it through each day. The indwelling Spirit fills the void of emptiness, and turns that loss into a hybrid realm of a "power-packed optimism" to aspire for upward mobility in life.

Consequently, the inward gaze of the born-again now beholds everyday realities through the "eyes of the Spirit." This helps to remove temporal limits of personhood so that the believer reinvents personality as a "new creature" with immeasurable power to accomplish in life (2 Co. 5:17; Phl. 4:13).

Although the "prosperity preachers" have hijacked this truth, Ogbu Kalu is right when he declares that, for most Neocharismatics, "prosperity is predicated on the quality of inner life."[66] Those who have prostituted the essence of the gospel for the personal gains of the "prosperity" message constitute the loudest and, unfortunately, the malcontents of Nigerian Pentecostal Christianity.

Landscape in the 1990s" (2002:6).
63. For details, see her article, "'God Is Not A Democrat': Pentecostalism and Democratisation in Nigeria" (1995:250).
64. William F. Kumuyi, "Deeper Christian Life Ministry" (1998:249).
65. Kumuyi (1998:249).
66. Ogbu Kalu, "Pentecostal and Charismatic Reshaping of the African Religious Landscape in the 1990s" (2002:7).

Summary

In summary, therefore, the three streams that I have identified as constituting Nigerian Christianity continue to exist simultaneously alongside each other. This is not to imply that there is a cessation of one epoch. Instead, they continue to impact eachother despite the fact that each continues to exist as was originally conceived. On the whole, these three epochs reflect ecclesiological paradigms profoundly different in experiences, practice and thought. Today, the overall frame of reference is that Nigerian churchgoers understand and experience Christianity in ways partially commensurable with denominations different from theirs.

On the whole, it is appropriate to say that the period of independency in Nigerian Christianity has demonstrated that Christianity does not have to be so intellectualized as to lose bearing with reality. A theology must be redemptive enough as to seek to save the totality of the human person, yet constructive enough as to address his existential aspirations. This is exactly what the Aladura and the Neocharismatics have done. Both have precisely articulated the absurd and anarchic realities of their respective ministry contexts with all the tension-ridden ambivalences. Yet, they have expressed these contextual issues in symbolic forms without the kind of disenchantment which expels them as figments of the imagination.

What they have done is to speak languages which render these situations understandable, offering the people the theological and psychological powers to deal with them in the process. It should not be surprising, therefore, that many people have and continue to secede from current churches to these new forms of churches, whether Aladura or Neocharismatic. As it is today, they continue to push the limits of ecclesiastical boundaries. In all practicality, the shift in the center of gravity of Christianity validates their claim and existence. Even more than that, they continue to represent a shorthand rubric of the pervasiveness and effectiveness of Nigerian Christian creativity.

PART V

From the Margins to the Center: The Political Origins of Unity in Nigerian Christianity, 1960-1993

The three historical streams that I have identified as constitutive of Nigerian Christianity reflect ecclesiological paradigms profoundly different in experiences and thought processes. This is not necessarily a negative thing considering the fact that an ecclesiology that accepts and affirms diversity as well as unity is an essential starting point for any ecumenical enterprise. The paradox, however, is that in Nigeria this diversity expresses itself in strong opposition to harmony. Therefore, what may be construed as disposition to ecumenism arose out of the pressure of a deepening religious antagonism and the resolve to survive in a pluralized democracy. The anxiety this brought has a long history, but it has received more attention in the ecumenical climate of the late 1970s than at any other time.

In what follows, I want to examine the fundamental aspect of religious ecumenism that was set in motion in the markedly anti-Islamic rhetoric and a new political activism of the Christian Association of Nigeria (CAN). I also want to examine the church's progress toward self-assertiveness, justice, and the termination of politico-religious quietism. The timeline is from 1976, the year CAN was inaugurated. This period is important because it highlights contemporary resurgence of religious politics in Nigeria as a natural rallying point for opposition.

CHAPTER 6

Reluctant Ecumenism: Historical Legacies of Christian Political Thoughts

A crucial factor in the new ecumenical paradigm in Nigerian Christianity is the complex nature of the socio-political and religious context of Nigeria itself. With a population of about 120 million people, the country is the most populous nation in Africa with approximately 250 ethnicities and languages. This diversity is further compounded by the demographic configurations of the country's main religious communities, namely Islam and Christianity.

The North is mainly Muslim, with the exception of the "minorities" of central Nigeria, (Middle Belt), whereas the Southeast is mainly Christian. It is only in the Southwest that both religions are equally represented. For their part, the "minorities" of the Middle Belt traditionally were made subordinate to the northern Islamic elite. However, in the last thirty years they have been turning to Christianity in great numbers as part of their assertion of political autonomy.[1]

This interaction of ethnicity with religion has become powerful ideological ground for intolerance, violence, and aggression. Today, most Nigerians no longer look at national issues from the standpoint of ethnicity, as was the case in the 1960s; the decade when the country won its independence. Instead, religion has become a powerful means of expressing popular aspirations and political opposition. This liaison is not new when one reflects carefully upon the contours of political theories and the religious dimensions of the colonial creation called Nigeria.

---

1. Paul Freston, *Evangelicals and Politics in Asia, Africa and Latin America* (2001:181).

A careful reading of Nigeria's history points to the fact that "religion and politics have been bedfellows throughout Nigerian history."[2] What seems to have changed is that since the late 1970s, religion has gained prominence, more than any other factor, as a vehicle for the struggle and legitimation of political power. Today, it has become as disruptive and as divisive as was the issue of ethnicity in the 1960s.

This politicization of religion has garnered aggressive competition for dominance between the country's two main religious rivals. The consequence is that proponents of Christianity or Islam have sought to "unseat the rival religion, to impose their own values, and to control the state."[3] What is observable in Nigeria today, therefore, is a new form of religious radicalism that has turned Africa's most populous nation into a volatile center of religious violence and aggression.

Consequently, the themes that best articulate the church's attempt at unity are those of marginalization and reluctance. This is because the strategy to present the church as a unified and homogenous phenomenon was not guided by basic ecumenical conviction towards Christian unity. Rather, the foundation of oneness was built on the need to shift the margins of religio-political boundaries which the Muslims have carved for themselves.

The Politicization of Religion in Modern Nigeria

A continuous history of the socio-political position of religion in Nigeria stretches back to pre-colonial times. In primordial, homogenous Nigerian societies, for example, religion was indissolubly linked to the political system. In the general African view, this has not changed. Religion and society are connected, even if not synonymous. Africans expect both to serve the people in a mutually benefiting way without harmful side effects. In a very significant way, this has no analogue in the radically different conditions in the West with its distinction between religion as private belief

---

2. Toyin Falola, *Violence in Nigeria* (1998:1).
3. Falola (1998:2).

and as public practice.⁴ The manipulation of religion for wresting political control was, in a sense, alien to indigenous structures.

What may be construed as the beginning of the use of religion as an instrument of political mobilization and legitimacy can be traced to an incursion of alien religions, starting with the jihadist Islam of the Muslim Fulani scholar, Usman dan Fodio (1804-1810), and then to the trailing civilizing humanism of the Protestant Missions (ca. 1841). Given the timeline of both foreign intrusions, we can fully comprehend the extent and consequences of religious politics by looking at the former.

Fulani Hegemony and Ethnic Politicking: The Legacy of Usman Dan Fodio's Jihad

Although Islam arrived in Nigeria sometime between 1000 A.D. and 1100 A.D., progress was largely sporadic and slow.⁵ What constituted the height of Muslim influence was the nineteenth century jihad of Usman dan Fodio.⁶ There was a case to be made in theory. The ostensible religious objectives of the jihad were to bring Islamic reforms to the state and its populace and to oppose the oppression, corruption, self-indulgence, and technical offences against the Islamic code by the ruling Hausa-Habe families of the time.⁷

Many of the Islamic reforms that dan Fodio set out to accomplish were achieved. He successfully conquered Hausaland, except for the Maguzawa, a large Hausa community which resisted the jihadist in faithful deference to its traditional religion. Other remarkable results of his campaign were the geographic expansion of Islam and the widespread adoption of its legal code, Sharia.

However, it is a misnomer to interpret dan Fodio's jihad purely on religious grounds. This, without doubt, obscures the equally important political reasons behind his Islamization campaigns. Although the Fulani

---

4. Lamin Sanneh, *Piety and Power: Muslims and Christians in West Africa* (1996:87).
5. See J. Spencer Trimingham, *The Christian Church and Islam in West Africa* (1956:9).
6. For a most detailed historical analysis, see Matthew Hassan Kukah, *Religion, Politics, and Power in Northern Nigeria* (1993).
7. See Hughes Johnston, *The Fulani Empire of Sokoto* (1967); and Yusufu Abba, "The 1804 Jihad in Hausaland as a Revolution" (1979).

scholar ostensibly wanted to create a "home for Islam," at issue was the dismantling of indigenous Hausa-Habe polities. Historically, the Fulani were not passive settlers. Johnston refers to them as "shepherd-kings," who upon settling in a community soon afterwards seized power.[8]

Usman dan Fodio's jihad was a classic case of "shepherd-king." As a nomadic race, his progenitors had migrated from Senegambia to settle in Hausaland around 1450 A.D.[9] An important aspect of his allegation of anti-Islamic practices against the ruling Hausa was the levying of taxes, especially the age-long *jangali*, the cattle tax. As a pastoral Fulani, dan Fodio vehemently questioned the legality of this tax, arguing instead that it was not one of the seven taxes recognized by the Islamic law.[10]

It should not come as a surprise, therefore, that an important feature of his jihad was the overthrowing of Hausa-Habe leadership. In its place, dan Fodio imposed a Fulani administration in consonance with his vision of Islam. That is, a constituent of emirates that would recognize the religious and political leadership of the Caliph or Sultan of Sokoto. Under dan Fodio's theocratic structure, no socio-political, economic, or religious decisions had legitimacy without the Sultan's approval.[11]

By the middle of the nineteenth century, Hausa rule in Northern Nigeria had been subjugated. Except for the mountainous districts of today's Plateau state, the Tiv in Benue state, and a few ethnic groups in southern Kaduna, much of the north passed under Fulani hegemony, or at least political dominance by Islamic structures. Dan Fodio's vision to bring the entire country under Islamic rule and leadership was only interrupted by British colonialism. Even then, his socio-political structure was what the British colonial administration inherited and upon which they founded their policy of "indirect rule."

---

8. Hughes Johnston, *The Fulani Empire of Sokoto* (1967:26).
9. James Kantiok, "Muslims and Christians in Northern Nigeria: Political and Cultural Implications for Evangelism" (2000:68).
10. Kantiok (2000:70).
11. Iheanyi Enwerem, *A Dangerous Awakening: The Politicization of Religion in Nigeria* (1995:50-51).

The Colonial Factor in the Hausa-Fulani/Northern Hegemony

The goal of the British was to set up their colonial administration to preserve as much as possible of the existing system. In fact, the British colonial administrators saw themselves as incorporating a system that was already in motion, not as initiating that process.[12] The leading elements in the system, without question, were the Fulani. The colonial system of "indirect rule" was predicated on the assumption that the Fulani were the country's natural rulers, and that it was through the Fulani that Nigeria could be governed "indirectly" and moved to the highest level of civilization. According to Frederick Luggard, the colonial governor of Nigeria, "indirect rule" means, among other things:

> To rule indirectly through the Native Chiefs, and in the North to maintain, strengthen, and educate the Fulani and Kanembu ruling races, so that regeneration of Nigeria may be through its own governing class and its own indigenous institutions.[13]

In deference to Fulani conquest and rulership, therefore, colonial policy was not only unfairly skewed towards Islam, it also showed to be tender of Islamic sensibilities. Two discrete factors, among others, are worthy of mention. The first was the setting up of a native administration in which the traditional and political power coalesced in the hands of the Muslim emirs. The result was the installation of Fulani hegemonic political control. This leads naturally to the second factor, the "Pax Islamica," which promised the emirs there would be no colonial interference with Islam.

The intellectual position of "Pax Islamica" was more than a mere promise. The axiomatic character of its benefits to Islam enabled the emirs

---

12. For a more insightful and succinct account, see Bulus Y. Galadima and Yusufu Turaki, "The Church in the African State Towards the 21st Century: The Experience of Northern Nigeria" (1998:43-51).
13. Frederick Lugard, *Political Memoranda: Revision of Instructions to Political Officers on Subjects Chiefly Political and Administrative* (1970:317). For Lugard's leading opinion on the policy of "indirect rule," see his earlier work, *The Dual Mandate in British Tropical Africa* (1922; reprint 1965).

to monopolize the civil sphere and religious territoriality. While the emirs could operate freely in non-Muslim areas, they could deny such access to Christian missionaries from operating within their emirates. In the race for the souls of Nigerians, therefore, the colonial administration encouraged and promoted the territorial interests of Islam by effectively blocking Christianization. In the words of Lamin Sanneh, "colonialism became the Muslim shield and the guarantor of Islam as the public alternative to Christianity for Africans."[14] Andrew Walls also puts it well when he declares:

> In Nigeria, the British maintained the emirates as the structures through which to rule, even though so much of the population was not Muslim. As a result, Islam spread far more effectively under colonial rule than it had ever done under the jihads. In general, the colonial powers were careful about Islamic sensibilities and did their best to avoid provocation, not least by damping down Christian missionary activity.[15]

The divide-and-rule policies of the colonial period help us to see the underlying structure that conditioned the religious and political behavior of postcolonial Nigeria. In fact, it is a form of historical amnesia to attempt to close off the legacy of the colonialists and lay the blame of the institutionalization of religious politics solely on Nigerians themselves. This note of embattlement is obvious in the colonial establishment of three unequal regions, the favored Islamic North over and against their Western and Eastern counterparts in the Christian South. The irony of this biased Nigerianization process was that it led to the rise of the politics of regional interests, the North versus the South.

Similarly, the colonial creation of two religious communities, namely, the Christian world and the Muslim world, has had unmistakable consequences. Primarily, it has trapped the nation in the labyrinthine religious politics of the North, and the Hausa-Fulani resolve to maintain an Islamic identity for modern Nigeria. The snowball effect of this, of course,

---

14. Lamin Sanneh, *Piety and Power: Muslims and Christians in West Africa* (1996:135).
15. Andrew Walls, *Cross-Cultural Process in Christian History* (2002:102).

is the institutionalization of interreligious competitions and nationalist aspirations that continue to poison the everyday existence of Nigeria even to the present. Perhaps a test case is to examine, however cursory, the political climate of postcolonial Nigeria.

Self-Government and Political Imagination: The Religious Dimension

The discussion so far has theorized that Nigeria's postcolonial, sociopolitical, and religious behavior corresponds to the internal contradictions of the colonization process. The result, as I have also noted, was the emergence of a set of polarities: between North and South, between Christians and Muslims, and between collective and individual goods. It is implicit to say, therefore, that the somewhat grudging acceptance of social difference and pluralism that Nigeria experiences today corresponds, in part, to what Mikael Karlström refers to as "the minimal civility of mutual tolerance."[16] It is not the highest virtue in the hierarchy of sociopolitical order.

There is legitimacy to this view. The era leading to an independent Nigeria, for example, was full of aspiring politicians who were concerned with symbols and ideologies that could sway public support and sympathy. Again, each party derived political support from one of the three regions on which the colonial government of Nigeria was organized: Obafemi Awolowo's Action Group (AG) received support from the Yoruba in the West, Nnamdi Azikiwe's National Council of Nigerian Citizens (NCNC)[17] received backing from the Igbo in the East, and the Northern region was geographically, religiously, and politically divided between the dominant Ahmadu Bello's Northern Peoples' Congress (NPC), Aminu Kano's

---

16. Mikael Karlström, "Civil Society and Its Presuppositions: Lessons from Uganda" (1999:116).
17. Although clinging to the same acronym (NCNC), the party had changed its name twice before finally adopting this one. It was first called "National Church of Nigeria and Cameroon", so-called in order to mobilize Christians against colonial administration. See T. Hodgkin, *Nationalism in Colonial Africa* (1956). Again, the party changed its name to "National Council of Nigeria and the Cameroon."

Nigerian Elements Progressive Union (NEPU), and the United Middle Belt Congress (UMBC).

Most of the political parties constructed their manifestos around issues of rapid development and distribution of power. For example, the AG put forward a welfarist program and the NCNC a socialist ideology, both attempting to appeal to all the strata of society, especially the lower and middle classes. The NPC had a totally different agenda. In the first place, it maintained its northern Islamic parochialism and prejudice by limiting membership only to northerners. And unlike the AG and the NCNC, the party made no pretense to socialism but conceived its program in such a way as to benefit the north.[18] There is no better starting point than the uses of religion in the high politics of the First Republic (1960-1966); looking particularly at the religious politics of Sir Ahmadu Bello, the Sardauna of Sokoto and the first premier of the northern region.

The First Republic: The Religious Politics of Sir Ahmadu Bello, 1960-1966

The place of Sir Ahmadu Bello in the history of the politicization of religion in Nigeria is so well documented as to require no more than a brief sketch here.[19] However, one thing that must be emphasized is that the determinant factor of his political life was his self-consciousness of being a descendant of Usman dan Fodio's caliphate. This awareness doubly reinforced what he perceived as a mandate to broaden the territorial boundaries of the Hausa-Fulani/North and Islam. He declares in no ambiguous way:

> I have never sought the political limelight or a leading position in [Nigeria]. But I could not avoid the obligation of my birth and destiny. My great-great-grandfather built an Empire in the Western Sudan. It has fallen to my lot to play a not inconsiderable part in building a new nation. My ancestor

---

18. Toyin Falola, *The History of Nigeria* (1999:100-101).
19. See J.N. Paden, *Ahmadu Bello, Sardauna of Sokoto: Values and Leadership in Nigeria* (1986).

was chosen to lead the Holy War which set up his Empire. I have been chosen by a free electorate to help build a modern state. . . . This, then, is the story of my life. The attempt of a Northern Nigerian to do his duty by his people and the principles of his religion [that is, Islam].[20]

Ahmadu Bello's remarks were not mere rhetoric. He developed instruments for carrying out his mission at the regional, national, and international levels. He was only cut short of fully realizing his vision by the military *coup d'état* of 1966 in which he was assassinated. At the regional level, he adopted a form of "political ecumenism" which "sought to bring northerners together under an Islamic political ideology."[21] There are, at least, two important political implications of this. On one hand, it fostered an unbroken continuity and a unifying Islamic identity for the North. On the other, it won his party, the NPC, political influence and consolidated its hold on power.

The move to capture the political center at the national level reflected Ahmadu Bello's very subtle calculations. An interesting feature of his scheme was the exaltation of the religious influence which was already at work or at hand. Perhaps it is fair to say that Ahmadu Bello's theology and outlook on the supremacy of Islam and the Hausa-Fulani/North were not different from those of Usman dan Fodio who combined conversion and conquest. The difference, ingenious when we consider the most restrained political climate of Ahmadu Bello's time, was the methodical way by which he embarked on his massive "conversion campaigns" to win over souls for Islam and the northern hegemony.

Ahmadu Bello understood that the extent to which his campaigns succeeded would become the groundswell of his capacity to combine both religious and political powers at the national level. Consequently, he instigated the founding of *Jama'atu Nasril Islamiya* (JNI, the "Society for

---

20. Paden (1986:viii-ix).
21. Toyin Falola, *Violence in Nigeria* (1998:30). The concept of "Political Ecumenism" was Matthew Hassan Kukah's construction. For details see his *Religion, Politics and Power in Northern Nigeria* (1993).

the Victory of Islam) and the Council of Mallams. Both organizations were supposed "to bring together various elements of religious leadership in the North for the purpose of discussion and general enlightenment."[22] Ahmadu Bello's greatest miscalculations, however, was that he did not understand or appreciate the aspects of Christianity that had already taken root among the minority tribes in central Nigeria.

It is perhaps not without significance that modern commentators interpret Ahmadu Bello's initiatives, especially his 1961 founding of JNI, in purely political terms.[23] Although JNI had all the trappings of a religious organization, it was practically "a political organ wearing a religious garb to serve a political purpose."[24] The constituency of JNI, for one thing, included the cadres of very influential people who were the doyen of early post-colonial Nigerian politics: traditional rulers, emirs, mallams (religious leaders), top civil servants, prominent businessmen, and powerful northerners in the NPC.

Similarly, Ahmadu Bello was not so naïve as to assume that achieving his political ambition was self-fulfilling. He understood the dialectical interaction between religion and politics much more than that, and he utilized it quite effectively. Rather than allowing the JNI to simply forge a strong Islamic identity in the North, he also found an important avenue in carving a political role for it. For example, a characteristic feature of the conversion campaigns of the JNI throughout northern and central Nigeria forced an acceptance of Ahmadu Bello's Islamic political ideology. In this way, the JNI became a *de facto* moral agent for an ideology that aimed inexhaustibly at the creation of a political community that upheld Islam as its constitutive value.

The political gains were enormous for NPC. On one hand, JNI succeeded in expanding Ahmadu Bello's religious views, using that at the same time to

---

22. J.N. Paden, *Ahmadu Bello, Sardauna of Sokoto: Values and Leadership in Nigeria* (1986:557).

23. For example, see Matthew Hassan Kukah's works, *Religion, Politics and Power in Northern Nigeria* (1993); and "Christians and Nigeria's Aborted Transition" (1995:225-238). See also Iheanyi Enwerem, *A Dangerous Awakening* (1995); and Toyin Falola, *Violence in Nigeria* (1998).

24. Iheanyi Enwerem, *A Dangerous Awakening* (1995:55).

qualify his political manifesto. By so doing, it (JNI) orchestrated a political center for NPC while pushing other rival parties and religions to the sidelines. On the other hand, and perhaps the more extreme gain for NPC, was that an extensive overlap that associated the state with Islam fulfilled Ahmadu Bello's strategy of setting the Muslims against the Christians and by implication, too, the North against the South.

In the attempt to voice a collective Christian outrage against the Sardauna's policies in 1964, the northern Christians inaugurated the Northern Christian Association (NCA). Unfortunately, the NCA was not able to swing back the pendulum of socio-political and religious ethos. Its position was weakened by the political dependence of its Christian politicians on the wide-ranging influence of the Sardauna himself.[25]

The exception to all the wrangling in the North, of course, was the Christian South. Even then, Ahmadu Bello did not simply throw up his arms in defeat. Instead, the JNI became his weapon of dramatic opposition. By the time the crucial federal election of 1964 was to be held, Ahmadu Bello had succeeded in capturing religious power beyond the northern region. The extent of his dual power (religious and political) was obvious. His party, the NPC, won a landslide victory in the election without his campaigning beyond the northern region. Enwerem says it well:

> For him [Ahmadu Bello], religion was a free-floating phenomenon which any class could effectively use to advance its interests.... On this score and in the context of the Nigerian world, Ahmadu Bello remained the master politician, far ahead of his Western-educated political peers.[26]

But the uneven quality of Ahmadu Bello's wide religio-political influences led to a polarization of relations, provoking the crisis that led to the Igbo-dominated military coup of January 1966. It was more of a political reappraisal and Ahmadu Bello and many other prominent northern leaders

---

25. For details, see Matthew Hassan Kukah, *Religion, Politics and Power in Northern Nigeria* (1993:54).
26. Iheanyi Enwerem, *A Dangerous Awakening* (1995:56).

were indivisibly caught up in the assassinations that followed. The whole political apparatus of the First Republic ended with these assassinations and heralded Nigeria's first military government. It also gave birth to regional suspicion and the ethnic animosity that led to the massacres of the Igbos living in the North and the subsequent outbreak of civil war in 1967.

The civil war compromised Nigeria's unity even further as bellicose propaganda, on both warring sides, "portrayed the conflict as a holy war between the forces of Christians and Islam."[27] The Igbo especially saw the war "as a genocidal one waged by the Muslims of Northern Nigeria who had declared *jihad* to exterminate Igbos from the face of the earth."[28] In a protest letter to the Pope and the prime minister of Italy, Col. Odumegu Ojukwu, an Igbo and commander-in-chief of the secessionist Biafran army, challenged "the sale of arms by 'Catholic' Italy to Muslim Northern Nigeria to be used in killing the 'Catholic' Igbos of Eastern Nigeria."[29] Ojukwu so welded religion and the war together that he won external support and sympathy, thereby stretching the war for as long as three years.

On the whole, it is important to note that the death of Ahmadu Bello did not weaken his religio-political organization, JNI, as much as it did its Christian rival, NCA. In a practical sense, the death of the Sardauna was for the NCA synonymous with idleness, irrelevance, and perhaps impotence. In the words of Aledeino, one of the founding members of NCA, "Sardauna was the reason why we founded the NCA. Since he was now dead, we saw no more reason to carry on the association."[30]

To this day, the JNI remains a formidable Muslim pressure group that continues to promote the interests of a unified North and the Islamic cause. Its activities, however, have collided with the equally powerful force of a new Christian organization, the Christian Association of Nigeria (CAN) that came into being in the wake of the Second Republic.

---

27. Bengt Sundkler and Christopher Steed, *The History of the Church in Africa* (2000:948).
28. Eghosa Osaghae, *Crippled Giant: Nigeria since Independence* (1998:66).
29. *Leader*, "Nigeria's Coming Civil War," June 3, 1967. See also http://odili.net/news/source/2003/may/31/65.html).
30. Matthew Hassan Kukah, *Religion, Politics and Power in Northern Nigeria* (1993:54).

The Political Dimension of Christian Ecumenism: The Christian Association of Nigeria Since 1976

Founded in 1976, the Christian Association of Nigeria (CAN) is an involuntary ecumenical child that emerged out of the military government's request for a single Christian group to deal with in connection to the latter's proposed "National Pledge" in schools.[31] As an ecumenical grouping, the constituency of CAN is broad and much better defined than those of its closest precursor, the NCA, that fruitlessly fought to resist the overwhelming influence of Ahmadu Bello during Nigeria's First Republic. It comprises the Catholics, Protestants, and the Aladura. From its inception, CAN has portrayed itself as the leading voice of Christians in Nigeria and is today reputed to be a *militant,* anti-Islamic Christian pressure group.

Although the military government may have orchestrated the founding of CAN, its life and activities have been a double irony. This is because CAN gradually became estranged from the founding motive in the government's invitation to participate in the discussions on "National Pledge." Instead, it launched itself fully into a confrontation with what was perceived as a systematic Islamization of Nigeria through the Muslims' constant efforts to implement Sharia law as the system of governance for all of Nigeria. It is fair to say, then, that the Muslim agenda, more than any other single factor, has provided legitimacy for the continued existence of CAN and explains its orientation to political activism and religious ecumenism.

Before this Christian "awakening," one of the features of Nigerian Christians, at least until early 1980s, had been their lack of interest in politics. This is not because the Christians are necessarily apolitical or overtly indifferent to politics. Rather, the core of the problem is that the Christians were trained to think that the realm of Caesar was of little importance in comparison to the ultimate goal of attaining heaven and was antithetical to authentic spirituality (Mt. 22:21; Mk. 12:17; Heb. 12:1-2).

---

31. For lack of space, I will not preoccupy myself with a review of the different theories that have been posited for the founding of CAN. A good resource, perhaps the most authoritative to date, is Iheanyi Enwerem's *A Dangerous Awakening: The Politicization of Religion in Nigeria* (1995).

However, there has been a paradigm shift. Today, the view of the Christians reverberates in the statement of Wilson Badejo, the general overseer of the Foursquare Gospel Church of Nigeria: "The Church must not just sit and watch. We must nurture the conscience of the nation, invest in the preparation of promising Godly character to man the affairs of our nation."[32]

One effect of the Islamic cycle of influence, therefore, has been to provoke the Christians into a form of religious ecumenism which, ironically, turned out to be a *de facto* triumph for a church that now wanted to free itself from political non-involvement. It should not come as a surprise, then, that the dominant ideology and goals of CAN have been political in appearance and inspiration. Putting all these together, we realize, then, that the entrance and recessional hymns at the inauguration of CAN—"Stand up, Stand up, for Jesus" and "Onward Christian Soldiers"—clearly demonstrate this new Christian awakening.[33]

It must be emphasized, however, that the political agenda of Christians is articulated through a platform that Muslims have constructed for their own purpose. This applies especially to three areas: CAN's objection to a progressive Islamization of Nigeria through Islamic Sharia, its relentless demands to the government to take the country out of OIC, and its insistence that the state upholds the constitutional secular principle of neutrality in religion. The obvious political consequence is that an agenda such as this confirms the perceived anti-Islamic posture of CAN, thereby setting the Christians on the Muslim side of the fault line.[34]

It is also worth noting that CAN has adopted a number of methodological approaches in order to achieve its political objectives. Enwerem has summarized them as falling under two broad categories: "politics of quiet diplomacy," or the "politics of persuasion," and "militant politics."[35] As its

---

32. See his statement, "Sustaining Nigeria's Nationhood," *This Day*, June 8, (2002:5).
33. Iheanyi Enwerem, *A Dangerous Awakening: The Politicization of Religion in Nigeria* (1995:84).
34. OIC is an abbreviation for "Organization of Islamic Conference." Formed in 1965 through the initiatives of the Muslim communities around the world, the purpose for the founding of the organization was to propagate Islam and acquaint the rest of the world with Islam, its issues, and aspirations.
35. Iheanyi Enwerem, *A Dangerous Awakening* (1995:119-120).

name implies, the first approach utilizes a variety of diplomatic means. These include the sending of delegations, the writing of letters or memoranda, and the lobbying of influential Christians in the army to seek government's concession on issues that affect the Christians.

The characteristics of the second approach are, in every sense of the word, "militant." This approach became dominant especially from 1987 during the presidency of Anthony Olubunmi Okogie, the fiery head of the Catholic archdiocese of Lagos. In his words, the first method "has been tried and we saw that it did not work; probably we got about, say, between 20-30 percent success."[36] This method adopts mass mobilization campaigns that range from pulpit preaching, effective use of the media, and civil litigations in court. The goal is to generate visible and constant publicity for the concerns of CAN and its members.

Perhaps the most drastic demonstration of militancy is CAN's goal of wrestling the control of the state from the hands of the Muslims through direct political involvement. This method was adopted in 1988 through a new understanding that the supposedly worldly realm of politics may overrun and marginalize the Christian church itself:

> If Christians distance themselves from politics that lead to leadership, then demons will have a field day as had been the case with Nigeria up till today. If demons govern and rule us and burn our churches and marginalize us and treat us like second class citizens in our country of posting, then why should the Christian complain?[37]

But the *modus operandi* of CAN, especially its politically charged statements, have been criticized by many modern commentators who believe that CAN is reflecting "a rather poor reading of the dynamics of political engineering." Notable among this group is Matthew Hassan Kukah, a Christian

---

36. Enwerem (1995:119).
37. Christian Association of Nigeria, *Leadership in Nigeria (To Date): An Analysis* (1987:viii). See also A. Edema, "Christians and Politics" (1989:12-18).

northerner.[38] Kukah faults as illusory CAN's protestations of Sharia and Nigeria's membership in OIC on a wrong assumption that "the constitution of Nigeria was as potent a weapon as it seemed on paper."[39] And to demonize Islam because of a perceived threat of Islamization is, in his own estimate, "to overdramatise its [CAN's] case."[40] Therefore, the many pronouncements of CAN are illegitimate and at best, given to "emotional relief."[41]

Kukah's observation is accurate to the degree that in both purpose and form, the model of Christian politics bears the deep imprint of the threat of Islamization. His case is even more compelling in light of the fact that CAN wanted the government to offset any concessions to Islam with similar concessions to Christianity. The most obvious being CAN's request for ecclesiastical courts for Christians, restoration of full diplomatic relations with Israel, and the setting up of pilgrim welfare boards for Christians.[42] He is equally accurate in his observation that the military rule is an illegitimate form of government and "an obstacle in itself to the realization of the goals and ideals of democracy." Consequently, CAN should not expect to make much gain if its only weapon was the suspended federal constitution.

This, precisely, means that criticisms of CAN's political agenda or its methodology must be tempered by the realities of the political engineering of military regimes. And compared to all before or after it, the repressive regime of Ibrahim Badamosi Babangida (1985-1993) stands out. For it was during his time that the crisis of religious politics and violence were most pronounced. It was also during this time that CAN was most vocal and militant. This is the missing aspect of Kukah's criticisms of CAN. At the risk of being mistaken for an advocate, a few observations and perhaps responses to Kukah are imperative.

In the first place, CAN did not have the means, although it had the desire, to reconstitute the pre-military politics in its integrity. Lacking no

---

38. For Kukah's argument see, "Christians and Nigeria's Aborted Transition" (1995:225-238).
39. Kukah (1995:226).
40. Kukah (1995:226).
41. Kukah (1995:227).
42. For details, see Joseph Kenny, "Sharia and Christianity in Nigeria: Islam and a 'Secular' State" (1996:338-364).

other resources to negotiate a fair treatment of the Christians as was most evident with the government's deference to their Muslim counterparts, CAN appealed rather unfortunately, to an abused and suspended federal constitution.

Kukah himself highlights an imbalance in government's dealing with Islam, "[t]here was evidence of... government funding of Islamic ventures (mosques, pilgrimages) from taxpayers' money. Also Muslims involved in riots had seemingly been treated with kid gloves."[43] This is where I locate the second point in assessing CAN's political agenda. That is to say, no amount of quarantine could have immunized CAN against such a flagrant disregard for the concerns of Christians. Perhaps, it is right to say that CAN became a victim of the scale of political balance it hoped to tilt and stabilize.

Lamin Sanneh captures this well when he declares that "[a]ll religious systems are equally vulnerable to the relentless incursions of temporal compromise and to the vagaries of human instrumentality even, or especially, where human stewardship is claimed in the service of revealed truth."[44] The ultimate challenge for CAN, as well as the other political players, is how to broaden their notion of fairness so that the rule of safeguarding and promoting one's own welfare does not become less valid when transferred to another's. In other words, conflicting demands must be dealt with without compromising the basic political principles of continued common existence.[45]

It is one thing to accuse CAN of political naïveté. It is totally a different thing to fault it for addressing its partisan concerns, especially when it sees itself as victim of the religio-political structures. CAN epitomizes a moral ground and catch-all repository of hopes and platform for fighting what it perceived as an old nemesis, Islam. It seems, however, that the struggle has just begun. The two constitutional debates of 1978 and 1988 respectively, would influence further, in very specific and conspicuous ways, the politicization of religion in Nigeria.

---

43. Matthew Hassan Kukah, "Christians and Nigeria's Aborted Transition" (1995:227).
44. Lamin Sanneh, *Piety and Power* (1996:128).
45. Simeon Ilesanmi, *Religious Pluralism and the Nigerian State* (1997:192).

Toward a Religio-Political Synthesis: The Constitutional Debates of 1978 and 1988

The discussion so far has demonstrated that the whole political apparatus of Nigeria's First Republic was the use of religion as a "free-floating phenomenon." To this extent, the history of the use of religion as an instrument of political mobilization is a single story. The civil war of July 6, 1967-January 12, 1970 complicates this story, but it does not determine it.

This distinction has implications for understanding the interrelated aspects of religion and politics in Nigeria and the bitter contention by the country's main religious rivals (Christianity and Islam) to increase the realms of their involvement. In no other area was this more apparent than in the process of re-democratization that was set in motion in the constitutional debates of 1978 and 1988 respectively. Both debates were efforts initiated by military governments to formulate federal constitutions that will guide the country in the Second and Third Republics. It is needless to say that the likelihood of taking up religious issues, including moral and philosophical concerns, provoked further the crisis of ideologies.

The Christians, through CAN, wanted a secularized polity so that the role of religion in the new Republics is depoliticized. To them, the bitter religiously motivated conflicts of the First Republic (1960-1966) and the civil war (1967-1970) constituted enough reasons. This attitude, which is doubtlessly integral to modern Western political theory, was not the theocracy of which the Muslims were most cognizant. Instead, the Muslims found the Christians' notion deficient on the ground that it had a clear affinity with European colonial policy which they also understood to be clearly Christian.

The state, however, found a remedy in the constituent assemblies composed of people from all walks of life. This way, the state attempted to show its neutrality but insofar as the constituent assemblies conducted themselves strictly on impartial grounds. This was not meant to be. When it came to acts and deeds, disputes and irreconcilable ideological differences between the religious agencies, notably Christians and Muslims, led to a clash of religio-political synthesis and secularized polities.

Toward the Second Republic: The First Constitutional Crisis of 1978-1979

At this point in our history of the politicization of religion in Nigeria, the assumption that "religious resurgence is a cyclical phenomenon" would not be mere rhetoric.[46] In no other aspects of the constitutional debates was this more apparent than in the fragile sections 23, 26, and 27. These sections, falling under the provisions of "Fundamental Human Rights," attempted to clarify three issues: define the status of religion, clarify the posture of the state in religious matters, and expose freedom issues and the status of Sharia.[47] The first issue was not so much of a contention as was the cynicism that attended the last two.

"The State in Religious Matters": Defining a Secular State

The Constitutional Conference of 1978-1979 was essentially a construct, attempting to oversee the drafting of a new federal constitution in anticipation of return to the civilian rule of the Second Republic. Colonial imposition of the constitution of the First Republic had specified that Nigeria was to remain a secular state. The substance of the provision was a split-level structure between the sacred and the secular. While the constitution did not imply indifference on the part of the state, it did prescribe that the state remain neutral in all matters of religion. In order to protect human rights and foster pluralism, the constitution further declared several freedoms. That is, freedom to practice, propagate, and change one's religion without coercion.

The interesting feature of this secularist ideology is the disjunction between the sacred and secular, and with neutrality which does not prescribe indifference. In other words, just precisely how the state would enforce this clause of the constitution while remaining neutral has always been a considerable dilemma. To Muslims, colonial laws were synonymous with Christianity by virtue of their shared "Christian-ness" and bolstered by their

---

46. Donald Smith, "The Limits of Religious Resurgence" (1990:34).
47. For details, see Ogbu Kalu, *Power, Poverty and Prayer: The Challenges of Poverty and Pluralism in African Christianity, 1960-1996* (2000).

shared "European-ness." Because of this affinity, Nigeria, in the Muslims' perception and interpretation, can neither be called secular nor Islamic.

They pointed to many spheres of the nation's public life to illustrate what they perceived as the state's adoption of Christian values and symbols. These included, among others, the observance of Saturdays and Sundays as free working days, the use of the cross as symbol for the nation's health institutions, and the use of Christian calendar to name school holidays such as Christmas and Easter Breaks.[48]

As was to be expected, the Christian members of the Constituent Assembly responded with a vigorous rebuttal. To them, the outcry of their Muslim counterparts was a disguise to concretely rework an Islamic agenda into the very fabric of the nation. Although the constitution of the First Republic prescribed a secularist ideology, the state, according to the Christians, had been undeniably Islamic in outlook and practice. To justify their claims, the Christians pointed to what may be regarded as an extensive overlap of state policies with the Islamic agenda to create a theocratic center for religion.

They did not make mere speculative allegations. They pointed to concrete instances of the use of state apparatus to further the cause of Islam. These included the use of state funds to build mosques and to finance other Muslim projects such as the trip to Mecca, the hajj. They also implicated the state in its establishments of the Pilgrims' Welfare Board and the Nigerian Pilgrims Board in 1958 and 1975 respectively. Both were ostensibly meant to facilitate government's subsidies of the pilgrimage and to coordinate logistical problems associated with the journey. The Christians also pointed to the pressure for Islamization as has been demonstrated in the limited practice of Sharia. Perhaps the strongest claim by the Christians was how Islam impinges on the imperatives of the state itself by holding the people captive to the political whims of the Muslim North.

To this crisis of disillusionment on what constitutes a "secular" state was added the crisis of rising expectations of how precisely this would play out in the Second Republic. The Muslims' position was that banishing religion from the public sphere is a negation of Sharia and by implication, inimical

---

48. Joint Muslim Advisory Council of Oyo State, "An Appeal to the Christian Association of Nigeria" (1989:2).

to the development and aspiration of *dár al-Islam* (the nation of Islam). A secular state, in their opinion, is nothing but an atheistic state.

Thus, the Christians' insistence on ideological secularism inspired widespread Muslim disenchantment as a disguise to "perpetuate Euro-Christian culture and neocolonialism."[49] To the Muslims, the political standard *lá hukm illá bi-illáhi* (no government except under God) is the reference point for an ideal state. To accept a secularist ideology for Nigeria, therefore, was a dangerous religious compromise capable of stripping its public square of the transcendent moral values of the Qur'an.

The Muslims' interpretation and popular disenchantment did not resonate with rank-and-file Christians. To the Christians, secularism is not synonymous with atheism. Rather, it denotes recognition of "separate and equally valid spheres of God and Caesar."[50] While a secular state was the political structure inherited from the British, Christians argued, it does not have to take the form of religious compromise as the West has modeled. To the Christians, the logic of secularism, of state neutrality in all matters of religion, is a lesser evil in comparison to Muslim theocratic demands.

Needless to say, neither side buckled under the intense pressure of argumentation. As a temporary measure for peaceful coexistence, therefore, the government adopted a compromising position that called Nigeria a religious country without an official religion. Even then, the issue of definition has still not been resolved. Instead, it has produced another ideological crisis, much more intense in nature, in the Muslims' demand for Sharia.

"Sharia in Toto*": The Political Challenge of Islam*

The failure to determine and clarify the official status of religion has not been the sole agency of Muslim-Christian opposition; but it formed the detonator of the vast explosion of religious violence of the 1980s. This has made an official position even more frustratingly problematic. Just precisely how the draft constitution of the Second Republic would fit

---

49. For details, see Umar Birai, "Islamic Tajdid and the Political Process in Nigeria" (1993:184-203).
50. Lamin Sanneh, *Piety and Power* (1996:112).

Nigeria's unique ethnic and religious heritage without falling victim to the structural problems that defeated the First Republic became one of the main contentions of the Constituent Assembly.

Still more problematic was "the extent to which concessions, if any, should be given to Muslims in the country's judicial system, and the extent to which Muslims could demand 'balance' and 'fairness' for perceived state concessions to Christians" without threatening public peace.[51] The Muslims have always held that a full implementation of Sharia (Sharia *in Toto*) is their inalienable religious and constitutional rights. To them, "[t]he Sharia is God's revealed law; it is therefore a collective duty of Muslims to obey it, just as it is the duty of the jurisprudents to determine what the Sharia is."[52]

This theological position became the instrument and the touchstone that prescribed for Muslims an uncompromising stand against an alien English law which is based on pagan Roman law.[53] The demand for an official recognition of the Sharia in the nation's judicial system, as a Muslim scholar has observed, remains "the most important and complex political issue dividing Muslims and Christians in Nigeria."[54]

Birai's observation is an accurate one. For no other religious issue has had as much religious and political ramifications as the issue of Sharia. Historically, Sharia courts, following the *Mālikī* School, had existed in pre-colonial northern Nigeria. Even the British recognized the importance of Sharia to Northern Muslims and conceded that it was equivalent to the customary courts.

This concession was embodied in the Native Courts Proclamation of 1900 as the British stated that "these courts are to administer native law and custom prevailing in the area of jurisdiction and might award any type of punishment recognized thereby except mutilation, torture, or any

---

51. Adigun Agbaje, "Travails of the Secular State: Religion, Politics, and the Outlook on Nigeria's Third Republic" (1990:292).
52. R.S. O'Fahey, "The Past in the Present? The Issue of the Sharia in Sudan" (1995:32).
53. For detailed discussions on the Sharia debates, see Matthew Hassan Kukah, *Religion, Politics, and Power in Northern Nigeria* (1993); W.I. Ofonagoro, *The Great Debate: Nigerians' Viewpoints on the Draft Constitution, 1976-77* (1978); David Latin, "The Sharia Debate and the Origins of Nigeria's Second Republic" (1982); and Joseph Kenny, "Sharia and Christianity in Nigeria: Islam and a 'Secular' State" (1996).
54. Umar M. Birai, "Islamic Tajdid and the Political Process in Nigeria" (1993:191).

other which is repugnant to natural justice and humanity."[55] However, it was not until 1956 that Sharia was formally written into the northern regional constitution of the First Republic. Even then, it was confined to the private and personal domains and had remained a non-issue until the constitutional debate of 1978-1979.

There was an important dimension to the constitutional crisis of 1978-1979. Whereas Sharia had been acceptable and appropriately confined to the Islamic North, the Muslims' desire for its legal and geographical extension to all of Nigeria quenched even the slightest flicker of any possible compromise between the Christian and Muslim members of the Constituent assembly. The Muslims argued from two standpoints, namely, the religious integrity of Sharia and the moral implications of a religion-free state. In the first place, the Muslims pointed to the nature of Sharia as a sacred law embracing the whole range of a Muslim's religious duties. Consequently, it is mandatory for them to obey the divine injunction since it constitutes "the totality of Allah's commands that regulate the life of every Muslim in all its aspects."[56]

The second unmistakable argument of the Muslims was the reality of a morally bankrupt Nigeria. To them, the religious minimalism of the so-called secular state has been detrimental just like the Western political ideologies on which it was modeled. The Muslims believed that by banishing religion from the public sphere, especially the criminal jurisdiction of Sharia, Nigeria has become a breeding place for iniquity. And in order to flourish on ill-gotten political and economic status quo, "[e]very politician tells lies, all army officers are rogues, people cannot train their mouths and minds, [and] women have no self control."[57] A foundational attachment in the Sharia, the Muslims concluded, would correct these moral lapses and promote social justice.

---

55. E. Keay and S. Richardson, *The Native Customary Courts of Nigeria* (1966:22). See also Matthew Hassan Kukah, *Religion, Politics, and Power in Northern Nigeria* (1993:116).
56. Joseph Schacht, *The Origins of Mohammedan Jurisprudence* (1959:1). See also S.K. Rashid, *Islamic Law in Nigeria: Application and Teaching* (1988).
57. Toyin Falola, *Violence in Nigeria: The Crisis of Religious Politics and Secular Ideologies* (1998:79).

But the Muslims' determination to solely occupy the religious center by "reject[ing] any new political order that does not recognize the uninhibited application of *Shari'a* law in Nigeria"[58] met with a parallel determination to suppress the contradictions of Muslim religious demands. The Christians refused to be marginalized on an important issue that would gravely affect their way of practicing their faith. Consequently, their objections to Sharia were based on two grounds—political and jurisprudential.[59]

First, the Christians invoked the secularist ideology of institutional separation and state neutrality to counter the Muslims' demand to make Sharia a political prerogative. To them, the inclusion of "religious laws or principles of any particular religion" in the constitution was tantamount to a new ideological and institutional establishment of religion.[60] Such an action, the Christians believed, was a decisive step oriented toward a theocratic state under the religio-political jurisdiction of Islam. Equally important was the political implication of giving public witness to "a religious system espoused by only the adherents of one particular religion."[61] Not only would this breach the constitutional "equality" of all citizens; to the Christians, it was also capable of making non-Muslims second-class citizens.

The second reason for Christian objections centered on the unusual legal procedures of Sharia. Although the Muslims claimed "the *Sharia* law is based on a set of particularized rules of the Islamic tradition,"[62] the Christians' perception of it was one of "backward legal system unfit for the modern age."[63] Its provisions (*huddi*) were seen to be riddled with draconian punishments. For example, the penal code on theft and adultery (*zina*) prescribed severance of limbs and death by stoning respectively (*rajmi*).[64]

---

58. *New Nigerian*, "Shari'a Law in Nigeria," September 29, 1986.

59. Much of the perspective and direction adopted here have been largely influenced by Simeon Ilesanmi. See his work, *Religious Pluralism and the Nigerian State* (1997:188-197).

60. Catholic Bishops of Nigeria, *Christian/Muslim Relations in Nigeria: The Stand of the Catholic Bishops* (n.d.). Also cited in Simeon Ilesanmi, *Religious Pluralism and the State* (1997:191).

61. Ilesanmi (1997:191).

62. David Latin, "The Sharia Debate and the Origins of Nigeria's Second Republic" (1982:413-414).

63. Toyin Falola, *Violence in Nigeria* (1998:78).

64. For a good analysis of the new phase of Sharia controversy in contemporary Nigeria,

To this end, the Christians' task had two complementary sides: to show that Sharia showed no potential for reworking into the constitution of the Second Republic and to find ways to represent secularism as the realization of Nigeria political destiny.

Overall, the ideological opposition during this period (1978-1979) without any doubt, had important political implications. Simply put, for Muslims it was a "hegemonial contention" for what was perceived as the best path toward Nigeria's political future. Islam, for the Muslim North, represents a better democratic polity since its codes of personal conduct, unlike the "bankrupt" Western values and ideologies, are fair and just. To the Christian South, however, imposing Islamic ideology was to set Nigeria on a deficient path, contoured with anti-modern, anti-progress, and anti-democracy culture that has come to be associated with the Arab world.[65]

These religious controversies have remained Nigeria's greatest perennial problem. To recognize the continuity in Nigeria's history, we only have to take a cursory look at the reign of Ibrahim Badamasi Babangida, the self-styled "evil genius," whose venal regime threw the country more into the very abyss of religious politics.

Toward the Third Republic: The Babangida Era, 1985-1993

> Look at the OIC meeting which Christians were shouting and bragging that it should not take place, was it not done? . . . Fellow Muslims, what do we want Babangida to do for us? Whatsoever we asked him, he has done it for us. He stood firm [on] Islam [being] preached in this nation, Nigeria; therefore we must support him.[66]

---

see Ogbu Kalu, "Safiyya and Adamah: Punishing Adultery with Shari'a Stones in 21st Century Nigeria" (2003:389-408).

65. Jeff Haynes, *Religion in Third World Politics* (1994:67-68). Haynes' work is an excellent analysis of the role and influence of religion in the politics of countries in Africa, Asia and the Middle-East.

66. Yusuf Sambo (the secretary of the Mullahs in Kaduna), "In Support of Babaginda," June 18, 1990. See also Iheanyi Enwerem, *A Dangerous Awakening* (1995:146).

Babangida inherited the old and common goal of both Christianity and Islam; in particular, the political exploitation of religion to control the state. Although a Muslim and northerner, Babangida appeared less concerned with the clash of incompatible religious interests. Instead, he showed himself to be a reformist with a mandate to return the country to civilian rule. The Third Republic, according to his plan, would be a departure from the "old party alliances and patronage networks" that corrupted Nigeria's First and Second Republics. Instead, it would operate under a new "political class" that "would emerge with a more contemporary and sophisticated political culture."[67]

At first, he seemed to be serious, banning from partisan politics all former senior-ranking politicians going back to the First Republic. This, indeed, was a false start for Babangida concealed a great deal. His insight became twisted into religion so that he became the very flagship of Northern interests. The distinctive characteristic of his regime was the rejuvenation of Islam as the only viable political force for Nigeria. It should not be too surprising, therefore, that he dismantled the machinery of civil society by annulling, on June 12, 1993, the election results that would have installed Moshood Abiola as president of Nigeria's Third Republic.[68] Although acclaimed as the undisputed winner of the presidential election, one of Abiola's "sins" was being a southerner whose type of Islam was at variance with the North's vision of "true Islam."

The scandal of Babangida's regime, therefore, was the uncanny ambivalence of his so-called "directed democracy." This involved the governing of Nigeria under responsibility or deference to one group, the Muslim North. In view of these many contradictions, any claim to authenticity and fairness in religious matters by Babangida, is self-conceiting. For during Babangida's tenure, Islam shored up the claims of the Muslim North to sustain a monopoly on power and political dominion. We only have to take a brief look at the Babangida era to see that it has harmed the Nigerian politico-religious psyche more than any before it.

---

67. Andrew Apter, "IBB = 419" (1999:280). Apter's work is, in my opinion, the best academic analysis of any work on Babangida's economic, political, and religious policies.
68. Apter (1999:267-307).

Nigeria and the Organization of the Islamic Conference (OIC)

My analysis at this point of the politicization of Christianity does have significance for understanding the violence of the late 1980s and beyond. So far, I have stressed that the issues of Sharia and secularism have provided substantive context for Christian-Muslim conflicts. Yet, given the fact that both had been brewing for decades, the controversial way by which Babangida pushed Nigeria into a full membership of the OIC in 1986 was a radical exacerbation of an already volatile religious environment.

Nigeria's association with the OIC dates back to 1969 when the country was first invited to attend the meeting of the then four-year-old Islamic organization. The decisive purpose of the organization was to propagate Islam and acquaint the rest of the world with the faith, its issues, and aspirations. However, the position espoused by all pre-1986 governments was that of an observer status, a possible compromise that was acceptable to most Nigerians.

Many theories have attempted to explain why "Babangida, like a thief in the night, had handed his country to the OIC." These have remained mere speculative conjectures. The consensus, however, is the surreptitious way by which Babangida actualized his plan without the knowledge of his deputy, Commodore Ebitu Ukiwe, the Ministry of External Affairs, as well as top functionaries within his so-called Armed Forces Ruling Council (AFRC).[69]

True to his controversial nature, Babangida denied any substantive claim to a systematic Islamization of Nigeria. Instead he formulated his arguments around the economic significance of upgrading the Islamic credentials of Nigeria to international standard. "Despite its name," he declares, "member nations of the OIC are distinguished more by their identity as third world nations than by religious affinities. Its business is strictly international cooperation and the struggle for economic development and self-reliance."[70]

The Christians and non-Muslims could not be persuaded otherwise. To them the government's action demonstrated that Islamization was a political prerogative and as such the state cannot be trusted in matters of moral

---

69. D. Olojede, "Trip to Fez" (1986:7).
70. Ibrahim Badamosi Babangida, "Address to the Inaugural Meeting of the Committee on Nigeria's Membership in the OIC" February 3, 1986.

truth and civility. Even more unsettling for the Christian community was Babangida's indifference to the role of the state as a fulcrum for balancing competing religious interests. In their view, "[t]here is no conceivable way by which full membership of OIC can be effective without using it to promote, canvass, or impose Islam on Nigeria."[71]

Therefore, to take the country into an organization that was distinguishably "religious in ideology and orientation was a direct violation of the secular status of the Nigerian constitution."[72] Recognizing that too much was at stake in the survival of the state, he hand-picked a committee and charged them, among other things, to create a permanent forum as "a clearing house for ideas on how religion can best serve the national issue, struggle for economic recovery and independence as well as for political cohesion and stability."[73]

Although this had an appearance of "democratic liberalism," Babangida has always held a utilitarian political view of religion. And in view of the utter inadequacy of his regime, religion became the anchor upon which to secure his despotic powers and bolster his partisan Northern interests.

Political Appointments, Authority, and Legitimacy

Whatever one's attitude toward the policy issue regarding Nigeria's membership of the OIC, there is no question that Babangida pursued a type of religion-based political ideology. Under his regime, the Muslim life endured and thrived simply because the muscle of a self-conscious Muslim leader could be harmonized to consolidate and preserve the status quo. And because of his concern with regime legitimization, Babangida utilized Islam to bolster his position and to appeal to Northern interests. This he achieved through indiscriminate and judicious appointments of influential Muslims and northerners into major government and military positions. As a result of these appointments, Babangida provided for himself a natural rallying point for deflecting criticisms from domestic economic failures.

---

71. Christian Association of Nigeria, memorandum no. 41 (1986).
72. Matthew Hassan Kukah, "Christians and Nigeria's Aborted Transition" (1995:225).
73. Toyin Falola, *Violence in Nigeria* (1998:99).

Examples of the dominating influence of Muslims in national politics are numerous. However, what perhaps stood out most clearly was his cabinet reshuffle of December 1989, and the widespread apparent absence of Christians in it. CAN's reaction was predictable indeed, vigorously decrying the inequality of a government dominated by about 80 percent Muslims, with the remaining 20 percent occupying inconsequential offices. Samuel Salifu, the self-described "fanatical Christian" secretary of the Kaduna branch of CAN was even more specific. According to him, of the total number of thirty-five ministers, twenty-seven were Muslims, five were Christians, and three did not declare their religious affiliation.[74]

The condemnation of the lopsided character of Babangida's cabinet reshuffle made headlines in the mainstream media. The African Guardian, for example, reported:

> Reaction to the December 29 changes followed predictable religious, sectional and ethnic lines. Christians, especially in the North, sought to draw attention to the fact that as a result of the changes, virtually all of the most important offices in the land: President, Chairman of the Joint Chiefs of staff, Army Chief of Staff, Inspector General of Police, Head of the Secret Service, Chief Justice of the Federation, Defence, External Affairs and Petroleum resources Ministership are now held by Moslems.[75]

If the mainstream media could react in this way, it should not be surprising, then, that CAN perceived Babangida as a powerful and unapologetic instrument of Northern interests:

> Since the Babangida Administration came to power it has unashamedly and in utter contempt for national unity manifested its naked discriminatory religious posture through overt and covert acts of patronage and preference for Islamic

---

74. Iheanyi Enwerem, *A Dangerous Awakening* (1995:122).
75. *African Guardian*, "Editorial on the Cabinet Reshuffle," January 29 (1990:12).

religion. One is therefore left with no alternative but to conclude that the Babangida Administration is the principal agent for the islamization of Nigeria. This administration, more than any before it, has built up religious tension in this country of a dimension that is capable of obliterating the foundations of our corporate entity as a country.[76]

These are strong accusations and not merely idle words. The obliteration of those foundations of "corporate entity" manifested in the religious violence of the late 1980s through the 1990s.

Violent Faces of Religion: The Christian-Muslim Clashes

Just like the political associations which preceded it historically, the state is a relationship of rule (*Herrschaft*) by human beings over human beings, and one that rests on the legitimate use of violence (that is, violence that is held to be legitimate). For the state to remain in existence, those who are ruled must submit to the authority claimed by whoever rules at any given time. When do people do this, and why? What inner justifications and what external means support this rule?[77]

The renowned sociologist, Max Weber, has observed that the stability of any form of rule, or any legitimation of it, depends largely on the condition that the ruled submit to be ruled. And in order to restrain impulsive conduct against any inequality in the distribution of power, any form of rule must justify itself and seek legitimacy. Confined to a state of silent isolation and political passivity, these legitimating doctrines are generally accepted by the ruled. But "when the inherent inequalities of social existence become

---

76. *Sunday Tribune*, "CAN on the Cabinet Reshuffle," April 23, 1990.
77. Max Weber, *Political Writings*. Peter Lassman and Ronald Speirs, eds. (1994:311).

visible, legitimating ideas are questioned, with intense and possibly violent struggles as a consequence."[78]

Although many of Weber's critics may not completely agree with his concept of "legitimacy," this, more apparent than real, is a problem of interpretation. But when his concept is applied to our context, Nigeria, it is instructive to reflect on the many violent clashes between Christians and Muslims as a corrective mechanism to the political quietism of the former. The ideological proximity of the Christians is the perceived imbalance between religion and the high politics of the state, and their resolve stretches beyond revealing the intrinsic weaknesses of a Muslim-dominated body polity to a complete modification of the status quo. The use of state apparatus by the Muslims to protect Islamic interests has burdened the Christians with spectacular ethical commitment to unseat their rivals and wrest the control of the state itself. This inflexible resistance to perceived political and religious superiority of the Muslims has naturally fueled the extreme determination to justify their continuing domination. The result, of course, is that violence has been woven into the fabric of mainstream religio-political orthodoxy.

Consequently, the proliferation of religious clashes has become rather inevitable. In Weberian term, therefore, the onus of responsibility has been mostly on the Muslims to assert control and relevance. As Enwerem has rightly argued:

> It is usually when Muslims fail to realize their objective—be it through diplomatic avenues or constitutional debate—that they resort to force. For, it is not an accident or mere coincidence that all the religious riots in modern Nigeria took place in the North, and most of them—in fact the major ones—took place after a significant failure by Muslims to realize a particular objective.[79]

---

78. Peter Lassman, "The Rule of Man Over Man: Politics, Power and Legitimation" (2000:91).
79. Iheanyi Enwerem, *A Dangerous Awakening* (1995:147).

It has been almost two decades since Enwerem made this observation. Yet, the agitations for Sharia under former President Olusegun Obasanjo and the incumbent, Goodluck Jonathan, both Christian southerners, have validated his claim quite prominently. From the 1980s, and especially with the compounding of the persistent religious problems of Nigeria by the Babangida government, Christian reaction has been quite radical. In those circumstances their resolve has been a dramatic shift from prayer and fasting, and between ideals and compromise. Instead, their implicit appeal has been to the reprisal aspect of the law of Moses—"an eye for an eye." Nowhere was such decision expressed more eloquently than in the statement by the Christian students of Ahmadu Bello University (ABU, Zaria) in the aftermath of the 1988 riot: "For too long [we] have been pushed to the wall . . . both cheeks have been slapped and there is no third cheek to slap."[80]

Several years after these statements were uttered, Nigeria's political landscape remains characterized by extremely high levels of religious violence. The flagrant disregard for peace and civility by the Islamic fundamentalist sect, Boko Haram, in the 2011 Christmas day bombings of Christians and subsequent murderous attacks well into 2012 have, once again, provided the rallying ground for Christian leaders to demystify perceived monopoly to superiority and coercion. The national president of CAN, Ayo Oritsejafor, and the immediate past Catholic Archbishop of Lagos, Anthony Olubunmi Okogie, have both renewed their call for self-defense. According to Oritsejafor, the killing that occured December 25, 2011,

> Has aptly confirmed what we have been saying that Christians should defend themselves since it has become obvious that the nation's security agencies are either overwhelmed by the terrorists or the hoodlums have infiltrated their ranks and therefore lack the capacity to do their duty of protecting lives and property of innocent Nigerians. I will not subscribe to

---

80. Enwerem (1995:150).

the notion that Christians should quit the North because of the ceaseless attacks; rather I will urge them to be vigilant and be prepared at all times to defend themselves, their family members and their churches, including their businesses with whatever is available to them.[81]

Needless to say, then, that the Muslims' push to assert control through violence means remains the single most important factor that has galvanized Christians into political awakening. The exasperating campaign of violence by Boko Haram right into 2012 makes it increasingly problematic to assume the Muslim agenda as merely imagined. Not at all! In fact, the ideological proximity of the deadly group can only crystallize in inflexible Christian resistance and determined prescriptions for survival and self-preservation. The inevitable concomitant of this, of course, is a further politicization of Christianity and the voiced determination of Christians to physically defend their lives, churches, and property. Perhaps this should be expected. Understanding that psychological or religious subservience is best perpetuated in a climate of intimidation and fear, justification for Christian ecumenism is encouraging a curious hybrid of Christian coalitions and alliances that seem to be moving beyond polarities that know only the categories of "Protestants," "Catholics," and "Indigenous" churches.

These developments have the realistic possibility of exacerbating an already volatile situation. Unfortunately such a conjunction of crises and the failure of governance are equally bound to accentuate primordial ethno-religious tension, political sloganeering, and systemic decadence. It is already inflaming suspicions and compounding over-rigid dichotomies between Christians and Muslims, between North and South, between us and them, and between competing socio-economic interests. Consequently, the defensive impulses on the part of the Christians are not only seen to be rational or merely formal, but are set to become rather normative and self-referential.

---

81. http://www.vanguardngr.com/2012/01/oritsejafor-okogie-adeboye-renew-call-on-christians-to-defend-selves/. Accessed January 13, 2012.

The following tables, although not an exhaustive listing, help to chronicle the violent face of Muslim-Christian relations since the 1980s:[82]

Table 1

Churches Attacked in the Kano Riots of October 30, 1982

Name	Type
Christ Redemption Church	Aladura
The Church of the Lord (Aladura)	Aladura
Cherubim & Seraphim Movement	Aladura
Pentecostal Church of Christ	Pentecostal
Eternal Sacred Order of C & S	Aladura
Cherubim & Seraphim Church	Aladura
Igbala Apostolic Church	Pentecostal
Christian Church of Light	Aladura

Table 2

The Maitatsine Uprisings of 1980-1985

Location	Date	Deaths	Arrests
Yan-Awaki Ward (Kano State)	Dec 18-20, 1980	1,171	1,673
Bulumkutu Ward (Borno State)	Oct 26-29, 1982	118	411
Rigassa/Tundun Wada (Kaduna State)	Sept 29 - Oct 3, 1982	53	116
Dobeli Ward, Jimeta (Gongola State)	Feb 27 - Mar 5, 1984	568	980
Pantami Ward (Bauchi State)	Apr 26-28, 1985	105	295

---

82. For exhaustive studies in this area, see Toyin Falola, *Violence in Nigeria* (1998). See especially chapters 5-7. For the most recent and up-to-date work on religious violence in Nigeria, see Jan H. Boer, *Nigeria's Decades of Blood, 1980-2002* (2003). I must also add that the following four tables have been adapted from Ogbu Kalu, *Power, Poverty and Prayer: The Challenges of Poverty and Pluralism in African Christianity, 1960-1996* (2000:150-151).

Table 3
Students and Religious Clashes of 1987-1988

Location	Date	Group Involved
Teachers' College, Kafanchan	Mar 1987	Fellowship of Christians
Funtua, Zaria Kankia, Daura (Kaduna State)	Mar 1987	Muslim Students' Society (MSS)
Queen Amina College (Kaduna State)	May 1987	Quest for Islamic Uniform
Ahmadu Bello University (Zaria)	Jun 13, 1988	MSS vs. Christians

Table 4
Ethno-Religious Clashes in Northern Nigeria, 1980-1996

Date	Location
1980	Kusuwan Magani, Kano
1982	Kano
1984	Zangon-Kataf (Kaduna)
1984	Yola (Gongola State)
1985	Wukari (Gongola)
1987	Kafanchan, Kaduna
1987	Kano
1989	Ilorin, Lere
1991	Katsina, Tafawa Balewa
1991	Bauchi City, Kano
1992	Zangon-Kataf (Kaduna)
1995	Kano & Kaduna

Table 5[83]

Attacks Attributed to Boko Haram from 2009 – December 2011

Boko Haram: Timeline of Terror		
Date	**Description**	**Location**
July 26, 2009	Starts a five-day uprising that caused almost 800 deaths	Maiduguri
Sept 7, 2010	Frees more than 700 prisoners, including former sect members	Bauchi
Oct 6, 2010	Kills two security guards and ANPP leader, Awana Ngala	Maiduguri
Oct 9, 2010	Assassinates Muslim cleric Bashir Kashara, one of his students, and a police officer	Maiduguri
Oct 11, 2010	Attacks a police station, destroying the station and injuring 3	Maiduguri
Dec 24, 2010	Christmas Eve bombing killing at least 38 people	Jos
Dec 28, 2010	Assassinates a senior police officer and 2 others at a hospital	Maiduguri
Dec 31, 2010	Mammy market blast killing 30 people	Abuja
Jan 3, 2011	Gunmen kill a policeman	Maiduguri
Jan 18, 2011	Sporadic shooting kill 4 people	Maiduguri
Jan 28, 2011	Assassinates ANPP gubernatorial candidate Modu Fannami Gubio and 8 others	Maiduguri
Feb 15, 2011	Attacks a church but no casualties confirmed	Maiduguri
Feb 20, 2011	Assassinates a policeman	Maiduguri
Feb 23, 2011	Kills another policeman	Maiduguri

---

83. Boko Haram has been behind a string of bombs and assassinations since 2009. The activities of the sect (both large and small) are too relentless to be accounted for fully in this listing. The following attacks have been compiled from many sources including: *Nigerian Tribune*, *Vanguard*, *The Guardian*, *The Moment*, BBC, CNN, and *Wikipedia* (http://en.wikipedia.org/wiki/Boko_Haram). For an extensive list of Islamic terror attacks since 9/11, see http://www.thereligionofpeace.com/Pages/ChristianAttacks.htm.

Date	Description	Location
Feb 28, 2011	Attacks a police commander's home, killing 2 policemen	Maiduguri
March 2, 2011	Killing of two policemen	Maiduguri
March 13, 2011	Gunmen assassinate Muslim cleric, Ibrahim Ahmed Abdullahi	Maiduguri
March 27, 2011	Assassination of ANPP leader, Alhaji Modu Gana Makanike	Maiduguri
April 9, 2011	Bombings at polling places injure several and killing at least one	Maiduguri
April 20, 2011	Bombing kills a policeman	Maiduguri
April 22, 2011	Frees 14 prisoners during a jailbreak	Yola
April 24, 2011	Four bombs explode in Maiduguri, killing at least 3	Maiduguri
May 17, 2011	Gunmen kill a policeman	Maiduguri
May 29, 2011	Anti-Jonathan presidency bombings and killings in multiple locations	Bauchi, Zaria, and Abuja
May 31, 2011	Assassination of Abba Anas Ibn Umar Garbai, brother of the Shehu of Borno	Maiduguri
June 6, 2011	Assassination of Muslim cleric, Ibrahim Birkuti	Maiduguri
June 7, 2011	Gunmen launch parallel attacks with guns and bombs on a church and police stations killing 5 people	Maiduguri
June 17, 2011	Bombing at police headquarters	Abuja
June 20, 2011	Gunmen attack a bank and a police station in Kankara	Katsina
June 26, 2011	Bombing attack on a beer garden killing 25 people	Maiduguri
June 27, 2011	Another bombing attack kill 2 girls and wounding 3 customs officials	Maiduguri

Date	Description	Location
July 10, 2011	Bombing at the All Christian Fellowship Church killing an unspecified number of people	Suleja, Niger
July 11, 2011	The University of Maiduguri temporarily closes down its campus citing security concerns	Maiduguri
Aug 26, 2011	Suicide car bombing of the UN headquarters, leaving at least 21 dead and dozens more injured	Abuja
Nov 5, 2011	A series of coordinated attacks primarily around Damaturu, killing at least 67 people	Borno & Yobe States
Dec 25, 2011	Series of bomb attacks on four churches across Northern Nigeria, claiming at least 39 lives with several injured	Madala, Jos, Damaturu, and Gadaka

CHAPTER 7

The Past in the Present: Toward Authentic Christian Ecumenism

The discussion so far has theorized that the justification for contemporary Christian ecumenism in Nigeria arose out of the threat of Islamization and not in any way as a result of basic ecumenical conviction toward Christian unity. It is crucial to highlight the Islamic factor since it constitutes the dynamic stimuli and reflector of Christian mobilization against what it perceived as those intensely political challenges of Islam. Whether the Muslim agenda is real or imaginary, it has encouraged a curious hybrid of Christian coalitions and alliances that move beyond polarities that know only the categories of "Protestants," "Catholics," and "Indigenous" churches. But then this is merely an antidote to a threat and an implicit ecclesial strategic response. The results, as I have noted, are highly complicated ideological, political, and religious conflicts between Muslims and Christians.

Of course, the church in Nigeria has a right to self-preservation, especially against unprovoked deadly attacks. My point, however, is that Christian unity has not been the result of an explicit strategic orientation toward self-representation or of a rational program marked by an ideological ecumenism. It is but a false image of a unified and homogenous phenomenon. This is because despite the gains of unity on the socio-political interface, these churches continue to coexist uneasily in disequilibrium, demonstrating incongruities in matters of thought, behavior, and institutional polities. Not only has this introduced a pattern that is inconsistent with true Christian ecumenicity, it has, more importantly, led to open and discernible intra-ecclesiastical antagonisms. The consequence, of course, is that there are perceived *winners* and *losers*.

In terms of mediating the sacred, for example, the Neocharismatics allege that the mainline churches are suffering from "power-failure" and are indulged in "dispensing Sunday-Sunday pills."[1] This, they argue, explains why members of these mainline churches are nominal Christians having one foot in the traditional religion and the other in "powerless Christianity."

Neocharismatics are particularly merciless toward the Roman Catholics and African Independent Churches (Aladura). Against the Catholics, they are quick to express their frustration by appropriating the biblical statement of Matthew 19:24 to allege that it is easier for a camel to go through the eye of a needle than for a Roman Catholic to be born again. Similarly, the de-Christianization of the Aladura in Pentecostal rhetoric is particularly aggravating. Because of the relative paucity of Aladura type of church in offering a distinctively indigenous expression of Christianity, they are bluntly referred to as "demonic" or "satanic." Consequently, members of the Aladura churches who convert to Neocharismatic pentecostalism are made to undergo "deliverance from covenant with familiar spirits."[2]

The Neocharismatic churches have not proven to be unassailable either. The philosophical foundation of their new type of church in radicalizing and restructuring the religious landscape has been relativized as "crossless Christianity." The critical rub in non-Pentecostal frame of reference is that Neocharismatic preachers engage in "sheep-stealing." They are seen as veritable false prophets and wolves in sheep's clothing whose primary preoccupation with the gospel of Christ is for personal enrichment. Reuben Abati gives a cold description of this strife when he writes:

> The popularity of the Pentecostal churches meant a loss of a substantial part of the congregation that used to patronize the old, inherited churches: the Anglican mission, the Methodist, the Seventh Day Adventist and so on. All of a

---

1. Ogbu Kalu, "Pentecostal and Charismatic Reshaping of the African Religious Landscape in the 1990s" (2002:1).
2. Kalu (2002:1).

sudden, the younger generation no longer thought God could be encountered in the sober environment of the Anglican Church and its traditions. They no longer think the bookish Catholic priest can speak to God and he would listen. The new [Pentecostal] Pastor became something of an attraction, particularly with his romantic ways and the urgency of his tone. The new Pastor is a spellbinder: he dresses well, he rides very flashy cars . . . he is also a businessman.[3]

What we see, therefore, are schisms paradoxically represented by a form of "ecumenism without unity."[4] The consequence is polarization as never before and a radical scaling down of what unity really implies. Instead, what is apparent today is that unity in one faith and in common life in Christ has become less of an ecumenical imperative as socio-political ecumenism.

This begs an important question as to the basic ecumenical conviction that should guide Christian unity; other secondary considerations can only be supplemental at best. That is to say that the challenge of ecumenism presupposes a rallying point for Christians and churches. But attempts at renewal and reawakening, as Wilbert Shenk has pointed out, requires moving from the ideal to the living situation.[5]

It is one thing for the church in Nigeria to have orchestrated an ecumenical system on the social-political interface. It is completely a different thing to engage in a parallel movement that takes Christian *ecumene* to its primary oneness in matters of Christian faith and confession. Perhaps it will be helpful to go back almost a century in the history of Christianity in Nigeria to find a remote parallel at Christian unity that can suggest useful principles for today.[6]

---

3. See his work, "The Clash of the Pastor-Generals" in *Nigeriaworld*. (Available from http://nigeriaworld.com/feature/publication/abati/111101.html.) Accessed November 14, 2001.

4. Henry Lederle, "The Spirit of Unity: A Discomforting Comforter: Some Reflections on the Holy Spirit, Ecumenism and the Pentecostal-Charismatic Movements" (1990:291).

5. Wilbert Shenk, *Write the Vision: The Church Renewed* (1995).

6. The history of early attempts at Christian unity in Nigeria has not received much scholarly attention. Apart from a few articles and chapters in books, there are about three published works (to the best of my knowledge) in this area: W.J. Wood, *Christian Union*

Early Attempts at Christian Unity in Nigeria

There are several strands to the history of church union in Nigeria. This history is inconceivable without the missionaries who articulated from the outset the vision for organic unity. Their vision for collaborative responsibility produced the momentous shift among Nigerian church leaders who allied themselves with the missionary initiative through a succession of church union conferences. As a result, a new ecclesiastical culture of interdenominational cooperation developed within the Nigerian church, orchestrating respectable projects that benefited both the church and the society.

Yet as lively as this ecumenical spirit was, it stirred a hint of an imbalance in church relations. The result was a crack in the fledging wall of church union, leading to a final collapse in November 1965. As we pursue this history and assess its different impulses and complex interplay, a thread that runs throughout is that these early attempts appealed to, and had their concern in, a commitment that is in the final analysis an endorsement of a truly Christian unity.[7]

The Formulation of Church Union: Impulses from the Missionaries

Sustained Christian presence in Nigeria began in the 1840s as part of the Evangelical undertaking toward global missions. Initially set within the ecclesiastical construct of the Western mind and its idealistic vision of the number of perishing "heathen," the Nigerian experience provided the occasion for Christian philanthropy. The result was the establishment of mainline denominations with deep roots in Western forms and theology.

Movements in Nigeria (1965); T.S. Garrett, and R.M.C. Jeffery, *Unity in Nigeria* (1965); and Ogbu Kalu, *Divided People of God* (1978).

7. Ogbu Kalu has written an extensive history of the church union movement in Nigeria, reviewing the original impulse and analyzing also the events leading to the failure of the talks. It is not my intention to duplicate what has been done. Rather, my approach is precisely as indicated above and that is to trace and show the interplay of the different strands in the efforts to foster unity in Nigerian Christianity. For details on Kalu's work, see *The Divided People of God* (1978)

Yet the Christianization of Nigeria, as it was with most of Africa, began on the treacherous voyages of the transatlantic slave trade, inhospitable climate, poor communications, and intertribal wars. It was within this paradox of horrible realities that the missionaries flourished under the broad banner of Christian brotherhood. This was not a simplistic turn to Christian unity. Instead, it was a pragmatic necessity arising out of a complex reality and a collective self-definition as allies in the business of the kingdom. As a result, these early missionaries to Nigeria saw the ecumenical benefits of adjusting practice for the sake of the kingdom. A few examples would suffice here.

When the CMS missionary, Henry Townsend, arrived in 1842, a Wesleyan Methodist missionary, Thomas Birch Freeman, was there to welcome him and to offer practical help. The pioneers of Sudan Interior Mission (SIM) and Sudan United Mission (SUM) learned from the experiences of CMS and moved into new frontiers where no Christian work was being done at all.[8] The same attitude of avoiding unnecessary competition was a fundamental principle in the work of the United Presbyterian Mission. Its missionary, Hope Waddell, sought practical help and consulted with the Baptists before moving on to establish a mission station at Calabar in 1846. In his words,

> It is not our wish to disturb any other body of Christians who may be engaged in similar labours. We would rather co-operate with them; and for that end, would respect their arrangements for the benefit of the natives and avoid disturbing their operations, even as we would expect the same consideration from them in respect to ours.[9]

Despite the shifting fortunes of Christian expansion, the measures for church union were reinforced at the turn of the twentieth century when in 1905, representatives of the Church of Scotland, the Niger Delta

---

8. For details, see Michael Marioghae and John Ferguson, *Nigeria Under the Cross* (1965). See also Ogbu Kalu, *The Divided People of God* (1978).
9. H.M. Waddell, *Twenty-Nine Years in the West Indies and West Africa* (1863:229).

Pastorate, and the Church Missionary Society met in Calabar and agreed to coordinate their expanding work. A timely boost for the burgeoning ecumenical climate was the Edinburgh Conference of 1910, which was itself a fresh appraisal of ecumenical concerns on matters of Faith and Order in the West. One year after the Edinburgh Conference, precisely in 1911, four of the Protestant missions in Nigeria (Presbyterians, Primitive Methodists, Niger Delta Pastorate, and Qua Iboe Mission) met in what is now historically described as the Calabar Conference.

This conference suggests the emergence of a distinctively Nigerian form of "Edinburgh," an eclectic blend infused with local flavor. Accordingly, principles of organic unity that were the backdrop of Christian ecumenism moved boldly to the foreground and received unanimous warrant in the resolution that was passed:

> The Conference solemnly declares the aim of missionary effort to be the establishment of one Church of Christ. The Conference resolves that to attain this unity there should be mutual and full recognition of the discipline of the churches of Southern Nigeria. That an effort be made to obtain corporate unity of the native churches . . . not episcopally ordained.[10]

Influenced by this new spirit in mission work, early missionaries saw the church as complementary and mutually dependent manifestations of the body of Christ. Arthur Wilkie, a Presbyterian, captured this well in his speech at the Calabar Conference:

> We are not here primarily to establish in Africa Presbyterianism or Methodism or any other –ism but to preach Christ and to take a lowly place under the guidance of the Spirit of God in laying the foundation of a church which shall not be foreign to the African.[11]

---

10. C.P. Groves, *The Planting of Christianity in Africa: 1878-1914*, vol. 3 (1955:279).
11. Minutes of the Conference of 1911, p. 77.

The Past in the Present: Toward Authentic Christian Ecumenism 217

In the context of such an ecumenical experiment, and following the quest for "unity of action," the 1911 conference assumed as its title the "Evangelical Union of Southern Nigeria" when it reconvened for the second time in 1923.[12] The 1923 conference involved a change in philosophy from an ecumenical enterprise among the original four bodies that participated in the 1911 conference, to focusing on a much broader participation and inclusion of other mission agencies. As a result, the conference invited the Yoruba Mission (Anglican), the Wesleyans, the Dutch Reformed church, the SIM, the Basal Mission, and the British and Foreign Bible Society.

The largeness of this conference was without precedent, and it affected much of Nigerian Christianity and shaped its ecumenical initiatives into the future. In fact, it glided naturally into the second strand in the efforts to foster church union in Nigeria. And to understand it we must turn to the inauguration of a service of conferences of Senior African Agents. A significant outcome of the 1923 conference, the meeting of African Agents in the following year at Ovim proposed, among other things, a central church in each town, a common form of worship, a common name and catechism, inter-church visitation, and the exchange of pulpits:

> In view of the great commission we have received from our Lord, and of his express desire that his people should be one, and of the desirability of presenting a united front to the world in the evangelization of our people; we the African delegates representing churches of Eastern regional section of the Christian Council of Nigeria deprecate the existence of division among us as a source of weakness and strongly urge that steps be taken to the consolidation of union among our churches.[13]

More than the passing of a resolution for organic unity, the body achieved a combination of two important things. First, it proved to have as pioneers a substantial corps of persons with the degree of commitment

---

12. Ogbu Kalu, *The Divided People of God* (1978:5).
13. Christian Council of Nigeria, "Minutes of the Calabar Conference" (1911:78).

capable of sustaining the vision for organic unity. Second, it inaugurated a series of conferences of senior African agents, a form of organizational viability, to mobilize and maintain the vision towards church union for themselves and others.

African Agents: Their Roles and Contributions

The inauguration at Ovim of a service of conferences of senior African agents could, in fact, be regarded as a change in approach from looking to missionaries as initiators, to the involvement of Nigerians as credible partners in an ecumenical project of national significance. Although the missionaries still largely sustained momentum for union, the collaborative efforts with African agents appropriated the invaluable theory of Henry Venn's euthanasia of the mission, "the settlement of a native church under a native clergy on a self-supporting system."[14]

But developments in Nigeria also benefited immensely from a growing global ecumenical revolution. For example, the founding of the Christian Council of Nigeria (CCN) in 1930, an association of missionary-oriented Protestant churches, was an ambitious scheme to import and pursue with such purpose and energy other ecumenical models such as the United Church of Canada in 1925.

Few events have shown the increased roles of Nigerian church leaders in the efforts toward church union as significantly as the CCN, and it was a sentiment many of them appreciated. From this point forward, we can trace the intensity of this indigenous contribution, as its dramatic effects on previously existing coalitions make clear. For example, the "Evangelical Union of Southern Nigeria" that was so-named in the Conference of 1923 became the "Eastern Regional Committee of the Christian Council" (ERCCC) in 1930, the same year CCN was founded.

It was possible to assume this name because despite regional claim to Christian alliance, it was only in eastern Nigeria that distinctive ecumenical attempts were noticeable. Efforts toward union did not take the same form in both the western and the northern regions but were much slower in

---

14. J.R. Harwood, "The Church Union Story" (1963:5-7).

pace. Nevertheless, ERCCC was an unprecedented compromise and an indication that Nigerian church leaders themselves would be the architects in mobilizing the regions into a national alliance.

It is important to highlight that the founding of CCN was a viable and logical step towards improving pre-existing regional inequalities in the move toward church union. And in order to provide evidence of its viability the council aimed at pursuing progressive projects such as education, pastoral training, medical, and urban ministry. Several years after its inauguration, its constitution still maintained as its aims:

a. to foster and express the fellowship and unity of the Christian church in Nigeria, to further the realization of its oneness with the church throughout the world;
b. to keep in touch with the International Missionary Council and the W.C.C.;
c. to preserve comity among churches and missions;
d. to be a medium for public statements and joint actions among the churches on social, moral, religious, and educational matters;
e. to be a forum for discussion of matters regarding the stability and expansion of Christianity in Nigeria.[15]

I have mentioned that there were disparities in the clarion calls for church union on a national scale. Here one must pause to ponder why it was comparatively easy for the churches in eastern Nigeria to co-operate and why its ecumenical body, the Eastern Regional Committee of the Christian Council (ERCCC), pursued the idea of organic unity more vigorously than their Protestant counterparts in the southern West and the northern regions respectively.

To this end, it is important to identify the Roman Catholic factor as an important aid to the church in mission. Here the dramatic expansion of the Catholic Church in the region provided the incentive for evangelical collaboration. The Catholics came late to the mission field, but aided by strong leadership, and evangelistic methods based upon a close

---

15. *Constitution of Christian Council of Nigeria* (1949).

understanding of Ibo religion, the Roman Catholics outstripped the Niger Mission of the Protestant churches combined.

Apart from the fact that the Roman Catholics were outside the sphere of church union, this energetic expansion into Protestant missions frontiers in the East was seen as a reckless territorial incursion. It became necessary, therefore, to develop a new strategy to combat and subvert Catholic influence and expansion. This enabled Protestant influences to be deployed actively against a common enemy, Roman Catholicism, in an implicit ecumenical strategy on the desirability of preserving a united front. This development laid a new requirement upon those for whom the need for church union, among other considerations, was Protestantism versus Catholicism.

The discussion so far has given positive value to the impulses for church union in eastern Nigeria. Yet this is a far cry to the vision of unity on a national scale. For example, in western Nigeria where the Catholic Church is smaller than in the East, the expanding frontiers of missionary activities brought about a cutthroat rivalry between the two dominant churches—notably the Anglicans and Wesleyan Methodists.[16] Perhaps this may have been influenced by a more localized religious competition which was a striking feature of Yoruba society.

As for the churches in the North, their concern was more with the challenges posed by Islam than with any discussion on church union. The structures in the North did not support any move to organic union either. The white-dominated missions, although smaller when compared with those of the South, were by no means undifferentiated. In spite of their utilization of Africans, the white missionaries saw the churches they had founded as infants still learning to walk.

Also, during the ecumenical conferences, and still more afterwards as the South (East and West) reflected on pushing the boundaries of organic unity, the North remained confined to the boundaries carved for them by the civil administration. The exigencies of the time forced them to shape their mission. This in itself had a serious implication. It marked the beginning of

---

16. T.S. Garrett and R.M.C. Jeffery, *Unity in Nigeria* (1965:25).

regional polarization that has become an integral part of Nigerian religio-political ethic.[17]

Despite the disparities that I have alluded to, the rhapsodic note in calls for church union during this period raised the issue of ecumenism in a new form. It gives us glimpses of eager, vigorous advocates of organic union who had the whole of Nigeria in their sights. These sights had as their prism the Pietist-Evangelical concern of "what could be done to draw the Protestant Evangelical forces in Nigeria together."[18] Among these advocates, J.T. Dean, a Presbyterian, occupied a unique position. It was he who first proposed back in 1931 that the Evangelical Church of West Africa should be comprehensive enough to embrace within it all the present missions.[19] His proposal was an attempt to provide practical direction to the declarations of African Agents at Ovim.

Ogbu Kalu has suggested that Dean's letter "is usually taken as the beginning of serious union negotiations in Nigeria."[20] This is an appropriate observation in the sense that Dean's letter became a unifying ideological referent. Nevertheless, it was not a simple matter to keep together a coalition which had been united only by the ecumenical zeal of the Christians in eastern Nigeria. Perhaps a mitigating factor was how to create a church union to suit the reality of the colonial political boundaries and to create a viable *modus operandi* for a populace divided by sharp ethnic, cultural, regional, economic, linguistic, and ecclesiastical differences.

Under the circumstances what appeared to give legitimacy to Dean's letter, which also showed to unite and focus disparate responses to church union in Nigeria, came in the form of yet another global manifestation, the Church of South India in 1947. This led to a degree of revival of Christian coalitions and a recovery of confidence in church union on a national scale. The result was that the Eastern Regional Committee of the Christian Council (ERCCC) appointed a subcommittee to work out the modalities for church union on a national scale. The proposed national conference

---

17. Ogbu Kalu, *The Divided People of God* (1978:22).
18. Kalu (1978:16).
19. Kalu (1978:16).
20. Kalu (1978:15).

met at Onitsha in 1947 and came up with their draft called the "Proposed Scheme of Church Union."

The 1947 "Proposed Scheme of Church Union" was unsurprisingly influenced by the cross-fertilization of ideas that arose out of the South Indian Scheme. And to heighten this development, modern commentators believe, the extensive tour of Nigeria in 1955 by Bishop Sumitra, moderator of the Church of South India, was carefully orchestrated "to combat the low degree of interest in church union in Western Nigeria."[21] More importantly, his visit provided opportunities for the Nigerians to ask questions on the thorniest issues in the mechanism of church union in the Third World.[22]

In assessing the participation of Nigerian leaders and churches in the move towards church union, the first and most obvious conclusion is that the historic national conference of 1947 was a significant turning point. It marked the beginning of serious ecumenical negotiations, with the resolutions to make solid connections between the Protestant churches and self-advancement in a series of comprehensive interdenominational programs. Ogbu Kalu refers to this year as the end of Phase I and the beginning of Phase II in the history of the church union movement in Nigeria.[23]

Interdenominational Cooperation

As I have already mentioned, the national conference of 1947 was a catch-all repository of hopes and ideals on Christian coalition. It was also decidedly the most enduring step towards union on a national scale. Looking at the spatial dimension of this event, the manifestations that made up ecumenical discussions were those of aspirations and intense negotiations. Present at the historic 1947 conference were representatives from Anglicans, Methodists, Presbyterians, the SUM, and the Qua Iboe Mission (QIM). The Southern Baptists, who had missions both in the South and North, refused to

---

21. For details, see Ogbu Kalu, "The Shattered Cross: The Church Union Movement in Nigeria, 1905-1966" (1980:343).
22. Ogbu Kalu, *The Divided People of God* (1978:10).
23. Kalu (1978:10).

participate in any ecumenical discussions. The foreword to the "Proposed Scheme of Union," the first of three such schemes, observed that:

> It is our earnest hope that before the union is inaugurated, it will embrace Christian churches in a wider area than the committee at present represents, and indeed it is doubtful whether the scheme can come to fruition unless it does embrace such a wider area. But the committee felt it was right to go forward in preparing a definite scheme.[24]

The program of organic unity during this period cannot be pursued fully, but it suggests something of the range that the study of early attempts at ecumenism in Nigerian Christianity opens up. To some of the participants at the 1947 national conference, the model of consensus was seen as appropriate only as long as federal rather than organic union was the goal. The divergence in ecumenical goals between organic and federal perceptions led to the voluntary withdrawal of the QIM and SUM. From this point on, ecumenical consultations and cooperation were products of the Joint Union Committee (formed in 1950) of the Anglicans, Methodists, and Presbyterians. Even then, the pattern of voting for union among these three churches was determined by the dynamics of church politics, and more importantly, by the influence of their overseas mentors.

After an extensive review of existing schemes and proposals for union, the Joint Union Committee presented its own scheme, thus orchestrating an alliance in education, social work, and medical projects. Here, a number of examples are important. The corps of competent training institutions in the West such as the famous Igbobi College for boys in Lagos, the establishments in Ibadan of Immanuel College for the training of ministers and the United Missionary College for the training of women teachers, remain as notable examples of joint educational work between Anglicans and Methodists.

---

24. Christian Council of Nigeria, "Proposed Scheme of Union," 1947. See also Ogbu Kalu, *The Divided People of God* (1978:16).

Other co-operative efforts include the establishment at Umuahia in Eastern Nigeria, the Trinity College for ministers, Women's Training College for teachers and a Union Secondary School for girls. The establishment of Queen Elizabeth Hospital at Umuahia by these three churches also furthers the idea of other united enterprises beyond the sphere of education[25] It is important to highlight these co-operative ventures not only because of their profound positive value for the church and the society at large, significant as that was, but also because they provide a framework from which to evaluate church unity in missional terms.

This interdenominational cooperation took a new turn in 1963 with the meeting of the standing committee in which the third and final draft of the scheme for church union was worked out and presented to the participating churches for approval, notably Presbyterians, Methodists, and seven Anglican dioceses from Eastern and Western Nigeria and Lagos. The scheme itself is divided into three parts. Part I was the Basis of Union, a foundation document which cannot be altered after union, but was to become an appendix to part 2 of the constitution. Part 3 dealt largely with the inauguration and interim arrangements for union. Again, the historian of the Nigerian church union movement, Ogbu Kalu, has categorized this event as marking the end of phase 2 and the beginning of phase 3.[26]

Denominational Interests

The meeting of the standing committee gave witness to the Church of Christ as being one by nature. As a result, the Committee resolved to form a solid Christian alliance by inaugurating the "United Church of Nigeria" in 1965. From here on discussions toward church union seemed to appear more substantive and decisive, yet it proved to be the most ironical. Initially, all the churches expressed ideal conformity to the inauguration of a united church. The Presbyterians were most eager, voting overwhelmingly for union in two successive years. The Methodists also showed commitment to union in principle by adopting a resolution in 1963 to join the United

---

25. For details, see Michael Marioghae and John Ferguson, *Nigeria Under the Cross* (1965:43-50); and T.S. Garrett and R.M.C. Jeffery, *Unity in Nigeria* (1965:31-33).
26. Ogbu Kalu, *The Divided People of God* (1978).

Church of Nigeria. The Anglicans appeared to be a promising ally with their sheer size, strong administration, and relationship with Lambeth.

Similarly, theological issues posed no great difficulty from a strictly ecumenical point of view. The Scheme of Union upheld the Bible, confessed Jesus Christ and accepted the biblical concept of the priesthood of all believers.[27] At the level of ecclesiastical polity, the scheme posited a threefold order: deacon, presbyter, and bishop. The draft also adopted what was referred to as "constitutional episcopacy." Although this episcopacy was for the most part Anglican, it was constitutional in the sense that the duties of the bishops were clearly defined in the constitution.

But the story developed in a completely unexpected way. The appeal to interdenominational cooperation, which had been enough to overcome immediate differences, became increasingly difficult to suppress as the standing committee worked out its third and final draft of the scheme for church union. As a result, the noble enterprise that was to culminate in the inauguration on December 11, 1965 of the United Church of Nigeria failed. To understand the stunning nature of the crisis that led to this failure, I must quickly highlight a number of factors.

Things Fall Apart

Ogbu Kalu has identified the factors responsible for the indefinite and ultimately the failure of church union during this period as: Methodist crisis, radical critique of the process, side effects of the pattern of negotiations, rumors, and tribalism.[28] There were other factors, too, that complicated and challenged the ecumenical enterprise.[29] But of all these factors the Methodist crisis represented one of the most immediate obstacles to unity.

Conscious participation in a pioneering venture such as church union should provoke positive thoughts in anyone with a strong sense of

---

27. For details, see T.S. Garrett and R.M.C. Jeffery, *Unity in Nigeria* (1965:43-50). See also ogbu Kalu's works, *The Divided People of God* (1978:52-65); and "The Shattered Cross: The Church Union Movement in Nigeria, 1905-1966" (1980:348-353).

28. Ogbu Kalu, *The Divided People of God* (1978:66-80).

29. For more information on the failure of church union as perceived by other observers, see D.T. Adamo and J. Enuwosa, "The Prospects of Intrafaith Dialogue in Nigeria" (2000:331-342).

providence. Yet the position of some Lagos congregations of the Methodist church, Tinubu, Olowogbowo, Agbeni, and Ago-Ijaye was one of strong opposition. Although there was no substantial criticism of the scheme of union per se, nevertheless, these congregations were embittered by the processes that had left them ignorant of the ecumenical process. Another issue, which undoubtedly proved to be a major sticking point for the Methodists, was who would control church properties.

In their quest for self-determination, and the disillusionment with the elite leadership of the Methodist church, the threats of legal action provided a platform on which these Lagos congregations could express their cynicism for the whole ecumenical enterprise. They were not empty threats. The result was a series of court injunctions. In the light of the tension and anxiety that gripped the union committee, the inauguration was postponed indefinitely. The church union had failed on the altar of institutional and personal factors.

It is hard to not identify specifically the Methodist factor as a major obstacle to church union. Yet, it is also through the eye of a Methodist, Bolaji Idowu, that we see the ideological inadequacies that made the ideal of a United Church of Nigeria difficult to implement. Idowu was a blunt and articulate churchman whose zeal for the Lord's house was beyond any doubt. One of his criticisms of the whole ecumenical enterprise was that the church leaders devoted more energy to organizational viability than to the nature of the product.

The main thrust of his argument was that most of the missionaries who were at the helm of the union movement gave no consideration to the particularities of Nigeria's cultural realities. For Idowu the defining issue was whether the United Church would speak "to Nigerian people in their own situation, or . . . merely be a Church imprisoned within a foreign structure."[30] It is only in a culturally relevant expression of the faith that the genius of church unity can be expressed and preserved. By ignoring this pertinent issue in the very form and procedures of the church union

---

30. Ogbu Kalu, "The Shattered Cross: The Church Union Movement in Nigeria, 1905-1966" (1980:358).

movement, Idowu believed that the whole ecumenical enterprise, although noble in its aims, was not well worked out.

It is fair to say, then, that among several factors (whether immediate or remote) two stand out as fuelling opposition to church unity. On one hand, there was the Methodist case of sentimental attachment to denomination, with the accompanying fear of being swallowed up into a single "super Church." On the other hand, and perhaps the more important, there was the failure to carefully formulate an authentic united Church whose mission and theology can be rooted into the culture of the people. Ogbu Kalu is straight to the point when he remarks that "[t]he collapse was a commentary on the predicament of the church in Nigeria."[31] In the final analysis, the irony is that Nigerian churches had the benefit of the Church of South India experience to study and benefit from. Unfortunately, specifically Nigerian issues prevailed over any idealism.

Toward Authentic Christian Ecumenism

The process of reflection on Nigerian Christian ecumenism has taken us deep into a realm of thought that focused almost exclusively on a conceptual sorting-out of old assumptions and constructs. This long, rather painful quest has raised the inescapability of the themes of reluctance and politicization of religion through a perceived threat of marginalization. Here, I have observed that the factor that prescribed for an increasingly unifying effect within the Christian community, especially since the 1970s, has been the Muslim threat. The crux of the case is the popular Christian belief "that colonialism strengthened the Muslims, who have increasingly dominated government and military since the 1970s and that government policies are discriminatory."[32]

Nothing better illustrates the ideological proximity of the Christians than this perceived imbalance between religion and the high politics of the state. But this tactic of associating anti-Islamic rhetoric with true Christian

---

31. Ogbu Kalu, *The Divided People of God* (1978:86).
32. Paul Freston, *Evangelicals and Politics in Asia, Africa and Latin America* (2001:183).

unity obscures a spirited formula for authentic ecumenism. Whatever may be the specific understanding of the church and its unity, an ecclesiology that accepts and affirms diversity as well as unity is an essential starting point for any ecumenical enterprise. This was the foremost agenda of the church union movement from 1905-1966. Its failure, as I have demonstrated, was due to the inability to successfully facilitate an ecumenical position that could overide denominational interests.

The justification and importance of the political impulses for ecumenism in contemporary Nigeria through the continued existence and operations of CAN, notwithstanding, have equally brought about a profound misunderstanding in what corresponds to authentic Christian unity. A key principle to recognize here is that national, political, social, and cultural distinctives, as important as they are, do not by themselves correspond to a model of union. This, at best, can only be viewed as a model of partial union. One can only speak of a model of union in the full sense, that is, as a form of the realization of visible unity of the church, only where there is a varying interplay of the ministry of the Word and sacraments and unity of action in witness and service to the world.[33]

The biblical ideal is that every sincere effort for church unity follows after God's own initiative in first assembling the one church. He creates the church as belonging to himself so that "it is not the faithful but God who is the subject when we speak of the church."[34] This perspective belongs in the realm of Christian faith and confession and it was how the primitive church understood its ecumenicity.

To take the early church, for example, the credo "one, holy, catholic, and apostolic church" (Nicene Creed) adheres to that to which the New Testament bears witness.[35] That is to say that unity, at least to the early church, was a matter of Christian faith, anchored on the metaphor of Christ as "head" of the body. The uniqueness of Christ, therefore, constitutes both

---

33. For insightful studies that encourage the Church toward authentic and biblical Christian ecumenism, see G.R. Evans, *The Church and the Churches* (1994); and Harding Meyer, *That All May Be One: Perceptions and Models of Ecumenicity* (1999).

34. Harding Meyer, *That All May Be One* (1999:9).

35. Meyer (1999:8).

the unity of those who are in him and the foundation of the church. In essence, the responsibility of the church is to the one Spirit, the one Lord, the one faith, the one baptism, and the one God and Father (Eph. 4:1-5).

Furthermore, the cosmological axis of the redemptive and reconciliatory work of Christ absolutizes the nature and mission of the church. It stands as corrective to the church's agenda of self-preservation. That is, the connection between God's plan of salvation in the world through Christ's suggests the connection between the church and her ministry in the world. In her engagement with the world, "the church has become a theologically thought-out salvation entity which must fulfill the role in the Redemption-event determined for her by God—admittedly never isolated from Christ but indispensable for his further work in the world."[36]

Summary

It is appropriate to affirm, therefore, that "the unity of the church is a matter of Christian faith and confession and not something subject to our disposition or a matter of considerations of mere utility."[37] Here lies the indestructibility of the church; it is first "his church" irrespective of the whole power of evil or of human desire for unity (Mt. 16:18). While the Nigerian church is to be commended for successfully fostering a socio-political ecumenism, thanks in part to the threat of Islamization, it has scored less than the pass mark in what constitutes true ecumenicity. The aim of any ecumenical enterprise should be "the bringing to men and society of the *civitas dei*, that divine commonwealth which must ultimately transform the kingdoms of this world till they become the kingdom of God and of Christ."[38]

As Shenk has reminded us, the Great Commission compels us to recognize that ever since the time of Jesus, mission must precede the church. It is imperative, therefore, that if the church in Nigeria is to

---

36. Rudolf Schnackenburg, *The Epistle to the Ephesians* (1991:295).
37. Harding Meyer, *That All May Be One* (1999:8).
38. J.T. Robinson, *On Being the Church in the World* (1960:19).

facilitate an authentic ecumenism, it must be based on a renewal that is linked to recovering this priority of mission.[39] This is the vision I seek for the church in Nigeria and it is precisely "the heart of the Gospel" and what is "distinctive and unique" in the Christian religion.[40]

---

39. Wilbert Shenk, *Changing Frontiers of Mission* (1999:131-132).
40. Edward Schillebeeckx, *Church: The Human Story of God* (1996:xiii).

PART VI

What on Earth is the Church? An Exploration in Biblical Understanding

"The greatest historical puzzle of the church's history," writes Leonhard Goppelt, "is her origin."[41] Even more so, the origin and formation of the church must be conceptualized in terms of her message since it is impossible to discuss one without the other. To this end, the apostolic witness has been the authoritative source that found its expression in what we have as the New Testament canon. Today, over two thousand years since the formation of the church, historical investigations have taken on new forms, indicating the lines of thought, and the forces that made for change.

Nevertheless, in the process of eccelesiastical scholarship, the New Testament documents set the stage for all church history. They offer a series of explanations for the transition from Jesus' earthly ministry to the development of the church. It is assumed in this book, therefore, that an understanding of the basic ecclesiological developments in the first century provides the *a priori* developmental principle that one can understand what the church should be today only when one has a thorough understanding of what the church "has been" or "ought to be."

It is an appropriate theological claim, then, to posit that there is a connection between historical and contemporary ecclesiological

---

41. Leonard Goppelt, *Apostolic and Post-Apostolic Times* (1970:8).

developments, whereby the former gives expression to the fundamental claims of the latter. What I want to do in this section is to explore the biblical understanding of the church and find relevant clues from ancient times that may inform Christian thought and practice today.

CHAPTER 8

The Relevance of a Biblical Starting Point

The purpose of a classical starting point is to enable us reflect on what the early church might contribute to our contemporary understanding of the church. This is necessary because our contemporary conception of the English word "church" is punctuated with so many confusions and ambiguities that many years after the Reformation, we still cannot securely determine what exactly is meant each time the word "church" is mentioned.[1] In other words, what is it that makes our own "church" painfully disparate with the church of both apostolic and post-apostolic periods? Even in cases where appeals have been made to the Greek word, *ekklēsia,* the same terminological confusion remains.[2]

This ambiguity is not limited to the conception of the church alone. Recent scholarship has emphasized the diversity of theological interests that have influenced responses to culturally related questions that are found within the New Testament itself. Similarly, ecclesiology, the field that

---

1. For an excellent example of how this word finds different expressions in contemporary interpretation, see Kevin Giles, *What on Earth Is the Church?* (1995).
2. Kevin Giles has observed that this appeal to the Greek finds advocacy especially among Protestant scholars among whom he listed F.J.A. Hort, *The Christian Ecclesia* (1914); Emil Brunner, *The Misunderstanding of the Church* (1952); E.D. Radamacher, *What the Church is All About* (1972); R. Saucy, *The Church in God's Program* (1972); R.P. Lightner, *Evangelical Theology* (1986:227-228); D.W.B. Robinson, *The Church of God* (1965). Building on the work of James Barr, *The Semantics of Biblical Language* (1961), Giles considers it a "seriously flawed approach" that Protestants continue to appeal to this word, *ekklēsia,* as a "common solution" to this terminological confusion (1995:4-25).

deals with the doctrine of the church, is not exempt from this problem.³ Although I do not intend to argue that an etymological study of the Greek word, *ekklēsia,* as used in the Bible is sufficient to formulate a theology of the church, it does help, however, to place our conception of the church in a proper perspective.

Etymological Analysis of Biblical Presuppositions

As already noted, the English word, "church," has become the primary term for designating the idea of the church either as an institution or as the Christian community. Although this English translation has largely assumed the meaning of the Greek word *ekklēsia* (assembly), its contemporary conception is misleading and does not correctly translate the common classical usage in New Testament Greek.⁴ Our conception of church today carries with it a translation of different Greek derivative, *kyriakon,* (that which is the Lord's).⁵

Opinions on the etymology of the word church differ today so much that Roberts has cautioned, "we ought to avoid the frequent error of etymological fallacy."⁶ It is not my intention to engage in a broad treatment of the word; nevertheless, a brief analysis of the designation of *ekklēsia* in the Scripture is necessary so as to understand the perspective adopted in this book.

---

3. See especially the works of James D.G. Dunn, *Unity and Diversity in the New Testament: An Inquiry into the Character of Earliest Christianity* (1990). See also E. Käsemann and Raymond Brown, "Unity and Diversity in New Testament Ecclesiology" (1963).

4. F.J.A. Hort, *The Christian Ecclesia* (1914:1-21); J.W. Roberts, "The Meaning of Ekklesia in the New Testament" (1972:27-36); William Stewart, *The Nature and Calling of the Church* (1958); and J.Y. Campbell, "The Origin and Meaning of the Christian Use of the Word Ekklesia" (1948:130-142).

5. Everett Ferguson, *The Church of Christ: A Biblical Ecclesiology for Today* (1996:129-130); William Stewart, *The Nature and Calling of the Church* (1958:5-6); George G. Findlay, *The Church of Christ as Set Forth in the New Testament* (1893:9-10).

6. J.W. Roberts, "The Meaning of *Ekklesia* in the New Testament" (1972:28).

Ekklēsia in the Old Testament

The popular etymology of the word *ekklēsia* is connected with the Greek verb *ekkaleo*, meaning "to call out" or to "summon." In classical Greek, the *ekklēsia* was clearly characterized as a political phenomenon. It referred to the conveyed assembly of the people of a city-state, the supreme legislative and judicial body in the democratic system. Usually the citizens were summoned by the trumpet of the *kerux* (herald) to the *ekklēsia* (assembly) in which fundamentally political and judicial decisions were made. The *ekklēsia* or the general assembly of the citizens thus constituted the ultimate power with unlimited rights to make decisions with regards to constitutional and state matters.

In the Greek translation of the Old Testament (*Septuagint*), the Jews adopted the same Greek word *ekklēsia* to translate the Hebrew word *Qahal*, which also originally meant a company summoned for a definite purpose by a trumpet call (Num. 10:2, 7).[7] The Jews seized on this Greek word because it was suitable to describe their assemblies before an "ultimate authority," the God of Israel. Deuteronomy 9:10, for example, records the first occurrence of the *ekklēsia* as a decisive moment in the history of Israel when the people were assembled before Jehovah at Sinai where he covenanted with them as his people.

Later assemblies of the people renew this *ekklēsia* of the Lord and are sometimes called the "assembly of the Lord" (Deu. 23:1-4), "assembly of God" (Neh. 13:1), "assembly of the people of the Lord" (Jud. 20:2), "assembly of the holy ones" (Ps. 149:1), "the people of Jehovah."[8] The importance of this *ekklēsia* as a holy assemblage unto the Lord is further demonstrated by the fact that those with bodily defects cannot enter (Deu. 23:1ff.).

Although *ekklēsia* was used mostly to translate the Hebrew equivalent, *qahal*, another Hebrew word that came to approximate in meaning is *edah*. *Edah*, however, was used to translate *synagogē*, the Hebrew word for "congregation." Unlike *qahal* which denotes the "assembly of the Lord," *edah* was used mostly in the sense of the Jewish people as a community, the

---

7. William Stewart, *The Nature and Calling of the Church* (1958:6).
8. Dean Gilliland, *Pauline Theology and Mission Practice* (1983:183).

assembly of the community, and finally for the building where the group met.[9]

The above analysis, therefore, suggests that while *qahal* (*ekklēsia*) was a word with theological potential in the sense that it described Israel as the people of God, *edah* functioned more as a name or a technical term for Jewish communities. Giles' position is, therefore, an agreeable one when he suggests that "[t]he early Christians generally found the word *synagōgē* uncongenial because this was a name for Jewish communities, and the buildings they met in, and so its close associate, *ekklēsia*, was preferred."[10]

Ekklēsia in the New Testament

Ekklēsia in the New Testament generally does not have as much emphasis in pre-Pauline conceptions as in the writings and usage of the apostle. The word occurs only in one of the four gospels, Matthew, and is used only two times in that gospel (16:18; 18:17). Considered along with its Pauline conceptions, however, the word has a basic two-fold meaning. First, it refers in some sense to a universal context as we can infer from Jesus' statement, "Upon this rock I will build my church" (Mt 16:18). Then it takes on a specific local context as in Paul's reference to, for example, "the church of the Thessalonians" (1 Th. 1:1). It is, therefore, important to do a brief analysis of the word in both its pre-Pauline and Pauline conceptions.

Ekklēsia in the Gospels

As I have already indicated, the word *ekklēsia* is confined to two passages of Matthew in the Gospels. We see its first occurrence in Matthew 16:18. Following Peter's confession, "You are the Christ, the Son of the living God," Jesus' response was, "On this rock I will build my church, and the gates of Hades shall not prevail against it." The precise meaning of Jesus' response has become a subject of hermeneutical controversy especially when consideration is given to the polemics deriving from later Christian

---

9. J.W. Roberts, "The Meaning of *Ekklesia* in the New Testament" (1972:34).
10. Kevin Giles, *What On Earth Is the Church?* (1995:25). Everett Ferguson also draws the same conclusion, *The Church of Christ: A Biblical Ecclesiology for Today* (1996:130-131). For more detailed discussions of this topic, see also J.A. Hort, *The Christian Ecclesia* (1914); and George Johnston, *The Doctrine of the Church in the New Testament* (1943).

history. My understanding, however, is the absolute universal sense of Jesus' usage of *ekklēsia* in this passage.

Although many scholars hold the view that its use by Jesus is an anachronism, depicting it strictly as a post-resurrection institution. This notwithstanding, its use within the context of Matthew 16:18 presupposes a messianic community which Jesus was already beginning to assemble at this time in his ministry.[11] Christ's church (*ekklēsia*), in this sense, is not limited to the assembly of Jesus' disciples alone but includes the great company of those who confess his messiahship. Our understanding of Christ's lordship of the universal church is further heightened by Jesus' promise of resurrection. The full force of evil will come against this divinely instituted community, but so powerful will the Messiah's people be that the opposition from the "gates of Hades" must give way before them.

This interpretation runs contrary to Oscar Cullmann and the Roman Catholic position on the papacy and the church. The identity of the "rock" on which the *ekklēsia* is to be founded is not on Peter (*petros*) but on the divine revelation of Peter's confession. That is, the truth about the Messiahship of Jesus that was revealed to Peter. Peter's "reward," however, does not stop at this divine revelation but also includes his future faithful stewardship of the Christ he has professed. He will be given the heavenly "keys" to "bind" and to "loose" (Mt. 16:18-19). Thus when Peter and all those who belong to the messianic community (the *ekklēsia*) are in obedience and in faithful stewardship to their Lord, Christ will recognize this and deal accordingly to them.

The second reference to the *ekklēsia* in the Gospels is Matthew 18:15-17. Unlike Jesus' usage of *ekklēsia* in chapter 16 that has both futuristic and universal connotations, the usage of *ekklēsia* in chapter 18 is rather present and local. Since it is virtually impossible to report one's brother's fault to the universal church, it makes sense to conclude then that the passage is referring to how the followers of Jesus are to settle disputes in a given *ekklēsia*. Hort puts it well when he states, "[t]he actual precept is hardly

---

11. R. Bowen Ward, "Ekklesia: A Word Study" (1958:164-179); Geoffrey Preston, *Faces of the Church: Meditations on a Mystery and Its Images* (1997:9); and J.W. Roberts, "The Meaning of *Ekklesia* in the New Testament" (1972:29).

intelligible if the *ekklēsia* meant is not the Jewish community, apparently the Jewish local community, to which the injured person and the offender belonged."[12] Even then, the universal reasonableness of this "principle holds good in a manner for all time."[13]

Ekklēsia in the Pauline Epistles

Ekklēsia is used 62 times in the Pauline corpus, and generally refers to "the reality of the Christian community" or "to the groups of those who met in the name of Christ."[14] Paul explicitly or implicitly used *ekklēsia* in various contexts. Although the meaning he attaches to *ekklēsia* depends on each particular context, his use is distinguished from the regular unconstitutional assembly (Ac. 19:32) or the political assembly (Ac 19:39, 41) as we see in other New Testament texts. For Paul, the *ekklēsia* "is in God the Father and in the Lord Jesus Christ" and are given four different expressions (1 Th. 1:1).[15]

Ekklēsia as a Local Assembly or Congregation

The first of Paul's usage, in chronological ordering, appears in 1 Thessalonica 1:1 and refers to the local congregation of the Christians at Thessalonica. In this case, and in many other similar instances, Paul's *ekklēsia* is "not a metaphor, but a term descriptive of an identifiable object."[16] For example, Paul's strong requests ("I charge you") to the believers at Thessalonica that his letter be read "to all the brothers" clearly indicates that he has a specific assembly in mind, the assembly of Christians at Thessalonica (1 Th. 5:25-27). Other instances of Paul's *ekklēsia* in reference to an identifiable reality include "the church in Cenchrea" (Rom. 16:1), "the church of God in Corinth" (1 Co. 1:2; 2 Co. 1:1), and "the church of the Laodiceans" (Col. 4:16).

---

12. F.J.A. Hort, *The Christian Ecclesia* (1914:10).
13. Hort (1914:10).
14. See Dean Gilliland, *Pauline Theology and Mission Practice* (1983:187); and James Dunn, *The Theology of Paul the Apostle* (1998:537).
15. See R. Bowen Ward "Ekklesia: A Word Study" (1958); and Gerald Hawthorne, Ralph Martin, and Daniel Reid, *Dictionary of Paul and His Letters* (1993:124-126).
16. Hawthorne, Martin, and Reid (1993:124).

Ekklesiai: Geographic and Generic

Paul also uses *ekklesiai* in the plural sense when he wishes to refer to more than one church. This plural usage, however, can be further subdivided into two categories: *ekklesiai* with reference to a larger geographical area,[17] and as a generic term.[18] First, Paul employs the plural word (*ekklesiai*) when he wishes to make a reference to a group of churches within a larger geographical area such as "the churches of Asia" (1 Co. 16:19), "the churches in Galatia" (1 Co. 16:1; Gal. 1:1), "the churches in Macedonia" (2 Co. 8:1), and "the churches of Judea" (Gal. 1:22; 1 Th. 2:14).

Second, Paul uses *ekklesiai* in a generic sense. For example, in addressing the issue of conduct in nonessential matters, he urges the Corinthians to have a tender concern for all, *Jews, Greeks* and *the church of God*, so as not to "cause anyone to stumble" (1 Co. 10:32). This intentionally inclusive language does not seem to address any of the "old categories" (Jews and Gentiles) but to a "new category" of those "being saved."[19]

Ekklēsia in the House

The third expression of *ekklēsia* in the Pauline corpus refers to those of smaller groups. Examples include "the church that meets at [the house of Priscilla and Aquila]" in Rome (Rom. 16:3-5), of the same couple in Ephesus (1 Co. 16:19), that of Nympha in Laodicea (Co. 4:15), and that of Philemon in Colosse (Phl. 2).

Ekklēsia as a Heavenly and Eschatological Entity

Paul's other usage of *ekklēsia* can be interpreted in the "already-not yet" eschatological framework. In a sense, Paul considers the earthly, historical *ekklēsia* to be a preliminary and partial ("already") rescuing "from the dominion of darkness" (Col. 1:12-14), with very important earthly responsibilities, shape and form (Col. 3:4; 4:6) striving towards eschatological ("not yet") reunion with Christ, "the head of the body, that

---

17. R. Bowen Ward, "Ekklesia: A Word Study" (1958:170).
18. Gerald Hawthorne, Ralph Martin, and Daniel Reid, *Dictionary of Paul and His Letters* (1993:124).
19. Gordon Fee, *The First Epistle to the Corinthians* (1987:489).

is the church" (Col. 1:18; 3:1; 3-4). This future *ekklēsia* is the "Jerusalem on high," an allegorical reference to the old Jewish personification of the holy city as the mother of many children (Gal. 4:26ff.).[20] "Christ is all, and is in all" in this eschatological *ekklēsia*, and in him "there is no Greek or Jew, circumcised or uncircumcised, barbarian, Scythian, slave or free" (Col. 3:11).

Paul, Israel, and the Church

The relationship between Israel and the church has become a crucial reference point in systematic theology, especially among dispensationalists and non-dispensationalists. It is not our intention, and neither is it within the scope of this work, to engage in the dispensationalist argument of a spiritual absorption of God's promises to Israel by the church. Our attempt in this work is to apply the term ("already-not yet") to interpret Paul's understanding of the relation between the earthly *ekklēsia* and the heavenly, future *ekklēsia*.

It should be noted that Paul's primary application of *ekklēsia* has to do with "the assembly of God" composed of Jews, Gentiles or a mixture of both. In such instances, "there is no indication that the *ekklēsia* is divided into *ekklesiai*, or vice versa."[21] Rather, the reality of the church for Paul finds expression and continuity in its universality with Christ as the head of the body (Eph. 1:22; Col. 1:24). Furthermore, this reality is metaphorically expressed in his application of the household code such as the unity between husband and wife in becoming "one flesh" (Eph. 5:31).[22]

---

20. For details, see Rudolf Schnackenburg, *The Church in the New Testament* (1965:84).
21. Roy Ward, "Ekklesia: A Word Study" (1958:170).
22. For an extensive systematic theology written by a dispensationalist, see Lewis Sperry Chafer, *Systematic Theology*, 8 vols. (1947). See also Robert Saucy, *The Case for Progressive Dispensationalism* (1993); Craig A. Blaising and Darrell L. Bock, *Dispensationalism, Israel and the Church* (1992); Arnold Fruchtenbaum, *Israelology: The Missing Link in Systematic Theology* (1992); and John S. Freiberg, *Continuity and Discontinuity: Perspectives on the Relationship Between the Old and New Testaments* (1988).

Having attempted an analysis of the different expressions undergirding the use of the word "church" in Scripture, I now turn to look at some selected New Testament churches in their different contexts. By so doing I hope to find those "relevant clues" in the attempt to formulate a theory of contextual ecclesiology and to establish the observation that the church by her calling and nature exists at the center of the continuum between Scripture and context.

Luke-Acts: The Primitive Church in Jerusalem

The Christian community in Jerusalem had a position of special privilege among the Jewish Christian communities of primitive times. As a parent-church of all the later communities, we gain insights into the beginnings of Christianity, not merely as a religion, but also as a system of life and action. It is, therefore, proper that we begin our discussion by setting the context of the church within its historical significance.

The Context of the Church

There is much dispensational distinction regarding the *actual* birthday of the church. While some scholars have ascribed the birth of the church to the Pentecost event, others see it as a significant event that functioned only as a "reconstitution of the church." The latter view holds that the Old Testament sacerdotal *kahal* has been replaced by the witnessing *ekklēsia* of the New Testament.[23] Both arguments have been given considerable attention.[24] However, there is need to place both the Old and the New

---

23. Harry Boer, *Pentecost and the Missionary Witness of the Church* (1955:105).
24. Following are a few that argue the Pentecostal constitution of the Church: George E. Ladd, *A Theology of the new Testament* (1993); W.L. Knox, *The Acts of the Apostles* (1948); G.B. Caird, *The Apostolic Age* (1955); E.F. Harrison, *The Apostolic Church* (1985); Dean S. Gilliland, *Pauline Theology and Mission Practice* (1983); R. Schnackenburg, *The Church in the New Testament* (1965); Chester K. Lehman, *Biblical Theology: New Testament* (1998). For a perspective that considers the Pentecost as merely "the inauguration of the evangelistic activity of the Christian Church," see Arthur McGiffert, *A History of Christianity in the Apostolic Age* (1906).

Testaments in a larger perspective of redemptive history, with the beginning of the church as the climatic point in that history.[25]

Pentecost and the Historical Significance of Jerusalem

When consideration is given to Luke's account of Jesus' valedictory charge to his disciples not to "leave Jerusalem, but wait for the gift my Father promised" (Ac. 1:4), and the response this elicited from the disciples about the restoration of the kingdom to Israel (Ac. 1:6), Luke places the church's origin, and growth firmly in history. The promise of the Holy Spirit and the geographical framework of Spirit-empowered witnessing will start from Jerusalem and then progress to the "uttermost part of the world" (Ac. 1:8). In this scheme of salvation history, Jerusalem takes a central place in the salvation occurrence and also represents some kind of continuity between Israel and the church.

In fact, New Testament scholars have observed that Luke "uses geography as a literary and theological instrument. The center of his story is the city of Jerusalem. The whole movement . . . is *toward* Jerusalem."[26] For example, in the infancy account, Jesus is presented in the Jerusalem temple (Lk. 2:22), he was discovered there after being lost (Lk. 2:41-51), the Matthean account of the temptation of Jesus is reversed by Luke so that it climaxed in Jerusalem (Lk. 4:9), at transfiguration, Jesus' journey and death is foretold to happen at Jerusalem (Lk. 9:31), and after resurrection, Jesus informs his disciples to remain in Jerusalem.

The same centrality of Jerusalem controls the book of Acts. The witnessing to Judea, Samaria, and to the end of the earth is *away from* Jerusalem (chapters 1-7), evangelization starts from Jerusalem (chapters 8-28) and circles back to Jerusalem (Ac. 12:25; 15:2; 18:22; 19:21; 20:16; 21:13; 25:1).[27]

---

25. Conzelmann has observed that in Luke-Acts history is divided into three stages: the period of Israel, the period of Jesus, and the period of the church, which is the greatest period of sacred history. See his work, *The Theology of St Luke* (1960).
26. Luke T. Johnson, *The Writings of the New Testament* (1999:220).
27. Johnson (1999:220).

Events on the day of Pentecost left no one with any doubts that the time had fully come for the promised Holy Spirit. The arrival of the Holy Spirit was accompanied by miraculous manifestations such as the "sound like the blowing of a violent wind," and a linguistic diversity that crosses the Palestinian borders into other "native language[s]" (Ac. 2:2-12). The tongues of fire that divided and rested on each of them not only suggested unity, but to a greater degree represented the universal scope of the new experience.

Peter's interpretation of Pentecost in light of the eschatological event announced by the prophet Joel (Ac. 2:16-21; Joel 2:28-32) demonstrates further the continuity between Israel and the church. It also carries an appeal that would influence the Jews in the direction of a favorable view of the church.[28] The Pentecost experience brings to fulfillment under the present dispensation that which Yahweh had promised his people (Ac. 2:16). It also defines many of the Old Testament pre-exilic prophecies of the eschatological event of the "last days" when God's rule will be established in all the earth, and all nations will worship the God of Israel (Isa. 2:2-4). It is a messianic future in the life of Israel when they will be saved under the rule of their king, which is the messianic King from the dynasty of David.

Part of this messianic Kingship was the coming of the Holy Spirit, and Peter's sermon thus affirms that *the last days* of eschatological salvation have come "for all people." The central motif of Acts in this respect is the development of the church from an assembly of a Jewish sect to a universal church through the exaltation and enthronement of Jesus, the messiah (Ac. 2:22ff.). In this "Pentecostal reconstitution of the church,"[29] Luke places the church in the context of redemptive history and the task to which it has been called (Ac. 1:8).

The micro *ekklēsia* made up of the disciples of Jesus, the women accompanying Mary, the mother of Jesus, and his brothers, has now become a new fellowship of a universal people, united in the Spirit. There is, therefore, more claim than to simply argue that Pentecost defines the

---

28. Donald Guthrie, *New Testament Introduction* (1990:367).
29. Harry Boer, *Pentecost and the Missionary Witness of the Church* (1955:104).

birthday of the church. Rather, one can argue that "[t]he coming of the Spirit and the church are inseparable."[30]

The church, therefore, is not a religious institution but is a creation of the Spirit of God in which heterogeneous groupings are joined together in a fellowship with Jesus and with each other. As Ladd rightly remarks, "The baptism with the Spirit is the act of the Holy Spirit joining together into a spiritual unity people of diverse racial extractions and diverse social backgrounds so that they form the body of Christ, the *ekklēsia*."[31]

Composition of the Jerusalem Church[32]

Studies on Jerusalem as an ancient city in the Roman period have expressed a common belief that it was a very diverse city both sociologically and culturally.[33] How then did the Jerusalem church reflect this socio-economic and cultural diversity? Put in another way, how did the socio-economic and cultural character of the city, Jerusalem, correspond to the composition of the church in Jerusalem?

Drawing from the works of historians, theologians, and archeologists, David Fiensy has observed, "the primitive church reflected to a great extent the rich diversity of Jerusalem itself."[34] In other words, the church was pluralistic in character, drawing its membership from among the different socio-economic and cultural matrix of the society. There were property owners who, in our contemporary method of social stratification, would suffice for the middle class. Examples of this class include Barnabas, Ananias, and Sapphira who possessed lands (Ac. 4:36f; 5:1), Mary, mother

---

30. George E. Ladd, *The Young Church* (1964:54).
31. George E. Ladd, *A Theology of the New Testament* (1993:384).
32. I acknowledge David Fiensy, whose work has largely influenced the perspective adopted here. See his work, "The Composition of the Jerusalem Church" (1995:213-234).
33. For works in this area, see J. Wilkinson, "Ancient Jerusalem, Its Water Supply and Population" (1974:33-51); M. Broshi, "Estimating the Population of Ancient Jerusalem" (1978:10-15); P. King, "Jerusalem" (1992:753). F.J. Foakes-Jackson and K. Lake, *The Beginnings of Christianity* (1920-33); and W.L. Blevins, "The Early Church: Acts 1-5" (1974:463-474).
34. David Fiensy, "The Composition of the Jerusalem Church" (1995:214).

of John Mark, owned a slave and a house large enough to serve as a place of assembly for the primitive church (Ac. 12:12-17).³⁵

The church also finds appeal among the outcast and marginal elements of society; for example, the beggars and the diseased people healed by the apostles (Ac. 3:1-10; 5:12-16). There were also significant numbers of impoverished people like the widows in Acts 6:1, other transient and destitute persons cared for by the church (Ac. 2:44f; 4:34), and also servile members like Rhoda (Ac. 12:13).

There can be no question to the fact that non-Jews also have their place in the church. Among the perplexed crowd that experienced the Pentecost event were also Gentiles from different nations (Ac. 2:7-12) who believed and were baptized in response to Peter's preaching that day—a total of three thousand (Ac. 2:41). In a few weeks the number had increased to five thousand men, not including women and children. Perhaps one of the best accounts of Luke was the brotherly recognition granted the uncircumcised Cornelius by the Jerusalem Council. Confronted by the council over his table fellowship with the Gentile, Peter's explanation of the Spirit coming upon the Cornelius brought a new reality to the Jerusalem church that God was now granting "even Gentiles repentance unto life" (Ac. 11:18).

In spite of the socio-economic and cultural differences, the young church was a community bearing a family character, the members' commitment to unity was inescapable, and thus was to an extent outwardly distinct group.

Contextual Issues in the Jerusalem Church

As I have already observed, the extended narrative of Acts provides for us a framework within which the church's orientation and direct continuity with Israel can be situated. It also provides us with contextual issues that arose as a result of the church's historical affiliation to Israel. Since the church's conception of identity is rooted in specific salvation history, continuity between her Jewish roots and the fledging Gentile frontiers, therefore, depends largely on how well these contextual issues are reconciled.

---

35. Fiensy (1995:227).

Legalism Battle: Is Salvation by Law or by Grace?

A major and threatening contextual issue that had to be resolved can best be described in the words of James Dunn. According to him, it is one of "classic confrontation between old revelation, confirmed by centuries of history, and a new insight, given . . . in the course of an expanding, developing mission."[36] Luke states very clearly that certain Jewish believers, allegedly representing the Jerusalem church, believed circumcision as axiomatic for the salvation of Gentiles and a requirement for sharing in Israel's blessings (Ac. 15:1).

Circumcision as Identity Marker

Circumcision is "Israel's essential identity marker" and constitutes its distinctiveness as a people. Laid down in Genesis 17:9-14, it is an everlasting covenant in their flesh, reminding them of the covenant between Yahweh, the God of Israel, and the patriarch Abraham and his descendants. To disregard circumcision, therefore, is to break the covenant and be deprived of the promises of Yahweh, losing in the process their sense of identity and ultimate status as God's people (Gen. 17:10-14).

To the protagonists of this unbroken tradition, the Jewish character of Christianity not only has to be secured but its continuity and efficacy have to be linked to this unbroken tradition. This poses a threatening situation for both the young church and the Gentile mission, which by this time was experiencing an impressive growth. Would Gentile believers be required to be circumcised in order to be justified? If that became a requirement for church membership, how then was one to be justified before God; through circumcision or by the saving faith in Jesus Christ?

Two key issues are central to this contextual issue. First, there is the threat of division in the church and the possibility of one side becoming apostate. Second, and perhaps the more important, is the deep theological concern and the soteriological implications this raises for both the mother church at Jerusalem and for the fledging Gentile mission. The question arising in

---

36. For details, see James Dunn, *The Acts of the Apostles* (1996:198-199).

both issues is the future assumption that one has to change cultures in order to be a follower of Jesus.

The Ministry of the Jerusalem Church

The life of the primitive church in Jerusalem provides us with a paradigm for ministry. We gain insight into the nature and strategy for ministry issues that become the test case against which our modern conception of ministry stands or falls (Jude 3-4). The interpretation of the movement up to Jerusalem, and from Jerusalem by many commentators as the story of Christian missions is not an inappropriate one. As important as this might be, however, it robs the book of Acts of its central theological purpose. As J.C. O'Neill has observed, "Acts is not primarily a history of the Christian missions. It is the account of how the church discovered its true nature in the way God dealt with it on the path from Jerusalem."[37]

The Lucan narrative sets this ideal for ministry with three distinct characteristics: the liturgical life and worship of the primitive church, harmony and community sharing, and the charismatic ministry of the apostles (Ac. 2:42, 46; 4:32-35; 5:12-16).

Liturgical Life and Worship

The early chapters of Acts provide us with the primitive church's patterns of behavior and piety that owe as much to pragmatic concerns as to dogma. In this embrace of a new life, the believers "devoted themselves to the apostle's teaching and to the fellowship, to the breaking of bread and to prayer" (Ac. 2:42). Four elements appear to characterize a Christian gathering in the primitive church: devotion to the apostles' teaching (*didache*), fellowship, breaking of bread, and prayer.[38]

First, "the apostles' teaching" or *didache* was central to the belief of the new believers and distinguished them from the adherents of other

---

37. J.C. O'Neill, *The Theology of Acts in its Historical Setting* (1961:170).
38. I. Howard Marshall, *The Acts of the Apostles: An Introduction and Commentary* (1980:83).

religions. Ladd summarizes this well when he remarks, "[the apostles' teaching] included the meaning of the life, death, and exaltation of Jesus, his enthronement as messianic King and Lord inaugurating the messianic age of blessing, and the future eschatological consummation."[39]

The second element was their sense of "fellowship." The reference is not simply to the apostle's fellowship or as something that the apostles were now opening up to accommodate more people; rather it denotes "the common life shared by believers."[40] The quality of their fellowship was one of active participation by all "rather than merely a feeling of oneness."[41]

The third element, "the breaking of bread" (Ac. 2:42, 46), was markedly an act of worship in the primitive church with a twofold expression. First, it recalled the Upper Room and other incidents in which Jesus resumed table fellowship with his disciples (Lk. 24:35; Jn. 21:12). Second, the common fellowship meals "form a bond with the Lord and impose the obligation of holy service for his sake."[42]

These fellowship meetings not only commemorate proximity and presence with the risen Lord, but also help to foster "inner cohesion among the faithful." As Schnackenburg has remarked, "In this . . . the nature of the 'Church of God' as the holy 'assembly' of the Lord or of the people of God found particularly clear expression."[43] Finally, prayer was an important part of their daily life, both in temple worship and in private meetings (Ac. 2:46).

Harmony and Community Sharing

The distinctive expression of fellowship in the Jerusalem community has been a subject of much controversy in New Testament studies. Some scholars have described the practice of sharing of possessions among the believers as primitive communism. It is, however, questionable if this is a fair assessment or the right word to use in describing the quality of

---

39. George E. Ladd, *A Theology of the New Testament* (1993:386).
40. Everett Harrison, *The Apostolic Church* (1985:179).
41. Harrison (1985:180).
42. Rudolf Schnackenburg, *The Church in the New Testament* (1965:43).
43. Schnackenburg (1965:43).

fellowship among these believers. First, we know that to be considered a communist system, whether primitive or otherwise, requires a "system of operation" to be put in place to ensure continuity. This was not the case with the Jerusalem church. Second, donations and contributions were not enforced but voluntary as the case of Ananias and Sapphira clearly indicates (Ac. 5:1-11).

Despite contemporary intellectual exercise, the more important thing is to recognize that an important element of early Christian behavior was the unity of mind and purpose.[44] This signified the mark of spiritual unity in worship that transcended the bounds of private possessions. The primitive church was compelled by such an outward expression of love that none considered their property as their own. Instead, holders of property held their wealth at the service of the church and lavishly used it for the good of all. In other words, the driving force was the recognition that the love of property was subordinate to the love of the Christian family.

The fact that Barnabas is especially commended for selling his field suggests that such generosity was a very rare occurrence and was completely voluntary. Similarly, the case of Ananias and Sapphira in Acts 5:4 clearly indicates that the couple was not condemned for failing to turn all their proceeds to the church but for pretending to be more generous than they really were.[45] The misconduct of Ananias and Sapphira, therefore, introduces us to different aspects in the life of the primitive church.

First, their action "underscored the necessity for holy living required of those engaged in worship."[46] Peter's unassuming stand portrays a powerful impulse for moral uprightness in which sin is taken seriously. It

---

44. Emil Brunner's criticism that "this kind of self-giving brotherly love was . . . exaggerated and unrealistic . . . and too direct a translation of *agape*" falls short of the character of love the disciples had learnt from Jesus and have carried over into their own apostolic teachings. Also, to blame the "impoverishment of the Jerusalem community" on this practice is a little over-reactionary. Rather than view this practice as purely communist, it should be considered that the primitive church was compelled to share the messianic blessings promised to the elect children of God. For details on Emil Brunner, see his work, *The Christian Doctrine of the Church, Faith, and the Consummation* (1962:33ff.).
45. Arthur McGiffert, *A History of Christianity in the Apostolic Age* (1906:67).
46. Chester Lehman, *Biblical Theology: New Testament* (1998:255).

also demonstrates the church's responsibility to deal with misconduct and ethical issues among the body of believers.[47]

The Theology of the Jerusalem Church[48]

The theology of the Jerusalem church corresponds exactly to the contextual character of the church. I have shown that in Lucan scheme of redemptive history, Jerusalem takes a central place in the salvation occurrence and also represents some kind of continuity between Israel and the Church. I have also examined the context of the Jerusalem church as comprising both Jewish and Gentile believers. The key theological issue, therefore, is one that seeks to reconcile the significance of circumcision to Jewish believers with the conditions placed on Gentile believers by which they could be admitted to full religious fellowship. In this instance, I refer once more to the Jerusalem church Council.

The Jerusalem Church Council

The Jerusalem Council requires delegates from the conflicting parties in deliberations that are pivotal to the very existence of the church. On the one hand are the legalistic Judaizers who see the continuity of Jewish tradition as essential to the Christian faith, while on the other are those of Paul and Barnabas leading the liberal Gentile delegation (Ac. 15:1-2). Two issues deserve special consideration here: circumcision versus salvation and the apostolic decree.

Legalism Battle: Is Salvation by Law or by Grace?

Here I want to revisit the issue of circumcision in the legislative battle between law and grace as the requirement for salvation and of admittance into the eschatological community. The issue of circumcision appears

---

47. See also Ernst Von Dobschütz, *Christian Life in the Primitive Church* (1904).
48. A full theology of Luke-Acts would have to deal with issues such as salvation history, Christology, the Spirit and the church, missiological ecclesiology, and persecution. My aim in this work is not to attempt this comprehensive exposition but to focus my theological interpretation on contextual issues that arose in the life of the Jerusalem church.

on the surface to be solely a contextual or cultural one. As much as it is a contextual issue, it is, however, one of deep theological concern with soteriological implications. Three factors make the circumcision issue a theological problem. First, the requirement of circumcision would greatly hinder the work of evangelism that had begun among the Gentiles (Gal. 2:2). Second, it poses a threat to unity, with the possibility of division and factions. Third, and perhaps the greatest, is the issue of justification by saving faith in Jesus Christ (Gal. 5:2-4).

That the Jerusalem Council reached a genuine consensus "not to burden" the Gentile believers with circumcision as basis for admission into full Christian fellowship holds itself to the fact "that God had taken an initiative which they could not gainsay."[49] This is where the lengthy account of Cornelius' conversion becomes the "decisive precedent" in the circumcision issue. Dunn here refers to Peter as "the bridge-man who spanned and held together the Gentile mission of Paul and the conservatism of the Jerusalem church under the leadership of James."[50]

The *initiative* was that God had shown Peter through the vision of the sheet filled with animals that no person is unclean in his eyes. Consequently, Peter was "forced by clear directive and approval from God to accept a Gentile as a new member of the new movement (indicated in baptism), without requiring him first to be circumcised" (Ac. 10:9-48).[51] The Cornelius episode was, however, not an isolated event when we take into account other similar incidents as confirmed by Paul and Barnabas with regards to their Gentile mission (Ac. 15:12). These occurrences were seen as having divine approval in that God had given the Holy Spirit to the Gentiles "just as he did to us" (Ac. 15:8; 11:15-17).

James alludes to the legitimacy of Peter's experience with Cornelius and also considers it to be the fulfillment of God's eschatological restoration of his people in the Messiah as prophesied by Amos (Ac. 15:15-18; Amos 9:11-12). More importantly, the gift of the Spirit was considered God's

---

49. I am indebted to James Dunn since my arguments here have built largely on his thesis. For details, see *The Acts of the Apostles* (1996:203, 195-211).
50. Dunn (1996:200).
51. Dunn (1996:200).

testimony of the Gentiles' acceptability to him, as well as an indication of the new paradigm concerning his redemptive purpose "in which the restoration of Israel would incorporate Gentiles . . . as also his people."[52]

By speaking of the Gentiles becoming "a people [*laos*]" for God's name (Ac. 15:14), James articulates the new understanding in which God radically redefines peoplehood or the people of God as coming from among all nations. As David Hesselgrave and Edward Rommen have observed, "it thus became apparent that salvation depended on the individual's relationship to God rather than to the tradition and institutions of any particular ethnic group."[53]

In summation, the results of the Jerusalem Council were a clear victory for the Holy Spirit. The Jerusalem church unanimously recognized that salvation was by grace alone and that the Gentiles needed only believe (Ac. 15:14-21). In the words of Dean Gilliland, this "was a radical move toward . . . contextualization [because] it signaled to Gentiles, as well as to Jews, that salvation no longer belonged only to Jews."[54] Dunn puts it equally well by interpreting the centrality of Acts 5:1-15 thus:

> that the grace of the Lord Jesus is both the necessary and the sufficient means of salvation for Jew and Gentile. The denial of any significance for ethnic or ritual factors enables unconditional recognition of every one's dependence equally on divine grace. Failure to acknowledge this is to "test"/resist God.[55]

The Apostolic Decree: Redefining the Covenant

The Jerusalem church Council did not make a total concession to the Gentile churches. Although the council recognized that circumcision was not a requirement for full Christian fellowship, it did send out to the Gentile

---

52. Dunn (1996:202).
53. David J Hesselgrave and Edward Rommen, *Contextualization: Meanings, Methods, and Models* (1989:11).
54. Dean Gilliland, *Pauline Theology and Mission Practice* (1983:39).
55. James Dunn, *The Acts of the Apostles* (1996:201-202).

churches a decree that "adopts some measure of Jewish legal prescriptions."[56] The first three prescriptions mentioned in Acts refer to food restrictions: to abstain from food that has been offered to idols (Ac. 15:20, 29; 21:25), to abstain from meat of animals which had been strangled and from which the blood had not been properly drained (Lev. 7:26-27; 17: 10-14). The fourth prescription was an ethical one and reflects on sexual immorality in general (Ac. 15:20), or of sexual union forbidden in Scripture (Lev. 18:6-18).

Facilitating Social Unity between Two Factions

There is much controversy in New Testament studies whether or not these restrictions are either ethical, ritualistic, or a combination of both.[57] Even more important is the interpretation that the decree is a "defeat" for Paul's teaching of "salvation through faith alone." Such an interpretation takes the Scripture, especially Acts 15:21, out of context. For Luke the decree cannot be considered burdensome nor surprising for Gentiles or "the resident alien" who, through their contact with the Synagogues, had become "familiar with the law of Moses and the sort of ritual provision found there which provided a basis for interaction between Jews and Gentiles."[58]

The issue, therefore, is not so much a contention as to who *won* or *lost* at the conference but rather of the terms necessary to facilitate social intercourse between Jewish and Gentile believers "by encouraging at least a minimum of ritual cleanness."[59] The decision of the apostolic church council, therefore, played a vital role as the basis of mixed churches. Not only did the church survive the greatest threat of division and of splitting into small groups, it solved the problem of the relationship between Jews and Gentiles. The oneness of the church was thus reinforced, bringing both Jewish and Gentile believers together around the one table of the Lord.

---

56. Marcel Simon, "The Apostolic Decree and its Setting in the Ancient Church" (1969:460).
57. For an insightful study in this area, see Marcel Simon, "The Apostolic Decree and Its Setting in the Ancient Church" (1970:437-460).
58. John Polhill, *Paul and His Letters* (1999:116).
59. David J. Hesselgrave and Edward Rommen, *Contextualization: Meanings, Methods, and Models* (1989:11).

CHAPTER 9

The Apostolic Churches as Models for Appropriate Ecclesiology

I have emphasized the *a priori* developmental principle that one can understand what the church should be today only when one has a thorough grasp of what the church "has been" or "ought to be." Again, I want to continue to explore the biblical understanding of the church by looking at the apostolic churches, the contextual challenges they had to contend with, and the theological responses to these challenges. By so doing, I hope to draw normative clues for the contemporary church in its mission to becoming what it is already by faith, the church of Jesus Christ.

Christianity in Rome

The epistle to the Romans has undoubtedly received overwhelming attention in contemporary biblical scholarship, more than any of the other undisputed Pauline epistles.[1] Although several reasons could be advanced for this massive attention, one important feature that cannot be overlooked is its substantive theological treatise that has had incalculable influence on the construction of Christian theology from primitive times to the present. Similarly, Paul's authorship of Romans is not in serious question. How Christianity reached Rome, however, is problematic since neither Paul nor any of the other apostles founded the Roman church. Regardless as

---

1. For a compilation of insightful studies, see Karl Donfried's *The Romans Debate* (1991).

to the origin of the Roman church, it is proper to attempt an enquiry in biblical scholarship.

The Church in Rome

The epistle to the Romans provides us with the earliest witness of the existence of a church in Rome, yet the question of determining the origin of this church is cloaked in historical obscurity. Several views that suggest a possible reconstruction of how Christianity reached the capital city of the Roman Empire have been advanced. The earliest view, held by the Roman Catholics, claims that the apostle Peter founded the church. This claim is fundamentally flawed when compared with the historical evidence that puts the arrival of Peter in Rome several years after the church has been founded.[2]

Another view attributes the origin of the Roman church to the efforts of the visiting Roman Jews and Proselytes who may have been converted on the day of Pentecost (Ac. 2:10). This view, however, lacks validity since there is no instance in the Scripture which shows that these Pentecostal converts returned to Rome to establish a Christian church. Moreover, these people would require more than what they brought away from Pentecost to lay the foundations of a Christian church.[3]

Still others argue that several small groups of Christians including those families of Christians from Pauline churches in the East settled in Rome and gathered for worship, thus founding the Roman church.[4] Since there

---

2. Some Roman Catholic scholars are also beginning to give up this claim because of its inconsistency with history and internal evidence of the New Testament. For example, J.J. Castelot in his work, "Peter, Apostle, St." writes, "An old tradition that he spent 25 years in Rome is quite unacceptable. All that can be said with certainty is that he went to Rome and was martyred there" (1967:173-176). A similar view is expressed by Alfred Wikenhauser in his *New Testament Introduction*, "The Apostle Peter cannot have founded the community, for his arrival in Rome probably took place in the fifties at the earliest" (1963:399). For Protestant disputation, see Donald Guthrie, *New Testament Introduction* (1990); and D. Edmond Hiebert, *Introduction to the New Testament* (1977).

3. William Sandlay and Arthur C. Headlam, *A Critical and Exegetical Commentary on the Epistle to the Romans* (1902:xxviii).

4. For details, see D. Edmond Hiebert, *Introduction to the New Testament* (1977);

is no allusion to an initial evangelization in Rome by any particular group of missionaries, it is reasonable to infer that the church in Rome came about through the activities of Christian laity who shared the gospel as they pursued their vocations or business. Priscilla and Aquila are a good example. Although the couple did not take the gospel to Rome, they, nevertheless, demonstrate how Christian laity shared the gospel wherever they went. As a couple, they seem to have taken the gospel from Rome to Corinth (Ac. 18: 2-3), and also to Ephesus (Ac. 18:26).[5] This and other activities of the laity are general probabilities for the origin of the church at Rome.

The Context of the Church

The epistle to the Romans manifests an antithesis that has led to differing conclusions on the context of the Roman church. Here I refer to the inconsistencies and conjectures regarding the composition of the Roman church. Was the church composed predominantly of Jewish-Christians or was it a predominantly Gentile congregation or a mixture of both? The school of criticism is widely divided over the church's composition. It is, however, important to place the issue in a proper perspective since our perceptions of this have direct ramifications for an overall understanding of the theological construct of the epistle.

Mainly Jewish Christians

Ever since Ferdinand Baur's supposition that the Roman church was mainly a Jewish-Christian congregation, discussions on the composition of the Roman church have generated more debate than did the origin of Christianity in Rome. Baur arrives at this conclusion by emphasizing the centrality of the addresses in the epistle which he believed had been made to Jewish Christians who had emerged from the Jewish community in Rome (1873).[6] Although this thesis has met with considerable opposition

---

and C.E.B. Cranfield, *A Critical and Exegetical Commentary on the Epistle to the Romans* (1975).

5. See John Polhill, *Paul and His Letters* (1999:279).

6. Ferdinand C. Baur, *Paul the Apostle of Jesus Christ: His Life and Work, His Epistles and His Doctrine* (1873). For further discussion in this area, see Wolfgang Wiefel's work, "The Jewish Community in Ancient Rome and the Origins of Roman Christianity" (1991:85-101).

within and outside his Tübingen School, he continues to appeal to scholars who believe that the Roman church composed mainly of Jewish Christians or at least formed the majority.[7]

Among several reasons that have been advanced for this position, a more compelling one takes Romans 9-11 as its point of reference. The evidence is made here of the debate between the Pauline gospel, the Old Testament, and rabbinic Judaism as dealing with issues that are more comprehensible and applicable to Jews than to Gentiles. This has been the strongest argument by the proponents in supporting the argument that the Roman church was predominantly Jewish Christians.

Nevertheless, there is no consensus among New Testament scholars. Some consider this argument to be "quite unjustified" on the premise that the "question of Israel was the question of God's faithfulness to his promises, and as such was the concern of the Gentile Christian just as much as it was the concern of the Jewish."[8]

Mainly Gentile Christians

Referring to indications supplied by the epistle itself, a second view argues that the church is either comprised primarily of Gentile Christians or that they are in the majority. There are inferences to Gentile elements that cannot be easily dismissed. For example, chapter 11:13-24 is a direct address to the Gentiles which, when compared with 11:28-31, provides strong indication of a Gentile Christian majority. Similarly, while in 1:5-7 the church at Rome is numbered "among all the Gentiles" who come under Paul's apostleship, 1:13-15 considers the apostle as being under obligation to preach to them so that he "might have harvest" among them just as he has had "among the other Gentiles."[9]

---

7. Among such scholars are Theodor Zahn, *Introduction to the New Testament* (1909); William Manson, *The Epistle to the Hebrews: An Historical and Theological Consideration* (1951); and T. Fahy, "St. Paul's Romans were Jewish Converts" (1960:182-191).

8. C.E.B. Cranfield, *A Critical and Exegetical Commentary on the Epistle to the Romans* (1975:19).

9. For a more detailed discussion, see J. Munck, *Paul and the Salvation of Mankind* (1959). See also William Sandlay and Arthur C. Headlam, *Critical and Exegetical Commentary on the Epistle to the Romans* (1902); and Werner Kümmel, *Introduction to the New Testament* (1984).

A Mixed Congregation

A third view, and perhaps the most probable, is that the Roman church was a mixed composition. The first evidence of this is the easy interchange of address by which the apostle addressed his audience, the Jews and the Gentiles alike. Apart from passages where Jews and Gentiles are mentioned together on the universal need of salvation (Rom. 1:14-16; 15:8-9), there are other references that pointedly suggest a mixed community. Romans 7:1 presumably addresses the Jews with its reference about those "who know the law," and "to those who are under the law" (3:19). Romans 11:13, on the other hand, is pointedly addressed to the Gentiles with the apostle's express declaration, "I speak to you Gentiles."

Perhaps a more striking indication of the Roman church as a mixed congregation is found in the greetings in chapter 16. There we have a collection of names that point to a mixture of nationalities. We have examples of Jewish names such as Aquila, Mary (Miriam), and Apelles. Andronicus and Junias and Herodion are described as "kinsmen" (tribesmen) of the apostle Paul. There are also Latin names as in the case of Urbanus, Ampliatus, Rufus, and Julia. The remaining ten names are, without any doubt, Greek names.[10]

One may not be able to determine with absolute certainty whether the majority of the Roman Christians were Jews or Gentiles. However, it is possible to conclude, as in the words of Cranfied, that "what is quite certain is that both the Jewish-Christian, and the Gentile-Christian, elements were considerable: it was clearly not a matter of an overwhelming majority and tiny minority."[11]

Contextual Issues in the Roman Church

Again, there are many differing interpretations over the exact situation of the Roman church and the reason for the writing of Romans. There are scholars like T.W. Manson, Günther Bornkamm, and Robert J. Karris who

---

10. For details, see William Sandlay, and Arthur C. Headlam, *A Critical and Exegetical Commentary on the Epistle to the Romans* (1902).
11. C.E.B. Cranfield, *A Critical and Exegetical Commentary on the Epistle to the Romans* (1975:21).

view Romans as a theological treatise. On the other side of the divide are also scholars such as Jacob Jervell, Wolfgang Wiefel, and Karl Donfried who insist that Romans is a situational or circular letter that relates to an audience in a similar way as in other Pauline letters.[12]

Yet others argue for a combination of purposes in the writing of Romans. That is, Paul was writing to address problems within the Roman church as well as out of his own personal concerns: the concerns of raising the support of a *unified* Roman church for his proposed mission trip to Spain and the concern of seeking the prayers of the Roman Christians with regards to his forthcoming trip to Jerusalem.[13]

Despite the irreconcilable differences among scholars, most believe that Romans is best understood when interpreted as a letter written to Rome on account of responding to the tension and dissension between the Jewish and Gentile segments of the church. This tension was one of animosity and division between the liberal-minded Gentile Christian majority (the "strong" in faith) and their unwilling attitude to have a fellowship with the "weak" in faith, the conservative Jewish Christian minority.[14]

James Dunn has helped to clarify the contrasting designations of the "strong" and the "weak." The "weak" were considered "weak in faith" not because they were weaker Christians but, precisely because they were holding to the "fundamental elements of their traditional faith and practice." On the contrary, the "strong" were so designated because like Abraham of old (Rom. 4:18-21), they trusted in God and Christ alone.[15]

Wolfang Wiefel seems to support the hypothesis of a Gentile majority. According to him, the Jewish Christians who had been expelled from Rome by Claudius in 49 CE, found upon their return during Nero's reign, a flourished and dominant Gentile Christian community who has established a new church structure different from the old synagogue fellowship. He

---

12. For details and references to the works of these scholars, see Karl Donfried's insightful compilation, *The Romans Debate* (1991).
13. John Polhill, *Paul and His Letters* (1991). For similar views in this regard, see F.F. Bruce, "The Romans Debate Continued" (1991:175-194), and A.J.M. Wedderburn, *The Reasons for Romans* (1988).
14. W.S. Campbell, "Why Did Paul Write Romans?" (1973:264-269).
15. James Dunn, *The Theology of Paul the Apostle* (1998:684).

considers Paul's letter a way of confronting the anti-Semitism present in the city and to encourage a Jewish-Gentile fellowship.[16]

Jewish/Gentile Disunity as a Contextual Issue

Romans 14:1-15-13 provides us with evidence as to the contextual problem that confronts the Roman church. The problem is one that has been rightly described as a "problem of the relation between faith and world view."[17] Although the problem divides the church along the contrasting titles of the "strong" and the "weak," it could well refer to a general designation that brings out the difference between segments of the church that are fundamentally opposed both in principle and in practice.[18] Not only are they fundamentally opposed in principle, their attitude is also described as judging and despising one another.

The "Weak" vis-à-vis the "Strong" in Faith[19]

As I have already mentioned, the "weak" are the converted Jews "whose Christianity does not relieve them of doubts in the exercise of Christian liberty" but rather on a dependence upon the Abrahamic covenant and on formal obedience to the Mosaic law.[20] Consequently, their weakness in faith consisted in the fact that they subjected themselves to dietary restrictions that placed strict vegetarianism over any kind of meat. They were not convinced that their faith could be supported without this God-pleasing practice (14:2). Similarly, they were not strong enough to view all days of the week as being equal. Instead, they honored some days, presumably the Sabbath and the Jewish festival days, as being more sacred than other days (14:5).

---

16. Wolfang Wiefel, "The Jewish Community in Ancient Rome and the Origins of Roman Christianity" (1991:85-101). For further discussion in this area, see A.J.M. Wedderburn, *The Reasons for Romans* (1988:54-65).

17. E. Käsemann, *Commentary on Romans* (1980:369).

18. Käsemann (1980:366).

19. For a detailed discussion on this issue, see Paul Minear, *The Obedience of Faith* (1971:8-23).

20. E. Käsemann, *Commentary on Romans* (1980:366).

The strong, on the other hand, stand in an antithetical position to the weak. They are the Gentile majority whose faith enabled them to exercise Christian liberty. They considered themselves strong in faith because of their freedom to eat anything without respect to dietary constraints (14:2, 14). Similarly, their religious freedom extended also to the calendar whereby all days are considered to be the same and equally sacred (14:5).

Disunity within the Church

The weak in faith constituted a problem to the unity of the church through their attitude of condemnation and accusation, while the strong added to it by abhorring the weak as incompatible with faith (14:4; 15:3). The result of these differing positions on the church, therefore, leaves little to the imagination. While the weak's "demands of both consistency and legality prevented table-fellowship and common worship with the strong," by scorning and despising the weak, the strong helps to stiffen the division thereby pushing the boundaries even further.[21]

The Ministry of the Roman Church

The New Testament provides evidence for a variety of forms of ministry in the first-century church. Although one cannot argue that the early church's ministry is necessarily normative in all instances, one can be sure that apostolic teachings certainly provide certain normative features that should appear in every expression of community life and ministry. The situation in the Roman church constitutes one of those instances where, although lacking the pattern of community life and ministry that is normative, yet is indicative of the meaning and pattern of church ministry. I will discuss the exhortation to the Roman church from two perspectives: sacrificial living as a mark of spiritual worship and the complemetarity of charismatic ministry.

---

21. Paul Minear, *The Obedience of Faith* (1971:9).

Sacrificial Living as a Mark of Christian Ministry

Although the division within the Roman church makes a formidable pattern of ministry an elusive one, by his allusion to sacrificial living Paul intends to set a corrective course for the Roman congregation. The corrective is the sacrificial offering of the body in its totality and not just in individual parts (12:1). Through his use of the cultic language, "offer" and "sacrifice," Paul wishes to contrast the Stoic and other philosophical polemics that intensify the "interiorizing of the ritual" with a fundamentally different understanding of true spiritual worship in which "bodily existence constitutively establishes worship."[22]

In other words, a true Christian worship is not one that is restricted to certain sacred practices or acts but one that has been "transformed" as to agree with "God's will to his praise in thought, will and act" (12:1-2).[23] Consequently, Paul reduces the Christian ministry to a simple description of doing God's will in the pattern of Christ to his Father (Jn. 6:38). It is at this stage every Christian is simultaneously sacrifice and priest (1 Pe. 2:8).[24]

Complementarity of Charismatic Ministry

There are many indications in the Pauline corpus that the concept of charisma is an important one to the apostle. This is demonstrated in the letters to his churches and in his address to the body of Christ. It is, therefore, not so surprising that he should exhort the Roman church on the significance of charisma in Christian ministry. Following his reference to the universal will of God for all believers expressed in the preceding two verses (12:1-2), Paul establishes further an identical universality of the priesthood of all believers and the divine authority for charismatic ministry (12:3-8).

While the charisma is a divinely given distinction for the individual, it is to be taken into the service of Christ and to facilitate the building up of his church. In other words, the capacities for charismatic service are not native to those who exercise them but are bestowed by the Spirit for the common energy of the church as the body of Christ. As Dunn has put it:

---

22. E. Käsemann, *Commentary on Romans* (1980:328).
23. Käsemann (1980:328).
24. Käsemann (1980:39).

> Each is a member of the body only in so far as the Spirit knits him into the corporate unity by the manifestation of grace through him. At no time did Paul conceive of two kinds of Christians—those who have the Spirit and those who do not. To be Christian in Paul's view was to be charismatic. One cannot be a member of the body without being a vehicle of the Spirit's ministry to the body.[25]

Consequently, the exercise of charismatic ministry must be mutual, devoid of arrogance, and reflecting soberness and satisfaction (12:3, 7-8).

The Theology of the Church

The contextual issue that I have pointed out as a problem of the relation between faith and world view is less a matter of ethnic strife than it was of differing theological positions. The consequence of these differing nuances for the Roman church was one of great division and one that required the apostle Paul to appeal precisely to the unity of God and his impartiality as the dynamics of a coherent Christian relationship. Many scholars agree that Paul was not driven to write the Romans by the need to support any of the warring factions. On the contrary, his guiding principle is theological and bothers on the unity of the church.[26]

Dynamics of a Coherent Christian Relationship

In responding to the division that was already ripping the Roman church apart, three issues deserve attention in our consideration of the apostolic construction of the dynamics of a coherent Christian relationship. These

---

25. James Dunn, *Unity and Diversity in the New Testament: An Inquiry into the Character of Earliest Christianity* (1990:110).
26. For details, see Wayne Meeks, *The First Urban Christians: The Social World of the Apostle Paul* (1983); Mark Seifrid, *Justification by Faith: The Origin and Development of a Central Pauline Theme* (1992); and Mark Reasoner, "The Theology of Romans 12:1-15:13" (1995:287-299).

dynamics fall under the rubric of the obligation of love, the call to worship, and the convergence in Christ.

The Obligation of Love

In his description of a functioning church, Paul sets the whole sequence of a coherent Christian relationship under the rubric of mutual forbearance in love. In his exhortation to the divided church, Paul first addresses the "strong" with regard to hospitality for the "weak" in faith. The strong, on one hand, are not only obligated to love but are to conduct themselves in a self-denying manner that does not cause hurtful feelings to their fellow weak Christian counterparts (14:3-4, 14-15, 21; 15:1-3). The weak, on the other hand, are obligated not to judge the strong for not sharing their scruples but to regard such practices as optional matters between the individual and God rather than as authoritative divine commands (14:3-4, 10-12).[27]

The Call to Worship

The injunction to "accept the one who is weak in faith" (14:1) is a call to the Roman church and an attempt by Paul to redefine what it means to be the people of God. To be the people of God is to be able to embrace divergent views and practices where there is no disposition to pass judgment on disputable matters. Instead, what the assembly needs is the "spirit of unity" so that in one accord ("with one heart and mouth") they may "glorify" God (15:5-6). Consequently, Paul echoes his earlier call for acceptance (14:1). But this time it takes on the form of an exhortation to both groups for a mutual acceptance of *all* "in accordance with Christ Jesus" as the one in and through whom fulfillment of covenant promise and gentile incoming have been made possible (15:7-13).[28]

Christ: The Point of Convergence[29]

Paul's overarching emphasis on unity for the divided church climaxes with his allusion to Christ. Two things are worthy of consideration in the reference

---

27. Francis Watson, *Paul, Judaism and the Gentiles: A Sociological Approach* (1986:97).
28. For details, see James Dunn, *Romans 9-16* (1988:846).
29. See James Edwards' commentary, *Romans* (1992:335-342).

to Jesus Christ. First, through his teaching and example, Jesus provided a model of self-denial and true acceptance of others (15:1-7). Thus, the exemplary life of Jesus becomes the basic hermeneutic for Christian worship and behavior and a focal point of unity within the church. Secondly, the plea for mutual acceptance and tolerance finds relevance in the universal dimension of Jesus' ministry.

Although Christ was a Jew by natural descent, his death and resurrection have a universal dimension that confirms God's faithfulness both to the Jews and also to the Gentiles. In other words, both the Jews and the Gentiles have now been brought into God's overall plan of salvation through his grace and by faith in Jesus Christ (15:7-13).[30]

Christianity in Corinth

I have affirmed Romans as Paul's major systematic doctrinal treatise in the construction of a Christian theology. By contrast, the epistles to the Corinthian church have a more pastoral and practical purpose for the church. Except for the way Paul refers to the cross and the resurrection, it is from the Corinthian epistles that we see the application of Paul's theological convictions expressed in the life of the church. As Findlay remarks about 1 Corinthians, it is "the doctrine of the cross in its social application."[31]

Since the purpose of this book is to present case studies of churches in the New Testament particularly as they relate to the *normative* (that which should be the ideal) and the *indicative* (that which ought to happen), my discussion on the Corinthian church will focus almost exclusively on 1 Corinthians. The reason for this is not far-fetched. 1 Corinthians presents an excellent case study for hermeneutical theories. It represents a church's encounter with practical problems, the theological implications of these problems and the apostolic grasp of the local situation.

In other words, not only does 1 Corinthians contribute to our understanding of primitive Christianity in its practical expression,

---

30. James Dunn, *Romans 9-16* (1988:685).
31. George Findlay, *St. Paul's First Epistle to the Corinthians* (1961:739).

it possesses both theological and ecclesiological value by which the contemporary church can interpret what it means to be the people of God. In 2 Corinthians, however, we see a more personal letter, occasioned by the intense conflict that had developed between the apostle and the church after the writing of 1 Corinthians.[32]

The Church in Corinth

The picture given us of the Corinthian church is far removed from what our contemporary understanding holds to be the *ideal* of a New Testament church. The inner relations, the disposition and thoughts of the people are such that Paul qualifies them as pagans (1 Co. 12:2). It is, therefore, important to attempt an understanding of the sociological characteristics of Corinth, together with its religious and philosophical milieu, since these have bearing on our understanding of a community that struggled to define its identity as the church of God in a complex and sophisticated urban setting.

The Context of the Church: "A Tale of Two Cities"[33]

Corinth was an ancient and powerful commercial city located on the Isthmus that linked the Peloponnese to the rest of Greece and separated

---

32. This study does not assume that the conflict between Paul and his church is entirely restricted to 2 Corinthians. In actual sense, the historical situation behind 1 Corinthians is fundamentally one of conflict between Paul and the Corinthian church. What is obvious, however, is that nowhere in 1 Corinthians does the apostle defend the appropriateness of his suffering nor have to defend the open rebellion against him and his gospel as we have in the deteriorated situation of 2 Corinthians. Rather, the apostle's purpose in writing 1 Corinthians is primarily didactic not apologetic, directive not combative. See Gerald F. Hawthorne, Ralph P. Martin, and Daniel G. Reid, *Dictionary of Paul and His Letters* (1993); Gordon Fee, *The First Epistle to the Corinthians* (1987); and for a sociological interpretation of the conflict between the apostle and his church, see Gerd Theissen, *The Social Setting of Pauline Christianity: Essays on Corinth* (1982).

33. For detailed sociological accounts, see Gerd Theissen, *The Social Setting of Pauline Christianity: Essays on Corinth* (1982) and Wayne Meeks, *The First Urban Christians: The Social World of the Apostle Paul* (1983). For references to ancient Corinth and archaeological evidence, see J. Murphy-O'Connor, *St. Paul's Corinth: Texts and Archaeology* (1983); J.G. O'Neill, *Ancient Corinth* (1930), and Oscar Broneer, "Corinth: Center of St. Paul's Missionary Work in Greece" (1951).

the Saronic and Corinthian gulfs. Corinth owed its wealth to this strategic position. Not only did it control the traffic between its two ports, Cenchrea on the side of the Aegean and Lechaeum at the edge of the Gulf of Corinth to the west, it also controlled the overland movement between Italy and Asia. This strategic location, therefore, sealed its fate as a prosperous city sitting at the crossroads of the world, tariffs, commerce, and ideas.[34]

The city, however, suffered destruction in 146 B.C. in the hands of a Roman army led by Lucius Mummius who attacked the city for its leading role in the revolt of the Achaian League. Corinth then lay in ruins for one hundred years, until it was re-founded by Julius Caesar in 44 B.C. as a Roman colony. Corinth quickly regained its prosperity and in 27 B.C. became the seat of the region's proconsul and the senatorial province of Achaia (southern and central Greece) in 44 A.D.

As the city regained its reputation as a center for commerce, so also did it regain its renowned vice as the center of sexual promiscuity and degrading worship. While the old city was renowned for its practice of treating visitors to free usage of the *Hieroduli* (consecrated prostitutes) at the temple of the goddess of love, Aphrodite, the new Corinth also restored the worship of Venus (the Roman counterpart of the Greek Aphrodite).[35] The city's reputation for sexual laxity was such that Aristophanes (c. 450-385 B.C.) coined the term *korinthiazesthai* ("to act like a Corinthian," meaning "to be promiscuous").[36]

Similarly, with the restoration of Corinth also came the restoration of most of the pagan worship. There were temples of various gods such as the Pantheon (temple of all the gods), the temple of Aesculapius (the god of healing), and other foreign cults such as the Egyptian gods Isis and Serapis.[37] By the time of Paul, Corinth had become a "pluralistic melting pot of cultures, philosophies, lifestyles, and religions."[38] This background,

---

34. Strabo, *Geography* (1932:20-23).
35. Ibid.
36. See Gerald F. Hawthorne, Ralph P. Martin, and Daniel G. Reid, *Dictionary of Paul and His Letters* (1993:172-173).
37. Edmond Hiebert, *Introduction to the New Testament* (1977:106).
38. See Gerald F. Hawthorne, Ralph P. Martin, and Daniel G. Reid, *Dictionary of Paul and His Letters* (1993:173).

therefore, explains the frequency of Paul's admonitions against sexual laxness, pagan idolatry and feasts in his Corinthian correspondence (1 Co. 6:9-11; 8:1-11; 12:2).

The Establishment and Composition of the Corinthian Church

It is important to place the establishment and the composition of the Corinthian church in proper perspective as a prelude to understanding the picture that emerges as we examine the contextual issues that preoccupy the life of the community.

Establishment of the Church

Internal evidences from the epistle itself leave us with no option to negotiate the fact that the apostle Paul himself founded the Corinthian church (1 Co. 3:6, 10; 4:15). Similarly, the antecedent conditions of the institution of the Corinthian church is further supplied in Acts 18:1-18. Paul was on his second missionary journey and had established several churches in Macedonia. However, the persecution in Macedonia drove him to Athens from where he left for Corinth after a brief and not too successful work. Arriving in Corinth alone (Ac. 18:5), Paul was soon joined by Silas and Timothy. With the coming of his helpers, Paul devoted himself to an intensive, full-time ministry in Corinth (Ac. 18:5). After one and a half years of intensive ministry (Ac. 18:11), Corinth became a center of the Pauline missionary work alongside Ephesus.

Composition of the Church

That the church is composed of members from both Jewish and Gentile backgrounds is supported from the account of Acts 18:8. However, that Gentiles predominated the believers in Corinth is illustrated by the problems and issues the church had to deal with (1 Co. 6:9-20; 7; 8:1-10; 22). Such highlights as participation in cultic banquets, civil litigation, and prostitution are overarching symbolism of a community with a pagan past (1 Co. 12:2).

By making allusion to internal evidences in the two Corinthian epistles, McGiffert has observed that the majority of Corinthian converts "seem to have come directly from heathenism." According to him, "there is nowhere in either of his epistles to the Corinthians a reference to the connection between Judaism and Christianity, or to the Christian's relation to Jewish law, of which he makes so much in his epistles to the Romans and Galatians." Even where the apostle makes use of the Torah, "he employs it only for the sake of illustrating or confirming what he has to say, and not as an authoritative code or a final court of appeal."[39]

The church also has a mixed social background. There were a few of noble rank in the church, such as the synagogue leader Crispus (Ac. 18:8; 1 Co. 1:14), and Erastus, who was the director of public works in the Corinthian city administration (Rom. 16:23). A number of the Corinthian Christians were also property owners (Ac. 18:2-8; Rom. 16:23; 1 Co. 1:16; 11:22a; 16:15ff.). Most of the church's membership was, however, from the lower strata (1 Co. 1:26-31). There were low-paying vocations such as "dockyards, potteries, and brass-foundries, from poor shopkeepers, bakers, brokers, fillers, and stray waifs in the motley crowds of Corinth."[40]

Theissen has stretched this further by affirming that the Corinthian situation had more to do with socially complex interactions of structures and not wholly determined by theological and religious factors as previously held. According to him, "the Corinthian congregation is marked by internal stratification" that pits the lower classes majority against the minority upper classes. This "internal stratification is not accidental" but has been rendered plausible by yet another factor, the "structural causes/elements," which could either "be found in the social structure of the city of Corinth itself or . . . from the structure of the Pauline mission."[41]

---

39. Arthur McGiffert, *A History of Christianity in the Apostolic Age* (1906:267-268). See also scripture references in 1 Corinthians 1:19, 31; 3:20; 9:9; 10:1-13; 2 Corinthians 6:2; 9:7.

40. McGiffert (1906:267-268). See also James Moffatt, *First Epistle of Paul to the Corinthians* (1944:xix). For a sociological analysis of the church's mixed status, especially with regards to the rich, the powerful, and the poor, see John K. Chow, *Patronage and Power: A Study of Social Networks in Corinth* (1992).

41. Gerd Theissen, *The Social Setting of Pauline Christianity: Essays on Corinth* (1982:69-119).

On top of the fact that the diverse social origins were enough reason for internal strife, it is important to add that the young church was equally influenced by its pagan environment, which continued to be a factor in the daily lives of its members.[42]

Contextual Issues in the Corinthian Church

The Corinthian epistles provide us with Paul's conception of the Christian way of life. Yet the urban Christians with whom he was dealing were a vivid "portrait of a community whose life together was a mixture of confusion, pettiness, and ambition, combined with enthusiasm and fervor."[43] The "mixture" in the Corinthian church was of a different kind. Unlike some of the other primitive churches (as in Jerusalem and Rome) where "mixed congregations" occasioned most of the contextual tensions; such a Jew-Gentile tension is in no way perceptible in the Corinthian letter. Rather, the larger agenda was how the Corinthians should relate to their culturally conditioned and pluralistic pagan environment now that they were Christians. Our intention, therefore, is to discuss in brief some of the problems of the Corinthian church, especially as they relate to their complex urban context.

The World in the Church

In a study that has shown to be a significant attempt at a reconstruction of the Roman world, John Chow has drawn attention to the power and social significance of patronage. According to him, the Roman society was built around a patron-client structure in which both patron and client obligated themselves to each other. It is, therefore, possible to infer that members of the Corinthian church had to operate within this patronal social order.[44]

---

42. Everett Harrison, *The Apostolic Church* (1985:202). For a middle position on the social and religious factors among the Corinthians and the first Christians, see Wayne Meeks, *The First Urban Christians: The Social World of the Apostle Paul* (1983).

43. Luke T. Johnson, *The Writings of the New Testament: An Interpretation* (1999:295).

44. John Chow's study about the patronal social order of ancient Corinth helps to highlight the cultural behavior of the Corinthian congregation. For details, see his work, *Patronage and Power: A Study of Social Networks in Corinth* (1992).

This is the agenda that the Corinthian church had on its hands. That is, the necessity of understanding the inner logic of what it means to be the "people of God" in a world that is marked by religious pluralism and cultural relativism. "Pulled between the movements of separation and assimilation," the following examples indicate the extent to which the Corinthian church patronized its world.[45]

Factions in the Church

In discussing the problems of the Corinthian church, Paul begins with the problem of division. The fact that Paul alludes to the factional allegiances and continues its discussion over four chapters indicates the seriousness of the issue (1 Co. 1:10-4:21). On first sight of 1 Corinthians 1:12, four ecclesiastical parties are evident in the Corinthian church, "each with a definite set of beliefs and practices." These parties include: a Paul faction, an Apollos faction, a Cephas faction, and a Christ faction.[46]

Attempts to identify the Corinthian factions have generated considerable scholarly disagreements. Of particular interest is Tidball's interpretation. He sees the divisions in the church as evidence of the social distinctions and an expression of cultural differences that have been brought about by the differences in the social classes of the church members. He notes that the preaching of Apollos may have appealed to the more educated; the preaching of Cephas to the more traditional Jews and the preaching of Paul, with its more direct style, may have appealed to the more common folk.[47]

C.K. Barrett seems to have approached the factions differently. By focusing on 1 Corinthians 1:13, he sees a link between baptism and the divisions in the Corinthian congregation.[48] This argument looks appealing especially when we are forced to probe the reason for the series of questions

---

45. Luke T. Johnson, *The Writings of the New Testament: An Interpretation* (1999:300).
46. William Baird, *The Corinthian Church: A Biblical Approach to Urban Culture* (1964:30).
47. Derek Tidball, *The Social Context of the New Testament: A Sociological Analysis* (1984:99).
48. C.K. Barrett, *Essays on Paul* (1982:29).

in 1 Corinthians 1:13, and the relief Paul expressed that he had baptized so few in Corinth himself (1 Co. 1:14-16).[49]

In all of this, one important factor that cannot be overlooked is the influence of the Hellenistic culture on the Corinthian Christians. By expressing their factional loyalty to their "favorite preacher," the Corinthians had demonstrated the influence of the tradition in which the Greeks were known for esteeming various schools of philosophy. And since the Corinthians had no famous teacher of philosophy, "there was a natural inclination to view Christianity as a system of thought that might be given varied interpretation and expression."[50]

Sexual Immorality in the Church

The situation at Corinth involved a variety of ethical issues. Most blatant was the issue of sexual laxity (*porneia*) that there was mention of an incestuous situation within the church. The incident was so severely reproachable that Paul describes it as "of a kind that is not found even among pagans" (1 Co. 5:1). Although the precise character of the situation is not clear, a church member was evidently cohabiting with his stepmother. This is a behavior that was forbidden both by Jewish law (Lev. 18:8) and the Roman law under which Corinth was being ruled.[51]

Sexual ethics, we have noted, had degenerated to a sodomic level with Hellenistic society. The deviation in the Corinthian church was of such a lower kind that the conduct seemed to have gone without it being censured by the congregation itself. Instead, there was both a display of flagrant pride and independent attitude necessitating the apostle's severe reproach, "And you are proud! Shouldn't you rather have been filled with grief?" (1 Co. 5:2).

---

49. For further discussions, see James Dunn, *1 Corinthians* (1995); William Baird, *The Corinthian Church: A Biblical Approach to Urban Culture* (1964); Nicholas Taylor, *Paul, Antioch and Jerusalem: A Study in Relationships and Authority in Earliest Christianity* (1991); N.A. Dahl, "Paul and the Church at Corinth according to 1 Corinthians 1-4" (1967); Gerd Theissen, *The Social Setting of Pauline Christianity: Essays on Corinth* (1982); and J.J. Gunther, *St. Paul's Opponents and Their Background* (1973).
50. Everett Harrison, *The Apostolic Church* (1985:203).
51. See William Baird, *The Corinthian Church* (1964:63).

Hensley Henson has observed that "[t]he disgraceful inactivity of the Ecclesia in the matter of the incestuous communicant indicated a singular inability to grasp the full greatness of its own position."[52] This view seems to have a common currency in contemporary scholarship. That is, that the Corinthians saw this as an example of their spiritual liberty and therefore one not to be censured.[53]

Besides the case of incest, the Corinthian church was also troubled by other varieties of sex-related problems. There was another example of sexual immorality relating to the patronizing of prostitutes, a conduct which the apostle strongly denounced (1 Co. 6:9-20). Perhaps the only area where the Corinthians could be credited for taking good initiative on sex-related issues was in the area of marriage.

Whereas an informant probably related the incestuous situation to Paul, the questions regarding marital problems were generated out of a written inquiry from the Corinthians themselves (1 Co. 7:1-40). There can be no doubt in affirming that the Corinthian way of life in its larger social context was one of immorality and sexual promiscuity against which even the church in Corinth had no immunity.

The Church in the World

As Chow has observed, scholars have largely concerned themselves with theological questions in Corinth at the expense of the underlying contextual factors.[54] It is my contention, too, that any contemporary attempts to reconstruct the Corinthian past must give assent to the socio-cultural milieu that informed the life and mission of the church. From the accounts in 1 Corinthians 6:1-11, we know that there was at least one case of legal dispute in the Corinthian church. Although Paul gives no specific information about the kind of dispute involved, he does hint at it as being of the "smallest matters" (*biōtika*).

---

52. Hensley Henson, *Apostolic Christianity* (1898:34-35).
53. For details in this regard, see James Dunn, *1 Corinthians* (1995:52); and John Polhill, *Paul and His Letters* (1999:239).
54. John Chow, *Patronage and Power: A Study of Social Networks in Corinth* (1992:122ff.).

The Corinthian Christians had a common practice of seeking litigation before the pagan courts over trivial cases that could have been settled within the church. This action fills Paul with indignation such that his reaction alternates between statements of horror (6:1, 6), rhetorical questions (6:2-4, 5b-7b), sarcasm (6:5), and threat (6:8-11).[55] Attempts at reconstructing Paul's understanding of the ethical issues involved in civil litigations can be hindered if one fails to recognize the social fabric of first-century Corinth. Roman Corinth was a society noted for its vexatious litigations whether civil or criminal.

In first-century Corinth, cases related to inheritance, legal possession, breach of contract, and the type described in 1 Corinthians 6:2 as the "smallest matters" (*biōtika*) would be categorized as civil. Although civil litigation was a common trait in Roman Corinth, an important feature of the system was that it tended to be prejudicial, serving only the interest of the governing elites.[56] It is, therefore, possible to attribute Paul's frustration not only to the church's failure to exercise its prerogative in settling internal feuds; but also to the inability to recognize its juridical authority over the world and angels alike (1 Co. 6:2-3).[57]

The Ministry of the Church

It hardly needs proof that the Corinthian peculiarities caused the apostle Paul severe pain. It is not merely the consciousness of the pull between the movements of separation and assimilation but of near complete immersion in a sea of paganism. William Baird puts it well when he remarks, "The church . . . was like a tiny boat tossed about in a vast sea of paganism. Its members had until recently flourished in that ocean, and its happy waves

---

55. Gordon Fee, *The First Epistle to the Corinthians* (1987:229).
56. For details, see P. Garnsey, *Social Status and Legal Privilege in the Roman Empire* (1970).
57. For further studies on the Roman legal system, see A.N. Sherwin-White, *Roman Society and Roman Law in the New Testament* (1969); J.A. Crook, *Law and Life in Rome* (1967); J.M. Kelly, *Roman Litigation* (1966); Bruce Winter, "Civil Litigation in Secular Corinth and the Church: The Forensic background to 1 Corinthians 6:1-8" (1991:559-572); and D. Engels, *Roman Corinth: An Alternative Model for the Classical City* (1990).

continued to beckon them."[58] There also existed within the church problems of worship that created tensions of theological and ethical significance.

Rather than be a community in ministry, the church itself was in need of a sustained ministry on what it means to be church in a defiled world of paganism. In all likelihood the Corinthian church was aligned with the world so much so that its members were unable to draw the "boundaries between the inside and the outside."[59] I will focus on two particular aspects of the world's inroad into the church: abuse of the Lord's Supper and misunderstanding of spiritual gifts.

Abuse of the Lord's Supper

Paul had no praises for the Corinthians in this regard but to strongly express that their "coming together" (*synerchesthai*) was not for the better but for the worse (1 Co. 11:17). Although a socially diverse congregation, the scandal for Paul was that the Lord's Supper, which was to be a solemn occasion for reconciliation, unity, and Christian love, had become the congregating point for flagrant displays of "schisms" (*schismata*) and "factions/sects" (*haireseis*; 1 Co. 11:18-19). There was a division between the rich and the poor; between the haves and the have-nots. While the rich over-indulged themselves with eating and drinking, the poor looked on with a sense of inferiority.

The Corinthians' abuse of the Lord's Supper may be attributed to the practice of public sacred feasting in both Judaism and Hellenistic religions. In both cases, meals served a congregational purpose for religious observance and socialization. The situation in the Hellenistic world was one in which there were meals associated with sacrifices, meals held by associations, meals celebrated in the cult of the dead, and the meals associated with the various mystery religions in Hellenism, Judaism, and the Gnostic sects.

Studies have also shown that it was common practice for clubs and associations to have common *agape* meals, or "love-feasts," with provisions being mainly contributed by the wealthy. The food was distributed inequitably with the rich taking gluttonous portions at the expense of the

---

58. William Baird, *The Corinthian Church* (1964:89).
59. Luke T. Johnson, *The Writings of the New Testament* (1999:300).

poor who remained empty. The "religious" gathering at Corinth paralleled this practice where meals were held in private homes, usually hosted by the richer members of the church.

Although the rich opened their houses to the church, they did so in a way that emphasized social divisions. Since most houses were large enough only to accommodate a few, the rich would be treated to quality foods in the *triclinium* (dining room) while the poor would dine on lesser fare in the larger *atrium* in the center of the home.[60] An alternative view holds that the rich feasted and reveled even to drunkenness while the poor had to "stand by with empty stomachs and envious glances."[61]

Despite the differences in interpretations, the important thing is that the coming together of the Corinthian church was a naïve expression of love and Paul did not mince words that such display of social distinction belonged in private homes and not in a Christian gathering.[62]

Misunderstanding of Spiritual Gifts

The church at Corinth was especially troubled by problems of spiritual gifts that the phrase, "now about," in 12:1 indicates that they had taken the initiative to ask Paul about the subject. To the Corinthian Christians, the most important demonstration of the indwelling Spirit was the pneumatic phenomenon of speaking with tongues (*glossolalia*). The outcome of this understanding was a free congregational worship that allowed some people to stand out as those from whom charismatic ministry could be expected.[63]

Two problems are identifiable from this misperception of spiritual gifts. First, it created disunity, elitism, and individualism between those who claimed the Spirit's endowment and those who felt left out. Second, the

---

60. J. Murphy-O'Connor, *St. Paul's Corinth: Texts and Archaeology* (1983:32-38).
61. Ernst Von Dobschütz, *Christian Life in the Primitive Church* (1904:61).
62. For further discussion in this area, see Gerald F. Hawthorne, Ralph P. Martin, and Daniel G. Reid, *Dictionary of Paul and His Letters* (1993:569-575); I. Howard Marshall, *Last Supper and Lord's Supper* (1980); Gerd Theissen, *The Social Setting of Pauline Christianity: Essays on Corinth* (1982:145-174); and B.W. Winter, "The Lord's Supper at Corinth: An Alternative Reconstruction" (1978:73-82).
63. Ronald Kydd, *Charismatic Gifts in the Early Church* (1984:10). Kydd's study is a very important study on the understanding and use of charismatic gifts in the Early Church.

uncontrolled display of spiritual manifestations naturally led to disruption in church worship.

As in our analysis of the abuse of the Lord's Supper, this is yet another example of how much of the pagan world was brought into the church's worship. The cults of the Hellenistic world were renowned for their pneumatic phenomenon and ecstatic behavior (1 Co. 12:2). It was common features in these pagan cults for devotees to behave in erratically unpredictable ways, to throw themselves about, and to speak in a frenzied manner.[64] The Corinthian Christians took this uninhibited behavior as a justification for the manifestation of the Spirit. It is, therefore, not out of place to conclude that part of the problem the Corinthian church was facing was largely due to its pagan environment out of which many of its members had been drawn.

The Theology of the Church

I have identified, as far as is practically possible, some of the problems that were confronting the church at Corinth. In doing so, we have also noted that there was a vast presence of doctrinal errors with very disruptive effects on both individual and corporate testimony of the Corinthian church. The picture which has emerged is that theological response to the Corinthian church needs to be coupled with the contextual issues and the problems that occurred within them. In the following paragraphs, I will attempt the theology which underpins Paul's response and thus his ecclesiology.

Factions in the Church

Paul destroys the validity of the Corinthians' factionalism by making reference to the nonessentiality of any individual person. Rather, the unity of every individual, including the church, is grounded in Christ and appropriated in baptism. He then follows logically by arguing the incompatibility of human wisdom with the divine wisdom of God (1 Co. 1:18ff.). By human standards the presentation of the message of the cross is foolishness to those who are perishing but the power of God unto salvation

---

64. Leon Morris, *1 Corinthians* (1985:162).

to those who believe. Paul then uses this argument to set revealed truth as the one centering on Christ and his atoning death over against human philosophical and religious wisdom (1 Co. 1:24).

The Corinthians' pursuit of human-centered wisdom and the factionalism that it has caused is descriptively referred to as "fleshly" (*sarkikos*). Through their behavior, the Corinthians have demonstrated not only their spiritual immaturity, but their incapability to understand the deeper spiritual truths (1 Co. 3:1-4).

The Problem of Sexual Immorality

Paul takes up the matter of sexual impropriety as an evil that does not belong in a Christian congregation (1 Co. 5:1-5). He uses the Greek word *porneia* to describe loose and licentious living. He rebukes the church for failing to act appropriately in relation to such flagrant displays of immorality. Rather than take pride in such unacceptable behavior, the church should rather engage in a mournful reflection. He instructed the Corinthian congregation to excommunicate the offender.

The purity of such discipline is the restoration of holiness to the community, "symbolized in the removal of leaven in the celebration of the OT Passover, which is fulfilled in Christ, 'our Passover Lamb'" (1 Co. 5:6-8).[65] He reminds the church that to enter into union with a prostitute is to become one flesh with her, which is contradictory to a believer's union with Christ (1 Co. 6:16).

Abuse of the Lord's Supper

Paul's response to the Corinthians' abuse of the Lord's Supper represents a significant teaching on sacramental theology. The focus of his response is to reclaim the real significance of the Supper as a memorial of the Lord's sacrificial death. He does this by making recourse to the "tradition," the tradition of the Last Supper when the Lord shared the bread and the cup with his disciples as a symbolic representation of his body and the new covenant in his blood. The "bread," representing the body of Christ,

---

65. W. Harold Mare, *1 Corinthians* (1976:217).

points to a constant reminder of his sacrificial death for all. Likewise the "cup," signifying the new covenant in Christ's blood, inaugurates a new relationship between God and his people.

Paul's teaching is that salvation through the sacrificial death of Christ has created a new community of people who have now become the new people of God. It is a community where those who share at the table of the Lord are brought into a unity with one another where social distinctions cannot be allowed to exist.[66] The exhortation for the Corinthians is for self examination before coming to the table lest they come under divine judgment.[67]

Misunderstanding of Spiritual Gifts

Paul does not challenge the Corinthians' understanding of the divine origin of gifts. Rather, his primary purpose is to correct the misunderstanding that undergirds their inordinate zeal for tongues so that the people might begin to understand spiritual gifts as God-given and for specific community function. In his effort to curb this misguided zeal for spirituality, Paul begins by offering a criterion for distinguishing between a frenzied ecstasy and a legitimate enthusiasm. A legitimate enthusiasm affirms the lordship of Jesus, "whereas ecstasy generates behavior hostile to the affirmation of Jesus' lordship." Consequently, his emphasis shifted from the "spiritually gifted" (*pneumatika*) to God's "gifts of grace" (*charisma*).

All Christians are endowed with diverse gifts for the common good (*sympheron*) of the church. The emphasis, therefore, is that if the community is truly to be "of the Spirit" (1 Co. 12:4-30), then it must embrace the diverse manifestations of gifts without recourse to individualism or pride. Since the believers *are* united into one body through the Lord's Supper, "then they *ought* in their everyday lives to live as members of the one body and realize the unity of the one body."[68]

---

66. Gerald F. Hawthorne, Ralph P. Martin, and Daniel G. Reid, *Dictionary of Paul and His Letters* (1993:572).

67. Hawthorne, Martin, and Reid (1993:573) elaborate the contemporary theological differences in the church, especially between Roman Catholic and Protestant interpreters.

68. Hans Küng, *The Church* (1968:229).

The motivating factor for seeking spiritual gifts, therefore, must be for the love of the community and to serve the faith, without which the gift counts for nothing (1 Co. 13:1-13). He concludes by exhorting the Corinthians to be motivated to seek after intelligible utterances and order (1 Co. 14:1-25, 26-40) so that through that the church might be built up (1 Co. 14:1-19, 26-33) and outsiders converted (1 Co. 14:20-25).

The Church in the Epistle to the Ephesians

This book has adopted a working pattern that looks at the church from three areas: (1) the context of the church, (2) the ministry of the church, and (3) the theology of the church. Also, while the Scriptures I have examined so far were considered to be responding to contextual and specific historical situation, the letter to the Ephesians, on the other hand, is less situational. There are neither references to any local situation nor does it have the same sense of urgency and response to specific discernible crises as do the other letters. The result of this is that the letter has been subjected to widely divergent conceptions over authenticity and purpose.[69]

Notwithstanding, there is a general consensus among scholars that Ephesians is markedly distinguished by its theological consistency of the church. In fact among the letters collected under the Apostle Paul's name, it has received some of the highest praise as, for example, C.H. Dodd's reference to Ephesians as "the crown of Paulinism."[70] As Ernest Best has also observed, "it is a thoroughly 'ecclesiastical' document—in the best sense of the word 'ecclesiastical'."[71] Hawthorne, Martin, and Reid have described it as an "advanced ecclesiology."[72] In the words of Peter O'Brien,

---

69. For an annotated summary of some of the major viewpoints on the authenticity of the epistle, see Gerald F. Hawthorne, Ralph P. Martin, and Daniel G. Reid, *Dictionary of Paul and His Letters* (1993:572).

70. C.H. Dodd, "Ephesians" (1929:1224).

71. Ernest Best, *One Body in Christ: A Study in the Relationship of the Church to Christ in the Epistles of Paul the Apostle* (1955:136).

72. Gerald F. Hawthorne, Ralph P. Martin, and Daniel G. Reid, *Dictionary of Paul and His Letters* (1993:240).

the letter presents a "high ecclesiology" not in a localized sense but in a distinguishingly universal way.[73] To Rudolf Schnackenburg, it is "an ecclesiology which is so extensively structured."[74]

Evangelical conviction about ecclesiology is that "discussions concerning the church should always be rooted in normative guidelines based on a study of the New Testament descriptions and teachings."[75] This perspective does not derive from a mindless logic of argumentation on ecclesiality, but on the conviction that "one can only know what the church should be now if one also knows what the church was originally [or was intended to be].[76] The epistle to the Ephesians offers such perspective, especially with its emphasis on cosmic reconciliation and unity in Christ. As Leslie Mitton has confirmed, "the epistle is essentially about Christ, and only about the church as it fulfills the purposes of Christ.[77]

If the epistle is "essentially about Christ," especially as "one *in whom* God chooses to sum up the cosmos, the one in whom he restores harmony to the universe," then Christ's sovereignty over the cosmos raises some implications for the church, his "body."[78] It begs the question of the church's relation to Christ's cosmic role, to the principalities and powers, and to God's eternal purpose.

Consequently, it is an agreeable persuasion that "the distinctive theology of Ephesians is no academic abstraction."[79] The present revival of academic concern for the ecclesiastical distinctiveness of the letter should, therefore, not be seen as a mere attempt at re-constructing ecclesiological concepts or theological assumptions. Rather, I am concerned with an "ecclesiology of responsibility."[80] That is, an ecclesiology that does not pay tribute to the letter as belonging only to ancient times but that recognizes it imposes an

---

73. Peter O'Brien, *The Letter to the Ephesians* (1999:25).
74. Rudolf Schnackenburg, *The Epistle to the Ephesians* (1991:293).
75. For details, see John Newport, "The Purpose of the Church" (1991:19); and Robert Webber, *Common Roots: A Call to Evangelical Maturity* (1978:41).
76. Hans Küng, *The Church* (1968:ix).
77. C. Leslie Mitton, *Ephesians* (1976:32).
78. Peter O'Brien, *The Letter to the Ephesians* (1999:58).
79. A. Skevington Wood, "Ephesians" (1978:19).
80. G.R. Evans, *The Church and the Churches* (1994:7).

obligation relevant for being the church of Christ in the world today. Based upon these facts, my approach in this chapter will focus primarily on Christ and about the church as it fulfills the purposes of Christ.[81]

Composition of the Church

The basis for the composition of the Church according to Ephesians centers on a cosmic secret that was part of God's eschatological plan laid "before the foundation of the world" (1:4). This cosmic secret is the "mystery" (*mystērion*, Eph. 1:9; 3:3, 4, 9; 5:32; 6:19) that accorded divine recognition to Gentiles as fellow heirs and co-partakers of God's promise with Israelites who have followed Jesus Christ (3:6).

The church exists truly as it is composed as the one body of Christ in which Gentiles have been united with the Jews as a public display of the grand redemptive purpose of God (Eph. 3:1-13). In this context, therefore, the church is one single "household of God" built on the foundation of the apostles and prophets and borne by Christ, the chief corner-stone (Eph. 2:19-20).[82]

The key paradigm of this "mystery" of unification as a spiritual blessing is especially complemented for the Gentile believers by "transfer terminology."[83] That is, those who were dead have been made alive in Christ (2:1-10), once "far off" but now have been "brought near" (2:13), excluded as aliens, now have received reconciliation and peace, (2:11-22). Given this context, "Christian Gentiles are considered representatives of

---

81. Ephesians offers us no option other than to interpret it as presenting a "cosmic Christology." This is based not only on the exaltation of Christ over all his enemies (Eph. 1:21-22), or on his role in bringing all of history to completion (Eph. 1:10), but also on his relationship to his church as the "head" (Eph. 1:23; 4:15-16) and "bridegroom" (Eph. 5:29). See also Ernest Best, *One Body in Christ* (1955) and F.W. Dillistone, *The Structure of the Divine Society* (1951).

82. See also Rudolf Schnackenburg, *The Epistle to the Ephesians* (1991:310).

83. Nils Dahl, "Gentiles, Christians, and Israelites in the Epistle to the Ephesians" (1986:33).

the entire non-Jewish part of humanity" whose "incorporation accords with the mystery of God's will to 'recapitulate' all things in Christ" (1:10).[84]

If Gentile believers represent the non-Jewish part of humanity, "it is reasonable," observes Dahl, "to think of Christian Jews as representatives of all Israel."[85] Both Jews and Gentiles constitute the "one new humanity" *in Christ* with equal access to the Father. The important thing, then, is to preserve this "unity" by means of mutual love, tolerance, and forgiveness (2:14-22; 4:1-6).

The Context of the Church

The train of thought in the letter to the Ephesians begins by espousing the cosmic plan of God "to bring all things in heaven and on earth together under one head, even Christ" (1:10). The letter then moves to Christ's position as "head" over the church, identified in her relationship to the exalted Christ as the "body," the fullness (*pleroma*) of him who fills all things (1:22-23). The implication of this is that the letter strikes a balance whereby the "cosmic Lord and reconciler of all things is also Lord over the church."[86]

It is important to state, therefore, that we cannot fully appreciate the connection between the church and its cosmic context without first acknowledging the connection between Christ and the cosmos since in Ephesians, "cosmology and ecclesiology intertwine."[87]

The Exalted Christ and the Cosmos

Ephesians presents us with a cosmic Christology in which the author stresses the cosmic range of Christ's function over "all things," including principalities and powers (1:22-23). Through human "trespasses and sins" (2:1), humanity is alienated from God, enslaved by the forces of evil, and thrown into a chaotic hostility towards one another (2:1-2). The point

---

84. Dahl (1986:33).
85. Dahl (1986:36).
86. Leland Ryken, James C. Wilhoit, and Tremper Longman III, *Dictionary of Biblical Imagery* (1998:238).
87. Stig Hanson, *The Unity of the Church in the New Testament: Colossians and Ephesians* (1946:125).

of reference for Ephesians, therefore, is God's plan to reverse this state of "cosmic-historical hostility" as a warrant for cosmic reunification between himself and humans and for the possibility of establishing unity among humans themselves.

God's plan, to "head up all things" (*anakephalaiōsasthai*) in Christ (1:10) then takes up a universal soteriological significance by which God is pacified. Christ's paradoxical death "heals the rupture between God and humanity, eradicates the cosmic forces that have enslaved humans to captivity, and reveals the possibility of a new way of being human, one that is not divided by hostility but united in peace" (1:7; 2:14-22).[88] Christ's immanence and transcendence is thus expounded through the redemption and reconciliation secured for the cosmos by his atoning blood on the cross (1:7; 2:16). Consequently, there is salvation for the cosmos both in the present dispensation, "realized" eschatology, and as a future reality (1:10, 14; 4:30; 5:6, 27).

The Church and the Cosmos

It can be argued, then, that the context of the church must be understood as being fundamentally dualistic. In other words, the cosmos must be understood as possessing both anthropocentric and theological dimensions. It is anthropocentric because in it is the visible church with the responsibility of playing an active role in the redemptive drama. On the other hand, the cosmos has a theological abstraction because it exists in the spiritual realms where the malignant pockets of principalities and powers exercise revolt against the authority of God (3:10). As Schnackenburg has noted, "the world is not regarded simply as God's creation, as the universe of the created things and the abode of humankind . . . but as a realm already darkened and occupied by the powers of evil."[89]

Although I have drawn a boundary of the cosmos as constituting the physical and the spiritual, the temporal and the eternal, the relationship of the Church to the cosmos cannot be given the same manner of expression.

---

88. See Luke T. Johnson, *The Writings of the New Testament* (1999:413).
89. Rudolf Schnackenburg, *The Church in the New Testament* (1965:177).

As an earthly institution, it functions singularly and simultaneously, yet in a state of tension between the "two worlds."

Through its physical existence, the church witnesses to the universal lordship of Jesus Christ over the cosmos. Its place in the cosmic context is one that is categorically dependent on the one who has authority over the cosmos itself. It will, therefore, be disillusioning for the church to identify itself as being autonomously related to the cosmos. Rather, the church exists in the world because of its origin in Jesus Christ, who is also the content of its message in and to the world.

Interestingly, nothing has been more divisive and problematic for the church than the inability to balance this cosmic dimension and task with the particularity of its existence in each local context. The problem of the relation of the church to the churches or the problem of some churches as being "more church" than others has substantially pit one segment of the church against the other. Consequently, the church exists in antithetical position to the divine mission, thus becoming a paradox of its own witness. In an age of globalization and unceasing universality, perhaps it is time the church realized that "the principle of 'separateness' can get in the way both of mission and of relationships with other churches" and ultimately with Christ himself.[90]

The Ministry of the Church

In her subordinate position as the "body" to the "head," the church is not a passive bystander in the cosmic drama. Instead, the church is enjoined to "live a life worthy of the calling you have received" (4:1, 4). The phraseology "worthy of the calling" is not so much a newer conception in defining the mystery of the church's existence but a development of what was implied earlier in 1:10-14, 18. Together they depict a church that was "included from the outset in the great divine Economy of Salvation" for a specific ministry in the world.[91]

---

90. G.R. Evans, *The Church and the Churches* (1994:23).
91. Rudolf Schnackenburg, *The Epistle to the Ephesians* (1991:294).

Hugo H. Culpepper has observed that this emphasis on calling "is the link between the theology and the ethics of the epistle."[92] If my interpretation of Culpepper is correct, then it means that we cannot reduce the conception (calling) to a logical or an abstract term but understand that in no precise way can the church separate the *meaning* of her calling from the *action* that defines that calling. It follows from here, therefore, that the church must understand that the basis for her ministry (calling) and presence in the world is explicitly and characteristically missionary in nature.

This conception is well articulated by David E. Garland when he declares, "[t]he church is not to be a curator of the theological wisdom of the ages, nor simply a cheerleader praising God for his splendid salvation scheme; it is to be an essential agent in the accomplishment of God's design."[93]

It suffices to say that the church's *essential agency* has a missionary purpose, and it is only in re-covering this that the church recovers her raison d'être. This is the theological and missional speculation of Ephesians which must find potency and integration in the life of the church. That is, appropriating in no uncertain term that "the church remains the mysterious *creatio Dei*" and exists for the *missio Dei* on behalf of the world.[94]

He would be a bold person who should suppose to have fully mastered all the aspects of the church's missionary dimension. However, my concern here is to attempt to interpret the ministry of the church in Ephesians from a missional perspective. For this purpose, I have identified three important missional dimensions: (1) the revelatory dimension, (2) the salvific dimension, and (3) the unity dimension.

The Revelatory Dimension of Ministry/Mission

As an agent of revelation, the church exists in the conflict between the sovereignty of God and the celestial adversaries of his divine purpose. It follows from the persuasion that the confusion and disorder in the original world ordered and led by God had been orchestrated by invisible evil

---

92. Hugo H. Culpepper, "Ephesians—A Manifesto for the Mission of the Church" (1979:553).
93. David Garland, "A Life Worthy of the Calling" (1979:517).
94. Charles Van Engen, *Mission on the Way: Issues in Mission Theology* (1996:107).

powers. But through his saving work in Christ's death and resurrection, God had re-established the cosmic order. The letter does not disavow the reality of "principalities and powers" but portrays an ecclesiology of power encounter and of the supremacy of God's power which is also accessible to the church (1:19-23; 4:8-10).

Although God had already defeated his celestial enemies, this still requires "progressive realization in the historical world."[95] Therefore, the church's existence is for this very purpose. That is, through her proclamation and life, "God's wise plan will be revealed to the powers and authorities that futilely contend with him for the allegiance of his own creatures" (2:2; 3:10).[96]

As Peter O'Brien has suggested, the existence of the church, especially in the reconciliation of formerly irreconcilable Jews and Gentiles into the one body of Christ, "is a reminder that the authority of the powers has been decisively broken, and that their final defeat is imminent."[97] The conception of the reconciliation of Jews and Gentiles is not merely that the two groups coalesce but that it reveals further God's new order.

Not only does the existence of the church reveal God's mystery and his plan of reconciliation in the present, there is also an eschatological dimension to the church's revelatory function. The "not-yet" aspect of the grand plan awaits "the fullness of the times" when "the things in heaven and on earth" will be brought together under one head, Christ (1:9-10). In the present dispensation, the church appears as "God's pilot scheme for the reconciled universe of the future."[98] The uniting of "Jews and Gentiles in Christ was . . . God's masterpiece of reconciliation, and gave promise of a time when not Jews and Gentiles only, but all the mutually hostile elements in creation, would be united in that same Christ."[99]

---

95. Rudolf Schnackenburg, *The Epistle to the Ephesians* (1991:308).
96. Luke T. Johnson, *The Writings of the New Testament* (1999:414-416); and J. Paul Sampley, "Ephesians" (1993:21).
97. Peter O'Brien, *The Letter to the Ephesians* (1999:63).
98. For details, see F.F. Bruce, *The Epistles to the Colossians, to Philemon, and to the Ephesians* (1984:321-322).
99. Bruce (1984:262).

To make this witnessing by existence possible, the Spirit prompts the church and equips her with powerful armory to demonstrate the superiority of the power of God by first overcoming in herself those corrupting forces of the unseen world who exert a bad influence on humanity (1:19-23; 3:16; 4:8-10; 6:10-20). Among these corrupting forces is disunity, which can only be overcome if the church grows in love and gains strength in unity. Johnson echoes this conviction that "it is only through a life in unity that the church stands as a witness to the world—in sharp contrast to the cosmic powers."[100]

The quality of the church as a *revelatory agent*, then, is that quality within her which has an influence on a world that is still separate from Christ and dominated by the influence of evil, the quality without which she is not recognizable as a revelatory agent of God's new order. As O'Brien puts it, "the church is not only the pattern but also the means God is using to show that his purposes are moving triumphantly to their climax."[101]

The Salvific Dimension of Ministry/Mission

The church exists in a privileged position as a mystical outflowing of Christ in the world. As the "body of Christ," the church is not only included in the great "divine economy of salvation," but she is also the channel through which salvation penetrates the world with the healing, liberating power of God. The church is the entity where God's presence in the world is acknowledged and realized and through which God is glorified (3:20-21). As Dale Moody noted, "God has called the church out from the world to send her back into the world with a message and a mission."[102]

Parallel to this emphasis on the church as an agent of salvation is an emphasis on the "indicatives of redemption."[103] By this is meant that the church is called specifically to eschew the works of darkness and thus reflect her understanding of God's redemptive purpose (5:1-18). Similarly, she is to live a life of good works through which the praise of God is actualized.

---

100. Luke T. Johnson, *The Writings of the New Testament* (1999:417).
101. Peter O'Brien, *The Letter to the Ephesians* (1999:63).
102. Dale Moody, *The Word of Truth* (1981:427).
103. F.W. Danker, "Epistle to the Ephesians" (1982:114).

This existential orientation is to reflect the church's understanding of her new status as members of Christ's body and also as a demonstration of God's extraordinary kindness in giving Jesus Christ (2:7).

Suffice it to say, therefore, "ecclesiology becomes a function of Christology, and the church's mission to the world is rooted in her understanding of the lordship of Christ."[104] It is not overstressing the ideal to echo Schnackenburg's estimate of the church's salvific agency that "if a church or Christian community no longer recognizes that it is bound to the *all-embracing task* of bringing salvation which is depicted in Ephesians, then it fails to understand what 'church' is by nature and mission."[105]

To speak of the church as "salvific agent," then, predicates its essence in the world so that soteriology, Christology, and ecclesiology are interconnected. Again Schnackenburg summarizes it well:

> The "church" does not mean an earthly institution, an entity marked out or identifiable in individual congregations or churches but an instrument of salvation created by God in Christ, which to be sure includes and combines the empirical congregations, is realized in them and through them encounters the world.[106]

The Unity Dimension of Ministry/Mission

It is never seriously in doubt that the theme of unity as a New Testament teaching comes to its clearest expression in Ephesians. The first three chapters of the epistle open with the broadest possible vista of the great divine wisdom. It begins with the cosmic scope of God's plan to unite all things in Christ (1:10), to ally Jews and Gentiles into the same body as one (2:11-19; 3:16), and to reconcile all of alienated humanity to himself (2:16, 18). This cosmic unity finds its corollary in chapter four with its emphasis on unity in matters of faith (4:3-6).

---

104. Danker (1982:114).
105. Rudolf Schnackenburg, *The Epistle to the Ephesians* (1991:309).
106. Schnackenburg (1991:308).

The task emerges for the church, therefore, "to maintain the unity of the Spirit through the bond of peace" (4:3). The exhortation "to maintain" (*tēreō*) unity suggests that the unity of the church is "bestowed" or "conferred" and arises from the fundamental oneness of all believers in the same body, the body of Christ (4:1-6). This understanding must take its clue from the meaning the word *ekklēsia* conveys as it is used in the epistle.

The conception of the word *ekklēsia* in Ephesians is singular and refers to the church in her entirety, the one body of Christ. The church is called to an understanding of this unity *in* Christ and the need to grow up into him and reach maturity (4:15-16). We can affirm then that the church is a body which is on her way to becoming what she is already by faith and affirmation. This call to unity absolutizes the nature and mission of the church and stands as corrective to the church's agenda of self-maintenance.[107]

In cases where talks of the universal expression of the Christian faith have been confused with the particular expression of the same faith in each local context, we do well to learn from the apostle Paul. For him, the "local 'being the church' was inseparable from [the] catholicity and unity with one another at the deepest level."[108] Ernest Best shares the same conviction when he declares, "for Paul there is no such thing as a solitary Christian; the faith that unites a man to Christ unites him also to other Christians; the church is more than an aggregate of Christians; it is a fellowship."[109]

It is to ensure the common consciousness of the Christian concord that the church has been endowed with ministry gifts (4:1-16). The purpose of the gifts is both "for the work of ministry" (*eis ergon diakonias*) and "for the building of the body of Christ" (*eis oikodomēn tou sōmatos tou Christou*). The heart of unity consists, therefore, in a dynamic interplay of charismatic ministry. As all the members play their part(s), the church will develop and express in the world a single personality that is reflective of her internal relationship with Christ. The church is *called* to seek unity that is

---

107. For insightful studies on the unity of the church, see G.R. Evans, *The Church and the Churches* (1994); and Miroslav Volf, *After Our Likeness: The Church as the Image of the Trinity* (1998).
108. G.R. Evans, *The Church and the Churches* (1994:18).
109. Ernest Best, *One Body in Christ: A Study in the Relationship of the Church to Christ in the Epistles of Paul the Apostle* (1955:193).

dependent on the one hope, one Lord, one faith, one baptism, one God, and Father of all (4:4-5).

It must be emphasized, however, that the unity of the church does not emerge out of a regimented conformity. It exists together with a diversity of gifts held together through the "bond of peace" (4:3). It is precise to say, therefore, that the "bond of peace" becomes the ecclesiological formulae for *maintaining* the unity of the church (4:2-7).

To transpose Mitton, "peace is here pictured as a rope which binds separate elements which are not naturally cohesive" (2:14-15, 17; 6:15).[110] As Garland has also observed, the church has a gospel of peace (6:15), peace is prominent in the mystery of the unification of Jews and Gentiles (2:11-22), Christ came to preach peace (2:17), he is the peace through whom humanity is united (2:14-15), and through Christ humankind has peace with the Father (2:18).[111]

The Theology of the Church

Millard J. Erickson has done a great service to biblical ecclesiology by exposing the attempt of contemporary transformers to develop a doctrine of the church based mainly on "empirical presence" in isolation of its "theoretical essence."[112] It is indeed a fact that our culture is dynamic and changing. This, however, begs the question as to how "dynamic" the church should be in order to keep up with our fast-changing culture? The church is in many respects analogical to the two sides of a coin. It is a true witness when it is concretely and historically recognizable in the world (existential/empirical) and normative to the extent it remains connected to biblical truth (quintessential).

It suffices to say, therefore, that a wholly existential/empirical perspective is intrinsically iconoclastic while a wholly quintessential framework is at best provocative. Neither is the only option in developing a doctrine of the church for the twenty-first century. Any discussion of what the church "concretely is" or "is becoming" must be guided by what the church "really

---

110. Leslie Mitton, *Ephesians* (1976:138-139).
111. David Garland, "A Life Worthy of the Calling" (1979:520).
112. For details, see Millard Erickson, *Christian Theology* (1998:1036-1045).

is" or "ought to be." In the words of John Macquarrie, our insights "need to be guided and correlated by a theological understanding of the church."[113] There is no better place to begin by allowing the imagistic language of Ephesians to inform our understanding of the nature and function of the church.

The Case for a Metaphorical Ecclesiology

What are the criteria for distinguishing the true church in the face of changing times? This is a highly complex issue and undoubtedly involves many factors. As Hans Küng has observed, the nature given to the church "was given it as a responsibility." This nature must be constantly "realized anew and given new form in history [since] changing times demand changing forms."[114]

The credal attributes have been the traditional point of departure for examining the "marks of the church." While one may not dismiss this approach as improper, the fact that the creed has assumed different interpretations and understanding in different ecclesiologies undercuts the credal approach as the *one* way to determine the marks of the true church.[115] This is not to suggest that the church should not aspire to *oneness*, *holiness*, *catholicity*, and *apostolicity*. On the other hand, the church is more a community of symbolic manifestation and can only be "true" to the degree that she lives and expresses fully the reality of that which she manifests.

Speaking of the church as a community of symbolic manifestation conjures up literary genres such as images, symbols, and metaphors. As imagistic language, they call into question their adequacy in bridging the gap between thought and life. That is to say that one expects to see the metaphoric process progress naturally from describing reality to that of constructing a corresponding reality. Therefore, the important thing is to note at how many points the symbol corresponds to the thing symbolized.

---

113. John Macquarrie, *Principles of Christian Theology* (1946:346).
114. Hans Küng, *The Church* (1968:263).
115. See Avery Dulles, *Models of the Church* (1987:137-138). For several of the most significant confessions of faith from various periods in the history of the Church, see Wayne Grudem, *Systematic Theology: An Introduction to Biblical Doctrine* (1994:1168-1207).

The choice of a metaphorical approach in understanding the nature or "marks of the church" is prompted by the conviction that metaphors are like an index finger pointing to a reality or something we know little about. M.H. Abrams has said it so descriptively that I will quote him at length:

> Any area for investigation, so long as it lacks prior concepts to give it structure and an express terminology with which it can be managed, appears to the inquiring mind inchoate—either a blank, or an elusive and tantalizing confusion. Our usual recourse is, more or less deliberately, to cast about for objects which offer parallels to dimly sensed aspects of the new situation, to use the better known to elucidate the less known, to discuss the intangible in terms of the tangible. This analogical procedure seems characteristic of much intellectual enterprise. There is a good deal of wisdom in the popular locution for "what is its nature?" namely: "What's it *like?*" We tend to describe the nature of something in similes and metaphors and the vehicles of these recurrent figures, when analyzed, often turn out to be attributes of an implicit analogue through which we are viewing the object we describe.[116]

The concern of this book is to inquire about the nature of the church. Ironically, nowhere in the Bible do we get a finite definition of the church. However, what we do find in the Bible are images, like the ones in the epistle to the Ephesians, which "are not simply pictorial comparisons but modes of expression which simultaneously depict the reality of the church."[117]

---

116. M.H. Abrams, *The Mirror and the Lamp* (1953:31-32). For other insightful studies in the areas of language, literature, and religion see Janet M. Soskice, *Metaphor and Religious Language* (1985); Philip Wheelwright, *Metaphor and Reality* (1962); Mary Gerhart and Allan Russell, *Metaphoric Process: The Creation of Scientific and Religious Understanding* (1984); Sallie McFague, *Metaphorical Theology: Models of God in Religious Language* (1982); and *Speaking in Parables: A Study in Metaphor and Theology* (1975). See also Edmund P. Clowney, "Interpreting the Biblical Models of the Church: A Hermeneutical Deepening of Ecclesiology" (1984).

117. Rudolf Schnackenburg, *The Epistle to the Ephesians* (1991:295). Paul Minear has suggested over one hundred images of the Church used in the New Testament, *Images of the Church in the New Testament* (1960). For images of the Church as applied to mission,

Without any attempt to be exhaustive, I must limit myself to only a few of the images that have dominated ecclesiological thought in the development of a doctrine of the church.

In Ephesians, four metaphors are used for the church: the church as a building, the body of Christ, the bride and wife of Christ, and as a brotherhood. These metaphors are distinct yet interconnected. More importantly, they are clearly used as a corresponding formulaic motif to bring the doctrine of the church closer to our understanding. For the purpose of this book, I will explicate the metaphor of the church as the "body of Christ." This does not mean that the other three are any less significant. Rather, as the most distinctive metaphor that is "related to reality and filled with reality,"[118] an understanding of its use can secure for us an appreciation of the other metaphors. Even then, it would be a bold claim to think that one can exhaust the depth of ideas that the "body" metaphor offers us in our attempt to better understand the meaning of the church as the body of Christ.

The Church as the Body of Christ

Although there are wide-ranging theories regarding the exact source of the concept, "the body of Christ,"[119] it is beyond any doubts that it is the most pervasive metaphor for the church. In the indisputably authentic Pauline letters, the body of Christ refers to the individual congregations with a call to Christian solidarity (Rom. 12 and 1 Co. 12). In 1 Corinthians 12, Paul draws upon the metaphor of the church as the body of Christ to establish the need for unity and Christian harmony. The church is one body but composed of individual parts that are uniquely endowed for specific tasks. In Romans 12, Paul reinforces the same principle of Christians' relation to one another, but the relationship to Christ is expressed in more intimate terms. Here, believers are not just "the body *of* Christ," but are now "one body *in* Christ" (Rom. 12:5). This emphasizes not just the connection of

---

see John Driver, *Images of the Church in Mission* (1997).
118. Rudolf Schnackenburg, *The Epistle to the Ephesians* (1991:298).
119. Ernst Best discusses seven of these theories in his work, *One Body in Christ* (1955:83-93).

the church with Christ, but "stresses the fact that Christ is the source of its unity."[120]

In both cases, the metaphor is incidental and emphasizes the primacy and continued affirmation of the corporate body above any individualism or self-aggrandizement. The importance of the metaphor of the church as the body of Christ, therefore, stresses a fact that there is a horizontal relationship that connects every member of the "body" one to another, as well as a vertical relationship "with Christ who is the 'body' that they are all members of."[121]

In Ephesians, however, there is a new dimension which puts a different spin on our understanding of the metaphor of the church as the body of Christ. Unlike Romans 12 and 1 Corinthians 12 where the congregation is the total body "of Christ," Ephesians injects a new line of thought that gives the head a special, characteristic position with regard to the body. This differentiation of Christ as head of his body, the church, suggests a new reality in our attempts to understand the mark of the church. The accent is not on the church as the body which represents the head, but on Christ as the head who imparts the body, the church, with the power to grow. Two important insights are identifiable from the use of this metaphor in Ephesians: the differentiation between the head and the body and the conditional growth of the body in relation to the head.

First, the specific differentiation of the superiority of the head over the body corrects the misunderstanding that the body constitutes the head and is primary vis-à-vis him.[122] There is truly a relationship between the head and the body, but it is a relationship of faith in which the body's position is more precisely a subordinate one. To describe the relationship between the head and the body in an exclusively organic way is also to undermine the preeminence of the head. There is no ontic identity since the head is not a member of the body as any other member but one that occupies a place of

---

120. Robert Banks, *Paul's Idea of Community* (1994:61).
121. Barbara Field, "The Discourses Behind the Metaphor 'the Church is The Body of Christ' as used by St Paul and the 'Post-Paulines'" (1992:90).
122. Walter Schmithals, *The Theology of the First Christians* (1997:160). See also Rudolf Schnackenburg, *The Epistle to the Ephesians* (1991:298).

pre-eminence. The body is totally dependent on the head for its existence, vitality, and growth.

It is imperative to apply theological understanding to this head-body image since in Ephesians 1:22-23, Christ is the head, and he remains the head at every level of reality. The connection between Christ and the church is one to be understood theologically as Lord over the church. This way, Hans Küng's observation is an accurate one when he declares, "the church receives from Christ its life and at the same time his promises and his direction, or rather his promises and his direction, and *therefore* its life."[123]

Implicit in this notion of head-body relationship is the complete dependence of the church upon Christ for its ministry in the world. It follows from the understanding that the domain of Christ's headship has both ecclesiastical and cosmic realities (Eph. 1:21). Consequently, as Christ's body, the church also receives the "fullness" (*plērōma*) of his Spirit and power so that it becomes the instrument of Christ in the world.

This spiritual endowment does not mean that Christ has abdicated his ecclesiastical and cosmic headship to the body, the church. Neither can the church play the "continuing life of Christ" or a "permanent incarnation."[124] Rather, the head has endowed the church, with the "fullness" (*plērōma*) of himself so that through the activities of the church in the world, his established reign is continually revealed in its "fullness" both to the world and to his defeated celestial adversaries. To this end, Küng's advice is worth emphasizing that "it is of vital importance for the church that it allows Christ to be its head; otherwise it cannot be his body [nor function effectively as his body]."[125]

The second important insight that is unique to Ephesians in the head-body metaphor is what we have identified as the conditional growth of the body in relation to the head. Just as precisely as the body depends on the head to exist, so also does it depend on the head for nourishment that brings growth (Eph. 4:15-16). This explicates the interior life of the body in two ways. First, the body grows towards its head as "she comes closer to

---

123. Hans Küng, *The Church* (1968:236-237).
124. Küng (1968:239).
125. Küng (1968:236).

him in everything, grows into him, reaches towards Christ in love" (4:16; 5:24).[126]

This means that the growth of the body, the church, is only possible in obedience to Christ who is her head. The body cannot move in flagrant disobedience to the head and expect to grow. It can only dry and wither away. As Küng has observed, "the church does not grow automatically and ontologically . . . real growth in the church occurs when Christ penetrates the world by the activity of his church in history.[127]

Secondly, not only does the body derive nourishment by being obedient to the head, it is also important that "the members interchange their blood, their energies, their assistance [so that] by the life-giving virtue of the head, the whole body has within itself its own principle of development and of growth."[128] The importance of this "interior life," by implication, is that the body increases unto its own upbuilding but not without assistance from Christ who is the source of its growth and upbuilding.[129]

As the church moves in faith in Christ and in love toward one another, the reign of Christ is not only established within her, but it also becomes a distinctive mark that differentiates the church from other well-meaning institutions. What we can infer, therefore, is that the church is not to be confined to the strictures of an organization (no matter how convenient and tempting this might be) but must be considered an organism. Even then, its unity, whether with Christ or its constitutive membership, should not be perceived as merely organic, but as one that is distinguishable by its spiritual dimension.

---

126. Rudolf Schnackenburg, *The Epistle to the Ephesians* (1991:301).
127. Hans Küng, *The Church* (1968:238).
128. Emile Mersch, *The Whole Christ: The Historical Development of the Doctrine of the Mystical Body in Scripture and Tradition* (1938:119).
129. Mersch (1938:119).

Summary

As I have demonstrated so far, the history of the church during the apostolic age as documented in the New Testaments presents the framework, not only for understanding what the church is, but of all other questions regarding the introduction of theology and contextual ecclesiology. I have shown the environment from which the church arose as the temporal framework and the material from which she gained her forms of expression. In all of this, I have demonstrated that despite being influenced by diverse contextual situations, apostolic responses upheld a community that is still separate, thus disrupting any direct continuity both in thought and practice.

I now conclude with the same question with which I began my exploration of biblical understanding, that is, what on earth is the church? In answer to this I affirm apostolic theological claim that the church is *true* to the extent that it functions in obedience to Christ. Biblical understanding gives us but one major hermeneutical approach. The ecclesiology of the New Testament is founded on its central focus on Christology. In Christ alone is summed up the totality of what the church *should be* and can ever *aspire to be.* The church is not only incomplete without Christ, but more precisely, "without him [Christ] there would be no church at all."[130]

---

130. Ernest Best, *One Body in Christ* (1955:166).

PART VII

Foundations for Orthodoxy in the Post-Apostolic Church

In this section, I hope to take my quest for a biblical and contextualized ecclesiology further by drawing insights from the struggle for orthodoxy in the post-apostolic church of the second and third centuries. This is important because whatever the church means to us today cannot be separated from historical events. Although I have deduced the various starting points within the primitive church through a biblical exploration of the New Testament, an examinination of the church's later development to the end of the third century helps to fill in a broader picture.

The post-apostolic age is particularly helpful because it reveals a new dimension in the life of the young church, that is, the earliest Christian mission in the world of Hellenism. In other words, it is in the post-apostolic age that we see the emergence of the church and her witness to Jesus Christ in serious struggle "with both Judaism and Hellenism from without as well as Nomism and Gnosticism from within."[1] Overall, this period of the church's history is useful in at least two ways. On the one hand, it outlines the development of the church and her message. On the other hand, it highlights the foundations for orthodoxy in what has remained for us today as historical legacy in Christian thought and practice.

---

1. Leonard Goppelt, *Apostolic and Post-Apostolic Times* (1970:vii).

CHAPTER 10

The Early Church and Hellenism

To write about the context of the early church is a complicated historical undertaking. Not only is it impossible to include all of its various constituents and sometimes overlapping parts in any single work, but also the multifarious and coexisting cultures make a generalized contextual description extremely difficult. This means that the choice of where to begin and what not to include has to be made from the outset. Although the rules guiding this decision-process might be considerably subjective, the historian is, however, obligated to be considerate of historical significance.

The Context of the Early Church

As I have mentioned, the difficulties in dealing with the long and complicated historical legacy of Hellenistic Christianity cannot be ignored. Similarly, perspectives on how to approach it have varied greatly among patristic scholars. They have ranged from gracious works that laid the foundation for young and contemporary scholars, to a near-absolute withdrawal by those, like Maurice Wiles, who chose "to take for granted a lively interest in the history of the early church and a proper sense of its practical and human dimensions."[1] Wiles considered himself "fortunate enough" to do this so he "could concentrate on [his] own particular interest in the development of Christian doctrine."[2] This, unfortunately, is hopelessly simple, even naïve.

---

1. Maurice Wiles, "Orthodoxy and Heresy" (1991:198).
2. Wiles (1991:198).

It is especially disturbing that Wiles failed to realize that Christian doctrine could not have developed without the inspiration of those "practical and human dimensions," the contextual factors, which he took for granted. Unfortunately he, in an almost apologetic tone, and with unbecoming rancor, laid "some of the responsibility" for his own failure "at the door of the verve and quality of [William Frend's] teaching," a man he claimed "has not had an altogether wholesome influence on [him]."[3]

For the purpose of this book, to discuss the context of the early church is to give appropriate consideration to those impulses, both internal and external, that deepened and influenced the early church during the second and third centuries. I cannot, however, claim to judiciously delineate these impulses in a limited paper such as this. Nevertheless, I have allowed historical significance to inform my choice, regardless of how subjective this might seem. My discussion on the context of the early church, therefore, will focus on three important trends in the life of the fledging church: (1) the religious, (2) the intellectual/literary, and (3) the socio-political.

The Religious Trends

Christianity had to find its own formulae for survival early in its inception in the polytheistic pagan culture of the second century within a cauldron of competing philosophies, religions, and syncretistic perplexity. This was by far one of the greatest challenges that the burgeoning church had to face. There were not only the host rival gods of Greece and Rome; there were also the more satisfying Oriental cults that had overtaken the Greco-Roman world from the first century. With these religious diversities, the church had to battle on three fronts: against those on the outside, especially the synagogue, and the Hellenistic religions on the one hand; and within the church against internal rival claims to exclusive truth on the other. The following is not an exhaustive account but is a rapid sketch of the polemical context within which early Christianity lived and fought to survive.

---

3. Wiles (1991:198). For Frend's detailed historical work on the development of Christianity, see *The Rise of Christianity* (1984).

Encounter with Hellenistic Religions

Religion in the Greco-Roman period was overwhelmingly varied. Cosmopolitanism opened the door to strange gods, thus amalgamating the varied foreign religious forms and rites with indigenous ones. Despite this marriage of the gods, the early church made its presence strongly felt in a world of "boundless syncretism of oriental and occidental religions."[4] Although syncretistic confusion had rendered the monumental presence of these cults and religions somewhat questionable, yet the church had much to contend with against Hellenistic religions and against the vogue of the mystery religions.

Interestingly, the echoes of the church's message, especially with its synthesis in the incarnation, fell on ears that were already yearning for a "monotheistic interpretation of the conventional polytheism."[5] More than anything, the parallels between pagan religions and Christianity proved to be instrumental to the early church's triumphant foray into the pagan world. Samuel Angus has put it so graphically that I will quote him at length:

> Christianity brought a harmony for the burdensome antinomies of that age. Revelation confirmed the truth of natural religion and reason, and added something indispensable. Christianity was the synthesis of and the authority for the truths proclaimed by all systems. It elevated the abstract monotheism of Greece, the henotheistic monotheism of Oriental cults, the deistic monotheism of Judaism into a universal spiritual Fatherhood; it corrected abstract monotheism by the truth of polytheism that the Godhead is not simple and jejune but has in itself a rich and manifold life; it blended the immanence of pantheism with the transcendence of skepticism, mysticism, and Hebrew thought; it glorified the human sympathy of Oriental cults through the historic life and death of a Man of sorrows. Christianity gave what the world most needed. . . . The Incarnation of the "Desire of all nations" answered the

---

4. David Bosch, *Transforming Mission: Paradigm Shifts in Theology of Mission* (1991:193).
5. J.N.D. Kelly, *Early Christian Doctrines* (1978:12-13).

universal question of Seneca: *Ubi enim istum invenies quem tot saeculis quaerimus?* "Where shall he be found whom we have been seeking for so many centuries?"[6]

It is important to state, therefore, that this polytheistic syncretism and the disenchantment with indigenous religions were weapons to be carefully utilized in the Christians' attempt to satisfy the yearnings for monotheism.

Encounter with Judaism

As I have already noted, the religious battle of early Christian survival was not only waged against Hellenistic religions, but also against "Jews who found Christian claims objectionable or even ludicrous."[7] Although the early Christians had a common factor with the religious symbol of the Jews in the Septuagint, and perhaps in their monotheistic confession and repugnance of idolatry, on every other front, the early church and the Jewish synagogue were fundamentally different and damningly polemical towards each other.[8]

Scholarly opinions differ on the "exact" roots of the problem. While some locate the roots of the problem "in the failure of the Christian mission to the Jews,"[9] others see the Jewish reaction as a defense of Judaism which was in this Greco-Roman period "an evangelical religion that was in the process of breaking its ethnic boundaries to become a universal faith."[10] Whatever the case, there is a scholarly consensus that there was a

---

6. Samuel Angus, *The Environment of Early Christianity* (1951:225-226).
7. Bart Ehrman, *After the New Testament: A Reader in Early Christianity* (1999:4).
8. For studies dealing with the ancient origins of modern anti-Semitism, see Rosemary R. Ruether, *Faith and Fratricide: The Theological Roots of Anti-Semitism* (1974); and John G. Gager, *The Origins of Anti-Semitism: Attitudes toward Judaism in Pagan and Christian Antiquity* (1983). For Jewish attitudes toward Christians, see Claudia Setzer, *Jewish Responses to Early Christians: History and Polemics 30-150 C.E.* (1994); R. Travers Herford, *Christianity in Talmud and Midrash* (1903); A.B. Hulen, "Dialogues with the Jews as Sources for Early Jewish Arguments Against Christianity" (1932); and Simon Marcel, *Versus Israel: A Study of the Relations between Christians and Jews in the Roman Empire (135-425)* (1986).
9. See Bart D. Ehrman's *After the New Testament: A Reader in Early Christianity* (1999:7-24).
10. Rosemary R. Ruether, *Faith and Fratricide* (1974:26).

fundamental problem on the interpretation of Scripture, with its genetic center on the theological dispute over the messiaship of Jesus.

The Jews found it inconceivable that Jesus, "a crucified criminal, was the messiah and that his Gentile believers, who did not follow the Jewish Law, were the true people of the God of Israel."[11] To confess followership was to become anathematized in the synagogue and ultimately before the God of the patriarchs. This was especially the case after the fall of Jerusalem and the rise to dominance of the Pharisaic party. To the Jews, Jesus was a criminal who was "rightly condemned as a deceiver" (Lev. 24:16).[12]

While the messiaship of Jesus was inconceivable to the Jews, the Christians were more concerned about making the divinity of Christ comprehensible by utilizing the *fulfillment motif* to portray him as the long-awaited Messiah. To think of Christianity and Judaism as belonging to the same symbolic system is also to amplify the incompatibility of church and synagogue. While the former is set toward mission and the conversion of all, the latter has no *equivalent* urge toward an all-inclusive evangelization.[13]

Encounter with "Heretics"

The Christian church in the second and third centuries had to combat disparate doctrinal beliefs that seemed to endanger crucial aspects of the Christian faith. For the sake of clarity, it is possible to identify (although not in a totally exclusive way) early Christian encounter with theological polemics on two fronts. On the one hand were the syncretistic religious systems of Gentile and Jewish non-believers that found valuable aspects of Christianity and adapted them to their own systems.

On the other hand were the conflicting beliefs of the many Judaizing movements and the multiplicity of groups that represented the exceptional diversity of early Christianity.[14] In the words of Ehrman, these were

---

11. Bart D. Ehrman, *After the New Testament* (1999:4).
12. William Horbury, "The Jewish Dimension" (1991:49).
13. Krister Stendahl, "Judaism and Christianity II: After a Colloquium and a War" (1967:2).
14. Modern historians of the later Roman Empire have attributed some of these conflicting beliefs (heresies and schisms) to national rather than purely religious movements. For a detailed analysis of this thesis, see E.L. Woodward, *Christianity and*

"believers in Christ who took radically different views on matters of practical and theological importance."[15] Among these groups can be identified Gnosticism, Marcion, Montanism, Monarchianism, Sabellius, and Adoptionism.[16]

The relationship of orthodoxy (from the Greek words *orthos*, "right," and *doxa*, "opinion" or "doctrine" = "true doctrine" or "true practice") to heresy (from the Greek word *hairesis*, "choice") had not been established during this period of the early church. However, the battle was already apparent on what ecclesiastical doctrines were considered "orthodox" from those that were deemed "nonorthodox" or "heretical."

Justo González has observed that "although the organization of the church during the second century was not such as to allow it to make quick and final decisions, the church at large reacted to the heresies in a surprisingly uniform way," adding that "the fundamental argument that could be adduced against the various heresies [was] apostolic authority."[17] In other words, apostolic authority became the "final argument that lies behind such antiheretical instruments as the New Testament canon, the rule of faith, the creeds, and the emphasis on apostolic succession."[18]

Walter Bauer has challenged this classical understanding of the relationship of orthodoxy and heresy. He argued that the early Christian church did not comprise a single orthodoxy from which emerged conflicting heresies. In his opinion, "early Christianity embodied a number of divergent forms, no one of which represented the clear and powerful

---

Nationalism in the Later Roman Empire (1916). See also A.H.M. Jones, "Were Ancient Heresies National or Social Movements in Disguise?" (1993).

15. Bart D. Ehrman, *After the New Testament* (1999:4).

16. For an account of the discovery of a large collection of Gnostic writings, see Jean Doresse, *The Secret Books of the Egyptian Gnostics: An Introduction to the Gnostic Coptic Manuscripts Discovered at Chenoboskion* (1960:116-136). For other important works in this area, see James M. Robinson, *The Nag Hammadi Library in English* (1988); Walter Bauer, *Orthodoxy and Heresy in Earliest Christianity* (1971); Bentley Layton, *The Gnostic Scriptures* (1987); Elaine Pagels, *The Gnostic Gospels* (1976); Kurt Rudolf, *Gnosis: The Nature and History of Gnosticism* (1983); Frederik Wisse, "The Nag Hammadi Library and the Heresiologists" (1971); Bart D. Ehrman, *The Orthodox Corruption of Scripture* (1993); and *After the New Testament: A Reader in Early Christianity* (1999).

17. Justo L. González, *A History of Christian Thought* (1970:146).

18. González (1970:146).

majority of believers against all others."[19] Ehrman has reiterated Bauer's thesis by saying that "this traditional understanding does not conform to historical reality." According to him, "there were . . . numerous Christian groups in the second and third centuries, with a wide range of beliefs and practices . . . each claim[ing] to represent the original teachings of Jesus and the apostles."[20]

Bauer's "reconstruction of orthodoxy and heresy," observes Ehrman, "was the deconstruction of the terms of the debate."[21] The Bauer challenge has fundamentally paved the way for the current historical *shibboleth* that sees the definition of "orthodoxy" as one-sided, one that has been "constructed" by the "winners" of this battle of doctrinal beliefs. It should be emphasized that a dose of historical relativism is welcome. However, as Carl Badger has observed, "to consider the resulting 'orthodox' positions to be 'orthodox' merely on account of their being espoused by the winning group among all numerous options in early Christianity is to throw away all critical theological responsibility."[22] This is at best the summation of Bauer's "winner takes it all" approach which has found a sympathetic audience in Ehrman.

A much better route, suggests Badger, "is to try to understand *in context* before judging."[23] Herein lies the significance of Badger's thesis. The allusion to apostolic doctrine or authority was a sufficient reason to unify a church that was still in the process of self-definition. The church did not deem it necessary "to construct a new system" but rather to "establish more firmly the truth which the church had possessed from the beginning, and to gain a clearer understanding of it."[24] Polemical confrontations of the early church require that we ask *in context* and examine historically why the "orthodox" position is of enduring value over against the other options that were considered an aberration and an adulteration of "true" apostolic doctrine.

---

19. Bart D. Ehrman, *The Orthodox Corruption of Scripture* (1993:7). For details on Walter Bauer's position, see his work, *Orthodoxy and Heresy in Earliest Christianity* (1971).
20. Bart D. Ehrman, *After the New Testament* (1999:131).
21. Bart D. Ehrman, *The Orthodox Corruption of Scripture* (1993:7).
22. Carl Badger, "Early Church History" (2000:13-14).
23. Badger (2000:13-14).
24. Reinhold Seeberg, *Textbook of the History of Doctrines* (1956:119).

The Intellectual-Literary Trends

The will to resist Christianity also intensified from nonliterary forms of opposition and found its accomplice in the genius of intellectual and literary sophistication of the opponents. On the one hand, the early church had to withstand the stamina of its opponents' intransigent appeal to philosophical justification, pamphlets, and books. On the other hand, perhaps the more subtle and dangerous, it had to battle noncanonical pseudepigrapha which had already become a phenomenon within Christianity itself. For the purpose of this sketch, I will concern myself with the literary trends by looking at: Greco-Roman intellectualism/philosophy, Gnosticism, and New Testament pseudepigrapha.

Greco-Roman Intellectualism/Philosophy[25]

The Romans were not noted for novel approaches to philosophy. Rather, much of what was to become Greco-Roman philosophy had been a Greek invention. This encounter between early Christianity and philosophy can be said to have "originated in pre-Socratic Greek thought, reach[ing] a fully developed form in Plato and Aristotle, and was continued in the various philosophical schools of Hellenism."[26]

True to its Greek origin, *philosophia* ("love of wisdom"), Greek philosophical thought was an attempt to understand the ultimate nature and principles of reality from every point of broad thought. Its romance with religion was in particular "a call to [humanity] to seek the synthesis of life in revelation and religion."[27] When Christianity came into the Greco-Roman world, it encountered a world that was already dominated by the spirit of intellectual aristocracy. Consequently, philosophy had come to be recognized as the deeper religion of most intelligent people.

To be considered an educated person, therefore, was to court Stoic and Platonic philosophy and be acquainted with Greek poets. Whether or not one was a Christian, the intellectual culture of the time was such

---

25. My concern here is a descriptive sketch of the milieu within which early Christianity existed and fought to survive.
26. David Balás, "Philosophy" (1999:914).
27. Samuel Angus, *The Environment of Early Christianity* (1951:174).

that philosophical concepts provided the intellectual framework for self-expression and ideas.[28] Ignorance was considered the source of sin and salvation remained only within the realm of cultivated understanding. Christianity at this time could not avoid being held in contempt by the culture of intellectualism for certain obvious reasons. First, it was considered to be lacking the philosophical reflection for articulating the transcendent. Secondly, and perhaps more important, it was composed largely of simple folk with little or no education.

A very good example of a late second-century philosopher who held Christianity in such contempt as intellectually absurd was Celsus. His polemic against Christianity was that it appealed to faith rather than rational knowledge; hence it converted only simple-minded people such as women, children, and slaves. According to him:

> Some [Christians] do not even want to give or to receive a reason for what they believe, and use such expressions as "Do not ask questions; just believe" and "Your faith will save you." Others quote the apostle Paul. "The wisdom in the world is evil and foolishness a good thing" (1 Co. 1:25-26).[29]

Celsus was not only concerned about this intellectually unsophisticated faith but also that these uneducated members of the lower classes were so involved with proselytizing that they pushed their opinions forward even when confronted by educated pagans. His work was a treatise that identified the "true doctrine" with the revered traditions of ancient doctrines and of the ancestors.[30] The work of Celsus is preserved for us only in fragments but may confidently be reconstructed from Origen's massive eight-volume reply.[31]

From the late second century onwards, an interesting twist to the encounter between early Christianity and Hellenistic philosophy took place.

---

28. J.N.D. Kelly, *Early Christian Doctrines* (1978:14).
29. Celsus, *On the True Doctrine: A Discourse against the Christians* 1.9.
30. Celsus, *On the True Doctrine* 1.14.
31. For Origen's eight-volume reply, see *Against Celsus*.

By this time, philosophy had raised questions which only religion could answer. From the works of early apologists like Justin Martyr, Clement of Alexandria, Origen, and others, a new Christian tradition emerged. It was a tradition of the "sophisticated Christian scholar who could match any pagan philosopher, particularly since they could make use of the same type of argument as the Greek teachers did."[32]

Gnosticism: Pathfinder for Christian Intellectualism

I have sketched the culture of intellectualism that dominated the Hellenistic world of the second century. Within this context of intellectual pride arose the Gnostics who wished to be distinguished from the "unlearned multitude" as those "who had grasped Christianity in its transcendent significance."[33] Derived from the Greek word *gnōsis* ("knowledge"), Gnosticism was however not altogether influenced by the rational knowledge of Hellenistic philosophy. Rather, it was more of esoteric knowledge with roots in oriental mysticism and other religious and quasi-philosophical movements of the Hellenistic world. David Bosch gives a graphic description of this amalgam of the speculative and the intellectual when he writes, "in spite of its air of sophistication Gnosticism really was not a philosophy, but a quasi-philosophy, one which despaired of human rationality."[34]

Gnōsis in this sense must be freed from the misleading associations suggested by the tradition of classical philosophy with its emphasis on "reason." Rather, it refers to a "revealed knowledge" or "secret teaching" available only to a select few. It was on the basis of this so-called privileged revelation that the Gnostics "were forward to claim that Christ had revealed to a select circle what he never had declared openly, and that this secret teaching had been transmitted continuously through a line of disciples, whose natures rendered them receptive of the mystery."[35] By its claim to apostolic doctrine Gnosticism became, not only an appealing alternative

---

32. David Bosch, *Transforming Mission* (1991:193).
33. Henry Sheldon, *History of the Christian Church* (1895:202).
34. David Bosch, *Transforming Mission* (1991:199).
35. Henry Sheldon, *History of the Christian Church* (1895:203).

to orthodox Christianity but an extreme Hellenization of the Christian faith.[36]

The most distinctive speculative construction of Gnosticism was its ontological dualism, professing a struggle between a transcendent God and some inferior deity who had created the world of matter. This material creation was intrinsically evil and was considered the result of some prehistoric disorder; some fall in the heavenly realm. By the activities of this renegade being, the universe was perceived as a prison from which the spirit must escape in its return to eternity. This was the Gnostics' way of explaining the riddle of existence, the antithesis of the good and evil, the temporal and the eternal, the earthly and the heavenly.[37]

On the account of this imprisonment arises the need for redemption, for a liberator from the transcendent world. This is where the Christian Gnostics located Jesus. However, theirs was a docetic Christology in that Christ's humanity was only a disguise worn by the heavenly liberator. Gnostic Christology affirmed that the spiritual Christ frequently entered the human Jesus at his baptism and departed prior to the crucifixion.[38] Thus, Gnosticism we can say was an integrative structure that attempted to develop a form of Christianity that provided an answer to some of the deepest metaphysical and theological problems.

How was the church to reconcile this radical perversion of the Christian truth with the inner spirit of its own profession of redemption that is available only through Christ, the revelation of the Father? To say that the church was merely challenged to a combat of doctrines is to undermine the mighty intellectual and philosophical polemics that threatened the church's very existence. On the contrary, the church implacably rejected

---

36. Adolf Von Harnack, *The Mission and Expansion of Christianity in the First Three Centuries* (1962:250).

37. Philip Schaff has summarized ideas that characterized all the Gnostic systems thus: (1) Dualism; the assumption of an eternal antagonism between God and matter. (2) The demiurgic notion; the separation of the creator of the world or the demiurgos from the proper God. (3) Docetism; the resolution of the human element in the person of the Redeemer into mere deceptive appearance. For details see his work, *History of the Christian Church* (1858:452ff.). For a similar summary, see J.N.D. Kelly, *Early Christian Doctrines* (1978).

38. Pheme Perkins, "Docetism" (1999:341).

this extreme Helenization of Christianity with a sophisticated and logical apprehension of its doctrines of salvation. To the church's eternal credit, she came forth victorious, thus setting the stage for "the task of developing the substance of the Christian truth in theoretical form."[39]

The Threat of New Testament Pseudepigrapha

I have already indicated that the claim to apostolicity was the primary weapon of early Christian struggles against heresy. It becomes imperative, therefore, that I take the religio-phenomenological discussion a step further by looking briefly at the problem of "forgeries" as this adds another dimension to our understanding of the complexities and diversities that characterized early Christianity. The twenty-seven books of the New Testament that have become the ecclesiastical Holy Writ for the modern church were not readily available to the early church. Instead, the early church evolved out of a world of "apostolic" writings, most of which were ostensibly forged in the name of Jesus' original apostles.

Pseudepigraphon (plural "pseudepigrapha") is a term from the Greek word *pseudepigraphos* that translates to "false superscription" in the English language. In reference to the New Testament and early Christian writings, "pseudepigrapha" refers to writings that were incorrectly ascribed to authors other than the real ones. Although pseudepigraphy was a common practice during the second century, it cannot be equated with literary forgery in the contemporary sense since many pseudepigrapha were not intended to deceive the reading audience.[40]

Rather, "many early Christians considered it proper to attribute thoughts or documents to someone who had inspired them."[41] Hence, the

---

39. Philip Schaff, *History of the Christian Church* (1858:509).
40. James H. Charlesworth, "Pseudepigraphy" (1999:961).
41. See Charlesworth (1999:961). For an extensive study of these pseudepigraphal writings, see David G. Meade, *Pseudonymity and Canon: An Investigation into the Relationship of Authorship and Authority in Jewish and Earliest Christian Tradition* (1986); James H. Charlesworth and J.R. Mueller, *The New Testament Apocrypha and Pseudepigrapha: A Guide to Publications with Excursuses on Apocalypses* (1987); B.M. Metzger, "Literary Forgeries and Canonical Pseudepigrapha" (1972); and K. Aland, "The Problem of Anonymity and Pseudonymity in Christian Literature of the First Two Centuries" (1965:1-13).

late second-century church saw a barrage of "apostolic" genres of writing in the form of gospels, acts, epistles, and apocalypses; writings that have now been regarded as pseudepigrahical.

Along with the other "admirable reasons" why early Christians would want to attribute their works to others, Charlesworth has singled out a "more important" reason for the frequent occurrence of forgery during these early days of Christianity. This was attributable to "the need to anchor a tradition in the apostolic period."[42] Although there was yet no "New Testament" as we have it today, the church also saw the *need* to respond to this superficial claim to apostolicity. Hence the proto-orthodox group was committed "to collect a group of 'apostolic' authorities that attested the orthodox understanding of the faith."[43] More importantly, the *need* was emphasized for a literal translation of the "textual authorities of these canons" so as to prevent "misuse" in the hands of heretics.[44]

Out of these theological debates and exigencies, there arose movements for the canonization of Scripture and the organization of the church with the aim of establishing an ecclesiastical norm "for life and doctrine, for the compass of Scripture and worship, and thus to make membership of the *one* church visible and manifest."[45]

The Socio-Political Trend

As the church progressed further into the Hellenistic civilization of the post-apostolic age, hostility and persecution continued. I have already attributed the first of these persecutions to the Jews who could not forgive the Christians for their apostasy from the faith of the fathers. The New Testament recorded numerous accounts of earliest persecutions of Christians by the Jews. An obvious case was Paul's own confession who, as a Jewish Pharisee, had persecuted the church "beyond measure" (Gal. 1:13), and that later, as a Christian, he had been treated with the same punishment by Jewish authorities (2 Co. 11:24).

---

42. James H. Charlesworth, "Pseudepigraphy" (1999:963).
43. Bart D. Ehrman, *The Orthodox Corruption of Scripture* (1993:25).
44. Ehrman (1993:25).
45. Edgar Hennecke, *The New Testament Apocrypha* (1991:23).

Hostility towards Christianity was, however, not limited to the Jews alone. There were also threats of mob violence resulting from both a widespread antipathy toward Christians and the great imperial persecutions. For the purpose of this paper, I will concern myself with those misconceptions that led to the persecutions of Christians.

The Conflict with the Romans

There can be little doubt that an ominous part of early church history was the persecution of Christianity by the pagan imperial power of Rome. While this was incidental, it is within a reasonable estimate of historicity to affirm Robert L. Williams' observation that "[t]he first Christians were conditioned to expect persecution even before they experienced it."[46] In this regard, three overlapping periods of Christian persecutions can be identified: (1) Jewish persecution of Christians from Jesus' death to the great fire in Rome, 64 A.D., (2) persecutions instigated by the Roman mobs, 64-250 A.D., and (3) persecutions initiated by the imperial State power, 250-313 A.D.[47]

Christianity as a Socially Offensive Religion

The negative perception of Christianity as a socially offensive religion can be attributed to the pagans' misunderstanding of Christian behavior and social life. On the social front, the Christians met secretly, withdrawn from both the social and ordinary civic society. The Christians' understanding of Christ's love also was expressed in mutual brotherly sharing and the Eucharist. These secret meetings and affirmation of brotherly love were incomprehensible to the Roman mind. Instead, they denounced the Christians for these practices and charged them with perpetrating the grossest immoralities of sexual promiscuity and cannibalism in their nocturnal meetings.

These and other charges are reflected in the writings of second-century pagan authors. For example, the Roman historian, Tactius, reports that

---

46. For details, see Robert L. Williams, "Persecution" (1999:895).
47. Williams (1999:895-899).

the Christians were derided as "haters of the human race," and that their tradition was "hideous and shameful," even "a deadly superstition."[48]

A more graphic description of the Christian practice finds expression in Pliny's well-known judicial investigations to Emperor Trajan. Pliny, the governor of Bithynia (111-113 A.D.), had investigated the Christian practice and reported that "they were in the habit of meeting on a certain fixed day before it was light . . . they sang in alternate verses a hymn to Christ, as to a god, and bound themselves together by a solemn oath."[49] By his account, Christians had formed a community joined together by myths, ritual practices, and doctrines about gods.

In Pliny's account, the Christian community was "nothing more than a pervert and extravagant superstition."[50] For his part, Trajan replied that Christianity was already viewed as criminal. Consequently, Christians were to be punished if they persisted in their profession and practices.[51]

Christianity as a Politically Dangerous Religion

Perception of Christianity as a politically dangerous religion was prompted by the disaffection of the Roman population as I have already highlighted. The threat for the imperial power also arose out of the Christians' refusal to participate in the pagan emperor-cult with all its idolatrous ceremonies and festivities. Instead, the Christians held strongly to their exclusive belief in the one God, thus invalidating the flourishing pantheons of the Roman gods.

This abstention had both religious and political ramifications for the Christians. First, they were dubbed atheists and also considered to be enemies of the Caesars and the Roman people. A more important implication, however, was the conviction that the Christians' abstention could bring divine retribution upon the state itself. Even more suspicious to Roman sensibilities was the Christian practice of secret meetings (*collegia*). The suspicion was aggravated because these secret meetings were similar to some of those Roman social clubs that had been considered disorderly due

---

48. Tacitus, *Annales* 15.44.
49. Pliny, *Letters* 10.96-97.
50. Ibid.
51. Ibid.

to their political agitations. The consequences for the earliest Christians were greviuos and took the form of state-sponsored persecutions.

Imperial Persecutions

The earliest example of imperial persecutions occurred in the second half of the first century under Nero after the great fire of 64 A.D. Tacitus' account describes the destruction as a conflagration that had been orchestrated by Nero himself. However, Nero found in the Christians scapegoats who, by the time of his reign, had become unpopular with the multitude. By the time that 1 Peter was written (ca. 90), suspicion against the Christians had reached such a level that the mere profession of Christianity was cause for incarceration (1 Pe. 4:12-17).[52]

Subsequent persecutions, those instigated by the society and those initiated by the governments, included those of Domitian (80-96), Trajan (98-117), Hadrian (117-138), Marcus Aurelius (161-180), Commodus (180-192), Caracalla and Geta (211), Maximinus Thrax (235-238), Philip (244-249), Decius (249-251), Valerian (253-260), Gallienus (260-268), and Diocletian (284-305). Although these persecutions were mostly occasional, the spate continued until the time of Constantine (312-337), the emperor who was to identify himself with the Christian God.[53]

I have sketched the context into which the post-apostolic church was born. This, however, begs the question as to how the early Christians were expected to live and minister in such an overwhelmingly hostile environment. Regarding the "how to" of ministry, there are no records except for the fact that the evidence comes from fragmentary exhortations and inferences from narratives. This is the focus of the next stage of this work as I investigate the life and ministry of the early church during the Hellenistic period.

---

52. Tacitus, *Annales* 15.38-44.
53. For a chronological survey of these persecutions, see Robert Lee Williams, "Persecution" (1999:895-899). See also Mark Reasoner, "Persecution" (1997:907-914).

The Ministry of the Early Church

I have attempted a brief description of the context within which early Christianity emerged and survived as a religious phenomenon. By so doing, I have examined the different practical and human dimensions of its most zealous and concerted adversaries. From this rapid sketch of the context, I have established that although the church was not a unitary religious phenomenon from the moment of inception, it had attained such a synthesis toward the Hellenistic society by the second century so that it came to be described by some Roman aristocracy as a "plague."

As already pointed out, there were no "how to's" either of ministry or theology since these were in the process of developing. Consequently, my conception of "ministry" in this paper should not be misunderstood. I use the word "ministry" from two perspectives. First, it refers to a brief historical sequence of the second- and third-century routinized hierarchy of ecclesiastical offices. Secondly, it refers to the inward necessity or the impulses to respond to external factors (or views and misconceptions) in the struggle to remain the church in historical existence.

These impulses have been interpreted as characterizing some form of *specialized* ministry. Consequently, my discussion will include such areas as: (1) ecclesiastical office as ministry, (2) the role of martyrdom, (3) missionary orientation as ministry, and (4) reasoned defense as ministry.

Ecclesiastical Office as Ministry

It is almost impossible to determine precisely the early church's understanding of ministry and leadership. Although the Greek word for "ministry" (*diakonia*) was a prominent term in New Testament times, its usage had many divergent and conflicting conceptions denying our ability to have a concise picture as to how the early church understood the office of public ministry and leadership. It is generally agreed, however, that the first set of documents clearly witnessing the ministry of the church as an office are *First Clement* (ca. 96), the *Didache* (ca. 100-150), and the letters of Ignatius (ca. 110-117).[54]

Although there is no consensus whether *First Clement* can in fact be regarded as the earliest example of this development, it is indisputable that it does witness to an official ministry. Consequently, it is appropriate to say that the development of ministry as an office, and the hierarchical institutionalization of it, is a second- and third-century phenomenon. By any standard, this period was particularly a critical one for the bourgeoning church and required a more distinct form of ecclesiastical organization different from the informal and fluid charismatic model of the apostolic period.

Factors Which Contributed toward a Hierarchical Order

Philip Schaff has described several important changes that appeared during this period, "the distinction of clergy and laity, and the sacerdotal view of the ministry becomes prominent and fixed; subordinate church offices are multiplied; the episcopate arises; the beginnings of the Roman primacy appear; and the exclusive unity of the Catholic church develops in opposition to heretics and schismatics."[55]

One of the primary factors for these changes was the growth of the church during this period. As the size of the church developed, along with the complexity of community life, several important changes had to be made in order to consolidate the existence and continuity of the church. Bernard Cooke has observed:

> As the church grew in size, it was inevitable that there be a certain dilution of the commitment and enthusiasms of the early decades, and it proved increasingly necessary to devise methods, such as the formalized catechumenate, to safeguard

---

54. For a full treatment of activities within the Christian Synagoue, see W.H.C. Frend, *The Rise of Christianity* (1984), especially chapters 4-7.
55. Philip Schaff, *History of the Christian Church* (1858:121).

and foster the spirit and insights upon which the community lived.[56]

A second factor arose out of the need to combat chaotic situations that I have mentioned as both internal and external to the church. Internally, the church was faced with the dangers of heretical falsifications and schisms, while it simultaneously faced the external challenges of socio-political antipathy and persecutions. These situations created the need to work out a theology of ecclesiastical offices, the body in which was to be invested the authority that would give potency to the church's profession of faith and its accepted canon.

This need to develop a theology of ecclesiastical offices was taken a step further by Ignatius.[57] His was a theology of the episcopate that advocated most eloquently for the "complete and unconditional bond of union between bishop and congregation."[58] His advocacy for "union" in the face of schisms naturally led to his understanding of the church as the "Catholic" church, the only precursor of the unity of doctrine and teachings.[59] Through this "union," the congregation was to respect the bishop as fully as they respect the authority of God,[60] and act in accord with his (bishop) mind (Eph. 4:1). Presbyters and deacons were likewise to be respected as people of authority, and together as a church should be in harmony before the Father through Jesus Christ (Eph. 4:2).

Bernard Cooke has attributed another factor to the church's attitude of "settling down." This conception was largely nourished by the realization that the church "was meant to continue in historical existence for a long period." Consequently, there was a shift of emphasis from an ardent hope in the approaching *parousia* "to the kingdom of God as it exists in the historical church." These convictions, observes Cooke, "changes people's

---

56. Bernard Cooke, *Ministry to Word and Sacraments: History and Theology* (1976:58).
57. For details on the Letters of Ignatius to the Ephesians, Magnesians, and Smyrneans, see Cyril C. Richardson, *Early Christian Fathers* (1996).
58. Karl Baus, *Handbook of Church History: From the Apostolic Community to Constantine* (1965:148-149).
59. Ignatius, *Smyrneans* 8.1-2.
60. Ignatius, *Magnesians* 3.2.

view towards those offices within the community that are necessary to make an earthly 'kingdom' run effectively! Ministry is still seen as having 'community' as its goal, but the idea of this community is undergoing change."[61]

The Beginnings of a Hierarchical Institutional Order

In so far as we can clearly identify ministry in the early church, our strongest biblical account are those churches associated with the apostle Paul. The structure of ministry in these churches has been described as "diaconal."[62] This is so called because of their sharp emphasis on charisma. Rather than being organized around ordained or official ministers, the general concept of "priesthood" in these charismatic communities was largely based on the spiritual endowment (*charisma*) of the individual by God to exercise for the good of the congregation.

Accordingly, Küng has observed that, "the church, being a fellowship of gifts of the spirits, is also a fellowship of different ministries."[63] Consequently, the diversity of ministry in any local church, especially in those of Paul, was as fluid and limitless as the diversity of charisms in that particular church (1 Co. 12:28-31; Rom. 12:6-8; Eph. 4:11-13; 1 Pe. 4:10-11).

By the second century, however, a new phenomenon is observable. This was the rise of monoepiscopacy where the bishop became the converging force within the church. It emphasizes a shift from the usual board of elders as the governing authority of a community to a single bishop who is vested with executive powers over a local community. Similarly, the charismatic teaching ministry and governance by apostles, prophets, and teachers was bequeathing its roles and influence to the administrative class of bishops, elders, and deacons.

The first example of this new trend was Ignatius, who became the single head of the church in Antioch as its bishop. His *corpus Ignatianum* not only provide valuable information regarding post-apostolic Christianity, his letters to the churches of Asia Minor reveal that monoepiscopacy had

---

61. For details, see Bernard Cooke, *Ministry to Word and Sacraments* (1976:58).
62. For details, see Hans Küng, *The Church* (1968:393ff.).
63. Küng (1968:393ff.).

gained ascent and had been adopted in places like Ephesus, Philadelphia, Magnesia, and Smyrna. I must add, however, that it is impossible to suppose that this trend was as at yet a universal practice.

Ignatius' insistence on ecclesiastical order and unity flows throughout all his letters, showing this theme to be his strongest after that of the desire for martyrdom. He unites in the bishop, not only doctrinal and liturgical authority,[64] but also disciplinary authority.[65] As an embodiment of unity and authority in the church, the bishop is to be respected and obeyed even if he is as young as Damas of Magnesia.

The bishop is the representative of God without whom no ecclesiastical activity can take place. As he declares emphatically, "where the bishop is present, there let the congregation gather, just as where Jesus Christ is, there is the Catholic Church."[66] To do anything contrary to this stipulation is synonymous to being in the devil's camp because "he who acts without the bishop's knowledge is in the devil's service."[67]

His advocacy for a monarchical episcopate followed a tripartite structure of "*One* eucharist, *one* body of the Lord, *one* cup, *one* altar, and therefore *one* bishop together with the presbyterium and the deacons, his fellow servants."[68] Thus, Ignatius established a definite three-tiered hierarchical structure in which the bishop was clearly distinguished (although closely connected with) the presbytery of which he was the leader (Eph. 4:1).[69] By so consolidating the ministry of the church after a threefold ministry, the division between "clergy" and "laity" was complete.

Although the Ignatian pattern did not immediately become an empire-wide practice in the beginning, it was, however, generally observed by the end of the second century. In this appeal to ministry as an office, Quentin Wesselschmidt observes that:

---

64. Ignatius, *Smyrneans* 8.1-2.
65. Ignatius, *Philadelphians*. 8.1.
66. Ignatius, *Smyrneans* 8.2.
67. Ignatius, *Smyrneans* 9.1.
68. Ignatius, *Philadelphians*. 4.1.
69. Ignatius, *Philadelphians*. 7.1.

> The bishop has increasingly assumed responsibility for the spiritual life of the church as the successor of the apostles and representative of Christ. . . . He also has become the primary preacher and spiritual leader, whose authority resided generally in the office passed down through a succession of bishops [apostolic succession], rather than by the call of the laity."[70]

As the church expanded, the tendency towards hierarchical structure led to the institution of additional orders of ministry below the diaconate, the *ordines minores*. By the middle of the third century there were added the offices of subdeacons, readers, acolytes, exorcists, precentors, janitors, and catechists.

Everett Ferguson has observed that "the orders of ministry in the church were increasingly thought of on the analogy of officers in the civil government, with the result that a person was expected to pass through the lower grades of the clergy in advancement to the higher offices."[71] Admission to clerical office was by ordination and was meant to connect to the earliest days of the church, and to act "as a sign of the bestowal of charismatic gifts, or separation for a special duty" (Ac. 6:6, 13:3; 1 Ti. 4:14, 5:20; 2 Ti. 1:6).[72]

Are we then to think that hierarchical development of ecclesiastical ministry sowed the seeds for potential corruption? This question is a relevant one for today especially with the current debates over the emergence of an official ministry. We should remember, however, that these earliest Christians responded in the best possible way known to them. That is, to "assure the theological solidarity of the Christian community ever in perils of its life from a hostile populace and an intermittently persecuting magistracy."[73]

---

70. Quentin Wesselschmidt, "The Concept and Practice of the Ministry in the Early Church: Structure, Formative Influences, and Scriptural Correspondence" (1988:257-258).
71. Everett Ferguson, "Ministry" (1999:751).
72. Williston Walker, *A History of the Christian Church* (1959:82-83).
73. George Williams, "The Ministry of the Ante-Nicene Church" (1956:28).

As Hanson has also observed, the church of the second and third centuries may have developed the concept of ministry as an office, it may have added new offices without "satisfactory theological interpretations" to them, the official ministry did not "become an intolerable burden and clog." Rather, the official ministry "was still flexible [and was] still capable of functioning effectively in ministering that which alone can give such a ministry justification, the communication of the gospel of Jesus Christ."[74]

The Ideal of Martyrdom

Phillip Schaff asks a provocative question in the preface to one of his church history volumes in a way that seemingly makes Christianity a different faith for the contemporary mind. Commenting on literary discoveries and the works of church historians, Schaff asks, "but who could now write a history of the first three centuries without recording the lessons of those rude yet expressive pictures, sculptures, and epitaphs from the homes of confessors and martyrs?"[75] As one reflects on Schaff's question, and in consideration of the fact that martyrdom became the ultimate and the most prominent expression of Christian life in the face of increased persecution, I cannot but write this history in a way that considers martyrdom as some form of *specialized ministry*.

Opinions differ widely as to whether or not the desire for death was credible enough to count for martyrdom, especially when we take into consideration the eagerness and the desire for death on the part of the would-be martyrs themselves. The overriding question has been whether the desire for death was an act of heroism (martyrdom), or some form of suicide. Regardless of one's position, the fact is that Christianity in the second and third centuries was an "emerging" alternative tradition that stood as a challenge to the already established cults of the gods and a threat to the existence of the State itself. As a result, we must reckon with the fact that martyrdom became evidently the single most visible expression of

---

74. Richard Hanson, *Studies in Christian Antiquity* (1985:143).
75. Phillip Schaff, *History of the Christian Church* (1858:vii).

Christianity and the medium through which many "pagans became aware of Christianity in the first place."[76]

As Christians came under increased persecution, so also did their heroic constancy in loyalty to Christ increase into the ideal of witness through death. Rather than employ revolutionary opposition to these persecutions, the attraction for the church was the connection between martyrdom and imitation of Christ. This conception finds its strongest expression in Ignatius who considered martyrdom as the highest manifestation of discipleship and fidelity to Jesus Christ[77] and as an act of imitating Jesus' passion.[78] Also, that the witness of the church was furthered decisively by the martyrdom of the faithful has been attributed to Tertullian, who is credited with saying: "The blood of the martyrs is indeed the seed of the church. Dying we conquer."[79]

Another justification for considering martyrdom as a form of *specialized* ministry of the early church can be attributed to the many writings of exhortation to martyrdom. Not only was violent death an expression of Christian life and the ultimate act of witnessing to Christ, Christian writers deliberately voiced enthusiasm for martyrdom. This was probably to encourage the believers in the face of an overwhelming defection and denial. Examples of such exhortations to martyrdom can be found in the writings of apologists such as Origen, Tertullian, and Cyprian.[80]

Cyprian particularly comforted and strengthened Christians facing martyrdom with the assurance that the Lord "himself contends in us, goes to battle with us, and in our hard struggle himself gives the crown and receives it."[81] Perhaps one of the most passionate and apologetic exhortations

---

76. G.W. Bowersock, *Martyrdom and Rome* (1995:66). For other excellent discussions of martyrdom and suicide among Christians in antiquity, see A. Droge and J. Tabor, *A Noble Death: Suicide and Martyrdom among Christians and Jews in Antiquity* (1992). See also Rodney Stark, *The Rise of Christianity* (1996).

77. Ignatius, *Romans*. 4.2.

78. Ignatius, *Romans*. 6.3.

79. For the reference to Tertullian, see A.B. Luter, "Martyrdom" (1997:720).

80. Origen, *Exhortation to Martyrdom*; Tertullian, *To the Martyrs*; and Cyprian, *To Fortunatus*.

81. Cyprian, *Epistles*. 10.4; 37.2; 76.7. See also Karl Baus, *Handbook of Church History: From the Apostolic Community to Constantine* (1965:293).

to martyrdom was the letter of Ignatius to the Romans. Not only did he convey a message of encouragement, the letter reflects his own "passion for death."[82] Moreover, he considers himself to be "voluntarily dying for God" and pleads with the Roman Christians not to do him "an unseasonable kindness" by interfering in the process.[83]

That martyrdom evolved to become a criterion for Christian perfection can be seen from the theological premises by which this heroic act was interpreted. Everett Ferguson has provided an excellent synthesis of the many theological interpretations by which martyrdom was understood and perhaps encouraged. According to his account of early Christian perspective, martyrdom was a grace not given by God to everyone but only to those who have been chosen by God for this experience. Also, to be a martyr was to be counted worthy by God.[84]

Martyrdom was an imitation of and a participation in the sufferings of Christ[85] who was present with the martyr, strengthening him or her.[86] The Holy Spirit filled the martyrs and inspired them with eloquence.[87] Martyrdom was a fight with the devil and his demons in which victory was won by the martyr.[88]

The fruit of the devotion to martyrdom as a form of ministry finds its uttermost reward in the number of conversions to Christianity.[89] John Foxe put it more graphically when he writes:

> The sight of their [Christians] cheerful countenances as they were led to execution, astonished the lookers-on, and made many inquire what this belief could be that seemed to rob

---

82. Ignatius, *Romans.* 7.2.
83. Ignatius, *Romans.* 4.1.
84. Hippolytus, *The Refutation of all Heresies*, and Polycarp, *Martyrdom of Polycarp* 14. See also Everett Ferguson, "Martyr, Martyrdom" (1999:724-727).
85. Polycarp, *Martyrdom of Polycarp* 1.6; and Origen, *Exhortation to Martydom* 42.
86. Polycarp, *Martyrdom of Polycarp* 2; and Eusebius, *Ecclesiastical History* 5.1.22.
87. Hippolytus, *The Refutation of all Heresies*.
88. Eusebius, *Ecclesiastical History* 5.1.23; Origen, *Exhortation to Martyrdom.* 42. See also Mark Reasoner, "Persecution" (1997).
89. Justin Martyr, *2 Apology* 12; and Tertullian, *Apology.* 50.

death of its terrors. Thus a desire was awakened in hundreds of troubled hearts to share in the consolations which the new faith afforded the believers.[90]

It is only reasonable to conclude that the martyrdom of the first three centuries "still remains one of the grandest phenomena of history."[91] Yet, the persecution of the church is not totally over. We are only now hearing about some of the atrocities that have been perpetrated against Christians who have demonstrated what it means to serve Christ under certain repressive Eastern European and Middle Eastern, Asian, and African regimes. We have seen the specter of persecutions as governments around the world have sought to suppress, infiltrate, compromise, limit, and destroy the church in our own time. One can only hope and pray that the testimony the early Christians bring to us will provide encouragement that the promise of God's presence in the midst of suffering is also relevant for the twenty-first century church.

Missionary Orientation as Ministry

One of the most significant facts of history is the remarkable rapidity of the church's expansion during the early centuries of its existence. Even more intriguing was the professed allegiance of the overwhelming majority to the Christian faith once it crossed the Jewish borders into the more intolerant frontiers of Hellenistic paganism. This expansion of the church defies any logical standard of expectation as can be seen in Tertullian's provocative remarks, "we are but of yesterday, and we have filled every place among you, cities, islands, fortresses, towns, market-places, the very camp, tribes, companies, palace, senate, forum; we have left nothing to you but the temples of your gods."[92]

This sentiment is carried further in Justin Martyr's assertion, "there is not one single race of men, whether barbarians or Greeks, or whatever they may be called, nomads, or vagrants, or herdsmen living in tents, among

---

90. John Foxe, *Foxe's Christian Martyrs of the World* (n.d.:43).
91. Phillip Schaff, *History of the Christian Church* (1858:77).
92. Tertullian, *Apology* 37.

whom prayers and giving of thanks are not offered through the name of the crucified Jesus."[93]

This remarkable spread of Christianity during the early centuries of the church's existence is certainly not without questions. We are compelled to ask about what was promised to loyal adherents to secure allegiance to the Christian faith over other religions that were competing to occupy the space of the divine? We are also tempted to investigate the extent by which this expansion could be attributed to, in the words of Henry Chadwick, "the tranquil operation of a wiser providence."[94] Unfortunately, our sources of information are too fragmentary to provide any adequate answers. Regardless of how imperfect this knowledge may be, one fact that is indisputable is that missionary activity, as "human intentions," played an important role in the expansion of early Christianity.

Missionary effort in the second century was intentional and mainly directed to the conversion of the heathen. As Cooke puts it, "Christianity remained essentially a missionary community: the gospel had been committed to the entire people, the responsibility of witnessing to it was the task of every Christian –by his words and by his life."[95] Early believers were engaged in the spread of the gospel through spontaneous witnessing. Their message remained focused on the historical Jesus as the kerygmatic Christ and called for total commitment to him. Against polytheistic and pagan worship came the call to the true worship that could only be found in God's son, Jesus. As an incentive to shifting allegiance, the converted would gain the benefits of divine grace, forgiveness of sins, eternal life, and the indwelling of the Holy Spirit.

Missionary witnessing offered a religious self-consciousness by pleading for repentance and the option of the "Two Ways."[96] Henry Chadwick calls this the "baptismal vows" which involved "a renunciation of sin and everything associated with demonic powers, idols, astrology, and magic; and a declaration of belief in God the Father, in the redemptive acts of

---

93. Justin Martyr, *Dialogue with Trypho* 117.
94. Henry Chadwick, *The Early Church* (1993:54).
95. Bernard Cooke, *Ministry to Word and Sacraments: History and Theology* (1976:64).
96. Justin Martyr, *1 Apology* 14.

Christ's life, death, and resurrection, and in the Holy Spirit active in the Church."[97]

Suffice it to say that the Christian message was authenticated by the quiet operation of a "wiser providence." Particularly significant was the testimony of the miracles which the early apologists like Quadratus, Justin Martyr, Ireneaus, Tertullian, and Origen confirmed to be a distinctive part of the preaching of missionaries for the conversion of the heathen.[98] Another divine intervention that complemented the church's exclusive truth claim was exorcism, in the display of Jesus' authority, "over the fiercest infestations of satanic power."[99]

The missionary effort of the Christians was, however, not without difficulties. They met with persistent opposition and severe persecution in the hands of the Roman populace and government who felt threatened that the new religion would upset the structure of the society. While their adversaries continued to persecute beyond measure, the tradition of martyrdom continued to pierce deeply the Christian mind. The devotion to missionary preaching was not regarded as a death knell or an act of fanaticism. Rather, the missionary Christians considered it a privilege and an opportunity to bear witness to Christ even in the face of death. The result was that rather than being silenced into obscurity, persecution fuelled missionary zeal, and the church continued to expand.

This indifference of Christians to death did more than expand the church. It won into the church highly educated individuals who later became the first defenders of the Christian faith.[100] Tertullian's conversion was a little out of his curiosity to ascertain what may have accentuated the Christians' defiance of pain and death. He asks rhetorically, "At the sight of it [that is, defiance of pain and death] who is not profoundly troubled, to the point of inquiring what may lie behind it all?"[101] His attempt to know "what may lie behind it all" set him in the path of an inquiry that culminated into

---

97. Henry Chadwick, *The Early Church* (1993:54).
98. For details, see Phillip Schaff, *History of the Christian Church* (1858:16).
99. Ramsay MacMullen, *Christianizing the Roman Empire, A.D. 100-400* (1984:27-29).
100. Justin Martyr, *2 Apology* 12.
101. Tertullian, *Apology* 50.15.

his declaring allegiance for the Christian faith. The works of these newly converted intellectuals to Christianity constituted a *specialized* ministry of a kind that I shall describe in the following paragraphs.

Reasoned Defense as Ministry

That a reasoned defense of the Christian faith constituted a *specialized* ministry in the life of the church can be seen from the ever-increasing hostility that faced Christians from every segment of public life. The hostility, orchestrated by prejudice and misinformation of the Christian faith and conduct, required an intellectually satisfying presentation of the fundamental truth of the Christian faith. This task of combining missionary and propagandist intentions thus became one of the distinctive features of second-century Christianity.

The task occasioned the development of a different form of literature, the "apology," as a defense against the criticisms and false accusations of the pagan world. It is for this reason that second-century Christianity is sometimes called "the age of the apologists," even though Christians of the third through the fifth centuries composed the most important apologies.[102] The accusations varied and so were the approach and choice of theme of the apologists. These apologetic writings came in at least four different forms although are more appropriately identified in their two distinct fronts, the Jewish and the Greco-Roman.[103]

Apologetics toward Judaism

By the time apologetics toward Judaism started in the second century, "the distinctions between Judaism and Christianity were clear both theologically and demographically, and mutual antagonism was commonplace."[104]

---

102. Harry Gamble, "Apologetics" (1999:81-82).
103. Although these apologists addressed several themes, four of them are distinctly pronounced and engaging: (1) apologetics toward Judaism, (2) apologetics toward the Roman government, (3) apologetics toward the intellectuals, and (4) apologetics toward non-Christian religions. Harry Gamble's categorization of the bodies of apologetic literature into two is, however, an accurate one. This is based on the fact that with the exception of the first (Judaism) that is distinct, the other three can be grouped as belonging together to the Greco-Roman world (1999:81-87).
104. Gamble (1999:82).

Christians' apologetic tracts focused almost exclusively on the messiaship of Jesus of Nazareth, as the person in whom alone the prophetic utterances of the Old Testament find their fulfillment. Through these dialogues, the apologists projected Christianity as the continuity and the fulfillment of the deepest longings and expectations of Judaism.

The best-known example of early apologetics toward Judaism is Justin Martyr's *Dialogue with Trypho* (ca. 155). Justin's dialogue was an attempt to refute some of the basic presuppositions of the Jews against Christianity as expressed by Trypho. "You place your hope in a crucified man," says Trypho. Although Trypho expressed the Jews' conviction that the scriptures "compel us to await One who is great and glorious, and takes over the everlasting kingdom from the Ancient of Days as Son of Man," it was, however, inconceivable that this scripture could have been fulfilled in a "crucified man" like Jesus. To him, a crucified man stands in an antithetical position to the hope of Israel.[105]

Justin Martyr's work engages contemporary Judaism in an extended debate regarding the merits and the superiority of Christianity. Like other Christian apologists, he alludes to the Old Testament prophetic predictions about the sufferings of the Messiah and his actual crucifixion. "By thus demonstrating the correspondence between the sufferings of Christ and the prophecies, they established the identity of the Christian Messiah with the one expected by Israel."[106] Suffice it to say that this particular apologetic piece reveals Justin Martyr as a man of considerable philosophical expertise. He is at home, not only with the philosophers, from Plato to Pythagoras, but with the books of the Old Testament as well.

Apologetics toward the Greco-Roman World

In debate with the Greco-Roman world, the apologists focused on the two themes that I have highlighted as orchestrating widespread dislike and persecutions of Christians. These are the perceptions of Christianity as a socially offensive and a politically dangerous religion. Against the allegation

---

105. Justin Martyr, *Dialogue with Trypho* 10.3; 32.1.
106. Simon Marcel, *Versus Israel: A Study of the Relations between Christians and Jews in the Roman Empire (135-425)* (1986:158).

of Christianity as a socially offensive religion, the apologists refuted the accusations with unequivocal unity both in themes and persuasion. They responded by establishing the innocence of Christians, the truth of the Christian claim and the ethic on which the religion was based. More importantly, the moral responsibility of Christianity was considered to be contradictory to allegations as gross as those of sexual promiscuity and esoteric cultic sacrifices. Justin Martyr's *Dialogue with Trypho* (10.1) and Athenagoras' *A Plea for the Christians* (177 A.D.) are good examples of such early apologies.

Apology toward the Roman government was addressed specifically to defending the Christians against "political suspicion" that had arisen due to the Christians' social behavior. Again, Christian apologists rose to the defense of the faith. First, they counter-attacked by pointing to the weaknesses in the pagan religions thus asserting the superiority of the Christian religion. Second, and perhaps even more engaging, they appealed distinctly to intelligence and to the Roman emperors. They emphasized that rather than be considered dangerous or as enemies of the State on matters of suspicion, Christians should be allowed to worship in any way they saw fit since they harm no one.[107]

More importantly, the apologists argued that Christians were good citizens who prayed for the welfare of the state and the ruler. The first of these apologetics was Quadratus' apologia to Emperor Hadrian around 125 A.D. A similar appeal was made by Aristides to Antoninus Pius about 140 A.D. And by far the most famous were Justin Martyr's defenses written at about 153 A.D. Justin Martyr, in particular, advocated for a fair hearing for Christians[108] and in the process did not fail to mention some of the contributions that Christians had made to the people of Rome.[109] Gamble summarizes well the ministry of these apologists when he writes:

---

107. For details, see Bart D. Ehrman, *After the New Testament: A Reader in Early Christianity* (1999:52).
108. Justin Martyr, *2 Apology* 1.
109. Justin Martyr, *2 Apology* 6.

The burgeoning number of apologies attests both the need and the effort of the church to respond. Apologists usually went beyond mere rebuttals of specific charges and pleas for toleration. They vigorously attacked popular religious ideas and practices and appealed to the thoughtful by representing Christianity as consistent with the best of classical philosophical reflection. They were defensive, polemical, and even evangelistic.[110]

Among other apologists that rose in defense of Christians against specific themes raised by their pagan opponents were: atheism,[111] cannibalism,[112] and incest.[113]

The Theology of the Early Church

So far we have seen that the ministry of the early church took form in the struggle with heretical and controversial points of view. The same corresponding reality characterized the theology of the early church. It developed within the complexities and paradoxes of differing doctrinal presentations. The problem was peculiarly difficult for the early church, as she needed to respond theologically to the objections and the speculations of other rival religious claims at a time when the boundary of orthodoxy had not been set. This struggle is strikingly evident in the theological argumentation of the early church fathers as portrayed in their writings.

These writings, which were mostly incidental in nature, do not constitute doctrinal presentations in themselves since this belonged only in the realm of the gospels and the apostolic letters.[114] Although the documents of the

---

110. Harry Gamble, "Apologetics" (1999:85).
111. Justin Martyr, *1 Apology* 5-6.
112. Justin Martyr, *Dialogue with Trypho* 10.1.
113. Athenagoras, *Plea Regarding the Christians*. For other apologetic responses, see Minucius Felix, *Octavus*; Tertullian, *Apology*; and Origen, *Against Celsus* (written as a direct response to Celsus' work, *True Doctrine*).
114. It should be noted that although the New Testament books were already in

Apostolic Fathers, including the *Didache*, may have contributed relatively little to the development of theology, they have helped to "furnish useful insight into the lines along which the church's unconscious theology was developing."[115]

For the purpose of this work, discussion on the theology of the early church will be undertaken from a two-fold perspective. First, I will consider early Christian worship and the witnesses of the early church fathers of the second century since they "shed light on the concept of faith and the church customs that prevailed in the earliest congregations."[116] This is necessary since ecclesiastical association of members, most of which had emerged from pagan background, required that their old habits be replaced with "Christian order and customs."[117]

The second aspect will focus on the beginnings of ecclesiastical doctrines that arose out of the pressure of absolute practical necessity, as well as in the inward development that transformed the gospel into a scientific theological system. Consequently, I will concern myself with the philosophical and theological vigor of the East (Origen) and the West (Tertullian), since both theologians were instrumental in providing the framework for subsequent systematization of theology.

Early Christian Worship

I have already mentioned that early Christians understood themselves to be a distinct social group, strikingly different from other religions in the Roman world. Although Christians had no sacred statues, temples, and rituals of sacrifice like other pagan cults, they did have religious gatherings

---

existence, there was, as of this time, no officially authorized New Testament Canon. The immediately accessible authorities for the early church fathers were the apostles who had worked with and had been commissioned by Jesus. The other authority being the Old Testament prophetic pronouncements about the person and ministry of Jesus Christ. A good reference point about this is Polycarp's summons to the Philippians to accept as their standard Christ himself along with "the apostles who preached the gospel to us and the prophets who announced our Lord's coming in advance," *Phil.* 6.3. See also J.N.D. Kelly, *Early Christian Doctrines* (1978:31).

115. Kelly (1978:90).
116. Bengt Hägglund, *History of Theology* (1968:15).
117. Hägglund (1968:16).

dedicated to the worship of the one true God. These gatherings occurred primarily on Sunday and involved a constellation of activities that had been taken over primarily from the Jewish synagogal rites rather than from cultic practices.[118]

Consequently, Christian gatherings embraced ritualistic practices such as baptism, the celebration of the eucharist (the Lord's Supper), the singing of Psalms and hymns, and the reading and exposition of Scripture. It should be mentioned, however, that "[d]espite the fact that Christian baptism, prayer, and sacral meals were rooted in Jewish traditions, the choice of new times and places for worship were means whereby Christians distanced themselves from Judaism."[119]

The Development of the Liturgy

Recent developments in Jewish liturgical study have made any single reconstruction of early Christian practices almost an impossible task.[120] Also, while the basic function of liturgical practices may have been to justify and consolidate congregational life, they also functioned in a way which tended "to dramatize and actualize the new, distinctively Christian norms and values" in a "hostile religious and cultural environment."[121] To this effect early Christians had "clear boundary markers"; those external rituals that showed who was in the group and who was not.[122]

---

118. I recognize the need to sketch liturgical parallels in Judaism and especially in the earliest Christian community of Jerusalem. But for lack of space, the reader is referred to Paul Bradshaw, *The Search for the Origins of Christian Worship* (1992); Everett Ferguson, *Worship in Early Christianity* (1993); David Aune, "Worship: Early Christian" (1992); and Edward J. Kilmartin, "Liturgy" (1999:683-686).

119. Reference should also be made to the letter of Ignatius, *Magnesians* 9.1. For the earliest descriptions of the Christian worship by a non-Christian, see the letter of the younger Pliny to Trajan (109 A.D.) which embodies the result of his judicial investigations in Bithynia, *Epistles*. 10.96-97. For a Christian description of the public worship, particularly as it was conducted about the year 140 A.D., see Justin Martyr, *1 Apology* 65-67. For contemporary investigations, see also David Aune, "Worship: Early Christian" (1992:973-974); and C. Perrot, "Worship in the Primitive Church" (1983:3-9).

120. For one of the earliest authoritative voices in this area, see Josef A. Jungmann's classic work, *The Early Liturgy: To the Time of Gregory the Great* (1959); and for the most recent addition, see Paul Bradshaw, *The Search for the Origin of Christian Worship* (1992).

121. David Aune, "Worship: Early Christian" (1992:974).

122. Bart D. Ehrman, *After the New Testament: A Reader in Early Christianity* (1999:343).

Baptism

In an attempt to identify Christianity as a distinctive religion in a world full of gods, most patristic scholars understand the primary function of baptism as an initiation rite for entry into the Christian community. This is in no way an incorrect interpretation, especially when we understand that early congregations were composed of members with pagan backgrounds. However, the overemphatic reference to baptism as an admission requirement has very imperfectly undermined its significantly important theological conception.

Although a doorway to Christianity, early Christians also held the theological conception that the effect of baptism consists in the forgiveness of sins. Justin Martyr, for example, finds authority for baptism in Isaiah 1:16-20 and John 3:3, 5. For him, baptism is "the water-bath for the forgiveness of sins and regeneration" and "the bath of conversion and the knowledge of God."[123]

This understanding of baptism as an avenue for the remission of sins is further emphasized in the epistle of Barnabas; "we descend into the water laden with sins and dirt, we rise up bearing fruit in our heart and with fear and hope in Jesus in our spirits" (11:11). And according to Hermas, the baptized "go down into the water dead and come up alive."[124] It is therefore clear that the early conception of baptism had as its effects regeneration, illumination, and remission of sins.[125]

The most common liturgical formula used in connection with baptism is the Christological phrase, "in the name of the Lord."[126] However, this formula was later expanded to a three-part Trinitarian formulation, "in the name of the Father and of the Son and of the Holy Spirit."[127]

I must emphasize that the above theological conception of baptism in the second and third centuries did not emerge out of a vacuum. Rather, it found its precedence in early New Testament teachings, especially in

---

123. Justin Martyr, *1 Apology* 61.
124. Hermas, *Similitudes*. 9.16.4.
125. J.N.D. Kelly, *Early Christian Doctrines* (1978:194).
126. Hermas, *Visions*. 3.7.3.; *The Didache* 9.5.
127. *The Didache* 7.1-3.

the Gospels and Acts and in Pauline understanding of baptism "as a ritual reenactment of the death and resurrection of Christ in which the believer experiences death to the old life of disobedience to God and resurrection to the new life of obedience (Rom. 6:3-11; Col. 3:1-3)."[128]

The Eucharist

If the above was the early church's understanding of baptism, the Eucharist was distinctively a Christian sacrifice. It was considered the holiest mystery of Christian worship and participation in it was generally forbidden to the unbaptized.[129] The earliest reference to the Eucharist probably comes from the *Didache* and contains eucharistic prayers without any reference to the theory of the Eucharist itself.[130]

Despite the disagreement on the origin of the Eucharist, there is however a scholarly consensus that from the second century on, *eucharistia* (with the generic Greek meaning "thanksgiving") was the predominant term applied to designate this Christian assembly.[131] Everett Ferguson remarks that, "the word could be applied to the prayer of thanksgiving (*Dididache* 9), to the elements for which thanks were said (Justin, *1 Apology* 66), and to the whole action (Ignatius, *Ephesians* 13.1)."[132]

Justin Martyr perhaps provides the first account of the Christian worship as a double description in the form of a prayer of thanksgiving and eucharistic celebration.[133] Attesting to this, Wainwright writes that "by the middle of the second century, Justin Martyr describes the church in Rome

---

128. David Aune, "Worship, Early Christian" (1992:986).

129. *The Didache* 9.5.; Justin Martyr, *1 Apology* 66.1.

130. There is a significant disagreement among scholars regarding the history of the Eucharist. This disagreement is traceable partly to the disparaging use of the terms *eucharistia* ("thanksgiving," *The Didache* 9.1), and the verb *eucharistein* ("to be thankful," *The Didache* 9.7; 14.1); and also to the actual dating of the *The Didache* itself. My concern is not to engage in this debate but to sketch the theological conception of the Eucharist during the second and third centuries. However, for works in this area see David Aune, "Worship, Early Christian" (1992:983-986). See also Paul Bradshaw's *The Search for the Origins of Christian Worship* (1992:47-55); and J.H. Srawley, *Early History of the Eucharist* (1947).

131. Ignatius, *Philadelphians* 4.

132. Everett Ferguson, "Eucharist" (1999:393).

133. Justin Martyr, *1 Apology* 67.

as holding a regular Sunday service of word and table, where the reading and exposition of the Scriptures are followed by prayers and the Eucharist of the Lord's body and blood."[134]

Ignatius, for his part, speaks of this sacrament in very strong mystical terms. He plainly declares that "the eucharist is the flesh of our Savior Jesus Christ, which suffered for our sins and which the Father in his goodness raised."[135] In another place, the bread is the flesh of Jesus, the cup his blood.[136] Ignatius especially uses this realism as his apologetic argumentation against the docetists' denial of the reality of Christ's body. To him, the Eucharist is the bond between Christians and Christ[137] "which is the medicine of immortality, the antidote we take in order not to die but to live forever in Jesus Christ."[138] Also, in his combat against Gnostic docetism, Irenaeus stresses the significance of the offerings of bread and wine as the gifts of thanksgiving which become the body and blood of Christ, able to preserve our bodies and souls to everlasting life.[139]

It is also important to mention that the early church naturally thought of the Eucharist not only as a sacrament but, also as a sacrifice. It is "the true and eternal sacrifice of the new covenant, superseding all the provisional and typical sacrifices of the old."[140] Justin, for instance, understands the bread and the wine to be the "pure offering" foretold by Malachi.[141] The bread and the wine are offered "in remembrance of the passion he endured for all those souls who are cleansed from sin."[142] And since the Eucharist brings Christians into union with their Lord, Christians are called to the sacrifice of renewed self-consecration as a sincere and faithful disposition to the Father for the offering of his Son.

---

134. G. Wainwright, "Lord's Supper, Lord's Feast" (1997:691).
135. Ignatius, *Smyrneans* 6.
136. Ignatius, *Romans* 7.3.
137. Ignatius, *Ephesians* 13.1.; *Philadelphians* 4.
138. Ignatius, *Ephesians* 20.2.
139. Irenaeus, *Against Heresies* 4.17-18.
140. Phillip Schaff, *History of the Christian Church* (1858:245).
141. Justin Martyr, *Dialogue with Trypho* 41.
142. Ibid.

This is probably why, from the *Didache*, we gather that the bread and wine are "holy."[143] As a result, Christians have to confess their sins before participating in the Eucharist so that their "sacrifice may be pure." They must also reconcile their quarrels or differences so that their "sacrifice may not be defiled."[144]

It is possible to infer from this sketch that the name *Eucharist*, which denoted the prayer of thanksgiving, referred to "a thank-offering of the whole church for all the favors of God in creation and redemption."[145] That it became afterwards a commemoration and renewed appropriation of the atonement can best be summarized in the words of Justin Martyr:

> For we do not receive these things as common bread nor common drink; but in like manner as Jesus Christ our Savior have been made incarnate by God's logos [Word] took both flesh and blood for our salvation, so also we have been taught that the food eucharistized through the word of prayer that is from him, from which our blood and flesh are nourished by transformation, is the flesh and blood of that Jesus who became incarnate.[146]

I have indicated the essential doctrinal ideas associated with the Eucharist. The fact is indisputable that the name, *eucharistia*, points to the congregational rendering of prayer of thanksgiving. Yet, the motive for this practice is fundamentally theological in the sense that the proceedings commemorated God's salvific initiative for humanity in the death and resurrection of his Son, Jesus Christ. As I will show further in my discussion of the development of ecclesiastical theology, this idea of Christ as a redemptive sacrifice became a dominant factor in western theological thinking.

---

143. *The Didache* 9.5.; 10.3.
144. *The Didache* 14.1-3.
145. Phillip Schaff, *History of the Christian Church* (1858:245).
146. Justin Martyr, *1 Apology* 66.2.

The Proclamation of the Word: Homily

One of the central features of early Christian worship was the familiar exposition of Scripture and exhortation to repentance and a holy life. Unlike the more structured "sermon," the homily was originally conversational and flexible, and was not bound to the strictures of rhetorical conventions. Instead, the homily was basically determined by the pattern of the material in the Scripture and public exposition emphasized the Christian moral life rather than a systematic exposition of theology.[147]

The oldest extracanonical Christian sermon that has survived is from the anonymous hortatory homily of the mid-second century formerly ascribed to Clement of Rome.[148] Based upon a text from Isaiah 54:1, *2 Clement* was a projection of the eloquence of Scripture on the need for repentance, on moral purity, and on triumphant faith that hopes in the reality of resurrection.[149] The second oldest is the late second-century Paschal homily of Melito, the bishop of the city of Sardis in Asia Minor. Entitled "On the Passover," the sermon is an intricately polemical exposition of the Passover meal of Exodus 12. For him, the "extraordinary mystery" of the Passover account was the replacement of the lamb with a man, even Christ, "who contains all things." This sermonic discourse by Melito is that "Jesus was the true Passover whose shed blood brings salvation."[150]

By far one of the most prolific authors of the second and third centuries, the oldest extant corpus of Christian homilies comes from Origen.[151] His homilies were a careful exposition of the text and were meant to extract

---

147. See George Kennedy, *Classical Rhetoric and Its Christian and Secular Tradition from Ancient to Modern Times* (1980:136). Joseph T. Lienhard has distinguished the homily from two other kinds of discourse in early Christianity: the missionary sermon and catechesis. According to him, "The homily had three characteristics: as liturgical, it belonged to the order of Christian worship; as exegetical, it explained a text from the Bible, God's living word to his people; as prophetic, it demonstrated the significance of the text for the hearers." For details, see his work, "Homily" (1999:539ff.).

148. There are conflicting theories on the authorship, date, and the stylistic structure of *2 Clement*. For an insightful analysis of the different schools of thought, see Karl P. Donfried, *The Setting of Second Clement in Early Christianity* (1974:1-48).

149. See John S. Chamberlin, *Increase and Multiply: Arts of Discourse Procedure in the Preaching of Donne* (1976:28).

150. Bart D. Ehrman, *After the New Testament: A Reader in Early Christianity* (1999:116).

151. For details, see Joseph Lienhard, "Homily" (1999:540).

doctrinal and ethical teachings for the congregation. Origen held a distinct perspective of the Bible as its own interpreter. This view of the Bible both influenced his theology and played an important role in the development of later Christian theology.

Theological Developments in the Early Church

I have said that the foundations for the development of theology were laid in the Alexandrian theological school in the East in the third century. It should be emphasized, however, that this was not an intentional innovation but one that was compelled by the fundamental need to consolidate the Christian faith from the speculations of heretics. Compelled by the consciousness to offer correctives to the objectionable philosophical speculations of Hellenism, Alexandrian theologians adopted the scientific and philosophic tradition of the day to project biblical revelation as the highest truth.

The general result of these pioneering attempts to legitimize the fundamental truth of biblical revelation by adopting a philosophical construct created the condition necessary to transform the gospel into a scientific theological system. In this work, I will concern myself to the philosophical and theological vigor of the East (Origen), and the West (Tertullian). These two, among others, give us insight into the framework for subsequent systematization of theology.

Origen

Origen, without any doubt, was one of the greatest minds in the history of Christianity and one whose intellectual sophistication and uncommonly prolific productions in biblical text-criticism and exegesis are still suggestive to patristic scholars today. Origen's theological point of view completed the scientific and philosophic process of interpreting Christian thinking in terms of Hellenistic thinking. As Williston Walker has observed, "he [Origen] gave to the Christian system the fullest scientific standing, as tested by the science of that age, which was almost entirely comprised in philosophy and ethics."[152]

Origen was a brilliant mind who understood the Scriptures as "the art of arts" and "the science of sciences." To him, the Scriptures had to be conceptualized as having a threefold representation: as literal (or "somatic"), moralistic (or "psychic"), and spiritual (or "pneumatic").[153] Whether or not interpretative efforts in the first two senses are reasonable, he held firmly to the view that one must hold strictly to the invisible, ever present spiritual meanings that lie behind every passage of Scripture. It is fair to say, then, that Origen's theological enterprise was motivated less by commitments to a synchronization of philosophical principles with Christian tradition, and more by the concern to better understand the Bible and thus use it to "create a right attitude in belief and true piety."[154]

It is from the above standpoint that his four-volume work, *On First Principles* (De Principiis) and *Against Celsus* (Contra Celsum) constitute major works on theology. In his dialogue with Celsus, for example, Origen refutes the former's polemic against Christianity by advancing the superiority of the wisdom of Scripture over Greek philosophy. Origen affirmed, "to those who have eyes to behold the venerable character of Scripture, the sacred writings of the prophets contain things more worthy of reverence than those sayings of Plata which Celsus admires."[155] Although Origen felt quite highly impressed with Greek and Plato's philosophies, he considered them as nothing more than precursors of the higher and fuller truth to be found in divine revelation.[156]

Origen appropriated the Hellenistic culture of intellectual reflection, and employed it to his careful formulation of Christian doctrine and systematization of biblical faith. Origen accomplished this in *Against Celsus*

---

152. Williston Walker, *A History of the Christian Church* (1959:75).
153. Bengt Hägglund, *History of Theology* (1968:64).
154. Karl Baus, *Handbook of Church History: From the Apostolic Community to Constantine* (1965:235). For further discussion in this regard, see also Bengt Hägglund's *History of Theology* (1968).
155. Origen, *Against Celsus* 6.18.
156. Roger Olson, *The Story of Christian Theology: Twenty Centuries of Tradition and Reform* (1999:102).

by juxtaposing Greek philosophy with Christian theology which he termed a "divine philosophy." According to him, Greek philosophy is neither capable of providing a saving knowledge of God nor does it have the ability to cure a person of sin because "in it the false is inextricably mingled with the true."[157]

In Origen's view, Christian theology is not to be equated with Greek philosophy but must be recognized as possessing higher philosophical concepts. This is because Christian theology has the "ability to identify a particular historical manifestation of the divine goodness—Jesus Christ." In this way, Christian theology, as a kind of "divine philosophy . . . surpasses and replaces all other philosophies and may use them as servants in its task of leading persons to a true knowledge of God and to salvation."[158]

Origen's *On First Principles* is a major work of Christian philosophy in which he "unfolded theological reflections on the nature of God and his Logos and creation and many other subjects."[159] Origen begins by setting out and affirming the faith expressed in the Church. He observed that this *regula fidei* ("rule of faith") is identical with the content of Scripture. However, he considered it ("rule of faith") to be rather ambiguous since it had no fixed formula for expressing the inner connections between the fundamental doctrines preached and taught by the Church.[160]

Consequently, he sets out to clarify what was only implicit in the faith by offering a systematic or speculative rendering of Christian doctrines in his four-volume work, *On First Principles*: (1) God, Jesus Christ, the Holy Spirit, (2) creation and the incarnation, the resurrection, and the judgment, (3) freewill, and (4) the inspiration, authority, and interpretation of Scriptures. Any examination of the contribution of Origen to the development of theology, therefore, must begin by reflecting on the conceptual framework of some of the doctrinal issues addressed in *On First Principles*. In this regard, I will offer a rapid sketch of the themes addressed in the first part of

---

157. Henri Crouzel, *Origen* (1989:158).
158. Roger Olson, *The Story of Christian Theology* (1999:102-103).
159. Ibid.
160. Origen, *On First Principles* 1.8.

On First Principles since it is here that Origen's theological system is most clearly presented.[161]

Trinitarian Theology: God, Son, and the Holy Spirit

Perhaps I should start by saying that one of the major difficulties of articulating Origen's interpretive framework on the doctrine of the Trinity is to be found in the pioneering nature of his work. Origen's Trinitarian theology was a re-construction of the Church's traditional threefold understanding of God in terms of middle Platonism. To him, God transcends being and mind and is thus incomprehensible to human intelligence.[162]

Human comprehension of God is possible only indirectly by inference from the intelligible, created world. God, being perfect and good, created an intelligible world of a purely spiritual kind endowed with freedom and dependence upon the Creator. As a result, the anthropomorphic language of Scripture has no literal significance but must be reinterpreted and understood metaphorically, typologically, or allegorically as a way in which a perfect God relates to creation and to humanity.

The Logos, Christ, is a part of this real world of spiritual reality. The Logos was not created but was eternally generated from God. It should be mentioned that Origen was not particularly concerned with an ontological constitution of Christ. Rather, his interest lay in projecting Christ as the revelation of the Father and as his "mediator" towards the world of creatures. In other words, while the Father is incomprehensible and transcendent, in the Son "the transcendent properties of the Father take form, as the expression of an objective, inexpressible reality."[163] Thus, Origen defines the relationship between God, the Father, and his Son, the Word (Logos)

---

161. Affirming that he (Origen) "inserted ideas from the Christian tradition into the framework of the Alexandrian world scheme," Bengt Hägglund has observed that three major themes are found in the first part of *De Principiis*. These are themes concerning "God and the transcendental world," "the fall into sin and the empirical world," and "salvation and the restoration of the finite spirits." These areas, he concludes, are those "in which . . . his theological system is most clearly presented" (1968:65ff.).
162. Origen, *On First Principles* 1.1.5-6.
163. Origen, *On First Principles* 1.2.6; 4.4.1. See also Aloys Grillmeier, *Christ in Christian Tradition* (1975:142).

along the lines of unity, divinity, and eternity and one that is borne out of knowledge, love, and action.[164]

This unity between the Father and the Son, however, is not without distinction. Although Origen considered the Son to be eternally generated from the Father, he still thinks in subordinationist tendencies that portrayed Father and Son as distinct in *hypostasis*. Origen did not dispute that the Son is God. However, the Son's deity is derivative and is best articulated as the "secondary God" or the "second God."[165] In other words, they are distinct as archetype, one that places the Son on a lower level in the divine hierarchy.

The consequence of this theological system is the question it raises regarding the relationship of the Son to the Father. In this regard, two currents run simultaneously in Origen's Platonic construction of theological system. First, that the Logos is of the same essence as the Father, and secondly, that the Son is nevertheless different from the Father and subordinate to him.[166] As Justo González has observed, this tension was to later divide Origen's followers into two "violently opposed groups."[167]

The same Platonic conceptuality characterizes Origen's understanding of the place of the Holy Spirit in the triadic Godhead. The Holy Spirit also originates from the Father; he is uncreated and thus coeternal with both the Father and the Son.[168] However, the divinity of the Holy Spirit is not as active in the world of creatures like the Father or the Logos but is limited only to the souls of the saints. In other words, the three are eternal yet distinct in the sense that the Father bestows existence, the Logos, rational creation, and the Spirit, sanctification.[169] He pushes this hypostasis even further by affirming: "The Son is less than the Father . . . for he is second to the Father; yet the Holy Spirit is lower, extending to the saints alone."[170]

---

164. Origen, *On First Principles* 1.2.2.
165. Origen, *Against Celsus* 5.39.
166. Bengt Hägglund, *History of Theology* (1968:66).
167. Justo González, *A History of Christian Thought* (1970:217).
168. Origen, *On First Principles* 1.3.4-8.
169. Ibid.
170. Ibid.

The Trinitarian Controversy

The hierarchical conception of the Trinity is apparently the primary reason why Origen was alleged to be teaching "a triad of disparate beings rather than a Trinity."[171] In a more sympathetic tone, however, William Rusch has observed, "when his Platonic background is noted, it is possible to see how he is holding to a genuine trinitarianism, although with a strongly pluralistic strain."[172]

I would like to echo Rusch's conviction that it is rather unfair to speak of Origen's theological system as "completely Hellenistic in nature [with] no relation to the Biblical proclamation."[173] On the contrary, the peculiar Platonizing errors of his theological system must be judged according to the possibilities of the age. As Karl Baus has noted, "he approached theological problems with the equipment and questions of a third-century man trained in philosophy; and most of the defects of his theology can be seen to derive from the limits and conditioning circumstances of this philosophy."[174] Instead, Origen's theological structure must be understood as the greatest intellectual creativity of the ante-Nicene church and one that was inspired by genuine ecclesiastical spirit.

Tertullian

The development of theology, as I have examined in Origen's *On First Principles*, and *Against Celsus*, emerged in the rationalistic and metaphysical interpretation of revelation as a demonstration of the superiority of Christianity over Hellenistic philosophical speculations. Tertullian was, however, not a speculative theologian like his Eastern counterpart. For him, "Christianity was a great divine foolishness, wiser than the highest philosophical wisdom of men, and in no way to be squared with existing philosophical systems."[175]

---

171. For details, see J.N.D. Kelly, *Early Christian Doctrine* (1978:131).
172. William Rusch, *The Trinitarian Controversy* (1980:15).
173. Bengt Hägglund, *History of Theology* (1968:67).
174. Karl Baus, *Handbook of Church History: From the Apostolic Community to Constantine* (1965:240).
175. Tertullian, *The Prescription* 7. See also Williston Walker, *A History of the Christian Church* (1959:65).

Tertullian's main concern lay, rather, in apologetic treatises that emphasized direct Christian ethics and ecclesiastical discipline in a society pervaded by paganism and idolatrous corruption.[176] This is not to infer that Tertullian did not play an important role in the development of early Christian doctrines. On the contrary, Tertullian is renowned for being the first ecclesiastical writer to use Latin in constructing theological terminologies, many of which were later adopted in subsequent Western Trinitarian and Christological discourses. In this regard, Tertullian was to the West what Origen was to the East.

Trinitarian Theology: God, Son, and the Holy Spirit

Tertullian's contributions to the developments of theology can best be seen in his *Against Praxeas*, a vitriolic treatise against a man named Praxeas. Praxeas had come to Rome and subsequently joined in combating Montanism while simultaneously helping to spread Monarchianism; a doctrine that emphasized the unity of divine being (*monarchia*, "one rule of power") while denying the trinitarian distinction of the Father, Son, and Holy Spirit in the Godhead. Thus, the importance of Tertullian's contribution to the doctrine of the Trinity in the ante-Nicene period can best be comprehended against this background.

Tertullian sets out against Praxeas by appealing to the *regula fidei* of the church. According to this rule, the mystery of Christianity is expressed in the *monarchia*, namely that God has a Son. This Son exercises the whole power of the Father in the world. It is a "unity of rule" analogous to an imperial government whereby "one and the same sovereignty could be exercised by coordinate agencies."[177] According to Tertullian's argumentation, the Son (and the Spirit) preexisted in God, both proceeding from God and into time in accordance with the order of salvation and redemption. He writes:

---

176. Tertullian's stringent demands for purity, especially in his understanding of the relation between the Christian faith and contemporary culture, have been attributed to the possibility of his own pagan past. Robert Sider has observed, "that he was a convert from paganism is suggested by his use of the first person plural in several passages: 'the kind of persons we ourselves once were—blind, without the light of the Lord' (*Paenit.* 1.1; *Fug.* 6.2; *Apol.* 18:4)." For Sider's work, see "Tertullian" (1999:1107-1108).
177. J.N.D. Kelly, *Early Christian Doctrines* (1978:113).

They are all of the one, namely by unity of substance, while none the less is guarded the mystery of that economy which disposes the unity into trinity, setting forth Father and Son and Spirit as three, three however not in quality but in sequence, not in substance but in aspect, not in power but in manifestation, seeing it is one God from whom those sequences and aspects and manifestations are reckoned out in the name of the Father and the Son and the Holy Spirit.[178]

Economic Trinity

The two technical terms that find appeal in Tertullian's argumentation are *persona* (person) and *substantia* (substance). The Son and the Spirit, as independent persons and existence, have derived from the Father in sequence and as such subordinate to him. Nevertheless, the trinitarian distinction of the three persons is not incompatible with the substance of their inner unity and indivisible power. In other words, the existence and the essential unity of the only one God are manifested within the framework of the economic Trinity.[179]

On the basis of this concept of substance and person, Tertullian affirms the distinction of the three persons of the economic trinity as "one substance in three who cohere."[180] Tertullian's trinitarian theology, especially his terminologies, eventually became the norm for the western Church in subsequent formulations of the doctrine of the Trinity.

It is appropriate to say at this point that both Origen (East) and Tertullian (West) contributed in some unique ways to the development of theology in the second and third centuries. Of particular significance is the fact that their theological enterprises emerged out of the objections and the heretical tendencies of Hellenism. In rising to this challenge, not only did they project the integrity and the fundamental elements of the Christian

---

178. Tertullian, *Against Praxeas* 2.
179. Tertullian, *Against Praxeas* 2, 7, 9.
180. Tertullian, *Against Praxeas* 12.

faith, they also presented the "Christian tradition as a superior counterpart to [Hellenistic] philosophy."[181]

Summary

As I attempt to formulate a theory of contextual ecclesiology that is also faithful to the Scripture, the concern is to identify a "hermeneutical key" that points in the way of the obligation to context and Scripture. This is where the extensive discussions of the various problems of the early church provide the hermeneutical principles for the contemporary Nigerian church. Although "we cannot turn to the past for solutions to the problems of the present," observes Kwame Bediako, "it is possible to find in the past analogues to the situations and circumstances in the present which raise some of the perennial questions that Christian reflection in every age is required to handle."[182]

Not only do we find "analogues" in the past but "the answers that were given in the past may illuminate the path of the modern inquirer after solutions to the problems of the present."[183] Problems such as cultural identification, worldview allegiances, traditional practices, secularization, nominality, and materialism are not new developments but phenomena that had prominence even in ancient times. What I hope to do in the remaining part of this book, therefore, is to apply the answers that were given in the past as hermeneutical principles in my attempt to develop a transforming ecclesiology that is biblical, missional, and contextual for Nigeria in the twenty-first century.

---

181. Bengt Hägglund, *History of Theology* (1968:59).
182. Kwame Bediako, *Theology and Identity: The Impact of Culture Upon Christian Thought in the Second Century and Modern Africa* (1992:427).
183. Ibid.

PART VIII

Between Past and Future: Transforming Ecclesiology in Twenty-First Century Nigeria

I have shown that the different expressions of church in Nigeria represent creative attempts to use cultural forms that connect with the experience of broad sectors of Nigerians. The significance of this, especially in the last couple of decades, is that Africa has acquired new gains in influence and respectability as "potentially the *representative* Christianity of the twenty-first century."[184] But when one reflects carefully on the experiences of the church in the West, that it was for so long the "*representative* Christianity" that pushed the boundaries of the gospel message to the geographical frontiers of Africa and Asia, then the present African success story reveals an irony arising out of history.

This "reminds us that the path of Christian discipleship calls us continually to press on toward the frontier but to do so in full awareness of the path the church has taken thus far."[185] It is precisely for this purpose, to distinguish to a degree between historical events and theological interpretations, that this book has gone back in time to the primitive Christianity of apostolic and post-apostolic times. The problems and struggles of the past call for the present fledging African church to be flexible and responsive. Failure to develop an articulate and renewed vision of the

---
184. Andrew F. Walls, *The Cross-Cultural Process in Christian History* (2002:85).
185. Wilbert R. Shenk, *Changing Frontiers of Mission* (1999:3).

nature, purpose, and characteristics of the church of the future should be as worrisome and challenging as the paralysis that attended the dominating ecclesiastical forces of previous centuries. This is what this part is about. It is geared towards providing guidelines that must be put in the foreground as an essential key toward the future.

CHAPTER 11

Toward a Biblical, Contextual, and Missional Ecclessiology in Nigeria

Beyond recognizing that the history of Christianity in Nigeria has been plagued with inconsistencies and a confusion of interests, this history, nevertheless, is the platform on which our people and nation stand as they face the future. So far, the historical analysis has revealed that Nigerians were interested in subscribing to a statement of faith, but the problem was whether the missionary heritage corresponded to their own construction of reality and cultural expressions. Therefore, what appeared to be contrary behavior, even defiance of missionary church forms and practices, was the result of a sustained battle of conflict between the "missionary gospel" and the daily needs of Nigerians. This brought about two unreconciled levels.

On one hand, converts associated Christian membership with benefits and social status. On the other, their Western-oriented Christian faith was in conflict with spontaneous beliefs in local traditions and customs. Because of this conflict of interests, most early Christian converts lived a dichotomous religious life in which they openly conformed to "Christian" forms while secretly patronizing the more relevant world of native beliefs and practices. This complex interplay of evangelical pietism and the need for interaction with Nigerian culture was what motivated Ajayi Crowther to warn the CMS to work "with due caution and with all meekness of wisdom."[1]

---

1. J. F. Ade Ajayi, *Christian Missions in Nigeria* (1965:224).

The insistence on monogamy as the biblical norm for marriage, for example, became a controversial issue once Nigerians discovered that the Old Testament patriarchs were polygamists and not condemned for it. Even the missionary appeal to the New Testament for monogamy was not convincing because it carries no direct references to the sanctity of monogamous marriage. At worse it tended to downgrade the Old Testament as authoritative Scripture.

In this respect, the missionaries faced a dilemma because Nigerians perceived that their culture was closer to the world of the Bible than the missionary cared to admit.[2] The developments in the early twentieth century of the African Independent Churches (AICs), and of the Charismatic/Pentecostal churches later in the same century were clear cases of indigenous efforts to address the theological and hermeneutical questions that constituted areas of tensions among Nigerian Christians.

Now that it is an undeniable fact that Africa is one of the most recognizable blocs of the Christian faith; the influence of Africa's socio-religious context on ecclesiology cannot be ignored. This means that contextual ecclesiology must proceed "with due caution and with all meekness of wisdom." We must preserve Christian commitment and objectivity as well as discover and affirm those traditional values that provide "the hermeneutical bridge" to Christian doctrine. This is a complex task involving a dynamic interplay of church, gospel, and society.

The choice facing the church, therefore, is to move toward a position of "critical contextualization." As Paul Hiebert has proposed, this involves a three-step formula that proceeds from an "exegesis of the culture," to an "exegesis of scripture," leading ultimately to a "critical response." This is the point where nationals "critically evaluate their own past customs in the light of their new biblical understandings and to make decisions regarding their response to their new-found truths."[3] The following diagram articulates this truth well:

---

2. Brian Stanley, *The Bible and the Flag: Protestant Missions and British Imperialism in the Nineteenth and Twentieth Centuries* (1990:168-169).
3. Paul Hiebert, *Anthropological Reflections on Missiological Issues* (1994:88-89).

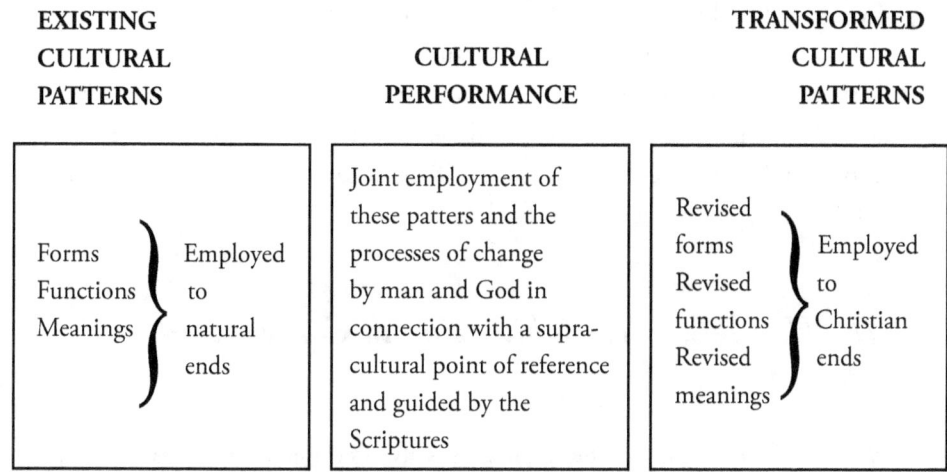

Figure 2
Christian Transformational Change[4]

The task of doing church in a way that connects the believer's transcendent experience of the sacred with the environment is not new. The early church, as I have shown, was forced into a critical hermeneutic approach that encouraged a dialogue between text and context in its Christianizing mission. The Bible is replete with accounts that testify to sharp differences among the earliest Christians as they attempted to connect their transforming message with their surrounding cultural contexts. As Leslie Newbigin has pointed out, "the passages in the epistles to the Romans and to the Corinthians referring to controversies about food offered to idols are ample evidence of this [sharp differences in relating to context and scripture]."[5] It can be argued, therefore, that the environment guides and shapes church forms, meanings, and practices.

At this point in this work, perhaps it is safe to say that hermeneutics, theology, exegesis, and context "flow into and out of each other with no

---

4. For details, see Charles H. Kraft, *Christianity in Culture: A Study in Dynamic Biblical Theologizing in Cross-Cultural Perspective* (1979:79).
5. Leslie Newbigin, *The Gospel in a Pluralist Society* (1989:148).

fixed dividing-lines."[6] Consequently, my task here is to engage in the delicate exercise of holding context and scripture in a creative tension without breaking the inescapable workings of the hermeneutical circle. The overall fundamental concern is the development of a hermeneutic and a corresponding ecclesiological practice oriented towards questions about a biblical and contextual ecclesiology.

The Hermeneutical Obligation to Context and Scripture

We know that theological hermeneutics is always influenced or determined by the context within which it evolves.[7] To begin with, it is important to state that theological hermeneutics not only reflect convictions arising from within certain historic theological perspectives but that these convictions also give attention to current social, economic, and political exigencies.[8] In other words, a critical and careful analysis of each particular context is required before any theological hermeneutic can be meaningful.

This does not mean theological hermeneutics is to "sell out" uncritically to cultural presuppositions and assumptions. What is important, however, is the establishment of a theological-hermeneutical framework that holds together in creative tension both context and scripture. For example, the Jerusalem Council settled on decrees for the Gentile churches with respect to the observance of Jewish dietary laws as a prerequisite for admission into Christian community. In doing so, the council acted not simply as the mother church or spiritual powerhouse, but also as the *supra-culture* of the then known world (Ac. 15).

Although the pressure on the Gentile churches to conform to Judaic practices appears to be largely culturally conditioned, it called for the

---

6. Francis Watson, *Text, Church, and World* (1994:241).

7. Friedrich Schleiermacher was one of the first theologians to espouse the view that the *modus operandi* of theologizing is fundamentally flawed. For details, see Stanley J. Grenz and Roger E. Olson, *20th Century Theology: God and the World in a Transitional Age* (1992:43).

8. David J. Bosch, *Transforming Mission* (1991:422-423).

necessity of understanding the complex "hermeneutical bridge" between context and the gospel.⁹ The hermeneutical obligation of context and scripture is, therefore, "a manifestation of the hermeneutical circle or spiral, in which whole and parts are dialectically related."¹⁰

If the roles of cultural, political, and socio-economic factors are agreeably pivotal elements in theological reflection, the question then confronts us as to how the church can navigate being church in the world and still remain authentically true to Scripture. It is helpful here to utilize Randolph Tate's integrative approach to biblical hermeneutics. Tate begins by exploring the three traditional methods of interpretation: *author-centered*, which looks at the world of the author for meaning; *text-centered*, which explores the world of the text for significance; and *reader-centered*, which focuses on the role of the reader in shaping the meaning of a text. His approach is a creative methodology where "the most viable meaning emerges out of an intersection of these three worlds: The world of the author and the world of the reader intersect[ing] in the world of the text to produce meaning."¹¹

New Testament Ecclesiology as "Hermeneutical Key" to Biblical and Contextual Ecclesiology

From my analysis of the churches in Jerusalem, Corinth, Rome, and the "high ecclesiology" of the epistle to the Ephesians, it is safe to claim that the New Testament establishes a theological-hermeneutical framework within which the formulation of a biblical and contextual ecclesiology may be understood. To illustrate, it is an oversimplification to interpret the book of Acts almost exclusively in terms of the great expansion of the church and of its frontier-crossing into the Gentile world. Although this fact cannot be ignored, the book of Acts also provides us with insights into the Jewish culture in a way that has no parallel in the New Testament.¹²

---

9. Paul Hiebert, "Critical Contextualization" (1987:104-112).
10. Francis Watson, *Text, Church, and World: Biblical Interpretation in Theological Perspective* (1994:222).
11. W. Randolph Tate, *Biblical Interpretation: An Integrated Approach* (1997).
12. For a detailed treatment of the Jewishness of Luke the writer and its influence on Luke-Acts, see David Bosch, *Transforming Mission* (1991:91ff).

The extended narrative of Acts places the life and orientation of the first church in direct continuity with Israel. Luke not only links the Pentecost event to the Old Testament prophecy of the prophet Joel, he also uses "geography as a literary and theological instrument."[13] The center of its narrative, for example, is the city of Jerusalem. The whole movement of the gospel is *toward* Jerusalem (Lk. 2:22), and movement is also *away from* Jerusalem (Ac. 1:8). These movements circle back to Jerusalem before reaching out still further (Ac. 12:25; 15:2; 18:22; 19:21; 20:16; 21:13; 25:1).[14] In this context, Acts' "highly concentrated theological symbol" of Jerusalem as "the sacred center of the world" shares a similar understanding with the Judaism of this time.[15] We have here problems of worldview allegiance, cultural continuity, and identificational allegiance.

Consequently, it does not come as a surprise that certain Judaizers would want to impose cultic practices on the Gentile Christians. It also does not surprise us that movement is once again back to Jerusalem. However, the narrative manifestly shifts focus from the interpretation of Christianity as the true successor to Judaism to God's redefinition of peoplehood (Ac. 15:14). The Jerusalem Council understood the reality that God's eschatological restoration of his people finds fulfillment in the Messiah.

These are a people gathered from among all nations and who are equally empowered by the Holy Spirit. The gift of the Spirit became God's testimony of the Gentiles' acceptability to him and was also indicative of the new paradigm in his redemptive purpose. The Jerusalem incident was a text-book case of biblical contextualization, illustrating a hermeneutical framework used by the first church to resolve the issue of cross-cultural application and communication of specific elements of Scripture.

The cultural situation in Rome is of a different kind. The Roman church was faced with distortions and deviations superimposed by the "problem of the relation between faith and worldview."[16] The "weak" and the "strong" in faith, each epitomizing segments of the church that were fundamentally

---

13. Luke T. Johnson, *The Writings of the New Testament: An Interpretation* (1999:220).
14. Ibid.
15. David Bosch, *Transforming Mission* (1991:93).
16. E. Käsemann, *Commentary on Romans* (1980:369).

opposed both in principle and practice, showed one side "boasting" of superiority over the other. The original vision of equality and unity is once again distorted, and the apostle Paul provides us with the hermeneutical grid for biblical contextualization.

The hermeneutical significance of what it means to be the people of God for Paul was seen by contrasting the schism in the Roman church with the life and teaching of Christ. By enhancing the distinctiveness of Jesus' life of self-denial and true acceptance of others (Rom. 15:1-7), Paul sets the basic hermeneutic for Christian life and practice in the exemplary life of Jesus Christ.

The picture given us of the ecclesial community at Corinth raises the question as to whether or not the community understands itself or its beliefs and practices enough to be authentically Christian. The Corinthian congregation was so immersed in its pluralistic pagan context that it could not draw the boundaries between the "inside" and the "outside." The church's struggle with disunity, sexual immorality, civil litigation, abuse of the Lord's Supper, and the misunderstanding of spiritual gifts all point to the problems of defining what it means to be "spiritual" and to be the "people of God" in a world that is marked by religious pluralism and cultural relativity (1 Co.).

Yet it is right to say that the Corinthian situation provides us with another classic example of a theological-hermeneutical framework for contextual ecclesiology. Apostolic response, and ultimately contextualization, was decidedly based on the hermeneutical application of "the twofold foundation of the Old Testament and Christology."[17] Paul mediates the unity and spirituality of every individual and the church as being grounded in Christ.

By so doing, "the cross" and "Christ crucified" are to be understood as oriented towards the restoration of unity and holiness to the community rather than in "'higher' knowledge and wisdom of spiritual existence" (1 Co. 1:17-19, 23; 2:2; 5:6-8). By adopting this hermeneutical framework, the apostle exemplifies a form of contextualization that is

---

17. See Gerald F. Hawthorne, Ralph P. Martin, and Daniel G. Reid, *Dictionary of Paul and His Letters* (1993:175).

responsive to both biblical truth and the aspirations of the world beyond the ecclesial community.

The Ephesians epistle, for its part, is markedly distinguished by its theological consistency of the church. The genius of this New Testament scripture is not only in offering a unique and independent conception of the church but also in presenting the church as having the capacity to manifest and proclaim the valid truth of the scripture in the cosmic context. The lordship of Christ is both religiously and cosmically inspired, and the church has the mandate to affirm and proclaim this "good news."

As Francis Watson has observed, "the world is the context of the church just as the church is the context of the biblical text . . . to renounce all claim to universality would be a drastic distortion of the Christian story itself, set as it is within the universal horizons of creation and eschaton."[18] The theological-hermeneutical framework for biblical contextualization, therefore, is the "conception of Christ as a corporate or inclusive personality" and of his church as being entrusted with the same incarnational mission of disclosing this fundamental reality in the world.[19]

The Challenge of Hellenism as "Hermeneutical Key" to Biblical and Contextual Ecclesiology

The advancement and the enrichment of the early church were equally and naturally influenced by religious, political, social, and philosophical pressures of Hellenism that sought to divest Christianity of its integrity. From this perspective, we can claim that the history of the church is the narrative of how it adapted itself to and assimilated the objectionable speculations of Hellenism without "selling out" the uniqueness of the Christian revelation.

The question, then, is what lesson is there for the Nigerian church in articulating the successful navigation of the early church through the turbulent ocean of Hellenism? It is rather a controversial enterprise to attempt to ascribe some form of normativity to the early church. Yet, the

---

18. Francis Watson, *Text, Church, and World: Biblical Interpretation in Theological Perspective* (1994:10).

19. Ernest Best, *One Body in Christ: A Study in the Relationship of the Church to Christ in the Epistles of Paul the Apostle* (1955:184).

legitimacy of this interpretative framework resides on the fundamental awareness that faithfulness to the truth does not lie within the strictures of modernity (or post-modernity) but in recognizing "the ancient as analogue of the modern."[20] Consequently, history itself becomes a continuum where one period grows into and emerges out of another by almost imperceptible degrees.

I have already highlighted the various Hellenistic trends that permeated every aspect of the church's historical development. Whether in the form of Hellenistic syncretism, or in the imperial systematic intention to suppress Christianity, or even in the propaganda of peripatetic philosophers, the early Christians disproved the insinuations leveled against them, maintaining instead that they had a special revelation to proclaim. It is a fair consideration to infer, then, that the interplay of Hellenism and early Christianity "supplies not only the temporal framework but also the material from which the new movement [Christianity] gained its form of expression."[21]

The strongest motivation for "the intellectual discipline of theology and the classical formulations of the faith," for example, can be credited to the Hellenistic philosophers.[22] For without the speculative philosophy of Gnosticism and Hellenistic thought, biblical and early Christian narratives would have remained self-contained and devoid of any form of systematization. However, in an Alexandrian theologian like Origen (and others who followed after him), we see the first successful "test-case" of contextual ecclesiology.

As Bosch has observed, "Origen and his colleagues were not interested in intellect for intellect's sake. They held on to the priority of faith over reason, and undertook rigorous intellectual pursuits precisely for the sake of the faith."[23] What is immediately clear, then, is that the Hellenistic world provided the church with sufficient reason to embark on an intellectual reflection and careful doctrinal formulation of the Christian faith. And by alluding to the *regula fidei* ("Rules of Faith") and the Scriptures, the earliest

---

20. Kwame Bediako, *Theology and Identity* (1992:426).
21. Leonard Goppelt, *Apostolic and Post-Apostolic Times* (1970:5).
22. David Bosch, *Transforming Mission* (1991:206).
23. Ibid.

Christians brought proofs to differentiate the uniqueness of Christianity as they dealt with the problematic task of being church in a pluralistic world.

Theological-Hermenutical Framework for a Biblical and Contextual Ecclesiology in Nigeria

The contextualization endeavor is so fraught with danger and difficulty that nearly forty years after the term was first coined there is still substantial confusion in contemporary scholarship.[24] The observations of Gilliland, Hesselgrave, and Rommen are accurate in that varying contextualization outcomes are a result of the specific framework within which different theological perspectives are set.[25] The orientation that has largely informed contextual theologizing is that in which the processes of acceptability or suitability of a particular contextualization outcome have usually derived from either theological judgments or novel re-constructions.

Similarly, my endeavor in this book may not be entirely devoid of this diachronic bias. However, my primary concern is to push further the construction of a workable paradigm for contextual ecclesiology in Nigeria, wherein the irreducibility of Scripture is fundamental to both the hermeneutical and contextualization process. Again, this is the genius of Stendahl's delineation of the autonomy of the historical task in theologizing. In order words, the contextualization continuum must give assent to the autonomy of Scripture as the authoritative text embodying an actual story of what God has in fact done, is doing, and will do.

Contextualization is not a springboard to relativism. Contextual ecclesiology fails when it allows the context to dictate the issues and the terms of the meeting. This is what has characterized the way of doing

---

24. For examples of such debates see Sam Schlorff's work, "The Translational Model for Mission in Resistant Muslim Society: A Critique and an Alternative" (2000:305-328); and Dean Gilliland's response, "Modeling the Incarnation for Muslim People: A Response to Sam Schlorff" (2000:329-338).

25. For details on the works cited, see Dean Gilliland's "Limits of Contextualization and the African Independent Churches" (1999:2); and David J. Hesselgrave and Edward Rommen *Contextualization: Meanings, Methods, and Models* (1989:144-157).

church in Nigeria. Although this has been a sincere attempt to make the church relevant, unfortunately, the result "is that the world is not challenged at its depth but rather absorbs and domesticates the gospel and uses it to sacralize its own purposes."[26] It is a fact, of course, that Scripture, church, and context are related to one another as three concentric circles; in the final court of appeal, both church and context are answerable to the Scripture. It is in this reflection that contextual ecclesiology stands either as a drastic distortion of the grand Christian story or as an affirmation and corresponding appropriation of its claim—a biblical Church. The following diagram articulates this truth in an impressive way:

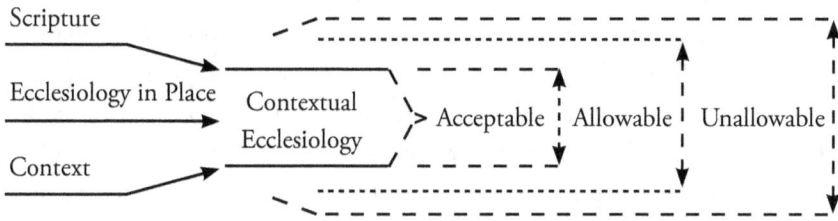

Figure 3
The Contextualixation Continuum[27]

My interpretation of the above diagram is not different from Gilliland's. The contextualization process or continuum, according to him, requires "a critical selection process." The "critical selection process" takes place as Scripture interacts with contextual phenomena. While much of the contextual phenomena can be accepted, other aspects "can [either] be modified and then incorporated" or rejected out rightly. Thus, the contextualization process flows within the continuum of what is "acceptable," "allowable," and "unallowable." In working with this continuum Gilliland explains:

---

26. Leslie Newbigin, *The Gospel in a Pluralist Society* (1989:152).
27. This diagram is an adaptation of Dean Gilliland's. For details, see "Limits of Contextualization and the African Independent Churches" (1999:2).

> (1) Acceptable: Belief and practice is clearly Biblical and cultural forms can be accommodated without distortion. (2) Allowable: Belief and practice can usually be reconciled with Christian truth and the Scripture but must constantly be tested. . . . (3) Unallowable: belief and practice is in conflict with the Scripture and is oriented in a direction which leads away from Christian teaching.[28]

Consequently, I now come to a point where it is perhaps safe to affirm that the witness of the first Christians establishes a theological-hermeneutical framework not only for comprehending biblical truth but also for manifesting an authoritative base in the contextualization process. The early Christians possessed contextual presuppositions that enabled them to maintain the essence of biblical truth while applying this truth to specific place and people. Whether in the misunderstanding of the Christian way of life (Corinth and Rome), or in the inability to postulate the starting-point of a new paradigm of redemptive history (Jerusalem), apostolic responses negotiated the delicate balance of context and Scripture in such a way that nothing of the essence of Christian truth is ever omitted in the contextualization process.

It is a bold claim, although a necessary one, that the Nigerian church stands between two worlds, the *descriptive* and the *prophetic*—"what it meant and what it means."[29] The *descriptive* represents the historical endeavor of discovering "what it meant" while the *prophetic* represents the theological-hermeneutical task of articulating "what it means" to be a biblical church. An understanding of this approach offers us objective criteria not only for the theological-hermeneutical process but also for constructing a biblical and contextual ecclesiology.

As Stendahl has suggested, one of the advantages of an autonomous descriptive method is that "once we confine ourselves to the task of descriptive biblical theology as a field in its own right, the material itself

---

28. Gilliland (1999:2).
29. Krister Stendahl, "Contemporary Biblical Theology" (1962:418-431).

gives us means to check whether our interpretation is correct or not."[30] My argument, therefore, is that regardless of the creative attempts to use cultural forms that make the church relevant to broad sectors of Nigerian church-goers, contemporary efforts at contextual ecclesiology must evolve out of the history of early Christian thought or theology as portrayed in the New Testament.

The following diagram is a visual representation of this process:

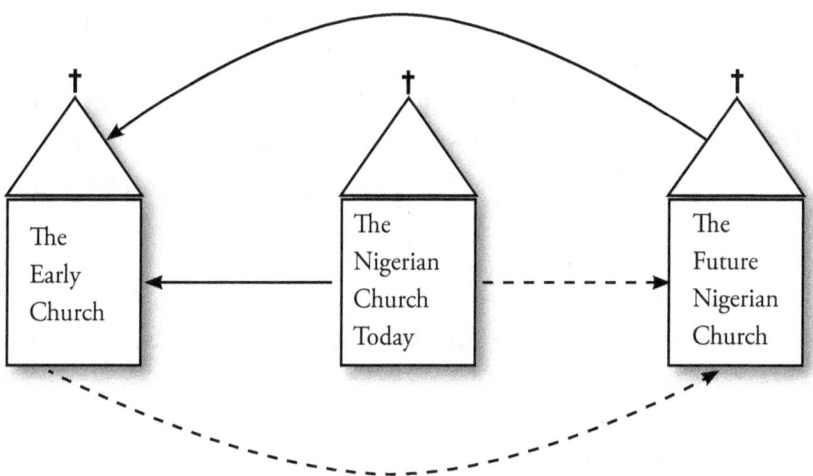

Figure 4
The Hermeneutical Spiral of Contextual Ecclesiology

As the above diagram shows, the Nigerian church is challenged to look back in time and place to historical precedents and use those insights to navigate its path on historically-becoming what it is already by faith. It is imperative to emphasize the wisdom of Hans Küng's warning that "the church must constantly reflect upon its real existence in the present with reference to its origins in the past, in order to assure its existence in the future."[31]

---

30. Stendahl (1962:422).
31. Hans Küng, *The Church* (1968:15).

In conclusion, therefore, two points are worthy of mention. First, I do not conceive contextual ecclesiology or even contextual theologizing as something new. It is rather very traditional and the "sine qua of all genuine theological thought."[32] What may be new is the understanding that in the rhetoric of superlatives, the context does not occupy a self-contained autonomous space. Rather, it (the context) must be treated in a way that is symbiotically located within the Scriptural space.

The second argument follows from here. That is, although this is not an attempt to ask the Nigerian church to replicate itself as the "early church" of the twenty-first century, it should nevertheless allow the "hermeneutic of description" to inform its churchness thus enabling it to function as the biblical representation for its own time and place. This way, there is no reason in principle why contextual ecclesiology should not be practiced as a theological enterprise.

Toward a Responsible and Missional Ecclesiology in Nigeria

I have argued that considerations about the rise and flowering of Christianity in Nigeria, as indeed with the rest of the non-Western world, cannot be discussed exclusive of the legacy of Christendom. But the vitality and commitment that gave witness to the first Christian presence, at least in Africa, soon faced the vigorous challenges of Ethiopianism and the cultural signification of Aladura-type churches. Right now, the entire edifice of Christian expressions epitomized by the first two strands of the Nigerian church is facing a fundamental assault about adequacy. What is immediately discernible is that the new paradigm of post-denominational Christianity has jettisoned aspects of existing church models claiming, instead, to bring rehabilitation and hope for the future.

But a fundamental question that must be asked at the outset is how we are to conceptualize this future. The distinctive contours and boundaries of

---

32. D.J. Hall, *Thinking the Faith: Christian Theology in a North American Context* (1989:21).

the future, as of yet, are not fully comprehensible. Yet it is absolutely urgent to envision how the church will face the future. If we are to learn any lesson from history, it is clear that even though the future may be an extension of the present, it will also be a new alternative, with the possible challenge of superceding the past.

Consequently, to begin to envision the future for the Nigerian church means we must not sell out to uncritical acclamation of the present, regardless of the current explosion of Christianity in the country. Instead, we do well to take stock of the contemporary church as it engages its cultural context and the missional challenges it has to face in the process. The present circumstance of the Nigerian church requires extreme caution. The following is not in any way an exhaustive list. Nevertheless, it is a tempered realism for understanding the great mission of God.

Doxological Challenge

A reflection on the life and experience of the church in Nigeria, especially its evangelistic ministry, seems to be in direct proportion to the normative guideline of the New Testament that identifies the mission dynamic as the *raison d'etre* of the church. Thankfully, the New Testament equally provides us with models of mission that are essential to the integrity of any missionary endeavor. The Acts of the Apostles and the Epistle to the Ephesians, for example, identify the reality of the reign of God as criterion for the presence and missionary witness of the church.

Similarly, the ultimate significance of the Great Commission is that God is a missionary God whose reign was thrust to the center of history in the Christ-event. Therefore, salvation means that the redemptive reign of God "is now being guided by a strategy that is being made explicit before the world in the ministry and life of Jesus the Messiah."[33] Consequently, the overall culmination of the Great Commission calls upon the church to enhance its mission consciousness, hence discover its true existence, in relation to the mission of God in the world. This is the extraordinary undertaking of the "gospel of the kingdom" (Mt. 24:14; Mk. 1:14-15).

---

33. Wilbert R. Shenk, *Changing Frontiers of Mission* (1999:9).

An understanding of the mission dynamic as being primarily God's and that the church is only participating on his invitation will subject our missiological objectives to rigorous scrutiny. Johannes Verkuyl describes this as the *doxological motif of mission*. This implies that "people who know the true and living God discover that he is such a delight that they want others to get acquainted with and live in fellowship with him as well."[34] The relevance of this to the contemporary church is that it provides a much-needed correction to our preoccupation with results and for achievement. It also reminds us that the results are for God's glory and not for the enhancement of our image.

There is no doubt that this was how the earliest Christians understood their missionary calling. The model for mission that becomes immediately clear in Luke's account of the Jerusalem church, for example, is that "witness to God's reign, present and coming, was at the heart of the disciple community's life."[35] This was also the basis by which the young church "challenged the regnant plausibility structure of their culture."[36] It should not surprise us, then, that the church grew organically.

But a line of distinction can be drawn with respect to the Nigerian church. This is because despite its fundamental importance to the Christian faith, the Nigerian church has not kept the reign of God at the center of its life and teaching. This diminution of the *doxological motif* of ministry/mission is especially a problem among the Charismatic/Pentecostal churches. Curiously, the Pentecostal revival in its early period of the 1970s was concerned with the creation of a powerful moral community. The values the revivalists espoused were radically antimaterialistic and demanded pure personal ethics. But as the movement expanded and developed stronger international ties, especially with their American counterparts, it lost its strict moral autonomy and was led away by the celebrity focus of American Pentecostal Christianity.[37]

---

34. Johannes Verkuyl, *Contemporary Missiology: An Introduction* (1978:166).
35. Wilbert R. Shenk, *Changing Frontiers of Mission* (1999:133).
36. Ibid.
37. See Ruth Marshall, "'God Is Not A Democrat': Pentecostalism and Democratisation in Nigeria" (1995:239-260). See also Steve Brouwer, Paul Gifford, and Susan D. Rose, *Exporting the American Gospel: Global Christian Fundamentalism* (1996).

The entire fabric of the church in twenty-first century Nigeria has changed, and the theological principle of God's rule seems not to provide the much-needed guidance for Christian missionary enterprise. Instead, the unprecedented exposure to the American social gospel and its doctrine of prosperity has led to large scale media-wise megachurches eager to build up and promote the image of their respective leaders. In the process, the Pentecostal pastor has become somewhat of a Christian superstar. The Pentecostal idiom of the "anointed man of God" legitimates his manipulative authoritarianism and militates, both in principle and practice, against Christian egalitarianism.

Nita Lafond Johnson of the America-based "World For Jesus Ministries" expresses a chilling and discomforting revelation:

> We spent days repenting, and weeping before God, for and over Nigerian Christian Leaders who demand worship and absolute submission from their followers. . . . It is a pitiful reality that was painful to unravel. The followers are guilty of the highest level of worshipping man. And, it is a worship the men require and demand. The end result has been a national church destitute of real power and joy. While it appears on the surface to be a rather healthy church, as you dig just a little below the surface the stench begins to rise. Therefore, what remains is a church that, in this case, prays often but they are without the sense and the tangible presence of their loving Savior; indeed without the favor of his great love because of their worship of man.[38]

The paradox of the Nigerian situation is a national church that appears spiritual and unimpeachable in its appearance yet internally it is condescending and trivialized because it is being disconnected from its *raison d'etre*. "The calling of the church," writes Wilbert Shenk, "is to glorify the Triune God (1) by faithfully witnessing to the reign of God, and

---

38. Nita Lafond Johnson, "Revival Fire" (2003:5).

(2) by living as a sign of that reign."³⁹ The superlatives and worship that surround the Nigerian church leaders are scandalous and inimical to the reign of God. An authentic witness to the reign of God disturbs the status quo, "exposes the egocentric structure of human nature . . . and challenges human motivation and character at the deepest levels."⁴⁰

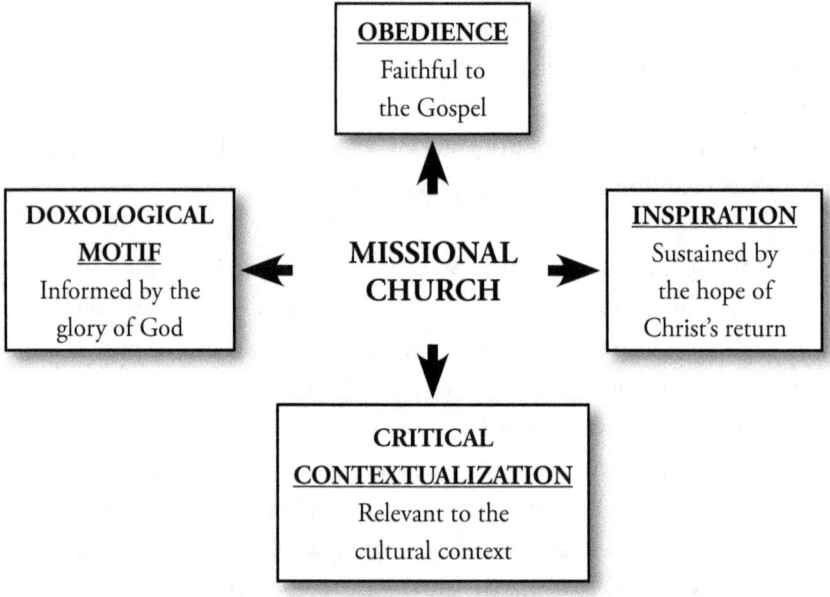

Figure 5
The Four Reference Points of a Missional Church⁴¹

The *doxological motif* of ministry/mission is neither a perfunctory bow of courtesy toward the missionary mandate nor a pious cause of the strongly established church. In fact, the respectability and power of the church's

---

39. Wilbert R. Shenk, *Changing Frontiers of Mission* (1999:15).
40. Shenk (1999:10).
41. This figure is an adaptation of Eddie Gibbs', "Evangelizing Nominal Christians" (2003:3).

witness can be judged only to the extent to which this *doxological motif* centering on the reign of God defines and shapes that witness.

The convictions which must guide the Nigerian church, and which must equally be the *sine qua non* of its advent toward the future, is the need to remember that "the church remains the mysterious *creatio Dei*" and exists for the *missio Dei* on behalf of the world.[42] As a living sign of the reign of God, therefore, the church must avoid the temptation to make its ministry relevant by rendering "respectable" service. When this happens, the church has "adopted an alien criterion and it becomes merely mundane."[43]

Leadership Challenge

> "Shared values are the glue that hold this organization together."[44]

There are important issues begging to be considered in terms of mentoring emerging leaders for the future of the church in Nigeria. On one hand, we must reflect on the extent to which Nigerian church leaders understand the nature of Christian leadership and its impact on the effectiveness of their witness to the world. On the other hand, the Nigerian church cannot afford to ignore certain biblical principles of leadership that even business organizations have appropriated as they work out the "witness" of their respective corporations.

Unfortunately, the church for so long has downplayed the importance of leadership. This has paralyzed her witness "by removing a crucial ability from the mix of abilities that are necessary for the church to be healthy, functional, and growing."[45] It is not surprising, therefore, that Jesus' parable of the shrewd manager resonates with embarrassment to the church, because

---

42. Charles Van Engen, *Mission on the Way: Issues in Mission Theology* (1996:107).
43. Wilbert Shenk *Changing Frontiers of Mission* (1999:16); citing Yinger J. Milton, *Religion, Society and the Individual: An Introduction to the Sociology of Religion* (1957:144ff.).
44. James M. Kouzes and Barry Z. Posner, *Credibility: How Leaders Gain and Lose it, Why People Demand It* (1993:119).
45. George Barna, *The Second Coming of the Church* (1998:103).

"the people of this world are more shrewd in dealing with their own kind than are the people of the light" (Lk. 16:8).

Robert Clinton has defined leadership as "a dynamic process in which a man or woman with God-given capacity influences a specific group of God's people toward his purposes for the group."[46] George Barna provides a definition that is compatible with the considerations that have been outlined by Clinton. According to him, "a Christian leader is someone who is called by God to lead and possess virtuous character and effectively motivates, mobilizes resources, and directs people toward the fulfillment of a jointly embraced vision from God."[47]

The singular failure of the Nigerian church in this regard is its narrowness about the interface between leadership as a God-given call and gift and the increasing responsibility to encourage the development of new leadership for the witness of the church. It is an undeniable fact that the church in Nigeria has witnessed rapid expansion because they are woven around individuals with charisma and clearly articulated personal visions. This, unfortunately, has also been the downside. The obvious problem with this charismatic leadership is the tendency for monopoly, arrogance, and autocracy.

The result is that the leader holds ultimate power over individual programs and almost unilaterally sets the vision that defines the institutional culture of the church. Even where leadership structure is seemingly put in place, these are often "dependency networks . . . which bolster their egos and ensure their position by making them indispensable."[48] In my opinion, the fact about a viable future for the Nigerian church, and indeed its vitality and effectiveness in the twenty-first century, puts a new emphasis on the mentoring, maturing, and empowering of emerging leaders.

---

46. J. Robert Clinton, *The Making of a Leader: Recognizing the Lessons and Stages of Leadership Development* (1988:14).

47. George Barna, *The Second Coming of the Church* (1998:107).

48. Eddie Gibbs has identified this as a universal problem especially among the new-paradigm churches epitomized by the new apostolic networks of Charismatic/Pentecostal churches. See his work, *ChurchNext: Quantum Changes in How We Do Ministry* (2000:84-87). For information on these new apostolic churches, see C. Peter Wagner, *The New Apostolic Churches* (1998).

Contrary to the church's truncated understanding, empowering leadership does not mean that the leader should be freed from performing the "real" ministry of preaching and teaching. Instead, it requires them to invert the pyramid of authority for the purpose of "motivating people to behave at specific times in certain ways for prescribed ends."[49] Such an enterprise requires various biblical tools and involves intersections with several disciplines, including social science and business management.

A number of studies can be cited to substantiate the contention that this is a workable idea. James Kouzes and Barry Posner, for example, highlight the following as important ingredients in the process of "liberating the leader in everyone": offering choices, encouraging ownership, inspiring confidence, creating a climate for learning, promoting communication and feedback, fostering mutual responsibility, and developing capacity.[50] The North American expert on leadership, John C. Maxwell, summarizes the leader's crucial task of nurturing potential leaders with his acronym, *BEST*: Believe in them, Encourage them, Share with them, and Trust them.[51]

Above all, rethinking the importance of nurturing potential leaders biblically and theologically requires that the Nigerian church leaders subscribe unconditionally to the approach of the master leader himself, Jesus Christ. In order to appreciate the genius of Jesus' approach, it is important to highlight the normative two-fold model by which he nurtured and trained his disciples. On one hand, Jesus seemed more intent on the quality of ministry and mentoring than on the quantity of people he was able to touch (Mt. 10:1-42; Mk. 3:13-19; Mk. 4:10-20; Lk. 6:12-19). On the other, he knew very well that effective ministry was a skill developed through practice; the more he allowed his disciples to apply what they had learned, the more capable they became. (Mt. 17:17-21; Mk. 9:14-29; Lk. 10:1-24).

If the Nigerian church is to embark on any viable leadership enterprise for the sake of its future, it is pointless to play the one approach out against

---

49. George Barna, *The Second Coming of the Church* (1998:106).
50. James Kouzes and Barry Posner, *Credibility: How Leaders Gain and Lose it, Why People Demand It* (1993:153-182).
51. John C. Maxwell, *Developing the Leaders Around You* (1995:61-82).

the other. As Eddie Gibbs has aptly put it, "theory informs practice, but equally important, practice develops new theories."[52] In order to actualize the true existence of the church in an effective and viable witness to the world, then, it is high time that the perspective of service to the kingdom be stressed forcefully in the mentoring, maturing, and empowerment of leaders for the twenty-first century Nigeria.

Discipleship Challenge

I have mentioned that Africa embodies a new hermeneutical center of Christian practice. Along with affirming the spectacular conversion stories on the continent, therefore, we also have to take cognizance of the post-conversion experiences of these new Christians. As Andrew Walls has rightly noted, "Christian mission is not simply about the multiplication of the church; it is about the discipling of the nations."[53] This means the task of winning souls for Christ must be balanced by an emphasis on what is to happen to the souls after they have been won.[54]

It is wrong, therefore, to suppose that making converts is more important than the making of disciples. The fact is that there is an indissoluble connection between "converting" and "discipling" such that we cannot play one against the other. But the difficult issue for the Nigerian church is how to be faithful to the command of Jesus Christ to make disciples of a nation in which the structure is one of "deep economic crisis, profound cynicism and disaffection towards political leadership . . . and a widespread sense of social and moral disintegration."[55]

While no consensus has been reached among New Testament scholars concerning the main elements of Christian discipleship, avoiding the issue altogether is a paralyzing defensiveness. This notwithstanding, we find in the biblical materials and the socio-historical context of the early Christian experience the positive features of faithful discipleship. In principle,

---

52. Eddie Gibbs, *ChurchNext* (2000:92-101).
53. Andrew Walls, *The Missionary Movement in Christian History* (1996:85).
54. Stephen Neill, "The Church" (1970:109).
55. Ruth Marshall, "'God Is Not A Democrat': Pentecostalism and Democratisation in Nigeria" (1995:246).

therefore, the term "discipleship" quite clearly carries a narrow as well as a broader definition. In its narrow sense, it can be understood technically and exclusively in terms of the teacher-learner dynamic (*mathētēs*) in which the pupil accepts and "follows" a given doctrine or teacher. In its broader definition, it can be understood as a way of thinking and speaking about the nature of the Christian life.[56]

In its Hellenistic context, the term implied the existence of a personal attachment between an apprentice or a pupil and a teacher. This meant that the master determined the type of adherency which could range from "being the pupil of a philosopher to being the follower of a great thinker and master of the past, to being the devotee of a religious figure."[57] The most important issue was that the personal attachment had an effect in shaping the whole life of the *mathētēs* and left no doubt as to who was the agent of formation, whether in knowledge or in action.

In spite of the term being a theological abstraction from Hellenism, a clear understanding calls for a response to the theological impulse of Christ's commission to the church. Although each Gospel narrative carries a message for the contemporary church, Luke-Acts appears to be more illuminating because the "treatment of the theme of discipleship is more extensively developed, more radically expressed, and more consistently sustained."[58]

In Luke-Acts, the idea for discipleship involves (1) a detachment from all other allegiances and a total allegiance to Jesus by "coming after" him (Lk. 14:26-27; 9:23), (2) repentance and baptism in the name of Jesus—symbolizing a detachment from old ties and attachment to a new authority (Ac. 2:38), and (3) a submission to the will and purpose of the living Lord and obedience to the heavenly vision (Ac. 9:1-19; 22:6-16; 26:12-19).[59]

---

56. Fernando Segovia, "Introduction: Call and Discipleship—Toward a Re-examination of the Shape and Character of Christian Existence in the New Testament" (1985:1-2).
57. Michael Wilkins, *Discipleship in the Ancient World and Matthew's Gospel* (1995:42).
58. Richard N. Longenecker, "Taking Up the Cross Daily: Discipleship in Luke-Acts" (1996:50).
59. The perspective I have adopted with regards to Christian discipleship in Luke-Acts depends heavily on the work of Charles H. Talbert, "Discipleship in Luke-Acts" (1985:62-75).

What is immediately observable in Luke-Acts, therefore, is the inseparability of the theme of discipleship from the model and tradition about Jesus. Again, this conforms to the literary genre of antiquity in which the biographies of certain founders of philosophical schools contained within themselves the life of the founder and were perpetuated by shaping the lives of his successors and disciples.[60] In other words, there were no generic philosophical or religious experiences and abstractions, only those that were common to specific traditions. In ancient time, this characteristic defined the structure of faithful discipleship.

Luke-Acts vividly portrays Jesus "as the founder of the Christian community who provides for its continuation after his departure."[61] Jesus embodied this tradition in his own life through an unconditional surrender to the will and mission of the Father. Through his own obedient life, he modeled for his disciples what are pointedly the most important elements that should define and shape the Christian walk. Luke 6:40, for example, is an explicit testimony about Jesus as model: "A disciple is not above his teacher, but everyone who is perfectly trained will be like his teacher." It should not surprise us, then, that his disciples reproduced in their careers the "prototypical events of the career of the earthly Jesus" (Ac. 20:17-35).[62]

The Jesus paradigm depicts the Christian *way to walk* not as something that can be postponed until one has achieved a high level of maturity as a follower of Christ but as an ongoing developmental process. Jesus' challenge to the Galilean fishermen, for example, was simultaneously about following and fishing (Lk. 5:1-11). For Jesus the emphasis was on the spiritual progress of his disciples, and he committed himself toward an experience-facilitating approach that enabled his disciples to actualize what they had learned in practical ways. In Luke 9:1-2, for example, we are told "he called his disciples together and gave them power and authority over all

---

60. See Charles Talbert, "Discipleship in Luke-Acts" (1985:63). See his other works, *What Is a Gospel? The Genre of the Canonical Gospels* (1977), and "The Gospel and the Gospels" (1981:14-26).
61. Charles Talbert, "Discipleship in Luke-Acts" (1985:64).
62. Ibid.

demons, and to cure diseases. He sent them to preach the kingdom of God and to heal the sick."

From the foregoing, we observe that the biblical model of discipleship, which finds its classical expression in the Jesus paradigm, runs counter to what is observable in contemporary Nigeria. The biblical archetype here is that faithful discipleship manifests in three ways: (1) being molded by a tradition, (2) being empowered by an experience, and (3) being a participant in a community.[63] In other words, the church has a single purpose, that of discipleship, which consists of three aspects. These three dimensions cannot be sustained in isolation from one another. They must be held together and allowed to interpenetrate if the church is to claim to be "coming after Jesus" and living a life that fulfills its mission. The following is a graphic depiction:

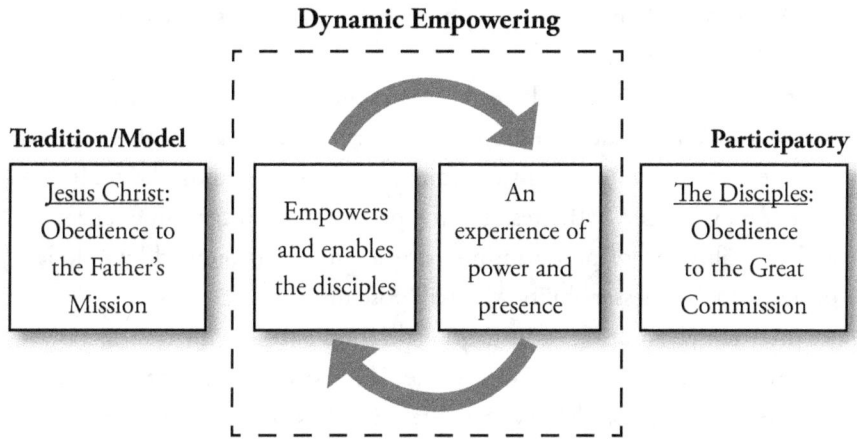

Figure 6
A Continuum of Faithful Discipleship

Apart from the mainline denominational churches, Deeper Life Bible Church stands out among the born-again strand as intentionally

---

63. Talbert (1985:62).

committed to disciple-making. Its purpose is clearly articulated in the words of William Kumuyi, the founding pastor, as "essentially a teaching ministry." The tripod on which the church rests, according to him, "is the Word, holiness and evangelism."[64] It is not surprising, then, that members of Deeper Life Bible Church are more theologically informed than the average Nigerian born-again Christian. It is appropriate to say that the vitality of the Nigerian church in the future and its missionary relevance to the world will be in direct proportion to the degree to which it engages with the model of discipleship exemplified by Jesus.

Nigerian church leaders have an obligation to lead their members after the model of Jesus through concrete teaching of the Word. They are equally responsible to provide ministry opportunities through which believers can actualize in experiential ways that which they have learned. In Luke-Acts, we find that "one fulfills the mission only as one is empowered, guided, and protected through an ongoing experience."[65] This is presently not the case in the Nigerian church.

Instead, there is the disenfranchisement of the people through a widespread "all-rounder" syndrome of Nigerian church leaders. This action is often legitimated by an egotistical claim to the so-called apostolic anointing of the "man of God." The result is the perpetration of institutionalization and centralization of power in one person who is surrounded by "'clones' or individuals of lesser ability who will pose no threat."[66]

Interestingly, a critic of institutionalization and legitimation of power comes from within the Pentecostal circle. This, however, is a false appearance because despite their claim which "delegitimises the authoritarian use of power . . . the idiom of born-again spiritual power is not radically different in its operation in terms of legitimating institutional authority."[67] Even in cases where so-called assistant pastors have been charged with ministerial responsibilities, this usually operates from a premise of distrust and

---

64. William Kumuyi, "Deeper Christian Life Ministry" (1998:243-256).
65. Charles Talbert, "Discipleship in Luke-Acts" (1985:69).
66. Eddie Gibbs, *ChurchNext* (2000:86).
67. Ruth Marshall, "'God Is Not A Democrat': Pentecostalism and Democratisation in Nigeria" (1995:256).

suspicion. The result is the endemic nature of bitter conflicts that have developed within the Pentecostal community.

If the Nigerian church is to survive its success, it must restructure its organizational character by democratizing access to the sacred. As Kingsley Larbi has observed with regards to the whole of Africa, "the obsession with numbers and the need to finish the Great Commission, have clouded the key issue embodied in the Great Commission, that is discipleship making.[68]" This, simply put, is analogous to putting the cart before the horse.

One of the defining convictions of biblical ecclesiology is that the church is a social community, a body of people who have been "called out" (*ekklēsia*) to live a missionary existence in the world. To this extent, it is appropriate to echo Karl Rahner's hopeful vision that "the church of the future would be built from the ground by base communities that were free to pursue their mission."[69] There is no reason to suppose that this cannot happen. The life of Jesus provides the normative model; the gifts of the Holy Spirit (*charismata*) guarantee divine empowerment; and the Great Commission challenges the church to keep the kingdom of God as its central focus.

To be a disciple of Jesus Christ and a member of his body, therefore, means that the church has to actualize its true existence in the world. There can be no doubt that "this was how the earliest Christians understood their calling."[70] In the long run, there is but one litmus test that will be applied to all the activities of the Nigerian church in her claim to obedience in mission. Do they or do they not produce disciples of Jesus Christ?[71]

---

68. E. Kingsley Larbi, "Response to Professor Ogbu U. Kalu's Paper, 'Pentecostal and Charismatic Reshaping of the African Religious Landscape in the 1990s" (2002:5).

69. Exact quotation is from Wilbert Shenk, *Write the Vision: The Church Renewed* (1995:101). For Shenk's reference to Karl Rahner, see the latter's work, *The Christian of the Future* (1967:78ff). See also Rahner's *The Shape of the Church to Come* (1983, first published in 1974).

70. Wilbert Shenk, *Changing Frontiers of Mission* (1999:132).

71. Arthur F. Glasser, *Announcing the Kingdom: The Story of God's Mission in the Bible* (2003:13).

Intellectual/Theological Challenge

> "Most Christians would rather die than think—in fact they do."[72]

Concerned about the lack of sustained intellectual life among North American Evangelicals, Mark Noll retorts with marked frustration that "the scandal of the evangelical mind is that there is not much of an evangelical mind."[73] Echoing Noll's observation and frustration, Os Guinness concludes that anti-intellectualism "has become the scandal of evangelicalism."[74] Interestingly both works were published in the same year, 1994, with one prophetic challenge to North American believers to start thinking again. According to them, this is the only way Evangelicals can escape the crippling sin of not loving God with their minds as well as their hearts (Mt. 22:37; Mk. 12:30).

While the intellectual renovation being envisioned for North America is not what is being addressed here, the present intellectual contradictions among Nigerian churches are even gravely more compelling. However, the scandal of anti-intellectualism in Nigerian Christianity is of a totally different sort. Whereas the North American situation is a retreat of the evangelical mind in the face of popular culture, the problem with Nigeria is the total lack of awareness of the urgent need for any kind of intellectual life. Ironically, the Protestant traditions (Anglican, Methodist, and Baptist) that brought Christianity to Nigeria developed out of vigorous theological principles, but unfortunately, these principles seem not to have engendered intellectual discipline in the new church movements.

Contemporary Christian thought, especially among the Aladura and the new Charismatic/Pentecostal churches, is best understood as a set of intellectual contradictions. This can be understood as arising from a synthesis of secular educational achievement, "in-house" apprenticeship,

---

72. Os Guinness, *Fit Bodies, Fat Minds: Why Evangelicals Don't Think and What To Do About It* (1994), see back cover.
73. Mark Noll, *The Scandal of the Evangelical Mind* (1994:3).
74. Os Guinness, *Fit Bodies, Fat Minds* (1994), see back cover.

and a complete misunderstanding of the spontaneous "anointing" of the Holy Spirit. Adding to these contradictions is the belief that the present growth of the church, its social vitality, and the spiritual passion for the gospel constitute a truly Christian life. The Nigerian situation is complex, yet the reasons for it can be highlighted, at least in certain specific ways.

First is the myriad of Pentecostal congregations founded and led by the upwardly mobile university graduates and professionals. Although not necessarily a bad thing, however, the concern hinges on the distinction between thoughts and expertise learned through the distinctives of secular life and thinking guided and inspired by Christian teaching. The problem is further compounded by the presupposition that these secular ideologies can glide effortlessly into ecclesiastical responsibilities with relatively little or no theological and missiological preparation. Before too long, ambitious young lawyers, teachers, engineers, doctors, and even showbiz stars became church founders and preachers. This became a syndrome to the degree that it helped in creating the faulty pathway for populist Pentecostal ecclesiology of the 1990s.

The long-term effect of the lack of theological and missiological preparation as well as the development of ministry skills is enormous. The first can be summarized by quoting Eddie Gibbs at length in his own observation of the North American situation:

> Without these training foundations, leaders will function without the benefit of a broader frame of reference beyond the norms and demands of their cultural context. They will lack the sensitivities developed through training in the biblical and missiological disciplines. They will not have the benefit of the lessons of church history. They will not be aware of how the Christian movement advanced in the face of the many challenges it faced in centuries past. They will not be aware of the periods when the church faltered in its advance because of failure to consolidate its gains, when it retreated because internal matters were neglected or, conversely, when domestic

issues became the overriding preoccupation and consumed far too much energy.[75]

The second implication of this theological anti-intellectualism is that most of these leaders labor under severe theological limitations that become increasingly more evident over time. This suggests why most Nigerian churchgoers are inept and lack the ability to do theological reasoning and criticism. And without thinking long and hard about the ramifications of their actions, each church leader presumes himself to be adequate to not only establish a church but also found Bible schools. Unfortunately, this problem is more profound and widespread than can be imagined.

The other problem is almost a universal problem, and cuts across all the three strands that constitute the Nigerian church. This is the "in-house" apprenticeship approach. While this initiative is commendable in many ways, it is not without great negative implications. As can be expected, the curricula are often shaped by the ministry needs of the local church such that they promote a rich breadth of competency but also an awful narrowness in theological and missiological adequacy.

Again, Eddie Gibbs' observation and warning to the churches of North America is equally valid for Nigeria. That is, the need to "be mindful of the fact that we reproduce after our own kind and our blind spots and false trails are likely to be perpetuated if there is not an adequate, broad-based critique."[76] So, while the first problem highlights the need to balance secular educational achievement with theological and missiological preparation, the second focuses on theological integrity and critical evaluation. The Nigerian church needs to take the long view and embrace a "new intellectualism" that would value and lay a solid theological foundation for what promises to be as demanding a theological frontier as the church has yet faced.

An appeal for theological and missiological learning is not to presume that this is the ultimate or only value. The call, rather, is for mutual interdependence and collaborative working relationship between the churches and the seminaries. As Eddie Gibbs has forcefully put it, "Each

---

75. Eddie Gibbs, *ChurchNext* (2000:87).
76. Gibbs (2000:100).

needs the other. Church leaders draw the attention of the scholarly community to the theological, philosophical, and ministry-skill related issues that they face. The scholarly communities act as consultants who provide the churches with an independent critique to grant correction and guidance."[77]

Ethical Challenge

> Miracles, expensive cars, exorcisms, and bodyguards: religion is big business in Nigeria. By promoting a dream of escaping poverty, they have turned their churches into corporations, which are changing the face of Christianity.[78]

It may not earn much adulation to raise issues of ethical challenge when the church appears to be active about its obligation to win lost souls. Yet, it is a sober reality that the church's evangelistic ministry has been largely verbal. While evangelism demands the verbal message, an equally valid dimension of ministry is that which reflects the life and experience of the messenger. As the Nigerian church stands now, there is a serious incompatibility between its evangelistic conviction and its moral obligation. Unless the church begins to act out of moral consciousness and develop a strong revolt against its own moral indifference it will become a hopeless contradiction even to those lost souls it is trying to win.

Perhaps in no other strand of the Nigerian church is this more apparent than in the born-again community of Neo-Charismatic/Pentecostal Christianity. It is difficult to imagine how the faithful have interiorized the materialistic to such an extent that everything connected with church or God has been identified primarily with one thing: irreducible material acquisition. Incidentally, the Pentecostal community is not a passing fad; it is instead a burgeoning one with its many pastoral, ecclesiastical, and theological implications.

---

77. Ibid.
78. Seyi Rhodes, "Nigeria's Millionaire Preachers" (2011).

The petrol price hike embroilment in Nigeria early in 2012 was a testament to this fact for it exposed a sizeable segment of the Pentecostal brand as ecclesial malcontents who have long since sold out to the god of Marmon. Names such as "El-Subsidy Church of Christ" and other expressive usage patterns like "Jehovah El-Subsidy Ministries," "Ijo Mimo Subsidy Lati Orun Wa," "CAC, Oke Subsidy" that permeated social networking sites, particularly Facebook, revealed disparaging adaptations and humorous lexical and semantic contortions of more authentic church names like "Ijo Mimo Kristi Lati Orun Wa" (Celestial Church of Christ), "Jehovah El Shaddai Ministries" (Jehovah God Almighty Ministries), "CAC, Oke Irapada" (CAC, Mount of Transfiguration), and so on. This vernacularization of the term "subsidy" and its associated contortions highlight the scandal in contemporary Nigeria and the outrageously unconscionable indulgences that exist in the realms of God and of Caesar—the religious and the civil.

The incongruous and unexpected association of these normally unrelated contexts (church and subsidy) allowed a mocking reappraisal of what being or doing church has become in contemporary Nigeria. To this extent, it is possible to assess the expressive usage pattern such as "El-Subsidy Church of Christ, Inc" not only as the limits of humor, but as both reflective of the state of the church in relation to the deeply conflicted subsidy removal itself and the associated corruption of our polity. The proliferation of churches, embodied by these distinctive church name variations, becomes the humorous reappraisal distancing authentic church practice from the upsetting scenario of present-day Nigeria.

The commercialization of evangelism, particularly among the Charismatic/Pentecostal strand of the Nigerian church, is disturbing, to say the least. Consumed by the "doctrine of prosperity" the church has found the "symbolic platform on which to integrate the born-again experience of redemption with social mobility, conspicuous consumption, and the legitimation of wealth in a time of scarcity."[79] It is, therefore, not surprising that expressions such as "My God is not a poor God" and Bible passages such as James 1:17: "Every good gift and every perfect gift is from above,

---

79. Ruth Marshall, "'God Is Not A Democrat': Pentecostalism and Democratisation in Nigeria" (1995:254).

and comes down from the Father of lights" are always on the lips of the "man of God." This explains why in many of these churches materialism is baptized. Unfortunately, it is only the leaders that are getting enriched while the naïve congregants get poorer each time they attend church.

The bold, radical, and even desperate attempts at becoming rich are out of bounds. In the process, the question of truth has been completely trivialized and the gospel itself robbed of its ultimate seriousness. Even the most elemental changes in human society for which the church has earned social respectability, such as building up morals and inculcating good behavior, have become lost by the inordinate greed of these "modern-day preachers." In contemporary Nigeria, it is not considered extreme for prosperity preachers to postulate that Jesus himself must have been very rich while on earth as he had a treasurer in the person of Judas Iscariot.

This exploitation of the psyche of the people through prosperity preaching has brought about criticism and even ridicule:

> As the world turns in Nigeria and as the economic situation deteriorates further, it seems that the ministry is the only profitable industry that can sustain a lifestyle of the rich and famous. It does not take much for one to be a pastor in Nigeria. One does not need a degree in divinity neither does one need to go to Bible school. All one needs is a Bible, and he does not need to know all its contents, just enough to get by. If he can recite a verse like John 3:16, "For God so love the world that he sent his only begotten son, that whosoever believeth in him shall not perish but have everlasting life", he will do just fine. He will also need a battery-powered micro-phone, a smiling face to give the impression that the Lord has been good to him, an eye catchy name for the church, something to the effect of "Give It All to Him Temple of God" or "Ask and It Shall be Given Church of God" and half a dozen to a dozen baskets several feet deep for the collection of tithes and offerings. Once all this are in place, the rest becomes history

and the pastor leaps to a higher tax bracket with immediate alacrity. Halleluia, isn't the Lord great?[80]

Although the above picture is pathetic, nevertheless, it is the true description. No less a towering figure in the Nigerian church, Anthony Olubunmi Okogie, the immediate past Roman Catholic Archbishop of Lagos, makes this clear. According to him, "the quickest and easiest way to make money in Nigeria is to carry a Bible on Sunday and start preaching."[81]

Borrowing Bosch's astute observation, it is appropriate to say that "the Jesus of [Pentecostalism] appears to have more in common with the Chamber of Commerce and the entertainment world than with a simple cave in Bethlehem or a rugged cross on a barren hill."[82] Unfortunately, the general dictum in Nigeria is "if you fail at a business, start a church." What we find, therefore, is that the Nigerian church like the prodigal son, is dissipating its prophetic witness, social respectability, and the morality of redemption at the altar of conspicuous materialism. This is cause for alarm and an overdue call for serious moral stocktaking.

If the Nigerian church ever desires to lift its battered image to a level that gives significance again to human society, the only alternative is a rediscovery of prophetic witnessing. That is, there must be a prophetic understanding of reality that is based in the notions that the poor is incontrovertibly a material reality and that all such social reality ultimately springs from the Word that became flesh. In other words, if we introduce Matthew 25 into the teaching and practice of the church, we find that the poor are not merely "the object of Christian love or the fulfilment of a moral duty; they are the latent presence of the coming Savior and Judge in the world, the touchstone which determines salvation and damnation."[83] This can only happen by revisiting the redemptive power of God and by

---

80. Tonye David-West, "Speaking of the Pastors of 'Show Me Thy Money Church of God' in Nigeria" (2001:3).
81. Norimitsu Onishi, "Africans Fill Churches That Celebrate Wealth" (2002:1).
82. David Bosch, *Transforming Mission* (1991:417); quoting James Armstrong, *From the Underside: Evangelism from a Third World Vantage Point* (1981:22, 41, 49).
83. Jürgen Moltmann, *The Church in the Power of the Spirit* (1993:127).

applying the revelational classics of the gospel message constructively to those problems which press most for solutions in a pragmatic way.[84]

Unfortunately, the church for too long has existed in a polarized climate that distinguishes between two different *mandates*, the one spiritual, the other social.[85] The result is that the church has neglected and become indifferent to the basic duties of human charity simply because of its religious orientation. Yet a fully biblical paradigm of ministry is one that is responsive to human well-being, aspirations, and justice. As Carl Henry has argued,

> the social implications of the Gospel are integral to evangelistic fulfillment, and social concern is an indispensable ingredient of the evangelistic message. Social concern cannot therefore be isolated and compartmentalized as a marginal or secondary consideration which the evangelist leaves to others because he has a special calling to evangelize.[86]

It is undoubtedly within the boundary of the missionary mandate of the Nigerian church to stake out programs aimed at empowering individuals to better manage themselves and to make appropriate contribution to the progress of their society. A useful starting point is to experiment with the concept of "Microenterprise Development" (MED). This has proven to be a poverty alleviation and value-based development enterprise in other two-third world countries.[87] MED is not charity, nor is it a subsidized program. Rather, it "involves providing credit and financial services and related training to poor microentrepreneurs to enable them to enhance

---

84. I am indebted to Carl F.H. Henry for his pioneering work in this regard, *The Uneasy Conscience of Modern Fundamentalism* (1947).

85. David Bosch, *Transforming Mission* (1991:403).

86. Carl F.H. Henry, "The Purpose of God" (1976:29).

87. For details see, Bruce J. Nicholls and Beulah R. Wood, *Sharing the Good News with the Poor* (1996); Tetsunao Yamamori, Bryant L. Myers, Kwame Bediako and Larry Reed, *Serving with the Poor in Africa* (1996); and United Nations Development Programme, *MicroStart: A Guide for Planning, Starting and Managing a Microfinance Programme* (1997).

their businesses and create employment and income for themselves and their communities."[88]

This does not mean that the church will abdicate its evangelistic responsibility and become instead a "Microfinance Institution" (MFI). On the contrary, it is an attempt to blend the evangelistic and socio-cultural mandates into one, so that the church's insistence on personal transformation finds leverage in "a vigorous application of Christian faith and values to sociopolitical [and economic] concerns."[89] Perhaps no one captures this better than Makonen Getu. He writes:

> The church can and should play a significant role in enhancing the MED industry as part of its mission to facilitate transformational change in people's lives. As an institution, the church has a wide constituency and social influence. The more people become obedient to God and apply Christian principles, the better the prospects for best-practice MED. Through its Christian teachings, the church could create a stronger presence of good stewardship, accountability, reliability, and integrity. These are important ingredients of best-practice MED because they promote financial discipline among clients.[90]

In the final analysis, Nigerian church leaders must recognize that although they may be the subject examining the socio-cultural context, they are equally the object of that examination. It is a serious sin, in itself, to remain morally indifferent to the disenfranchised, let alone exploit them in the name of God. The higher morality of the gospel, which should be the hermeneutical locus of our witness, is the Word that became flesh (Jn. 1:14).

---

88. I am grateful for the insightful work of Makonen Getu that has been adopted here, "Poverty Alleviation and the Role of Microcredit in Africa" (2001:165-179).

89. Wilbert Shenk, *Changing Frontiers of Mission* (1999:25).

90. Makonen Getu, "Poverty Alleviation and the Role of Microcredit in Africa" (2001:177).

Jesus was not simply interested in telling self-contained stories about the kingdom, rather he demonstrated that the kingdom had arrived in very practical ways. In other words, his kingdom perspective awakened faith and brought wholeness. For the Nigerian church, and even more so for the future of the church, this can only mean one thing. That is, missiological integrity requires that "the deed without the word is dumb; the word without the deed is empty. Words interpret deeds and deeds validate words."[91]

Conclusion

I have attempted to demonstrate that the changing face of Christianity is one that bears the deep imprints of Africa. Andrew Walls is therefore not mistaken when he declares "African Christianity as potentially the *representative* Christianity of the twenty-first century."[92] But while we celebrate the unique African experience, we must also not forget that the phenomena that characterize the history of Christianity are full of wholesale transformations that have made past "representative Christianity" peripheral to the grand Christian story. Andrew Walls himself alludes to this fact when he writes:

> The representative Christianity of the second and third and fourth centuries was shaped by events and processes at work in the Mediterranean world. In later times it was events and processes among the barbarian peoples of northern and western Europe, or in Russia, or modern western Europe, or the North Atlantic world that produced the representative Christianity of those times[93]

---

91. Leslie Newbigin, "Cross-Currents in Ecumenical and Evangelical Understandings of Mission" (1982:146-151).
92. Andrew Walls, *The Cross-Cultural Process in Christian History* (2002:85).
93. Ibid.

The historical situation in the above is a sober analysis. Yet there is an element of curiosity about it. It suggests that being a "representative Christianity," as pivotal as this may be, is not an automatic ticket to surviving that success. The more important work of critical evaluation is necessary in order to facilitate a sustaining and penetrating success. In the words of Ogbu Kalu, "a definition of the church as *ekklēsia* must perforce mean that church history is the reconstruction of the experience of what God has done in Christ through the power of the Holy Spirit in individuals and among communities, in time perspective."[94]

Christianity is not new to Africa and it cannot be treated as a product of imperialist expansion. The North African church of the early centuries, the Coptic Church of Egypt, and the Ethiopian Orthodox Church testify to the historic manifestations of Christianity on the continent. Yet the euphoria that characterized these early manifestations of Christianity in Africa as well as other "representative Christianity" of the past has evaporated almost completely. Presently, there has been a turning of the tide in other parts of Africa.

But if we must reflect on the past and look upon it as a compass for navigating our mission to the world, it is equally important that we see the future as an extension of the present. The church in Nigeria, as in the rest of Africa, is poised at the "strategic inflection point." Andrew Grove, former CEO of Intel, defines this as "a time in the life of a business when its fundamentals are about to change."[95] While the African phenomenon is ultimately the work of the Holy Spirit, leaving the "fundamentals" unattended will only weaken and leave the church open to secularizing forces.

This means that we must perceive the Nigerian church as an ellipse with two foci. In and around the first it calls for an acknowledgement and a celebration of this new Christian vitality. From and through the second focus on the interface of history and theology the church must challenge

---

94. Ogbu Kalu, "Enstranged Bedfellows?: The Demonization of the Aladura in African Pentecostal Rhetoric (2001:7-8).

95. Andrew S. Grove, *Only The Paranoid Survive* (1996:3, 32). For a perspective that relates this concept to the North American context, see Eddie Gibbs, *ChurchNext* (2000:32-35).

itself to practice a "transformational hermeneutics."[96] In other words, while I do not intend to undervalue "the extent to which African Christianity represents a new chapter in Christian history,"[97] what I am emphasizing is that our purely triumphant perspectives must be counterbalanced by a critical theological response. This way the Nigerian church can be radically transformed by reconceptualizing its nature and existence in relation to the great mission of God in the world.

This is an appropriate time, a "strategic inflection point," where discernible strengths and limitations of the Nigerian Christian experience must be juxtaposed with a fresh articulation and a renewed vision of the nature, purpose, and characteristics of the church of the twenty-first century. Failure to engage in this type of "transformational hermeneutics" is to concede to the same contradictions of the post-Christian West.

Moving beyond our present triumphalism means that we are constantly engaged in thought processes that provide interpretive framework for the way we do church in Nigeria. This, as a matter of priority and urgency, must include the role of Scripture in the task of the church, the value of past theological constructs for the twenty-first century, and the effect of our pluralistic context on the message and mission of the church. This way there is no reason, whether in principle or in practice, why the church in Africa (Nigeria) cannot be transforming representative model that Andrew Walls envisions for the future.

---

96. James P. Martin, "Toward a Post-Critical Paradigm" (1987:378).
97. Andrew Walls, *The Cross-Cultural Process in Christian History* (2002:116).

Bibliography

Abati, Reuben
    2001   "The Clash of the Pastor-Generals." *Nigeriaworld.* Accessed November 14, 2001. <http://nigeriaworld.com/feature/publication/abati/111101.html>.

Abba, Yusufu
    1979   "The 1804 Jihad in Hausaland as a Revolution." In *Studies in the History of the Sokoto Caliphate: The Sokoto Seminar Papers.* Y.B. Usman, ed. Pp. 20-33. Zaria, Nigeria: Ahmadu Bello University.

Abimbola, Wande
    1973   *Ifa Divination Poetry.* Bloomington, IN: Indiana University Press.
    1976   *Ifa: An Exposition of Ifa Corpus.* London: Oxford University Press.

Abrams, M.H.
    1953   *The Mirror and the Lamp.* London: Oxford University Press.

Achebe, Chinua
    1958   *Things Fall Apart.* London: Heinemann.

Adamo, D.T., and J. Enuwosa
    2001   "The Prospects of Intrafaith Dialogue in Nigeria." *Missiology* 29(3):331-342.

Adegboyega, S.G.
    1978   *Short History of the Apostolic Church of Nigeria.* Ibadan, Nigeria: Rosprint.

Adejobi, Emmanuel A.
    1965   *The Observances and Practices of the Church of the Lord (Aladura) in Light of Old Testament and New Testament.* Lagos, Nigeria: Charity Press.

Adekola, Moses Akinwumi
    1989   "The Redeemed Christian Church of God." Ph.D. dissertation, Obafemi Awolowo University, Ile-ife, Nigeria.

Ademakinwa, J.A.
    1945   *Iwe Itan Ijo Wa (History of Our Church).* Lagos, Nigeria: CSS Press.

Adogame, Afeosemime U.
    1999   *Celestial Church of Christ.* Frankfurt, Germany: Peter Lang.

African Church Organization
    1910   *Report of Proceedings of the African Church Organizations for Lagos and Yorubaland, 1901-1908.*

African Guardian
    1990   "Editorial on the Cabinet Reshuffle." January 29:12. Lagos, Nigeria.

Agbaje, Adigun
    1990   "Travails of the Secular State: Religion, Politics, and the Outlook on Nigeria's Third Republic." *Journal of Commonwealth and Comparative Politics* 28(3):288-308.

Agbeti, Kofi
    1986   *West African Church History, Christian Missions and Church Foundations: 1482-1919.* Leiden: E.J. Brill.

Ajayi, J.F. Ade
    1959   "Nineteenth Century Origins of Nigerian Nationalism." *Journal of the Historical Society of Nigeria* 1(4):121-124.
    1965   *Christian Missions in Nigeria, 1841-1891: The Making of a New Élite.* Evanston, IL: Northwestern University Press.
    1999   "From Mission to Church: The Heritage of the Church Mission Society." *International Bulletin of Missionary Research* 23(2):50-55.

Ajayi, Olusola
    1997   *Warrior of Righteousness: The Life and Ministry of Rev. J.O. Akindayomi.* Abeokuta, Nigeria: Ordinance Publishing House.

Akinjogbin, I.A.
    1967   *Dahomey and Its Neighbors, 1708-1818.* Cambridge, UK: University of Cambridge Press.

Akinsanya, Gbolahan Olukayode
    2000   "'You Shall Receive Power': The Establishment of the Pentecostal Movement in the Nigerian Context." Ph.D. dissertation, Drew University.

Akpaekong, Obong
    1999   "The Miracle Man." *Newswatch* 20(December):8-14.

Aland, Kurt
    1965   "The Problem of Anonymity and Pseudonymity in Christian Literature of the First Two Centuries." In *The Authorship and Integrity of the New Testament.* SPCK Theological Series, 4. Aland Kurt, et al. Pp. 1-13. London: SPCK.

Allen, Roland
    1965   *Missionary Methods: St. Paul's or Ours?* Grand Rapids, MI: William B. Eerdmans.

Alokan, Adeware
    1991   *The Christ Apostolic Church, 1928-1988.* Ibadan, Nigeria: Ibukunola Printers Nigeria Limited.

Anderson, Allan H.
  1999   "Pentecostal Pneumatology and African Power Concepts: Continuity or Change?" *Missionalia* 19(1):65-74.
  2001a   "Types and Butterflies: African Initiated Churches and European Typologies." *International Bulletin of Missionary Research* 25(3):107-113.
  2001b   *African Reformation: African Initiated Christianity in the 20th Century*. Trenton, NJ: Africa World Press, Inc.

Angus, Samuel
  1951   *The Environment of Early Christianity*. New York: Charles Scribner's Sons.

Apostolic Faith of Nigeria, The
  n.d.   *The Man with a Vision: The Biography of Timothy Gbadebo Oshokoya*. Lagos, Nigeria: The Apostolic Faith.

Apter, Andrew
  1999   "IBB = 419: Nigerian Democracy and the Politics of Illusion." In *Civil Society and the Political Imagination in Africa*. John L. Comaroff and Jean Comaroff, eds. Pp. 267-307. Chicago, IL: The University of Chicago Press.

Armstrong, James
  1981   *From the Underside: Evangelism from a Third World Vantage Point*. Maryknoll, NY: Orbis Books.

Atanda, J.A., ed.
  1988   *Baptist Churches in Nigeria, 1850-1950, Accounts of the Foundation and Growth*. Ibadan, Nigeria: University Press Limited.

Athenagoras
  n.d.   *A Plea for the Christians*. In *The Ante-Nice Fathers: The Writings of the Fathers Down to A.D. 325*. Vol. 2 (1978). Alexander Roberts and James Donaldson, eds. Pp. 129-148. Grand Rapids, MI: William B. Eerdmans.

Aune, David
  1992   "Worship: Early Christian." In *Anchor Bible Dictionary*. David Noel Freedman, ed. Pp. 973-989. New York: Doubleday.

Ayandele, E.A.
  1966   *The Missionary Impact on Modern Nigeria 1842-1914: A Political and Social Analysis*. London: Longmans.
  1970   *Holy Johnson: Pioneer of African Nationalism, 1836-1917*. New York: Humanities Press.
  1978   "The Aladura Among the Yoruba: A Challenge to the 'Orthodox' Churches." In *Christianity in West Africa: The Nigerian Story*. Ogbu Kalu, ed. Pp. 384-390. Ibadan, Nigeria: Daystar Press.

1980 "The Missionary Factor in Northern Nigeria, 1870-1918." In *The History of Christianity in West Africa*. Ogbu U. Kalu, ed. Pp. 133-158. London: Longmans.

Babangida, Ibrahim Badamosi
1986 "Address to the Inaugural Meeting of the Committee on Nigeria's Membership in the OIC." February 3, 1986. Abuja, Nigeria.

Badejo, Wilson
2002 "Sustaining Nigeria's Nationhood." *This Day* 8(June):5.

Badger, Carl
2000 "Early Church History," CH500, class syllabus. Pasadena, CA: Fuller Theological Seminary, School of Theology.

Baëta, C.G., ed.
1968 *Christianity in Tropical Africa*. London: Oxford University Press.

Baird, William
1964 *The Corinthian Church: A Biblical Approach to Urban Culture*. New York: Abingdon Press.

Baker, Robert A.
1974 *The Southern Baptist Convention and its People, 1607-1972*. Nashville, TN: Broadman Press.

Balás, David L
1999 "Philosophy." In *Encyclopedia of Early Christianity*. 2nd edition. Everett Ferguson, ed. Pp. 914-917. New York: Garland Publishing.

Bankole, Olusegun
1999 *The Trees Clap Their Hands*. Lagos, Nigeria: El-Shalom Publishers.

Banks, Robert
1994 *Paul's Idea of Community*. Revised edition. Peabody, MA: Hendrickson.

Barber, Karin
1991 *I Could Speak Until Tomorrow: Oriki, Women, and the Past in a Yoruba Town*. Washington, DC: Smithsonian Institution Press.

Barna, George
1998 *The Second Coming of the Church*. Nashville, TN: Word Publishing.

Barr, James
1961 *The Semantics of Biblical Language*. Oxford: Oxford University Press.

Barrett, C.K.
1982 *Essays on Paul*. Philadelphia, PA: The Westminster Press.

Barrett, David B.
1982 *Schism and Renewal in Africa: An Analysis of Six Thousand Contemporary Religious Movements*. Nairobi, Kenya: Oxford University Press.
2001 "The Worldwide Holy Spirit Renewal." In *The Century of the Holy Spirit*. Vinson Synan, ed. Pp. 381-414. Nashville, TN: Thomas Nelson Publishers.

Barth, Karl
  1936   *Church Dogmatics.* Vol. 1. Edinburgh, Scotland: T. and T. Clark.
Bascom, William
  1960   "Urbanization Among the Yoruba." In *Cultures and Societies of Africa.* Simon Ottenberg and Phoebe Ottenberg, eds. Pp. 255-267. New York: Random House.
Bauer, Walter
  1971   *Orthodoxy and Heresy in Earliest Christianity.* Robert Kraft et al., trans. Robert Kraft and Gerhard Krodel, eds. Philadelphia, PA: Fortress Press.
Baur, Ferdinand C.
  1873   *Paul the Apostle of Jesus Christ: His Life and Work, His Epistles and His Doctrine.* 2 vols. A. Menzies, trans. London: William and Norgate.
Baus, Karl
  1965   *Handbook of Church History: From the Apostolic Community to Constantine.* Hubert Jedin, trans. New York: Herder and Herder.
Becker, Jürgen
  1993   *Paul: Apostle to the Gentiles.* O.C. Dean, Jr., trans. Louisville, KY: Westminster/John Knox Press.
Bediako, Kwame
  1992   *Theology and Identity: The Impact of Culture Upon Christian Thought in the Second Century and Modern Africa.* Oxford: Regnum Books.
Beecroft, J.
  1851   "Letter to Palmerston." CMS, F.O. 84/858. October 27, 1851. CMS Archives.
Bernard, J.H.
  1907   "The Connexion between the Fifth and Sixth Chapters of 1 Corinthians." *The Expositor* 7(3):433-443.
Best, Ernest
  1955   *One Body in Christ: A Study in the Relationship of the Church to Christ in the Epistles of Paul the Apostle.* London: S.P.C.K.
         Ephesians. New Testament Guides, 49. Sheffield: JSOT Press.
Bevans, Stephen B.
  1992   *Models of Contextual Theology.* Maryknoll, NY: Orbis Books.
Beyerhaus, P.
  1969   "An Approach to the African Independent Church Movement." *Ministry* 9:73-77.
Biobaku, O. Saburi
  1952   "An Historical Sketch of Egba Traditional Authorities." *Africa* 22(1):35-49.
  1957   *The Egba and Their Neighbours, 1842-1872.* Oxford: Clarendon Press.

Birai, Umar M.
1993   "Islamic Tajdid and the Political Process in Nigeria." In *Fundamentalisms and the State: Remaking Polities, Economies, and Militance*. Martin E. Marty and R. Scott Appleby, eds. Pp. 184-203. Chicago, IL: Chicago University Press.

Blaising, Craig A., and Darrell L. Bock, eds.
1992   *Dispensationalism, Israel and the Church: The Search for Definition*. Grand Rapids, MI: Zondervan Publishing House.

Blevins, W.L.
1974   "The Early Church: Acts 1-5." *Review and Expositor* 71:463-474.

Bloesch, Donald G.
1983   *The Future of Evangelical Christianity: A Call for Unity Amid Diversity*. Garden City, NY: Doubleday and Company.

Blyden, E.W.
1878   "Africa and the Africans." *Fraser's Magazine* 28(August):178-196.
1903   "West Africa before Europe." *Journal of African Society*. Pp. 361-365.
1908   *The Three Needs of Liberia*. London: Oxford University Press.

Boer, Harry R.
1955   *Pentecost and the Missionary Witness of the Church*. Amsterdam, Netherlands: T. Wever.

Boer, Jan H.
2003   *Nigeria's Decades of Blood, 1980-2002*. Belleville, Ontario, Canada: Essence Publishing.

Bosch, David
1991   *Transforming Mission: Paradigm Shifts in Theology of Mission*. Maryknoll, NY: Orbis Books.

Bowen, T.J.
1851   Letter to Taylor. July 10.
1857   Letter to Taylor. November 23.
1968   *Adventures and Missionary Labours in Several Countries in the Interior of Africa from 1849-1856*. London: Frank Cass and Company Limited. (Original: 1857).

Bowersock, G.W.
1995   *Martyrdom and Rome*. Cambridge, UK: Cambridge University Press.

Bradshaw, Paul F.
1992   *The Search for the Origins of Christian Worship*. Oxford: Oxford University Press.

Broneer, Oscar
1951   "Corinth: Center of St. Paul's Missionary Work in Greece." *Biblical Archaeologist* 14:78-96.

Brooke, G.W.
   1890   Letter to General J. Touch. CMS, G3/A3/93, June 5. CMS Archives.

Broshi, M.
   1978   "Estimating the Population of Ancient Jerusalem." *The Biblical Archaeology Review* 4(2):10-15.

Brouwer, Steve, Paul Gifford, and Susan D. Rose, eds.
   1996   *Exporting the American Gospel: Global Christian Fundamentalism*. New York: Routledge.

Bruce, F.F.
   1984   *The Epistles to the Colossians, to Philemon, and to the Ephesians*. Vol. 51 of *The New International Commentary on the New Testament*. Grand Rapids, MI: William B. Eerdmans.
   1991   "The Romans Debate-Continued." In *The Romans Debate*. Karl Donfried, ed. Pp. 175-194. Peabody, MA: Hendrickson Publishers.

Brueggemann, Walter
   1978   *The Prophetic Imagination*. Minneapolis, MN: Fortress Press.

Brunner, Emil
   1952   *The Misunderstanding of the Church*. London: Lutterworth.
   1962   *The Christian Doctrine of the Church, Faith, and the Consummation*. Philadelphia, PA: The Westminster Press.

Burgess, Stanley, ed.
   2002   *The New International Dictionary of Pentecostal and Charismatic Movements*. Revised and expanded edition. Grand Rapids, MI: Zondervan Publishing House.

Burks, Edgar H.
   1994   *Planting the Redeemer's Standard: A Life of Thomas J. Bowen, First Baptist Missionary to Nigeria*. Columbus, GA: Brentwood Christian Press.

Burns, Alan C.
   1969   *History of Nigeria*. 7th edition. London: Allen and Unwin.

Butterfield, Herbert
   1949   *Christianity and History*. New York: Charles Scribner's Sons.

Buxton, Thomas. F.
   1968   *The African Slave Trade and Its Remedy*. London: Pall Mall. (Original: 1839).

Caird, G.B.
   1955   *The Apostolic Age*. London: Gerald Duckworth.

Campbell, J.Y.
   1948   "The Origin and Meaning of the Christian Use of the Word Ekklesia." *Journal of Theological Studies* 49:130-142.

Campbell, W.S.
   1973   "Why Did Paul Write Romans?" *Expository Times* 85:264-269.

Castelot, J.J.
    1967   "Peter, Apostle, St." Vol 11 of *New Catholic Encyclopedia*. Pp. 173-176. New York: McGraw-Hill.

Catholic Bishops of Nigeria
    n.d.   *Christian/Muslim Relations in Nigeria: The Stand of the Catholic Bishops*. Lagos, Nigeria: Catholic Secretariat.

Cauthen, Baker James
    1970   *Advance: A History of Southern Baptist Foreign Missions*. Nashville, TN: Broadman Press.

Celsus
    n.d.   *On the True Doctrine: A Discourse against the Christians*. R. Joseph Hoffmann, trans. (1987). New York: Oxford University Press.

Chadwick, Henry
    1993   *The Early Church*. Revised edition. The Penguin History of the Church, 1. New York: Penguin Books.

Chafer, Lewis Sperry
    1947   *Systematic Theology*. 8 vols. Dallas, TX: Dallas Seminary Press.

Chamberlin, John S.
    1976   *Increase and Multiply: Arts of Discourse Procedure in the Preaching of Donne*. Chapel Hill, NC: University of North Carolina.

Charlesworth, James H.
    1999   "Pseudepigraphy." In *Encyclopedia of Early Christianity*. 2nd edition. Everett Ferguson, ed. Pp. 961-963. New York: Garland Publishing.

Charlesworth, James H., and J.R. Mueller
    1987   *The New Testament Apocrypha and Pseudepigrapha: A Guide to Publications with Excursuses on Apocalypses*. Metuchen, NJ: Scarecrow.

Chirenje, J. Mutero
    1987   *Ethiopianism and Afro-Americans in Southern Africa, 1883-1916*. Baton Rouge, LA: Louisiana State University.

Chow, John K.
    1992   *Patronage and Power: A Study of Social Networks in Corinth*. Sheffield, UK: JSOT Press.

Christian Association of Nigeria (CAN)
    1987   *Leadership in Nigeria (To Date): An Analysis*. Kaduna, Nigeria: CAN Northern Zone.

Christian Council of Nigeria (CCN)
    1911   "Minutes of the Calabar Conference."
    1947   "Proposed Scheme of Union."
    1949   *Constitution of Christian Council of Nigeria*.

Church Missionary Society (CMS)
    1841   "Bishops in Foreign Countries Act." (The Jerusalem Bishoprics Act, 5 Vict. c6). CMS Archives.
    1842   "Instructions of Local Committee." CMS, CA1/0218, November 9. CMS Archives.
    1844   "Instructions of Local Committee." CMS, CA2/11, October 25. CMS Archives.
    1851   "Minute upon the Employment and Ordination of Native Teachers." CMS, G/AZ1/1, no. 71. CMS Archives.
    1857a   "Proceedings of the CMS." Pp. 49-50.
    1857b   "Secretaries to Missionaries in Yoruba." CMS, CA2/L2, February 17. CMS Archives.
    1858   *The Church Missionary Intelligencer*. CMS Archives.
    1859   *The Gospel on the Banks of the Niger: Journals and Notices of the Native Missionaries Accompanying the Niger Expedition of 1857-1859*. London: CMS.
    1861   "Minute of the Parent Committee on the Ogboni System." CMS, CA2/L3, November 23. CMS Archives.
    1864   "Minute on the Constitution of the Anglican Native Bishopric on the West African Coast." CMS Archives.
    1876   "Instructions of the Parent Committee to James Johnson." CMS, CA2/056, December 8. CMS Archives.
    1879   "Minutes of the Parent Committee on Domestic Slavery in the Yoruba Mission." CMS, CA2/L4, August 6. CMS Archives.
    1880a   "Annual Reports, 1869 to 1880." CMS, CA3/04(b). CMS Archives.
    1880b   *The Church Missionary Intelligencer*. CMS Archives.
    1889a   *The Church Missionary Intelligencer*. CMS Archives.
    1889b   CMS Agents: Letter to the CMS Secretariat. CMS, G3/A2/05, June 14. CMS Archives.

Clement of Alexandria
    n.d.   *The Stromata*. In *The Ante-Nice Fathers: The Writings of the Fathers Down to A.D. 325*.Vol. 2 (1978). Alexander Roberts and James Donaldson, eds. Pp. 299-568. Grand Rapids, MI: William B. Eerdmans.

Clarke, Peter B.
    1982   *West Africa and Islam: A Study of Religious Development from the 8th-20th Century*. London: Edward Arnold Publishers.
    1986   *West Africa and Christianity*. London: Edward Arnold Publishers.

Clinton, J. Robert
    1988   *The Making of a Leader: Recognizing the Lessons and Stages of Leadership Development*. Colorado Springs, CO: NavPress.

Clowney, Edmund P.
    1984   "Interpreting the Biblical Models of the Church: A Hermeneutical Deepening of Ecclesiology." In *Biblical Interpretation and the Church:*

The Problem of Contextualization. D.A. Carson, ed. Pp. 64-109. Nashville, TN: Thomas Nelson.

Coleman, J.S.
   1958   *Nigeria, Background to Nationalism.* Berkeley, CA: University of California Press.

Collins, Travis M.
   1993   *The Baptist Mission of Nigeria, 1850-1993.* Ibadan, Nigeria: Associated Book-Makers Limited.

Committee of Correspondence
   1879   "Minute on the Niger Mission." CMS, CA3/L1, October 21. CMS Archives.

Conzelmann, H.
   1960   *The Theology of St Luke.* London: Faber and Faber.
           1 Corinthians. Philadelphia, PA: Fortress Press.

Cook, Henry
   1947   *What Baptists Stand For.* London: Carey Kingsgate Press.

Cook, Norton A.
   1943   *British Enterprise in Nigeria.* Philadelphia, PA: Fortress Press.

Cooke, Bernard
   1976   *Ministry to Word and Sacraments: History and Theology.* Philadelphia, PA: Fortress Press.

Cooper, Frederick
   1979   "The Problem of Slavery in African Studies." *Journal of African History* 20(1):103-125.

Corten, André
   2000   "Transnationalised Religious Needs and Political Delegitimisation in Latin America." In *Between Babel and Pentecost: Transnational Pentecostalism in Africa and Latin America.* André Corten and Ruth Marshall-Fratani, eds. Pp. 106-123. Bloomington, IN: Indiana University Press.

Corten, André, and Ruth Marshall-Fratani, eds.
   2000   *Between Babel and Pentecost: Transnational Pentecostalism in Africa and Latin America.* Bloomington, IN: Indiana University Press.

Cranfield, C.E.B.
   1975   *A Critical and Exegetical Commentary on the Epistle to the Romans.* Vol. 1. Edinburgh, Scotland: T and T Clark.

Crook, J.A.
   1967   *Law and Life in Rome.* London: Thames and Hudson.

Crouzel, Henri
   1989   *Origen.* A.S. Worrall, trans. San Francisco, CA: Harper and Row.

Crowther, S.A.
- 1844 Journals, Quarter ending March 25. CMS, CA1/079 no. 3. CMS Archives.
- 1856 Letter to T.J. Hutchinson. September 10.
- 1857 Letter to Venn. CMS, CA2/031, January 2 1857; March 4 1857. CMS Archives.
- 1860 Letter to Venn. CMS, CA3/04, April 4. CMS Archives.
- 1873 Annual Report. CMS, CA3/04 (b). CMS Archives.
- 1875 Letter to Venn. CMS, CA2/031, January 3. CMS Archives.
- 1885 "A Brief History of the Niger Mission since 1857." CMS, G3/A3/O2, October 8. CMS Archives.
- 1891 Letter to Lang. CMS, G3 A3/O, no. 15, December 1. CMS Archives.

Crowther, S.A., and J.C. Taylor
- 1968 *The Gospel on the Banks of the Niger: Journals and Notices of the Native Missionaries Accompanying the Niger Expedition of 1857-1859.* London: Dawsons. (Original: 1859.)

Crumbley, D.H.
- 2000 "On Being First: Dogma, Disease and Domination in the Rise of an African Church." *Religion* 30(2):169-184.

Culpepper, Hugo H.
- 1979 "Ephesians—A Manifesto for the Mission of the Church." *Review and Expositor* 76(4):553-558.

Cyprian
- n.d. *Epistles.* In *The Ante-Nice Fathers: The Writings of the Fathers Down to A.D. 325.* Vol. 5 (1978). Alexander Roberts and James Donaldson, eds. Pp. 275-409. Grand Rapids, MI: William B. Eerdmans.
- n.d. *To Fortunas.* In *The Letters of St. Cyprian of Carthage.* Vol. 46 (1986). G.W. Clarke, trans. Pp. 53-54. New York: Newman Press.

Dahl, N.A.
- 1967 "Paul and the Church at Corinth according to 1 Corinthians 1-4." In *Christian History and Interpretation.* W.R. Farmer, et al. Pp. 313-336. Cambridge, UK: Cambridge University Press.
- 1986 "Gentiles, Christians, and Israelites in the Epistle to the Ephesians." *Harvard Theological Review* 79(1-3):31-39.
- 1988 "Ephesians." In *Harper's Bible Commentary.* James L. Mays, ed. Pp. 1212-1219. New York: HarperCollins Publishers.

Danjuma, Theophilus
- 2002 Speech Delivered at the "Northern (Nigeria) Christian Elders Forum (NOCEF)." April 20. Abuja, Nigeria.

Danker, F.W.
- 1982 "Epistle to the Ephesians." In *The International Standard Bible Encyclopedia.* Vol. 2. Geoffrey W. Bromiley, ed. Pp. 109-114. Grand Rapids, MI: William B. Eerdmans.

David-West, Tonye
    2001   "Speaking of the Pastors of 'Show Me Thy Money Church of God' in Nigeria." *Nigeriaworld*. Accessed November 29, 2001. <http://nigeriaworld.com/feature/publication/david-west/111101.html>.

Davies, J.G.
    1965   *The Early Christian Church: A History of Its First Five Centuries*. Grand Rapids, MI: Baker Books.

Dayton, Donald W.
    1987   *Theological Roots of Pentecostalism*. Metuchen, NJ: Scarecrow Press.

Deissmann, A.
    1927   *Light from the Ancient Near East*. Revised edition. Lionel R.M. Strachan, trans. New York: George H. Doran Company.

Desai, Ram, ed.
    1962   *Christianity in Africa as Seen by Africans*. Denver, CO: Allan Swallow.

Didache, The
    n.d.   In *The Apostolic Fathers*. Revised edition (1999). Michael W. Holmes, ed. Pp. 246-269. Grand Rapids, MI: Baker Books.

Dike, K.O.
    1956   *Trade and Politics in the Niger Delta, 1830-1885*. Oxford: Oxford University Press.

Dillistone, F.W.
    1951   *The Structure of the Divine Society*. London: Lutterworth Press.

Dobinson, Henry H.
    1894   Letter to Baylis. CMS, G3 A3/O, nos. 47 and 60, March 29. CMS Archives.

Dodd, C.H.
    1929   "Ephesians." In *The Abingdon Bible Commentary*. Frederick C. Eiselen, Edwin Lewis, and David G. Downey, eds. Pp. 1224-25. New York: Abingdon Press.
    1936   *The Apostolic Preaching and Its Developments*. New York: Harper and Row.

Donfried, Karl P.
    1991   *The Setting of Second Clement in Early Christianity*. Leiden: E. J. Brill.

Donfried, Karl P., ed.
    1991   *The Romans Debate*. Revised edition. Peabody, MA: Hendrickson Publishers.

Doresse, Jean
    1960   *The Secret Books of the Egyptian Gnostics: An Introduction to the Gnostic Coptic Manuscripts Discovered at Chenoboskion*. New York: Viking Press.

Driver, John
    1997   *Images of the Church in Mission*. Scottdale, PA: Herald Press.

Droge, A., and J. Tabor
  1992   *A Noble Death: Suicide and Martyrdom among Christians and Jews in Antiquity*. San Francisco, CA: HarperCollins Publishers.
Dulles, Avery
  1987   *Models of the Church*. Expanded edition. New York: Image Books.
Dunn, James D.G.
  1988   *Romans 9-16*. Vol. 38b of *Word Biblical Commentary*. Dallas, TX: Word Books.
  1990   *Unity and Diversity in the New Testament: An Inquiry into the Character of Earliest Christianity*. 2nd edition. London: SCM.
  1995   *1 Corinthians*. New Testament Guides. Sheffield, UK: Sheffield Academic Press.
  1996   *The Acts of the Apostles*. Valley Forge, PA: Trinity Press International. *The Theology of Paul the Apostle*. Grand Rapids, MI: William B. Eerdmans.
Duval, Louis, M.
  1928   *Baptist Missions in Nigeria*. Richmond, VA: Foreign Mission Board, Southern Baptist Convention.
Edema, A.
  1989   "Christians and Politics." *Thelia* 2(3):12-18.
Edwards, James
  1992   *Romans*. New Testament Series, 6. Peabody, MA: Hendrickson Publishers.
Ehrman, Bart D.
  1993   *The Orthodox Corruption of Scripture*. New York: Oxford University Press.
  1999   *After the New Testament: A Reader in Early Christianity*. New York: Oxford University Press.
Elsbree, Oliver W.
  1928   "The Rise of Missionary Spirit in America, 1790-1815." Ph.D. dissertation, Columbia University.
Engels, D.
  1990   *Roman Corinth: An Alternative Model for the Classical City*. Chicago, IL: University of Chicago.
Enwerem, Iheanyi
  1995   *A Dangerous Awakening: The Politicization of Religion in Nigeria*. Ibadan, Nigeria: IFRA.
Ernest, Best
  1955   *One Body in Christ: A Study in the Relationship of the Church to Christ in the Epistles of the Apostle Paul*. London: SPCK.
Erickson, Millard J.
  1998   *Christian Theology*. 2nd edition. Grand Rapids, MI: Baker Books.

Eusebius
n.d. *Ecclesiastical History.* Kirsopp Lake, trans. (1932). New York: G.P. Putnam's Sons.

Evans, G.R.
1994 *The Church and the Churches.* Cambridge, UK: Cambridge University Press.

Fage, J.D.
1969 "Slavery and the Slave Trade in the Context of West African History." *Journal of African History* 10(3):393-404.

Fahy, T.
1959 "St. Paul's Romans were Jewish Converts." *International Theological Quarterly* 26:182-91.

Falola, Toyin
1986 "Missionaries and Domestic Slavery in Yorubaland in the Nineteenth Century." *Journal of Religious History* 14:181-192.
1998 *Violence in Nigeria: The Crisis of Religious Politics and Secular Ideologies.* Rochester, NY: University of Rochester Press.
1999 *The History of Nigeria.* Westport, CT: Greenwood Press.

Fee, Gordon D.
1987 *The First Epistle to the Corinthians.* The New International Commentary on the New Testament. Grand Rapids, MI: William B. Eerdmans.

Feinberg, John S., ed.
1988 *Continuity and Discontinuity: Perspectives on the Relationship Between the Old and New Testaments.* Wheaton, IL: Crossway.

Felix, Minucius
n.d. *Octavius.* In *The Ante-Nice Fathers: The Writings of the Fathers Down to A.D. 325.* Vol. 4 (1978). Alexander Roberts and James Donaldson, eds. Pp. 173-198. Grand Rapids, MI: William B. Eerdmans.

Ferguson, Everett
1996 *The Church of Christ: A Biblical Ecclesiology for Today.* Grand Rapids, MI: William B. Eerdmans.
1999a "Eucharist." In *Encyclopedia of Early Christianity.* 2nd edition. Everett Ferguson, ed. Pp. 393-397. New York: Garland Publishing.
1999b "Martyr, Martyrdom." In *Encyclopedia of Early Christianity.* 2nd edition. Everett Ferguson, ed. Pp. 724-727. New York: Garland Publishing.
1999c "Ministry." In *Encyclopedia of Early Christianity.* 2nd edition. Everett Ferguson, ed. Pp. 750-752. New York: Garland Publishing.

Ferguson, Everett, ed.
1993 *Worship in Early Christianity.* New York: Garland Publishing.

Ferguson, James
   1841   Letter to Thomas Dove. March 2, 1841. NRO:ECC 2/1096. CMS Archives.

Field, Barbara
   1992   "The Discourses Behind the Metaphor 'the Church is The Body of Christ' as used by St Paul and the 'Post-Paulines.'" *Asia Journal of Theology*. 6(1):88-107.

Fiensy, David A.
   1995   "The Composition of the Jerusalem Church." In *The Book of Acts in Its Palestinian Setting*. Richard Bauckham, ed. Pp. 213-234. Grand Rapids, MI: William B. Eerdmans.

Findlay, George G.
   1893   *The Church of Christ as Set Forth in the New Testament*. Edinburgh, Scotland: Morrison and Gibb.
   1961   *St. Paul's First Epistle to the Corinthians*. Expositor's Greek Testament, 2. Grand Rapids, MI: William B. Eerdmans.

Fiorenza, E.S.
   1988   "1 Corinthians." In *Harper's Bible Commentary*. James L. Mays, ed. Pp. 1168-1188. San Francisco, CA: Harper and Row.

Fisher, Humphrey J.
   1973   "Conversion Reconsidered: Some Historical Aspects of Religious Conversion in Black Africa." *Africa* 43:27-40.
   1983   "The Juggernaut's Apologia: Conversion to Islam in Black Africa." *Africa* 55:153-173.

Flint, J.E.
   1974   "Economic Change in West Africa in the Nineteenth Century." In *History of West Africa*. Vol. 2. J.F.A. Ajayi and Michael Crowther, eds. Pp. 380-401. New York: Columbia University Press.

Florin, Hans W.
   1960   "The Southern Baptist Foreign Mission Enterprise in Western Nigeria: An Analysis." Ph.D. dissertation, Boston University.

Foakes-Jackson, F.J., and K. Lake, eds.
   1920-33 *The Beginnings of Christianity: The Acts of the Apostles*. 5 vols. London: Macmillan and Company.

Foster, R.S.
   1961   *The Sierra-Leone Church: An Independent Anglican Church*. London: SPCK.

Foxe, John
   n.d.   *Foxe's Christian Martyrs of the World*. Chicago, IL: Moody Press.

Freiberg, John S.
   1988   *Continuity and Discontinuity: Perspectives on the Relationship Between the Old and New Testaments*. Westchester, IL: Crossway Books.

Frend, W.H.C.
    1984   *The Rise of Christianity*. Philadelphia, PA: Fortress Press.

Freston, Paul
    2001   *Evangelicals and Politics in Asia, Africa and Latin America*. Cambridge, UK: Cambridge University Press.

Fruchtenbaum, Arnold G.
    1992   *Israelology: The Missing Link In Systematic Theology*. Revised edition. Tustin, CA: Ariel Ministries Press.

Gager, John G.
    1983   *The Origins of Anti-Semitism: Attitudes Toward Judaism in Pagan and Christian Antiquity*. New York: Oxford University Press.

Galadima, Bulus Y., and Yusufu Turaki
    1998   "The Church in the African State Towards the 21st Century: The Experience of Northern Nigeria." *Journal of African Christian Thought* 1(1):43-51.

Gallagher, J.
    1958   "Fowell Buxton and the New African Policy, 1838-1842." *The Cambridge Historical Journal* 10(1):36-58.

Gamble, Harry
    1999   "Apologetics." In *Encyclopedia of Early Christianity*. 2nd edition. Everett Ferguson, ed. Pp. 81-87. New York: Garland Publishing.

Gammell, William
    1849   *A History of American Baptist Missions in Asia, Africa, Europe and North America*. Boston, MA: Gould, Kendall, and Lincoln.

Garland, David E.
    1979   "A Life Worthy of the Calling." *Review and Expositor* 76(4):517-527.

Garlock, Ruthanne
    1981   *Benson Idahosa: Fire in His Bones*. Tulsa, OK: Praise Books.

Garnsey, P.
    1970   *Social Status and Legal Privilege in the Roman Empire*. Oxford: Claredon Press.

Garrett, T.S., and R.M.C. Jeffery
    1965   *Unity in Nigeria*. London: Edinburgh House Press.

Gerhart, Mary, and Allan Russell, eds.
    1984   *Metaphoric Process: The Creation of Scientific and Religious Understanding*. Fort Worth, TX: Texas Christian University Press.

Getu, Makonen
    2001   "Poverty Alleviation and the Role of Microcredit in Africa." In *Faith in Development: Partnership between the World Bank and the Churches of Africa*. Deryke Belshaw, Robert Calderisi, and Chris Sugden, eds. Pp. 165-179. Oxford: Regnum Books International.

Gibbs, Eddie
   2000   *ChurchNext: Quantum Changes in How We Do Ministry*. Downers Grove, IL: InterVarsity Press.
   2003   "Evangelizing Nominal Christians," MC532, lecture notes. Pasadena, CA: Fuller Theological Seminary, School of Intercultural Studies.

Giles, Kevin
   1995   *What on Earth is the Church? An Exploration in New Testament Theology*. Downers Grove, IL: InterVarsity Press.

Gilliland, Dean S.
   1983   *Pauline Theology and Mission Practice*. Surulere, Lagos: Tryfam Printers.
   1986   "How 'Christian' Are African Independent Churches?" *Missiology* 14(3):259-272.
   1986   *African Religion Meets Islam: Religious Change in Northern Nigeria*. Lanham, MD: University Press of America.
   1989   "Contextual Theology as Incarnational Mission." In *The Word among Us: Contextualizing Theology for Mission Today*. Dean S. Gilliland, ed. Pp. 9-31. Dallas, TX: Word Publishing.
   1999   "Limits of Contextualization and the African Independent Churches," MT510, lecture notes. Pasadena, CA: Fuller Theological Seminary, School of World Mission.
   2000   "Modeling the Incarnation for Muslim People: A Response to Sam Schlorff." *Missiology* 28(3):329-338.

Gilliland, Dean S., ed.
   1989   *The Word among Us: Contextualizing Theology for Mission Today*. Dallas, TX: Word Publishing.

Glasser, Arthur F.
   2003   *Announcing the Kingdom: The Story of God's Mission in the Bible*. Grand Rapids, MI: Baker Books.

González, Justo L.
   1970   *A History of Christian Thought*. Vol. 1. Revised edition. Nashville, TN: Abingdon Press.

Goodykoonthz, Colin B.
   1939   *Home Missions on the American Frontier*. Caldwell, ID: The Caxton Printers Limited.

Goppelt, Leonard
   1970   *Apostolic and Post-Apostolic Times*. London: Adam and Charles Black.

Greenberg, Joseph
   1946   *The Influence of Islam on a Sudanese Religion*. Seattle, WA: University of Washington Press.

Grenz, Stanley J., and John R. Franke
   2000   *Theology for the Community of God.* Grand Rapids, MI: William B. Eerdmans.
   2001   *Beyond Fundamentalism: Shaping Theology in a Postmodern Context.* Louisville, KY: Westminster John Knox Press.

Grenz, Stanley J., and Roger E. Olson
   1992   *20th Century Theology: God and the World in a Transitional Age.* Downers Grove, IL: InterVarsity Press.

Grillmeier, Aloys
   1975   *Christ in Christian Tradition.* Vol. 1. 2nd revised edition. John Bowden, trans. London: Mowbrays.

Grove, Andrew S.
   1996   *Only The Paranoid Survive.* New York: Currency Doubleday.

Groves, C.P.
   1948   *The Planting of Christianity in Africa.* 3 vols. London: Lutterworth Press.
   1953   *The Planting of Christianity in Africa.* Vol. 2. London: Lutherworth Press.

Grudem, Wayne
   1994   *Systematic Theology: An Introduction to Biblical Doctrine.* Grand Rapids, MI: Zondervan Publishing House.

Guinness, Os
   1994   *Fit Bodies, Fat Minds: Why Evangelicals Don't Think and What To Do About It.* Grand Rapids, MI: Baker Books.

Gunther, J.J.
   1973   *St. Paul's Opponents and Their Background.* Leiden: Brill.

Guthrie, Donald
   1990   *New Testament Introduction.* Revised edition. Downers Grove, IL: InterVarsity Press.

Hackett, Rosalind I.J.
   1998   "Charismatic/Pentecostal Appropriation of Media Technologies in Nigeria and Ghana." *Journal of Religion in Africa* 28(3):258-277.

Hägglund, Bengt
   1968   *History of Theology.* J. Lund Gene, trans. St. Louis, MO: Concordia Publishing House. (Original: *Teologins Historia*, 1966.)

Hall, D.J.
   1989   *Thinking the Faith: Christian Theology in a North American Context.* Minneapolis, MN: Augsburg.

Hanciles, Jehu J.
   1995   "The Sierra Leone Native Pastorate Church (1850-1890): An Experiment in Ecclesiastical Independence." Ph.D. dissertation, Edinburgh University.

1997 "The Legacy of James Johnson." *International Bulletin of Missionary Research* 21(4):162-167.
2001a "Anatomy of an Experiment: The Sierra Leone Native Pastorate." *Missiology* 29(1):63-82.
2001b "Bishop and Archdeacon Crowther: Inter-Generational Challenge and Opportunity in the Building of an African Church." Unpublished manuscript.
2002 *Euthanasia of a Mission: African Church Autonomy in a Colonial Context*. Westport, CT: Praeger Publishers.

Hanson, Richard
1985 *Studies in Christian Antiquity*. Edinburgh, Scotland: T and T Clark.

Hanson, Stig
1946 *The Unity of the Church in the New Testament: Colossians and Ephesians*. Uppsala: Almqvist and Wiksells Boktryckeri AB.

Harnack, Adolf Von
1909 *New Testament Studies, III: The Acts of the Apostles*. J.R. Wilkinson, trans. New York: Putnam.
1962 *The Mission and Expansion of Christianity in the First Three Centuries*. New York: Harper and Brothers. (Original: 1908.)

Harries, Lyndon
1953 "Christian Marriage in African Society." In *Survey of African Marriage and Family Life*. Arthur Phillips, ed. Pp. 329-456. London: Oxford University Press.

Harrison, Everett F.
1985 *The Apostolic Church*. Grand Rapids, MI: William B. Eerdmans.

Harrison, Norman B.
1930 *His Very Own, Paul's Epistle to the Ephesians*. Minneapolis, MN: The Harrison Service.

Harwood, J.R.
1963 "The Church Union Story." *Church Union News* 1(1):5-7.

Hastings, Adrian
1994 *The Church in Africa, 1450-1950*. Oxford: Clarendon Press.

Hawthorne, Gerald F., Ralph P. Martin, and Daniel G. Reid, eds.
1993 *Dictionary of Paul and His Letters*. Downers Grove, IL: InterVarsity Press.

Haynes, Jeff
1994 *Religion in Third World Politics*. Boulder, CO: Lynne Rienner Publishers.
1996 *Religion and Politics in Africa*. London: Zed Books.

Heidegger, Martin
1971 *Poetry, Language, Thought*. New York: Harper and Row.

Hennecke, Edgar
    1991   *The New Testament Apocrypha*. 2 vols. 3rd edition. R.M. Wilson, trans. W. Schneemelcher, ed. Louisville, KY: Westminster/John Knox.

Henry, Carl F.H.
    1947   *The Uneasy Conscience of Modern Fundamentalism*. Grand Rapids, MI: William B. Eerdmans.
    1976   "The Purpose of God." In *The New Face of Evangelicalism*. Rene C. Padilla, ed. Pp. 17-32. London: Hodder and Stoughton.

Henson, Hensley
    1898   *Apostolic Christianity*. London: Methuen and Company.

Herford, R. Travers
    1903   *Christianity in Talmud and Midrash*. London: Williams and Norgate.

Hermas
    n.d.   *Similitudes*. In *The Apostolic Fathers*. Vol. 2 (1913). Kirsopp Lake, trans. Pp. 139-305. Cambridge, MA: Harvard University Press.
    n.d.   *Visions*. In *The Apostolic Fathers*. Vol. 2 (1913). Kirsopp Lake, trans. Pp. 6-71. Cambridge, MA: Harvard University Press.

Hesselgrave, David J., and Edward Rommen
    1989   *Contextualization: Meanings, Methods, and Models*. Grand Rapids, MI: Baker Books.

Hewitt, Gordon
    1971   *The Problems of Success: A History of the Church Missionary Society, 1910-1942*. London: SCM Press.

Hiebert, D. Edmond
    1977   *Introduction to the New Testament*. Vol. 2. Revised edition. Chicago, IL: Moody Press.

Hiebert, Frances F.
    1997   "Beyond a Post-Modern Critique of Modern Missions: The Nineteenth Century Revisited." *Missiology* 25(3):259-275.

Hiebert, Paul G.
    1987   "Critical Contextualization." *International Bulletin of Missionary Research* 11(3):104-112.
    1994   *Anthropological Reflections on Missiological Issues*. Grand Rapids, MI: Baker Books.

Hiebert, Paul G., R. Daniel Shaw, and Tite Tiénou
    1999   *Understanding Folk Religion*. Grand Rapids, MI: Baker Books.

Hinderer, Anna
    1872   *Seventeen Years in the Yoruba Country: Memorials of Anna Hinderer, Wife of the Rev. David Hinderer, Church Missionary Society Missionary in West Africa*. London: The Religious Tract Society.

Hippolytus
n.d. *The Refutation of all Heresies*. In *The Ante-Nice Fathers: The Writings of the Fathers Down to A.D. 325*.Vol. 5 (1978). Alexander Roberts and James Donaldson, eds. Pp. 9-153. Grand Rapids, MI: William B. Eerdmans.

Hopkins, A.G.
1973 *An Economic History of West Africa*. London: Columbia University Press.

Hodgkin, T.
1956 *Nationalism in Colonial Africa*. London: Muller.

Horbury, William
1991 "The Jewish Dimension." In *Early Christianity: Origins and Evolution to A.D. 600*. Ian Hazlet, ed. Pp. 40-51. Nashville, TN: Abingdon Press.

Horsley, Richard
1980 "Gnosis in Corinth: 1 Corinthians 8: 1-6." *New Testament Studies* 27:32-51.

Hort, F.J.A.
1914 *The Christian Ecclesia*. London: Macmillan.

Horton, Robin
1971 "African Conversion." *Africa* 41:85-108.
1975a "On the Rationality of Conversion, Part I." *Africa* 45:219-235.
1975b "On the Rationality of Conversion, Part II." *Africa* 45:373-399.

Howse, E.M.
1952 *Saints in Politics: The "Clapham Sect" and the Growth of Freedom*. London: George Allen and Unwin.

Hulen, A.B.
1932 "Dialogues with the Jews as Sources for Early Jewish Arguments Against Christianity." *Journal of Biblical Literature* 51:55-58.

Hurd, John Coolidge
1965 *The Origin of 1 Corinthians*. New York: Seabury Press.

Hutchinson, E.
1879 Letter to James Johnson. CMS, CA2/L4, August 6. CMS Archives.
1880 Letter to Bishop Crowther. CMS, CA3/L1, November 20. CMS Archives.

Idowu, Bolaji
1962 *Olódùmarè: God in Yorùbá Belief*. London: Longmans.
1965 *Towards an Indigenous Church*. London: Oxford University Press.
1968 "The Predicament of the Church in Africa." In *Christianity in Tropical Africa*. C.G. Baeta, ed. Pp. 417-437. London: Oxford University Press.

Ifemesia, C.C.
    1962   "The 'Civilizing' Mission of 1841." *Journal of Historical Society of Nigeria* 2(3):291-310.

Ige, O.
    1965   "Joseph Babalola—A Twentieth Century Prophet." *African Historian* 1(3):38-42.

Ignatius
    n.d.   *Ephesians*. In *The Apostolic Fathers*. Revised edition (1999). Michael W. Holmes, ed. Pp. 136-151. Grand Rapids, MI: Baker Books.
    n.d.   *Magnesians*. In *The Apostolic Fathers*. Revised edition (1999). Michael W. Holmes, ed. Pp. 150-159. Grand Rapids, MI: Baker Books.
    n.d.   *Philadelphians*. In *The Apostolic Fathers*. Revised edition (1999). Michael W. Holmes, ed. Pp. 176-185. Grand Rapids, MI: Baker Books.
    n.d.   *Romans*. In *The Apostolic Fathers*. Revised edition (1999). Michael W. Holmes, ed. Pp. 166-177. Grand Rapids, MI: Baker Books.
    n.d.   *Smyrneans*. In *The Apostolic Fathers*. Revised edition (1999). Michael W. Holmes, ed. Pp. 184-195. Grand Rapids, MI: Baker Books.

Ilesanmi, Simeon O.
    1997   *Religious Pluralism and the Nigerian State*. Athens, OH: Ohio University Press.

Irenaeus
    n.d.   *Against Heresies*. In *The Ante-Nice Fathers: The Writings of the Fathers Down to A.D. 325*.Vol. 1 (1978). Alexander Roberts and James Donaldson, eds. Pp. 315-567. Grand Rapids, MI: William B. Eerdmans.

Isaacson, Alan
    1990   *Deeper Life: The Extraordinary Growth of the Deeper Life Bible Church*. London: Hodder and Stoughton.

Isichei, Elizabeth
    1977   *History of West Africa Since 1800*. New York: Africana Publishing Company.
    1983   *A History of Nigeria*. London: Longmans.

Johnson, James
    1873   Memo to M. Taylor and Others. CMS, CA1/0123, April 19. CMS Archives.
    1877   Report on Ibadan. CMS, CA2/056, August. CMS Archives.

Johnson, Luke T.
    1999   *The Writings of the New Testament: An Interpretation*. Revised edition. Minneapolis, MN: Fortress Press.

Johnson, Nita Lafond
    2003   "Revival Fire." *World For Jesus Ministries* 3(8):1-8.

Johnson, Samuel
    1921   *The History of the Yoruba*. London: Routledge.

Johnston, Hughes
    1967   *The Fulani Empire of Sokoto*. London: Oxford University Press.

Johnston, George
    1943   *The Doctrine of the Church in the New Testament*. Cambridge, UK: Cambridge University Press.

Joint Muslim Advisory Council of Oyo State
    1989   "An Appeal to the Christian Association of Nigeria (CAN)." *National Concord* 25 (April):2.

Jones, A.H.M.
    1993   "Were Ancient Heresies National or Social Movements in Disguise?" In *Orthodoxy, Heresy, and Schism in Early Christianity*. Studies in Early Christianity, 4. Everett Ferguson, ed. Pp. 314-332. New York: Garland Publishing.

Jones, G.I.
    1963   *The Trading States of the Oil Rivers*. London: Oxford University Press.

Journal of the African Civilization Society
    1842   *Friend of Africa*. Cambridge, UK: The Central Committee on the United Study of Foreign Missions.

Judge, E.A.
    1960   *The Social Pattern of Early Christian Groups in the First Century*. London: Tyndale Press.

Jungmann, Josef A.
    1959   *The Early Liturgy: To the Time of Gregory the Great*. Francis A. Brunner, trans. Notre Dame, IN: University of Notre Dame.

Kalu, Ogbu
    1978   *Divided People of God: Church Union Movement in Nigeria, 1875-1966*. New York: NOK Publishers.
    1980   "The Shattered Cross: The Church Union Movement in Nigeria, 1905-1966." In *The History of Christianity in West Africa*. Ogbu Kalu, ed. Pp. 340-364. London: Longman Group Limited.
    1992   "Beyond Nationalist Historiography: White Indigenizers of the Igbo Church, 1876-1892." Paper presented at the Centre for the Study of Christianity in the Non-Western World, University of Edinburgh, November 1992.
    1998   "The Third Response: Pentecostalism and the Reconstruction of Christian Experience in Africa, 1970-1995." *Journal of African Christian Thought* 1(2):3-16.
    2000a   *Power, Poverty and Prayer: The Challenges of Poverty and Pluralism in African Christianity, 1960-1996*. Frankfurt am Main, Germany: Peter Lang.

2000b "Doing Mission Through the Post Office: The Naked Faith People of Igboland, 1920-1960." *Neue Zeitschrift für Missionswissenschaft* 56 (4):263-280.

2000c "Ancestral Spirituality and Society in Africa." In *African Spirituality: Forms, Meanings, and Expressions*. Jacob K. Olupona, ed. Pp. 54-84. New York: Crossroad Publishing Company.

2001 "Enstranged Bedfellows?: The Demonization of the Aladura in African Pentecostal Rhetoric." Unpublished manuscript.

2002 "Pentecostal and Charismatic Reshaping of the African Religious Landscape in the 1990s." Paper presented at a Round Table Discussion, held at Center for Religion and Civic Culture, University of Southern California, February 15, 2002, Pp. 1-25. Los Angeles, CA.

2003 "Safiyya and Adamah: Punishing Adultery with Shari'a Stones in 21st Century Nigeria." *African Affairs* 102(408):389-408.

Kantiok, James
2000 "Muslims and Christians in Northern Nigeria: Political and Cultural Implications for Evangelism." Ph.D. dissertation, Fuller Theological Seminary.

Kärkkäinen, Veli-Matti
2002 *An Introduction to Ecclesiology: Ecumenical, Historical and Global Perspectives*. Downers Grove, IL: InterVarsity Press.

Karlström, Mikael
1999 "Civil Society and Its Presuppositions: Lessons from Uganda." In *Civil Society and the Political Imagination in Africa*. John L. Comaroff and Jean Comaroff, eds. Pp. 104-123. Chicago, IL: The University of Chicago Press.

Karris, R.J.
1991 "Romans 14:1-15:13 and the Occasion of Romans." In *The Romans Debate*. Karl Donfried, ed. Pp. 65-84. Peabody, MA: Hendrickson Publishers.

Kasdorf, Hans
1980 *Christian Conversion in Context*. Scottdale, PA: Herald Press.

Käsemann, E.
1969 *New Testament Questions of Today*. Philadelphia, PA: Fortress Press.
1980 *Commentary on Romans*. Geoffrey W. Bromiley, trans. Grand Rapids, MI: William B. Eerdmans.

Käsemann, E., and Raymond Brown
1963 "Unity and Diversity in New Testament Ecclesiology." *Novum Testamentum* 6:293-308.

Kearney, Michael
1984 *World View*. Novato, CA: Chandler and Sharp Publishers.

Keay, E., and S. Richardson
  1966   *The Native Customary Courts of Nigeria*. London: Sweet and Maxwell.
Keller, Charles R.
  1942   *The Second Great Awakening in Connecticut*. New Haven, CT: Yale University Press.
Kelly, J.M.
  1966   *Roman Litigation*. Oxford: Clarendon Press.
Kelly, J.N.D.
  1978   *Early Christian Doctrines*. Revised edition. New York: Harper Collins Publishers.
Kelsey, David H.
  1975   *The Uses of Scripture in Recent Theology*. Philadelphia, PA: Fortress Press.
Kennedy, George
  1980   *Classical Rhetoric and Its Christian and Secular Tradition from Ancient to Modern Times*. Chapel Hill, NC: University of North Carolina.
Kenny, Joseph
  1996   "Sharia and Christianity in Nigeria: Islam and a 'Secular' State." *Journal of Religion in Africa* 26(4):338-364.
Kilmartin, Edward J.
  1999   "Liturgy." In *Encyclopedia of Early Christianity*. 2nd edition. Everett Ferguson, ed. Pp. 683-686. New York: Garland Publishing.
King, P.
  1992   "Jerusalem." In *The Anchor Bible Dictionary*. D.N. Freedman, ed. P. 753. New York: Doubleday.
King, Roberta R.
  1989   "Pathways in Christian Music Communication: The Case of the Senufo of Cote d'Ivoire." Ph.D. dissertation, Fuller Theological Seminary.
  1990   "The Role of Music in Theological Education." *Africa Journal of Evangelical Theology* 9(1):35-41.
  1999   *A Time to Sing: A Manual for the African Church*. Nairobi, Kenya: Evangel Publishing House.
Kirby, J.C.
  1968   *Ephesians, Baptism, and Pentecost: An Inquiry into the Structure and Purpose of the Epistle to the Ephesians*. London: SPCK.
Klein, Martin, ed.
  1993   *Breaking the Chains: Slavery, Bondage, and Emancipation in Modern Africa and Asia*. Madison, WI: The University of Wisconsin Press.
Knight, William
  1880   *Memoir of the Rev. Henry Venn: The Missionary Secretariat of Henry Venn*. London: Longmans Green and Company.

Knox, W.L.
    1948   *The Acts of the Apostles*. Cambridge, UK: Cambridge University Press.

Kouzes, James M., and Barry Z. Posner
    1993   *Credibility: How Leaders Gain and Lose it, Why People Demand It*. San Francisco, CA: Jossey-Bass.

Kraft, Charles H.
    1979   *Christianity in Culture: A Study in Dynamic Biblical Theologizing in Cross-Cultural Perspective*. Maryknoll, NY: Orbis Books.

Kukah, Matthew Hassan
    1993   *Religion, Politics, and Power in Northern Nigeria*. Ibadan, Nigeria: Spectrum Books Limited.
    1995   "Christians and Nigeria's Aborted Transition." In *The Christian Churches and the Democratisation of Africa*. Paul Gifford, ed. Pp. 225-238. Leiden: E.J. Brill.

Kümmel, Werner G.
    1984   *Introduction to the New Testament*. Revised English edition. Nashville, TN: Abingdon Press.

Kumuyi, William F.
    n.d.   "The Good Old Days." Lagos, Nigeria: Zoe Publishing and Printing.
    1975   *Have Compassion on Them*. Lagos, Nigeria: Zoe Publishing and Printing.
    1983   *Holiness Made Easy*. Lagos, Nigeria: Zoe Publishing and Printing.
    1989   *Deeper Life*. Lagos, Nigeria: Zoe Publishing and Printing.
    1998   "Deeper Christian Life Ministry." In *The New Apostolic Churches*. C. Peter Wagner, ed. Pp. 243-256. Ventura, CA: Regal Books.

Küng, Hans
    1968   *The Church*. Ray and Rosaleen Ockenden, trans. New York: Sheed and Ward.

Kydd, Ronald A.N.
    1984   *Charismatic Gifts in the Early Church*. Peabody, MA: Hendrickson Publishers.

Ladd, George E.
    1964   *The Young Church*. Nashville, TN: Abingdon Press.
    1993   *A Theology of the New Testament*. Grand Rapids, MI: William B. Eerdmans. (Original: 1974.)

Laird, Macgregor, and R.A.K. Oldfield
    1837   *Narrative of an Expedition into the Interior of Africa*. 2 vols. London: Oxford University Press.

Lang, R.
    1882   Letter to J.B. Wood. CMS, G3A3/12, March 17. CMS Archives.

Larbi, E. Kingsley
   2002   "Response to Professor Ogbu U. Kalu's Paper, 'Pentecostal and Charismatic Reshaping of the African Religious Landscape in the 1990's." Paper presented at the University of Southern California, held at the Center for Religion and Civic Culture, February 15, 2002. Los Angeles, California.

LaRue, Cleophus J.
   2000   *The Heart of Black Preaching*. Louisville, KY: Westminster/John Knox Press.

Lassman, Peter
   2000   "The Rule of Man Over Man: Politics, Power and Legitimation." In *The Cambridge Companion to Weber*. Stephen Turner, ed. Pp. 83-98. Cambridge, UK: Cambridge University Press.

Latin, David
   1982   "The Sharia Debate and the Origins of Nigeria's Second Republic." *Journal of Modern African Studies* 20(3):411-430.

Latourette, Kenneth S.
   1939   *A History of the Expansion of Christianity: Three Centuries of Advance, A.D. 1500-A.D. 1800*. Vol. 3. New York: Harper and Brothers Publishers.

Layton, Bentley
   1987   *The Gnostic Scriptures*. Garden City, NY: Doubleday.

Leader
   1967   "Nigeria's Coming Civil War." June 3.

Lederle, Henry I.
   1989   The Spirit of Unity: A Discomforting Comforter: Some Reflections on the Holy Spirit, Ecumenism and the Pentecostal-Charismatic Movements." *The Ecumenical Review* 42(3-4):291.

Lehman, Chester K.
   1998   *Biblical Theology: New Testament*. Scottdale, PA: Herald Press.

Lewis, I.M., ed.
   1966   *Islam in Tropical Africa*. London: Oxford University Press.

Lewis, P. Jack
   1958   "The Jewish Background of the Church." *Restoration Quarterly* 2(4):154-163.

Lienhard, Joseph T.
   1999   "Homily." In *Encyclopedia of Early Christianity*. 2nd edition. Everett Ferguson, ed. Pp. 539-540. New York: Garland Publishing Inc.

Lightner, R.P.
   1986   *Evangelical Theology*. Grand Rapids, MI: Baker Books.

Little, K.L.
   1960   "The Role of the Secret Society in Cultural Specialization." In *Cultures and Societies of Africa*. Simon and Phoebe Ottenberg, eds. Pp. 199-213. New York: Random House.

Longenecker, Richard N.
   1996   "Taking Up the Cross Daily: Discipleship in Luke-Acts." In *Patterns of Discipleship in the New Testament*. Richard N. Longenecker, ed. Pp. 50-76. Grand Rapids, MI: William B. Eerdmans.
   1999   *New Wine into Fresh Wineskins: Contextualizing the Early Christian Confessions*. Peabody, MA: Hendrickson Publishers.

Lugard, Frederick
   1965   *The Dual Mandate in British Tropical Africa*. London: Frank Cass. (Original: Blackwood and Sons, 1922.)
   1970   *Political Memoranda: Revision of Instructions to Political Officers on Subjects Chiefly Political and Administrative*. London: Frank Cass.

Luter, A.B., Jr
   1997   "Martyrdom." In *Dictionary of the Latter New Testament and Its Developments*. Ralph Martin and Peter Davids, eds. Pp. 717-722. Downers Grove, IL: InterVarsity Press.

Lynch, Hollis R.
   1967   *Edward Wilmot Blyden: Pan Negro Patriot, 1832-1912*. London: Oxford University Press.

MacCormac, Earl R.
   1960   "The Transition from Voluntary Missionary Society to the Church as a Missionary Organization among the American Congregationalists, Presbyterians, and Methodists." Ph.D dissertation, Yale University.

Mackay, John A.
   1957   *God's Order: The Ephesian Letter and This Present Time*. New York: Macmillan.

MacMullen, Ramsay
   1984   *Christianizing the Roman Empire, A.D. 100-400*. New Haven, CT: Yale University Press.

Macquarrie, John
   1946   *Principles of Christian Theology*. New York: Scribner.

MacQueen, James
   1822   *A Geographical and Commercial View of Northern Central Africa*. London: Oxford University Press.

Manson, T.W.
   1962   *Studies in the Gospels and Epistles*. Manchester, UK: Manchester University Press.

Manson, William
  1951   *The Epistle to the Hebrews: An Historical and Theological Consideration.* London : Hodder and Stoughton.
Marcel, Simon
  1986   *Versus Israel: A Study of the Relations between Christians and Jews in the Roman Empire (135-425).* H. McKeating, trans. Oxford: Oxford University Press.
Mare, W. Harold
  1976   *1 Corinthians.* Vol. 10 of *The Expositor's Bible Commentary.* Frank E. Gaebelein, ed. Pp. 175-297. Grand Rapids, MI: Zondervan Publishing House.
Marioghae, Michael, and John Ferguson
  1965   *Nigeria Under the Cross.* London: The Highway Press.
Marshall, I. Howard
  1980a *The Acts of the Apostles: An Introduction and Commentary.* Grand Rapids, MI: William B. Eerdmans.
  1980b *Last Supper and Lord's Supper.* Exeter: Paternoster Press.
Marshall, Ruth
  1993   "'Power in the Name of Jesus': Social Transformation and Pentecostalism in Western Nigeria Revisited." In *Legitimacy and the State in twentieth-Century Africa.* Terence Ranger and Olufemi Vaughan, eds. Pp. 213-246. London: The Macmillan Press Limited.
  1995   "'God Is Not a Democrat': Pentecostalism and Democratisation in Nigeria." In *The Christian Churches and the Democratisation of Africa.* Paul Gifford, ed. Pp. 239-260. Leiden: E.J. Brill.
Marshall-Fratani, Ruth
  1998   "Mediating the Global and Local in Nigerian Pentecostalism." *Journal of Religion in Africa* 28(3):278-315.
  2000   "Mediating the Global and Local in Nigerian Pentecostalism." In *Between Babel and Pentecost: Transnational Pentecostalism in Africa and Latin.* André Corten and Ruth Marshall-Fratani, eds. Pp. 80-105. Bloomington, IN: Indiana University Press.
Martin, James P.
  1987   "Toward a Post-Critical Paradigm." *New Testament Studies* 33:370-385.
Martyr, Justin
  n.d.   *1 Apology.* In *The Ante-Nice Fathers: The Writings of the Fathers Down to A.D. 325.* Vol. 1 (1978). Alexander Roberts and James Donaldson, eds. Pp. 159-187. Grand Rapids, MI: William B. Eerdmans.
  n.d.   *2 Apology.* In *The Ante-Nice Fathers: The Writings of the Fathers Down to A.D. 325.* Vol. 1 (1978). Alexander Roberts and James Donaldson, eds. Pp. 188-193. Grand Rapids, MI: William B. Eerdmans.

n.d. *Dialogue with Trypho*. In *The Ante-Nice Fathers: The Writings of the Fathers Down to A.D. 325*.Vol. 1 (1978). Alexander Roberts and James Donaldson, eds. Pp. 194-270. Grand Rapids, MI: William B. Eerdmans.

Mathieson, W.L.
1929 *Great Britain and the Slave Trade, 1839-1865*. London: Oxford University Press.

Maxwell, John C.
1995 *Developing the Leaders Around You*. Nashville, TN: Thomas Nelson Publishers.

McFague, Sallie
1975 *Speaking in Parables: A Study in Metaphor and Theology*. Philadelphia, PA: Fortress Press.
1982 *Metaphorical Theology: Models of God in Religious Language*. Philadelphia, PA: Fortress Press.

McGiffert, Arthur C.
1906 *A History of Christianity in the Apostolic Age*. Revised edition. New York: Charles Scribner's Sons.

McKenzie, P.R.
1976 *Inter-Religious Encounters in West Africa*. Leicester Studies in Religion, 1. Leicester: Blackfriars Press Limited.

Meade, David G.
1986 *Pseudonymity and Canon: An Investigation into the Relationship of Authorship and Authority in Jewish and Earliest Christian Tradition*. Tübingen, Germany: Mohr.

Medaiyese, J.A.
n.d. *Itan Igbedide, Woli Joseph Babalola Fun Işe Ihinrere* (A Life of Babalola). Ibadan, Nigeria.

Meeks, Wayne
1977 "In One Body: The Unity of Humankind in Colossians and Ephesians." In *God's Christ and His People*. Jacob Jervell and Wayne A. Meeks, eds. Pp. 209-221. Oslo, Norway: Universitetsforlaget.
1983 *The First Urban Christians: The Social World of the Apostle Paul*. New Haven, CT: Yale University Press.

Meillassoux, Claude, ed.
1971 *The Development of Indigenous Trade and Markets in West Africa*. London: Oxford University Press.

Mersch, Emile
1938 *The Whole Christ: The Historical Development of the Doctrine of the Mystical Body in Scripture and Tradition*. John R. Kelly, trans. London: Dennis Dobson.

Metzger, B.M.
: 1972 "Literary Forgeries and Canonical Pseudepigrapha." *Journal of Biblical Literature* 91:3-24.

Meyer, Harding
: 1999 *That All May Be One: Perceptions and Models of Ecumenicity*. Grand Rapids, MI: William B. Eerdmans.

Miers, Suzanne, and Igor Kopytoff, eds.
: 1977 *Slavery in Africa: Historical and Anthropological Perspectives*. Madison, WI: University of Wisconsin Press.

Milton, Yinger J.
: 1957 *Religion and the Individual: An Introduction to the Sociology of Religion*. New York: Macmillan.

Minear, Paul S.
: 1960 *Images of the Church in the New Testament*. Philadelphia, PA: Westminster Press.
: 1971 *The Obedience of Faith: The Purposes of Paul in the Epistle to the Romans*. Studies in Biblical Theology, 19. Naperville, IL: Alec R. Allenson.

Mitton, C. Leslie.
: 1976 *Ephesians*. New Century Bible, 49. London: Marshall, Morgan and Scott.

Mobley, Harris
: 1970 *The Ghanaian's Image of the Missionary*. New York: E.J. Brill.

Mockler-Ferryman, A.F.
: 1900 *British West Africa*. London: Oxford University Press.

Moffatt, James
: 1944 *The First Epistle of Paul to the Corinthians*. New York: Harper and Brothers.

Moltmann, Jürgen
: 1993 *The Church in the Power of the Spirit*. Minneapolis, MN: Fortress Press.

Moody, Dale
: 1981 *The Word of Truth*. Grand Rapids, MI: William B. Eerdmans.

Morris, Leon
: 1985 *1 Corinthians*. Tyndale New Testament Commentaries, 7. Revised edition. Grand Rapids, MI: William B. Eerdmans.

Morton-Williams, Peter
: 1960 "The Yoruba Ogboni Cult in Ọyọ." *Africa* 30(3):362-374.

Mudimbe, V.Y.
: *The Invention of Africa: Gnosis, Philosophy, and the Order of Knowledge*. Bloomington, IN: Indiana University Press.

Mulago, V.
    1965   *Un Visage Africain du Christianisme (The African Face of Christianity)*. Paris, France: Présence Africaine.

Munck, J.
    1959   *Paul and the Salvation of Mankind*. Richmond, VA: John Knox.

Murphy-O'Connor, J.
    1983   *St. Paul's Corinth: Texts and Archaeology*. Wilmington, DE: Michael Glazier.
    1984   "House Churches and the Eucharist." *Bible Today* 22:32-38.

Nair, Kannan
    1972   *Politics and Society in South Eastern Nigeria: 1841-1906*. London: Frank Cass.

Neill, Stephen
    1957   *The Unfinished Task*. London: Lutterworth Press.
    1966   *Colonialism and Christian Missions*. New York: McGraw-Hill Book Company.
    1970   "The Church." In *Concise Dictionary of the Christian World Mission*, Stephen Neil, Gerald H. Anderson, and John Goodwin, eds. Pp. 109-110. London: Lutterworth Press.
    1986   *A History of Christian Missions*. Harmondsworth, UK: Penguin Books.

Newbigin, Leslie
    1982   "Cross-Currents in Ecumenical and Evangelical Understandings of Mission." *International Bulletin of Missionary Research* 6:146-151.
    1989   *The Gospel in a Pluralist Society*. Grand Rapids, MI: William B. Eerdmans.

New Nigerian
    1986   "Shari'a Law in Nigeria." September 29. Lagos, Nigeria.

Newport, John P.
    1991   "The Purpose of the Church." In *The People of God: Essays on the Believers' Church*. Paul A. Basden and David S. Dockery, eds. Pp. 19-40. Nashville, TN: Broadman and Holman Publishers.

Nicholls, Bruce J., and Beulah R. Wood, eds.
    1996   *Sharing the Good News with the Poor*. Grand Rapids, MI: Baker Books.

Noel, Baptist
    1842   *Christian Missions to Heathen Nations*. London: SPCK.

Noll, Mark A.
    1994   *The Scandal of the Evangelical Mind*. Grand Rapids, MI: William B. Eerdmans.

O'Brien, Peter Thomas
    1999   *The Letter to the Ephesians*. Grand Rapids, MI: William B. Eerdmans.

O'Connor, Thomas
1970   *Outlined Notes on the Expansion of Baptist Work in Nigeria, 1850-1939*. Ibadan, Nigeria: The Caxton Press Limited.

O'Fahey, R.S.
1995   "The Past in the Present? The Issue of the Sharia in Sudan." In *Religion and Politics in East Africa*. Holger Bernt Hansen and Michael Twaddle, eds. Pp. 32-44. London: James Currey Limited.

Ofonagoro, W.I.
1978   *The Great Debate: Nigerians' Viewpoints on the Draft Constitution, 1976-77*. Lagos, Nigeria: Times Publications.

Ogundare, T.O., ed.
1993   *A Christian Church on the March: A History of the First Baptist Church, Isokun, Oyo, 1858-1992*. Ibadan, Nigeria: Vantage Publishers.

Ojo, G.J. Afolabi
1966   *Yoruba Palaces*. London: London University Press.

Ojo, John Odunayo
1988   *The Life and Ministry of Apostle Joseph Babalola*. Lagos, Nigeria: Prayer Band Publications.

Ojo, Matthews
1988   "Deeper Christian Life Ministry: A Case Study of the Charismatic Movements in Western Nigeria." *Journal of Religion in Africa* 18(2):141-162.
1992a "The Contextual Significance of the Charismatic Movements in Independent Nigeria." *Africa: Journal of the International African Institute*. 2(58):175-192.
1992b "Deeper Life Bible Church of Nigeria." In *New Dimensions in African Christianity*. Paul Gifford, ed. Pp. 135-156. Nairobi, Kenya: All African Conference of Churches.
1995   "The Charismatic Movement in Nigeria Today." *International Bulletin of Missionary Research* 19(3):114-118.
1996   "Charismatic Movements in Africa." In *Christianity in Africa in the 1990s*. A.F. Walls and Christopher Fyfe, eds. Pp. 92-110. Edinburgh, Scotland: Center of African studies, University of Edinburgh.
1999   "The Church in the African State: The Charismatic/Pentecostal Experience in Nigeria." *Journal of African Christian Thought* 1(2):25-32.
2001a "African Charismatics." In *Encyclopedia of African and African-American Religions*. Stephen D. Glazier, ed. Pp. 2-6. New York: Routledge.
2001b "Christ Apostolic Church." In *Encyclopedia of African and African-American Religions*. Stephen D. Glazier, ed. Pp. 84-86. New York: Routledge.

Ojo, Tunde
    1995   "Forty and Forceful: The Story of Foursquare in Nigeria." *Foursquare Advance*. Pp. 5-15. Lagos, Nigeria: Foursquare Gospel Church.

Okafor, Gabriel Maduka
    1992   *Development of Christianity and Islam in Modern Nigeria*. Würzburg, Germany: Echter.

Okorocha, Cyril
    1987   *The Meaning of Religious Conversion in Africa: The Case of the Igbo of Nigeria*. Avebury, England: Aldershot.

Olagunju, T., A. Jinadu, and S. Oyovbaire.
    1993   *Transition to Democracy in Nigeria, 1985-1993*. Ibadan, Nigeria: Safari and Spectrum.

Olisa, Michael S.O.
    1971   "Political Culture and Political Stability in Traditional Igbo Society." In *Igbo Traditional Life, Culture and Literature*. M.J.C. Echeruo and E.N. Obiechina, eds. Pp. 16-29. Austin, TX: Conch Magazine Limited.

Olojede, D.
    1986   "Trip to Fez." *Newswatch* 22(February):7.

Olson, Roger E.
    1999   *The Story of Christian Theology: Twenty Centuries of Tradition and Reform*. Downers Grove, IL: InterVarsity Press.

Olukayode, Akinsanya
    2000   "'You Shall Receive Power': The Establishment of the Pentecostal Movement in the Nigerian Context." Ph.D. dissertation, Drew University.

Olupona, Jacob K., ed.
    2000   *African Spirituality: Forms, Meanings and Expressions*. New York: The Crossroad Publishing Company.

Omoyajowo, J. Akinyele
    1982   *Cherubim and Seraphim: The History of an African Independent Church*. New York: NOK Publishers.

Omoyajowo, J. Akinyele, ed.
    1994   *The Anglican Church in Nigeria: 1842-1992*. Lagos, Nigeria: Macmillan.

O'Neill, J.C.
    1961   *The Theology of Acts in its Historical Setting*. London: SPCK.

O'Neill, J.G.O.
    1930   *Ancient Corinth*. Oxford: Oxford University Press.

Onishi, Norimitsu
    2002   "Africans Fill Churches That Celebrate Wealth." *The New York Times* 13(March):1-4.

Ononyemu, Lugard
1993 "Stop the Delphic Games! Another Demonic Invasion Looms on Nigeria." *True Light* 1(1):40-41.

Origen
n.d. *Against Celsus*. In *The Ante-Nice Fathers: The Writings of the Fathers Down to A.D. 325*.Vol. 4 (1978). Alexander Roberts and James Donaldson, eds. Pp. 395-669. Grand Rapids, MI: William B. Eerdmans.
n.d. *Exhortation to Martyrdom*. Rowan A. Greer, trans. (1979). New York: Paulist Press.
n.d. *On First Principles*. In *The Ante-Nice Fathers: The Writings of the Fathers Down to A.D. 325*.Vol. 4 (1978). Alexander Roberts and James Donaldson, eds. Pp. 239-382. Grand Rapids, MI: William B. Eerdmans.

Oritsejafor, Ayo
1993 "Jesus on the Offensive." Message preached at the Lagos National Theatre, May 13, 1993. Lagos, Nigeria.

Oroge, E.A.
1971 "The Institution of Slavery in Yorubaland, with Particular Reference to the Nineteenth Century." Ph.D. dissertation, University of Birmingham.

Osaghae, Eghosa E.
1998 *Crippled Giant: Nigeria since Independence*. Bloomington, IN: Indiana University Press.

Oshun, C.O.
1981 "Christ Apostolic Church of Nigeria: A Suggested Pentecostal Consideration of its Historical, Organizational and Theological Developments, 1918-1975." Ph.D. dissertation, University of Exeter.

Paden, J.N.
1986 *Ahmadu Bello, Sardauna of Sokoto: Values and Leadership in Nigeria*. Zaria, Nigeria: Hudahuda Publishing Company.

Page, Jesse
1908 *The Black Bishop: Samuel Adjai Crowther*. London: Hodder and Stoughton.

Pagels, Elaine
1976 *The Gnostic Gospels*. New York: Random House.

Parliamentary Papers
1985 "Report of the Select Committee on the State of British Settlement in West Africa."

Parrinder, Geoffrey
1953 *Religion in an African City*. London: Oxford University Press.

Peel, J.D.Y.
- 1968 *Aladura: A Religious Movement Among the Yoruba*. London: Oxford University Press.
- 1983 *Ijeshas and Nigerians: The Incorporation of a Yoruba Kingdom, 1890s-1970s*. London: Cambridge University Press.
- 2000 *Religious Encounter and the Making of the Yoruba*. Bloomington, IN: Indiana University Press.

Perkins, Pheme
- 1999a "Docetism." In *Encyclopedia of Early Christianity*. 2nd edition. Everett Ferguson, ed. Pp. 341-342. New York: Garland Publishing.
- 1999b "Gnosticism." In *Encyclopedia of Early Christianity*. 2nd edition. Everett Ferguson, ed. Pp. 465-469. New York: Garland Publishing.

Perrot, C.
- 1983 "Worship in the Primitive Church." *Concilium* 162:3-9.

Phillips, Arthur, ed.
- 1953 *Survey of African Marriage and Family Life*. London: Oxford University Press.

Pityana, N.
- 1973 "What is Black Consciousness?" In *Black Theology: The South African Voice*. B. Moore, ed. Pp. 58-63. Atlanta, GA: John Knox Press.

Pliny
- n.d. *Letters*. Betty Radice, trans. (1969). Cambridge, MA: Harvard University Press.

Polhill, John B.
- 1999 *Paul and His Letters*. Nashville, TN: Broadman and Holman Publishers.

Polycarp
- n.d. *Martyrdom of Polycarp*. In *The Apostolic Fathers*. Vol. 2 (1913). Kirsopp Lake, trans. Pp. 307-345. Cambridge, MA: Harvard University Press.

Porter, Andrew
- 1976 "Evangelical Enthusiasm, Missionary Motivation and West Africa in the Late Nineteenth Century: The Career of G.W. Brooke." *The Journal of Imperial and Commonwealth History* 6(1):23-46.

Preston, Geoffrey, O.P.
- 1995 *Faces of the Church: Meditations on a Mystery and Its Images*. Grand Rapids, MI: William B. Eerdmans.

Radamacher, E.D.
- 1972 *What the Church is All About*. Chicago, IL: Moody Press.

Rahner, Karl
- 1967 *The Christian of the Future*. New York: Herder and Herder.

1983   *The Shape of the Church to Come*. New York: Crossroad. (Original: Seabury Press, 1974).

Rambo, Lewis R.
1993   *Understanding Religious Conversion*. New Haven, CT: Yale University Press.

Rashid, S.K., ed.
1988   *Islamic Law in Nigeria: Application and Teaching*. Lagos, Nigeria: Islamic Publications Bureau.

Ray, Benjamin C.
1976   *African Religions: Symbol, Ritual, and Community*. Englewood, NJ: Prentice-Hall.
1993   "Aladura Christianity: A Yoruba Religion" *Journal of Religion in Africa* 23(3):266-291.

Reasoner, Mark
1995   "The Theology of Romans 12:1-15:13." In *Pauline Theology*. Vol. 3. David M. Hay and E. Elizabeth Johnson, eds. Pp. 287-299. Minneapolis, MN: Fortress Press.
1997   "Persecution." In *Dictionary of the Latter New Testament and Its Developments*. Ralph Martin and Peter Davids, eds. Pp. 907-914. Downers Grove, IL: InterVarsity Press.

Richardson, Cyril C., ed.
1996   *Early Christian Fathers*. New York: Touchstone.

Roberts, J.W.
1972   "The Meaning of *Ekklesia* in the New Testament." *Restoration Quarterly* 15:27-36.

Robinson, D.W.B.
1965   *The Church of God*. Sydney, Australia: Jordan.

Robinson, J.A.
1889   Letter to Lang. CMS, G3/A3/04, June 20. CMS Archives.
1890   Letter to Lang. CMS, G3/A3/122, August 5. CMS Archives.

Robinson, J.T.
1960   *On Being the Church in the World*. Philadelphia, PA: Westminster Press.

Robinson, James M., ed.
1988   *The Nag Hammadi Library in English in English*. 3rd edition. San Francisco, CA: Harper-SanFrancisco.

Roelofs, Gerard
1994   "Charismatic Christian Thought: Experience, Metonymy, and Routinization." In *Charismatic Christianity as a Global Culture*. Karla Poewe, ed. Pp. 217-233. Columbia, SC: University of South Carolina Press.

Routh, Eugene
    1958   "Foreign Mission Board of the Southern Baptist Convention." In *Encyclopedia of Southern Baptists*. Vol. 1. Pp. 457-474. Nashville. TN: Broadman Press.

Rudolph, Kurt
    1983   *Gnosis: The Nature and History of Gnosticism*. Robert M. Wilson, ed. and trans. San Francisco, CA: Harper-SanFrancisco.

Ruether, Rosemary R.
    1974   *Faith and Fratricide: The Theological Roots of Anti-Semitism*. New York: The Seabury Press.

Rusch, William, ed.
    1980   *The Trinitarian Controversy*. Philadelphia, PA: Fortress Press.

Ryder, A.F.C.
    1960   "Missionary Activity in the Kingdom of Warri to the Early Nineteenth Century." *Journal of the Historical Society of Nigeria* 2(1):1-20.
    1961   "The Benin Missions." *Journal of the Historical Society of Nigeria* 2(2):231-259.

Ryken, Leland, James C. Wilhoit, and Tremper Longman III, eds.
    1998   *Dictionary of Biblical Imagery*. Downers Grove, IL: InterVasity Press.

Sambo, Yusuf
    1990   "In Support of Babangida." *The African Gurdian*, June 18.

Samples, Bob
    1976   *The Metaphoric Mind: A Celebration of Creative Consciousness*. Reading, MA: Addison-Wesley Publishing Company.

Sampley, J. Paul
    1993   "Ephesians." In *The Deutero-Pauline Letters: Ephesians, Colossians, 2 Thessalonians, 1-2 Timothy, Titus*. Proclamation Commentaries. Revised edition. Gerhard Krodel, ed. Pp. 1-23. Minneapolis, MN: Fortress Press.

Sandlay, William, and Arthur C. Headlam
    1902   *A Critical and Exegetical Commentary on the Epistle to the Romans*. 5th edition. Edinburgh, Scotland: T and T Clark.

Sanneh, Lamin
    1983   *West African Christianity: The Religious Impact*. Maryknoll, NY: Orbis Books.
    1987   "Christian Missions and the Western Guilt Complex." *The Christian Century* 104(11):330-334.
    1989   *Translating the Message: The Missionary Impact on Culture*. Maryknoll, NY: Orbis Books.
    1991   "The Yogi and the Commissar: Christian Missions and the African Response." *International Bulletin of Missionary Research* 15(1):2-11.

1993   *Encountering the West*. Maryknoll, NY: Orbis Books.
1997   *Piety and Power: Muslims and Christians in West Africa*. Maryknoll, NY: Orbis Books.

Sasime, Ibiba
1976   "The Church Missionary Society and the Establishment of British Rule in Nigeria, 1849-1894." Ph.D. dissertation, University of Nebraska.

Saucy, Robert
1972   *The Church in God's Program*. Chicago, IL: Moody Press.
1993   *The Case for Progressive Dispensationalism*. Grand Rapids, MI: Zondervan Publishing House.

Schacht, Joseph
1959   *The Origins of Mohammedan Jurisprudence*. Oxford: Clarendon Press.

Schaff, Philip
1858   *History of the Christian Church*. Vol. 2. New York: Charles Scribner's Sons.

Schillebeeckx, Edward
1996   *Church: The Human Story of God*. New York: Crossroad.

Schlorff, Sam
2000   "The Translational Model for Mission in Resistant Muslim Society: A Critique and an Alternative." *Missiology* 28(3):305-328.

Schmidt, Wilhelm
1931   *The Origin and Growth of Religion*. London: Methuen and Company Limited.

Schmithals, Walter
1971   *Gnosticism in Corinth: An Investigation of the letters to the Corinthians*. John E. Steely, trans. New York: Abingdon Press.
1997   *The Theology of the First Christians*. O.C. Dean, Jr., trans. Louisville, KY: Westminster/John Knox Press.

Schnackenburg, Rudolf
1965   *The Church in the New Testament*. Montreal, Canada: Palm Publishers.
1991   *The Epistle to the Ephesians*. Helen Heron, trans. Edinburgh, Scotland: T and T Clark.

Schön, J.F., and S.A. Crowther
1970   *Journals of the Rev. James Frederick Schön and Mr. Samuel Crowther*. London: Frank Cass and Company. (Original: 1842.)

Schultze, Quentin J.
1991   *Televangelism and American Culture: The Business of Popular Religion*. Grand Rapids, MI: Baker Books.

Schwarz, Christian A.
   1999   *Paradigm Shift in the Church: How Natural Church Development Can Transform Theological Thinking.* Carol Stream, IL: ChurchSmart Resources.

Seeberg, Reinhold
   1956   *Textbook of the History of Doctrines.* Vol. 1. Charles E. Hay, trans. Grand Rapids, MI: Baker Books.

Segovia, Fernando F.
   1985   "Introduction: Call and Discipleship—Toward a Re-examination of the Shape and Character of Christian Existence in the New Testament." In *Discipleship in the New Testament.* Fernando F. Segovia, ed. Pp. 1-23. Philadelphia, PA: Fortress Press.

Seifrid, Mark A.
   1992   *Justification by Faith: The Origin and Development of a Central Pauline Theme.* New York: E. J. Brill.

Setzer, Claudia
   1994   *Jewish Responses to Early Christians: History and Polemics 30-150 C.E.* Minneapolis, MN: Fortress Press.

Shaull, Richard, and Waldo Cesar
   1996   *Pentecostalism and the Future of the Christian Churches.* Grand Rapids, MI: William B. Eerdmans.

Sheldon, Henry C.
   1895   *History of the Christian Church.* Vol. 1. New York: Thomas Y. Crowell and Company.

Shenk, Wilbert R.
   1975   *Bibliography of Henry Venn's Printed Writings with Index.* Scottdale, PA: Herald Press.
   1977   "Henry Venn's Instructions to Missionaries." *Missiology* 5(4):467-485.
   1983   *Henry Venn—Missionary Statesman.* Maryknoll, NY: Orbis Books.
   1995   *Write the Vision: The Church Renewed.* Harrisburg, PA: Trinity Press International.
   1996   "Toward a Global Church History." *International Bulletin of Missionary Research* 20(2):50-57.
   1997   "Mission, Renewal, and the Future of the Church." *International Bulletin of Missionary Research* 21(4):154-159.
   1999   *Changing Frontiers of Mission.* Maryknoll, NY: Orbis Books.
   2001   "Recasting Theology of Mission: Impulses from the Non-Western World." *International Bulletin of Missionary Research* 25(3):98-107.

Shepperson, George, and Thomas Price
   1958   *Independent Africa.* Edinburgh, Scotland: Edinburgh University Press.

Sherwin-White, A.N.
    1969   *Roman Society and Roman Law in the New Testament*. Oxford: Clarendon Press.

Sider, Robert
    1999   "Tertullian." In *Encyclopedia of Early Christianity*. 2nd edition. Everett Ferguson, ed. Pp. 1107-1108. New York: Garland Publishing.

Simon, Marcel
    1969   "The Apostolic Decree and its Setting in the Ancient Church." *Bulletin of John Rylands Library* 52:437-460.

Smith, Donald Eugene
    1990   "The Limits of Religious Resurgence." In *Religious Resurgence and Politics in Contemporary World*. E. Sahliyeh, ed. Pp. 34-39. Albany, NY: State University of New York Press.

Soards, Marion L.
    1999   *1 Corinthians*. Peabody, MA: Hendrickson Publishers.

Søgaard, Viggo
    1996   *Research in Church and Mission*. Pasadena, CA: William Carey Library.

Soskice, Janet
    1985   *Metaphor and Religious Language*. Oxford: Clarendon Press.

Spittler Russell
    1990   "Theological Style among Pentecostals and Charismatics." In *Doing Theology in Today's World*. John D. Woodbridge and Thomas E. McComiskey, eds. Pp. 291-318. Grand Rapids, MI: Zondervan Publishing.

Srawley, J.H.
    1947   *Early History of the Eucharist*. 2nd edition. Cambridge, UK: Cambridge University Press.

Stanley, Brian
    1990   *The Bible and the Flag: Protestant Missions and British Imperialism in the Nineteenth and Twentieth Centuries*. Leicester, UK: Apollos.

Stark, Rodney
    1996   *The Rise of Christianity: A Sociologist Reconsiders History*. Princeton, NJ: Princeton University Press.

Stendahl, Krister
    1962   "Contemporary Biblical Theology." In *Interpreter's Dictionary of the Bible*. Vol. 1. George A. Buttrick, ed. Pp. 418-431. Nashville, TN: Abingdon Press.
    1967   "Judaism and Christianity II: After a Colloquium and a War." *Harvard Divinity Bulletin* 1:2-9.

Stewart, William
   1958   *The Nature and Calling of the Church*. Mysore City, India: Wesley Press.

Stock, Eugene
   1899   *The History of the Church Missionary Society, Its Environment, Its Men, and Its Work*. 4 vols. London: CMS.

Strabo
   1932   *The Geography of Strabo*. Vol. 8. Horance Leonard Jones, trans. Cambridge, MA: Harvard University Press.

Sumitra, Bishop
   1955   "Comments on Polygamy." Lagos, Nigeria. Quoted in Michael Marioghae and John Ferguson, *Nigeria Under the Cross*. London: The Highway Press, 1965.

Sunday Tribune
   1990   "CAN and the Cabinet Reshuffle." April 23. Lagos, Nigeria.

Sundkler, Bengt
   1961   *Bantu Prophets in South Africa*. London: Oxford University Press.

Sundkler, Bengt, and Christopher Steed
   2000   *The History of the Church in Africa*. Cambridge, UK: Cambridge University Press.

Sword of the Spirit Ministries
   1986   *Sword of the Spirit*. No. 27. Ibadan, Nigeria.

Synan, Vinson, ed.
   2001   *The Century of the Holy Spirit: 100 Years of Pentecostal and Charismatic Renewal, 1901-2001*. Nashville, TN: Thomas Nelson Publishers.

Tacitus
   n.d.   *Annales*. In *Tacitus: Selections from His Works*. Frank Burr Marsh and Harry J. Leon, eds. (1936). Norman, OK: University of Oklahoma Press.

Talbert, Charles H.
   1977   *What Is a Gospel? The Genre of the Canonical Gospels*. Philadelphia, PA: Fortress Press.
   1981   "The Gospel and the Gospels." In *Interpreting the Gospels*. J.L. Mays, ed. Pp. 14-26. Philadelphia, PA: Fortress Press.
   1985   "Discipleship in Luke-Acts." In *Discipleship in the New Testament*. Fernando F. Segovia, ed. Pp. 62-75. Philadelphia, PA: Fortress Press.

Talbot, Percy A.
   1969   *The Peoples of Southern Nigeria*. Vol. 3. London: Frank Cass and Company.

Tasie, G.O.M.
 1978 *Christian Missionary Enterprise in the Niger Delta, 1864-1918*. Leiden: E.J. Brill.
 1982 "The Prophetic Calling: Garrick Sokari Braide of Bakana." In *Varieties of Christian Experience in Nigeria*. Slizabeth Isichei, ed. Pp. 99-115. London: Macmillan.

Tate, W. Randolph
 1997 *Biblical Interpretation: An Integrated Approach*. Revised edition. Peabody, MA: Hendrickson Publishers.

Taylor, Nicholas
 1991 *Paul, Antioch and Jerusalem: A Study in Relationships and Authority in Earliest Christianity*. Sheffield: Sheffield Academic Press.

Temples, P.
 1959 *Bantu Philosophy*. Paris, France: Presence Africaine.

Tertullian
 n.d. *Against Praxeas*. In *The Ante-Nice Fathers: The Writings of the Fathers Down to A.D. 325*.Vol. 3 (1978). Alexander Roberts and James Donaldson, eds. Pp. 597-627. Grand Rapids, MI: William B. Eerdmans.
 n.d. *Apology*. In *The Ante-Nice Fathers: The Writings of the Fathers Down to A.D. 325*.Vol. 3 (1978). Alexander Roberts and James Donaldson, eds. Pp. 17-55. Grand Rapids, MI: William B. Eerdmans.
 n.d. *The Prescription*. In *The Ante-Nice Fathers: The Writings of the Fathers Down to A.D. 325*.Vol. 3 (1978). Alexander Roberts and James Donaldson, eds. Pp. 243-265. Grand Rapids, MI: William B. Eerdmans.
 n.d. *To the Martyrs*. In *The Ante-Nice Fathers: The Writings of the Fathers Down to A.D. 325*.Vol. 3 (1978). Alexander Roberts and James Donaldson, eds. Pp. 693-696. Grand Rapids, MI: William B. Eerdmans.

The Economist
 1993 "Survey." August 21:14.

Theissen, Gerd
 1982 *The Social Setting of Pauline Christianity: Essays on Corinth*. Philadelphia, PA: Fortress Press.

Tidball, Derek
 1984 *The Social Context of the New Testament: A Sociological Analysis*. Grand Rapids, MI: Academie Books, Zondervan Publishing House.

Townsend, Henry
 1843 "Journal on a Mission of Research." CMS, CA1/0215, January 5. CMS Archives.
 1851a Letter to Henry Venn. CMS, CA2/085, October 21. CMS Archives.

1851b   Letter to Major Straight. CMS, CA2/016, October 29. CMS Archives.
1857   Letter to Henry Venn. CMS, CA2/085, July 21. CMS Archives.

Trimingham, J. Spencer
1956   *The Christian Church and Islam in West Africa*. London: SCM Press.
1959   *Islam in West Africa*. Oxford: Clarendon Press.
1968   *The Influence of Islam upon Africa*. London: Longmans.

Tucker, Ruth A.
1983   *From Jerusalem to Irian Jaya*. Grand Rapids, MI: Zondervan Publishing House.

Turaki, Yusufu
1995   "The Socio-Political Context of Christian-Muslim Encounter in Northern Nigeria." *Studies in World Christianity* 3(2):121-137.

Turner, Harold W.
1965   *Profile through Preaching*. London: Edinburgh House Press.
1967   *History of an Independent African Church: The Church of the Lord (Aladura)*. 2 vols. London: Oxford University Press.
1979   *Religious Innovation in Africa: Collected Essays on Religious Movements*. Boston, MA: GK Hall and Company.

United Nations Development Programme
1997   *MicroStart: A Guide for Planning, Starting and Managing a Microfinance Programme*. Version 1.0. New York: United Nations.

Van der Ven, Johannes A.
1996   *Ecclesiology in Context*. Grand Rapids, MI: William B. Eerdmans.

Van Engen, Charles E.
1996   *Mission on the Way: Issues in Mission Theology*. Grand Rapids, MI: Baker Books.

Van Hooff, Anton
1990   *From Euthanasia to Suicide: Self-Killing in Classical Antiquity*. London: Routledge.

Van Unnik, W.C.
1959   "Dominus Vobiscum: The Background of a Liturgical Formula." In *New Testament Essays in Memory of T.W. Manson*. A.J.B. Higgins, ed. Pp. 270-305. Manchester: Manchester University Press.

Vaughan, Idris
1991   *Nigeria: The Origins of Apostolic Church Pentecostalism, 1931-52*. London: Ipswich Book Company.

Venn, Henry
1851   "Minute Upon the Employment and Ordination of Native Teachers." CMS, G/AZ1/1, no. 71. CMS Archives.
1858   Letter to Samuel Crowther. CMS, CA3/L2, July 22. CMS Archives.
1862   *The Missionary Life and Labours of Francis Xavier*. London: Longman.

1864a Letter to Lamb. CMS, CA2/L3, January 23. CMS Archives.
1864b Letter to Missionaries in the Yoruba Mission. CMS, CA2/L3, July 23. CMS Archives.
1865a *Retrospect and Prospect of the Operations of the Church Missionary Society*. 2nd edition. London: CMS.
1865b Letter to Townsend. CMS, CA2/L3, September 22. CMS Archives.

Verkuyl, Johannes
1978 *Contemporary Missiology: An Introduction*. Dale Cooper, trans. Grand Rapids, MI: William B. Eerdmans.

Volf, Miroslav
1998 *After Our Likeness: The Church as the Image of the Trinity*. Grand Rapids, MI: William B. Eerdmans.

Von Dobschütz, Ernst
1904 *Christian Life in the Primitive Church*. George Bremner, trans. New York: G. P. Putnam's Sons.

Wach, Joachim
1944 *Sociology of Religion*. Chicago, IL: University of Chicago Press.

Waddell, H.M.
1863 *Twenty-Nine Years in the West Indies and West Africa*. London: Cambridge University Press.

Wagner, C. Peter
1998 *The New Apostolic Churches*. Ventura, CA: Regal Books.

Wainwright, G.
1997 "Lord's Supper, Lord's Feast." In *Dictionary of the Latter New Testament and Its Developments*. Ralph Martin and Peter Davids, eds. Pp. 686-694. Downers Grove, IL: InterVarsity Press.

Walker, F. Deaville
1930 *The Romance of the Black River*. London: CMS.

Walker, Williston
1959 *A History of the Christian Church*. New York: Charles Scribner's Sons.

Walls, Andrew F.
1980 "Missionary Vocation and the Ministry: The First Generation." In *The History of Christianity in West Africa*. Ogbu U. Kalu, ed. Pp. 22-35. London: Longman.
1992 "The Legacy of Samuel Ajayi Crowther." *International Bulletin of Missionary Research* 16(1):15-21.
1996 *The Missionary Movement in Christian History*. Maryknoll, NY: Orbis Books.
2002 *The Cross-Cultural Process in Christian History*. Maryknoll, NY: Orbis Books.

Walls, Andrew F., and Christopher Fyfe, eds.
    1996   *Christianity in Africa in the 1990s*. Edinburgh, Scotland: Center of African studies, University of Edinburgh.

Warburton, J.
    1842   "Instructions of Local Committee." November 9. CMS, CA1/0218. CMS Archives.
    1844   "Instructions of Local Committee." October 25. CMS, CA2/11. CMS Archives.

Ward, R. Bowen
    1958   "Ekklesia: A Word Study." *Restoration Quarterly* 2(4):164-179.

Warren, Max
    1971   *To Apply the Gospel: Selections from the Writings of Henry Venn*. Grand Rapids, MI: William B. Eerdmans.

Watson, Francis
    1970   "The Two Roman Congregations: Romans 14:1-15:13." In *The Romans Debate*. Karl Donfried, ed. Pp. 203-215. Peabody, MA: Hendrickson Publishers.
    1986   *Paul, Judaism and the Gentiles: A Sociological Approach*. Cambridge, UK: Cambridge University Press.
    1994   *Text, Church, and World: Biblical Interpretation in Theological Perspective*. Grand Rapids, MI: William B. Eerdmans.

Weber, Max
    1994   *Political Writings*. Peter Lassman and Ronald Speirs, eds. Cambridge, UK: Cambridge University Press.

Webber, Robert E.
    1978   *Common Roots: A Call to Evangelical Maturity*. Grand Rapids, MI: Zondervan Publishing House.

Webster, J.B.
    1964   *The African Churches Among the Yoruba*. London: Oxford University Press.

Wedderburn, A.J.M.
    1988   *The Reasons for Romans*. Edinburgh, Scotland: T and T Clark.

Weiss, J.
    1937   *The History of Primitive Christianity*. New York: Wilson-Erikson.

Wesselschmidt, Quentin
    1988   "The Concept and Practice of the Ministry in the Early Church: Structure, Formative Influences, and Scriptural Correspondence." *Concordia Journal* 14:248-265.

West, Martin
    1975   *Bishop and Prophets in a Black City*. Cape Town, South Africa: David Philip.

Wheelwright, Philip.
   1962   *Metaphor and Reality*. Bloomington, IN: Indiana University Press.

Wiefel, Wolfgang
   1993   "The Jewish Community in Ancient Rome and the Origins of Roman Christianity." In *The Romans Debate*. Karl P. Donfried, ed. Pp. 85-101. Peabody, MA: Hendrickson Publishers.

Wikenhauser, Alfred
   1963   *New Testament Introduction*. New York: Herder and Herder.

Wiles, Maurice
   1991   "Orthodoxy and Heresy." In *Early Christianity: Origins and Evolution to A.D. 600*. Ian Hazlet, ed. Pp. 198-207. Nashville, TN: Abingdon Press.

Wilkie, Arthur
   1911   "Minutes of the Calabar Conference." Calabar, Nigeria: CCN.

Wilkins, Michael J.
   1995   *Discipleship in the Ancient World and Matthew's Gospel*. Grand Rapids, MI: Baker Books.

Wilkinson, J.
   1974   "Ancient Jerusalem, Its Water Supply and Population." *Palestine Exploration Quarterly* 106:33-51.

Williams, George H.
   1956   "The Ministry of the Ante-Nicene Church." In *The Ministry in Historical Perspective*. H. Richard Niebuhr and Daniel D. Williams, eds. Pp. 27-59. San Francisco, CA: Harper and Row.

Williams, C. Peter
   1986   "From Church to Mission: An Examination of the Official Missionary Strategy of the Church Missionary Society on the Niger, 1887-93." In *Voluntary Religion*. W.J. Sheils and Diana Wood, eds. Pp. 391-409. London: Blackwell.
   1990   *The Ideal of the Self-Governing Church: A Study in Victorian Missionary Strategy*. New York: E.J. Brill.
   2000   "'Not Transplanting': Henry Venn's Strategic Vision." In *The Church Mission Society and World Christianity 1799-1999*. Kevin Ward and Brian Stanley, eds. Pp. 147-172. Grand Rapids, MI: William B. Eerdmans.

Williams, Robert Lee
   1999   "Persecution." In *Encyclopedia of Early Christianity*. 2nd edition. Everett Ferguson, ed. Pp. 895-899. New York: Garland Publishing.

Winter, Bruce
   1978   "The Lord's Supper at Corinth: An Alternative Reconstruction." *Reformed Theological Review* 37:73-82.

1991 "Civil Litigation in Secular Corinth and the Church: A Forensic Background to 1 Corinthians 6: 1-8." *New Testament Studies* 37:559-572.

Wisse, Frederik
1971 "The Nag Hammadi Library and the Heresiologists." *Vigiliae Christianae* 25:205-223.

Wobo, M. Sam
1955 *A Brief Résumé of Dr. J.O. Oshitelu* Shagamu, Nigeria: Ibukunola Printers.

Wood, A. Skevington
1978 "Ephesians." In *The Expositor's Bible Commentary*. Vol. 11. Frank E. Gaebelein and J.D. Douglas, eds. Pp. 3-92. Grand Rapids, MI: Zondervan Publishing House.

Wood, J.B.
1880 Report after a Visit to the Niger Mission in 1880. CMS, CA3/04. CMS Archives.

Wood, W.J., ed.
1965 *Christian Union Movements in Nigeria*. Ibadan, Nigeria: Daystar Press.

Woodward, E.L.
1916 *Christianity and Nationalism in the Later Roman Empire*. London: Longmans.

Woodward, Kenneth L.
2001 "The Changing Face of the Church." *Newsweek* 16(April):46-52.

Yamamori, Tetsunao, Bryant L. Myers, Kwame Bediako, and Larry Reed, eds.
1996 *Serving with the Poor in Africa*. Monrovia, CA: MARC.

Yates, Timothy E.
1978 *Venn and Victorian Bishops Abroad: The Missionary Policies of Henry Venn and Their Repercussion upon the Anglican Episcopate of the Colonial Period, 1841-1872*. London: SPCK.

Zahn, Theodor
1909 *Introduction to the New Testament*. John Moore Trout, et al. trans. Edinburgh, Scotland: T and T Clark.

Index

Abacha, Sanni, 151, 153
Abati, Reuben, 212-213
Abba, Yusufu, 175
Abeokuta, 43-46, 64, 80-81, 104
Abiara, S.K., 107
Abimbola, Wande, 113
Abiola, Moshood, 198
Abrams, M.H., 294
Abubakar, Abdulsalami, 151
Achebe, Chinua, 53
Adamo, D.T., 225
Adeboye, E.A., 107, 142, 145
Adegboyega, S.G., 104, 106, 109-110, 140
Adejobi, Emmanuel A., 127
Adekola, Moses Akinwumi, 139, 145
Ademakinwa, J.A., 104
Adogame, Afeosemime U., 102
African, xix, xx, 1-2, 7, 9, 14-16, 18, 20-21, 23-24, 27-29, 31-33, 40-44, 46, 48, 50, 52, 54-55, 57, 59-60, 62-70, 72-74, 76, 79, 82-85, 87-88, 91, 93-102, 104-105, 108, 111-114, 117, 120-121, 123-126, 130, 137-139, 142, 148, 151, 158, 162, 166, 168-169, 174, 177, 191, 201, 206, 212, 216-218, 221, 328, 351, 354, 362-363, 379, 389-391
African agents, 15, 55, 66-67, 69-70, 72, 82, 217-218, 221

African Church Bethel, 69-70
African Church Organization, 98
African Guardian, The, 201
Agbaje, Adigun, 194
Agbẹbi, Mọjọla, 72, 96-98
Agbeti, Kofi, 52
Ajayi, J.F. Ade, 14-15, 20, 25, 32, 34-35, 40-42, 50, 53-54, 62-65, 67, 73, 85, 94, 125, 140, 145, 162, 353
Ajayi, Olusola, 14-15, 20, 25, 32, 34-35, 40-42, 50, 53-54, 62-65, 67, 73, 85, 94, 125, 140, 145, 162, 353
Akindayomi, Josiah Olufemi, 139-140, 144-145, 162
Akinjogbin, I.A., 11
Akinsanya, Gbolahan Olukayode, 104, 110
Akinsowon, Abiodun, 105
Akinyele, Isaac (Olubadan), 55, 102, 104, 106, 108-110
Akpaekong, Obong, 145
Aku, 43
Aladura, xix, 96, 99-103, 105-133, 138, 149, 165, 167, 170, 185, 212, 380, 390
Aland, Kurt, 314
Aledeino, Rev., 184
Alokan, Adeware, 104, 121, 129

Anderson, Allan H., 58, 93, 99, 113, 126, 130
Anglican (see also CMS), 15, 33-35, 45, 55, 58, 63-64, 68, 70, 75, 78-79, 95, 97, 99, 102-104, 107, 110, 126, 138-139, 146, 212-213, 217, 224-225, 380
Angus, Samuel, 305-306, 310
apologists, 123, 312, 326, 330-334
Apostolic Faith Mission, 139-140, 146
Apter, Andrew, 152-153, 198
Armstrong, James, 386
Ashcroft, J.A., 66
Assemblies of God (AOG), 138, 140
Atanda, J.A., 55
Athenagoras, 333-334
Aune, David, 336, 338
Awolowo, Obafemi, Chief, xx, 179
Ayandele, E.A., 14, 32, 34, 49, 53, 67, 73, 81, 83, 85, 88, 95, 97-98, 100, 132
Azikiwe, Nnamdi, Chief, 179
Babalola, Joseph Ayodele, 105-106, 109-110, 119, 129
Babangida, Ibrahim Badamosi, 149, 151, 153, 188, 197-202, 204
Badagry, 33, 39, 43-45
Badejo, Wilson, 186
Badger, Carl, 309
Baëta, C.G., 89
Baikie, William, Dr., 47
Baird, William, 272-273, 275-276
Baker, Jim, 142
Baker, Robert A., 39
Balás, David, 310
Balewa, Tafawa, 151
Bankole, Olusegun, 140
Banks, Robert, 48, 296
Barber, Karin, 128

Barna, George, 371-373
Barrett, C.K., 272
Barrett, David B., 93, 135-136
Barr, James, 233
Bascom, William, 19
Bauer, Walter, 308-309
Baur, Ferdinand C., 257
Baus, Karl, 321, 326, 343, 347
Bediako, Kwame, 350, 361, 387
Beecroft, J., 13
Bello, Ahmadu, Sir, 179-185, 204
Benin, 11, 24, 33-34, 104
Best, Ernest, 78, 83, 96, 99, 118, 174, 178, 188, 197-198, 200, 205, 213, 228, 245-246, 260, 281, 283, 291-292, 295, 299, 309, 324, 334, 340, 346, 348, 360, 373, 380
Bevans, Stephen B., 124
Beyerhaus, P., 130
biblical, xix, xx, 2-4, 26, 77, 116-117, 119, 123, 126, 146, 149, 155-156, 160, 163, 212, 225, 228, 231-234, 236, 241, 249, 255-256, 272-273, 284, 292-294, 299, 301, 322, 342-343, 347, 350, 353-364, 366, 371, 373-374, 377, 379, 381, 387
Biobaku, O. Saburi, 14, 85
Birai, Umar M., 193-194
Blaising, Craig A., 240
Blevins, W.L., 244
Blyden, Edward, 95-97
Bock, Darrell L., 240
Boer, Harry, 241, 243
Boer, Jan H., 149, 206
Bornkamm, Günther, 259
Bosch, David, 305, 312, 356-358, 361, 386-387

Bowen, Thomas J., 27, 39, 45-46, 50-51, 72, 86, 237-239
Bowersock, G.W., 326
Boyejo, James Abayomi, 140
Braide, Garrick, 101, 138
Brand, Consul, 21, 93, 98, 138, 384
British Apostolic Church (BAC), 109, 138, 142
Broneer, Oscar, 267
Brooke, G.W., 67-69, 94
Broshi, M., 244
Brouwer, Steve, 153, 368
Brown, Raymond, 98, 234
Bruce, F.F., 260, 275, 288, 387
Brueggemann, Walter, 121-122
Brunner, Emil, 233, 249
Buhari, Muhammadu, 151, 153
Burks, Edgar H., 39, 86
Butler, Bishop, 34
Caird, G.B., 241
Campbell, J.Y., 234
Campbell, W.S., 260
Castelot, J.J., 256
Catholic Bishops of Nigeria, 196
Cauthen, Baker James, 39
Celestial Church of Christ (CCC), 102, 384
Celsus, 123, 311, 334, 343, 346-347
Chadwick, Henry, 329-330
Chafer, Lewis Sperry, 240
Chamberlin, John S., 341
Charismatic/Pentecostal churches, 1, 133, 136-137, 143, 212, 354, 368, 372, 380
Charlesworth, James H., 314-315
Cherubim and Seraphim (C & S), 102, 105, 139, 144
Chirenje, J. Mutero, 93
Chow, John K., 270-271, 274
Christ Apostolic Church (CAC), 101-102, 104, 107, 110-111, 118, 121, 129-130, 138-139, 384
Christian Association of Nigeria (CAN), 1, 3, 7, 23, 25, 40, 45-46, 53-54, 58, 62, 65, 70-72, 75, 79, 84, 86-87, 94, 96-97, 99-100, 105, 108, 113, 116-118, 120, 122-124, 126, 128-129, 132-133, 140, 143, 145, 151, 155-156, 158, 160, 165, 167-168, 171, 175, 184-190, 192, 200-202, 204-205, 213, 218, 223, 226-228, 231, 236, 239, 244-246, 255-256, 262, 267, 274-275, 282, 285-287, 289, 291, 293-295, 297-299, 308, 310, 313, 316, 320, 322-323, 325-328, 331, 340, 347-348, 355-357, 360-361, 363-364, 368, 371, 373, 375-376, 378-382, 385-386, 388-389, 391
Christian Council of Nigeria (CCN), 217-219, 223
Christianization, 3, 7, 9, 29-30, 33, 47, 55, 57, 72, 83, 178, 215
Chukwu (Chineke), 25
Church Missionary Society (CMS), 15, 33, 35-36, 49, 59, 63-64, 66, 68, 76-77, 83-84, 216
Church of God Mission, 142, 144
Church of the Lord (Aladura), xix, 96, 99-103, 105-133, 138, 149, 165, 167, 170, 185, 212, 380, 390
Clapham Sect, the, 35
Clarke, Pastor, 105
Clarke, Peter B., 28, 49
Clarkson, Thomas, 35
Clement of Alexandria, 123, 312
Clinton, J. Robert, 372

Clowney, Edmund P., 294
Colley, W.W., Rev., 47
Collins, Travis M., 55
colonial, 40, 54, 58, 60, 81, 84-85, 87-89, 104, 108-109, 138, 150, 152, 173, 176-179, 190-191, 221
Committee of Correspondence, 66
contextual, xx, 2-4, 60, 116, 124, 141, 154, 170, 241, 245-246, 250-251, 255, 259, 261, 264, 269, 271, 274, 278, 281, 299, 303-304, 350, 353-354, 356-357, 359-366
contextual ecclesiology, 2, 60, 241, 299, 350, 354, 356-357, 359-366
contextualization, 89, 115, 118, 120, 124, 252-253, 354, 357-360, 362-364
Cooke, Bernard, 320-322, 329
Cook, Henry, 70
Cook, Norton A., 41
Cooper, Frederick, 21
Corten, André, 167
Cranfield, C.E.B., 257-259
Crook, J.A., 275
Crouzel, Henri, 344
Crowther, Samuel A., 15, 23, 25-26, 41-42, 45, 47-50, 54, 62-70, 77, 84, 94-95, 125, 353
Crumbley, D.H., 121
Culpepper, Hugo H., 287
culture, xix, xx, 1-2, 7, 10-11, 18, 24, 26, 28-29, 32, 64, 77, 82, 84-85, 88-89, 93, 96, 101, 111-112, 114-115, 117, 122-124, 131-132, 137, 147-148, 153-154, 161, 168, 193, 197-198, 214, 227, 272-273, 292, 304, 310-312, 343, 348, 350, 353-355, 357, 368, 372, 380
Cyprian, 326
Dahl, N.A., 273, 283-284
Dan Fodio, Usman, 28, 175-176, 180-181
Danker, F.W., 289-290
David-West, Tonye, 386
David, W.J., Rev., 47, 62, 73, 84, 86, 93, 98, 103, 126-127, 135-136, 144, 166, 194, 196, 243-244, 252-253, 287, 292, 305, 310, 312, 314, 336, 338, 356-358, 361-362, 386-387
Dean, J.T., 28, 120, 221, 235, 238, 241, 252, 362-363
Deeper Life, 107, 142-146, 155-156, 162-164, 169, 377-378
de Graft, William, 44
democracy, 10, 144, 152, 171, 188, 198
Desai, Ram, 85
Didache, the, 247, 320, 335, 337-338, 340
Dike, K.O., 19
Dillistone, F.W., 283
Dobinson, Henry H., Archdeacon, 69-70
Dodd, C.H., 281
Donfried, Karl, 255, 260, 341
Doresse, Jean, 308
Dove, Thomas, Rev., 44
Driver, John, 106, 295
Droge, A., 326
Dulles, Avery, 293
Dunn, James D.G., 234, 238, 246, 251-252, 260, 263-266, 273-274
Duval, Louis M., 55, 87
early Christians, 115, 236, 306, 314-315, 318, 328, 335-337, 361, 364

Early Church, xix, 228, 233, 244, 262, 277, 303-306, 308-310, 314, 316, 318-319, 322, 324, 326, 329-330, 334-335, 338-339, 342, 350, 355, 360, 366
ecumenism, 3, 171, 173, 181, 185-186, 205, 211, 213, 216, 221, 223, 227-230
Edema, A., 187
Edinburgh Conference, 216
Edwards, James, 265
Ehrman, Bart D., 306-309, 315, 333, 336, 341
Ejiwumi, Theophilus, 140
ekklēsia, 233-241, 243-244, 291, 379, 390
Ekpe (Egbo), 13
Elsbree, Oliver W., 36
Elton, S.G., Rev., 142
emirs, 49-50, 177-178, 182
Engels, D., 275
Enuwosa, J., 225
Enwerem, Iheanyi, 176, 182-183, 185-187, 197, 201, 203-204
episcopate, 55, 58, 63, 94, 320-321, 323
Erickson, Millard J., 292
Ethiopianism, 93, 95, 366
Eusebius, 327
Evans, G.R., 228, 282, 286, 291
Fage, J.D., 20, 24
Fahy, T., 258
Falola, Toyin, 149-151, 153, 174, 180-182, 195-196, 200, 206
Fee, Gordon, 35, 239, 267, 275
Felix, Minucius, 334
Ferguson, Everett, 234, 236, 324, 327, 336, 338
Ferguson, John, 79, 215, 224
Fergusson, James, 44

Field, Barbara, 59, 65, 71, 120, 148, 150, 187, 219, 233, 249, 296, 364
Findlay, George G., 234, 266
First Republic, 151, 180, 184-185, 190-192, 194-195, 198
Fisher, Humphrey J., 112
Flint, J.E., 18
Foakes-Jackson, F.J., 244
Fortescue, Chichester, 16
Foster, R.S., 59, 105, 158, 191, 214, 217, 219, 248, 321
Foursquare Gospel Church, 139-140, 186
Foxe, John, 327-328
Franke, John R., 124
Freeman, Thomas Birch, 44, 215
Frend, W.H.C., 304, 320
Freston, Paul, 173, 227
Gager, John G., 306
Gallagher, J., 40
Gamble, Harry, 331, 333-334
Gammell, William, 38
Garland, David E., 287, 292
Garlock, Ruthanne, 142
Garnsey, P., 275
Garrett, T.S., 214, 220, 224-225
Gerhart, Mary, 294
Getu, Makonen, 388
Gibbs, Eddie, 370, 372, 374, 378, 381-382, 390
Gifford, Paul, 153, 368
Giles, Kevin, 233, 236
Gilliland, Dean S., 28-29, 120, 235, 238, 241, 252, 362-364
Glasser, Arthur F., 379
Gnosticism, 301, 308, 310, 312-313, 361
Gollmer, C.A., 16, 45, 62
González, Justo L., 308, 346

Goodykoonthz, Colin B., 36
Goppelt, Leonard, 231, 301, 361
Gowon, Yakubu, 151
Grant, Charles, 35, 383
Grenz, Stanley J., 124, 356
Grillmeier, Aloys, 345
Grove, Andrew S., 390
Groves, C.P., 35, 43, 47, 216
Grudem, Wayne, 293
Guinness, Os, 380
Guthrie, Donald, 243, 256
Hägglund, Bengt, 335, 343, 345-347, 350
Hanciles, Jehu J., 40, 54, 60, 95, 97
Hanson, Richard, 325
Hanson, Stig, 284
Harden, Sarah, 46, 72-73
Harnack, Adolf Von, 313
Harries, Lyndon, 16
Harrison, Everett F., 241, 248, 271, 273
Harwood, J.R., 218
Hastings, Adrian, 98, 100, 106
Hausa, 28-29, 48, 50-51, 175-176
Hawthorne, Gerald F., 238-239, 267-268, 277, 280-281, 359
Haynes, Jeff, 29, 197
Headlam, Arthur C., 256, 258-259
Heidegger, Martin, 147
Hellenism, 276, 301, 303, 310, 342, 349, 360-361, 375
Hennecke, Edgar, 315
Henson, Hensley, 274
Herford, R. Travers, 306
Hermas, 337
hermeneutic, 70, 123, 126, 266, 355-356, 359, 366
hermeneutical bridge, 101, 354, 357
Hesselgrave, David J., 252-253, 362
Hewitt, Gordon, 83

Hiebert, D. Edmond, 256, 268
Hiebert, Frances F., 88
Hiebert, Paul G., 114, 354, 357
Hinderer, Anna, 62, 83-84, 127
Hinderer, David, 62, 83-84, 127
Hippolytus, 327
Hodgkin, T., 179
Hopkins, A.G., 21
Hopkins, Samuel, 36
Horbury, William, 307
Hort, F.J.A., 233-234, 236-238
Horton, Robin, 112
Hulen, A.B., 306
Hutchinson, E., 15, 66-67
Ibadan, 45, 64, 80, 104, 106-107, 109, 141, 158-159, 223
Ibiam, Akanu, 140
Idahosa, Benson, 142
Idowu, Bolaji, 26, 83, 113, 117, 226-227
Ifemesia, C.C., 40
Igboho, 45-46
Ige, O., 106
Ignatius, 320-323, 326-327, 336, 338-339
Ijaye, 22, 46
Ilesanmi, Simeon, 189, 196
Ilesha, 104, 106-107, 109
independency, 1, 3, 70, 72-73, 90, 93-95, 98-101, 114, 170
indigenous, 1, 3, 7, 16, 20-21, 23, 25, 27-29, 32, 52-54, 58-59, 61, 63-65, 69, 74, 80, 83, 85, 88-89, 91, 94, 97-98, 100-101, 112, 116, 124-125, 131, 133, 138, 141, 149, 167, 175-177, 205, 211-212, 218, 305-306, 354
indirect rule, 176-177
Irenaeus, 339
Ironsi, Aguiyi, 151

Isaacson, Alan, 143, 146
Isichei, Elizabeth, 51
Jaja of Opobo, King, 23
Jeffery, R.M.C., 214, 220, 224-225
Jerusalem Act, 63
Jervell, Jacob, 260
Jinadu, A., 144
Johnson, Harry, 44
Johnson, James (Holy Johnson), 80, 95-97, 100
Johnson, Luke T., 242, 271-272, 276, 285, 288-289, 358
Johnson, Nita Lafond, 369
Johnson, Samuel, 11
Johnston, George, 175-176, 236
John, William, 35, 66, 79, 106, 124, 129, 215, 224, 240, 245, 253, 257, 260, 270-271, 274, 282, 293, 295, 306, 327-328, 337, 341, 373, 385
Jones, G.I., 19, 308
Jungmann, Josef A., 336
Kalabari, 22, 50
Kalu, Ogbu, 26, 94, 104, 137, 140-141, 161, 168-169, 191, 197, 206, 212, 214-215, 217, 221-227, 379, 390
Kano, Aminu, Alhaji, 48, 104, 179, 206
Kantiok, James, 176
Karlström, Mikael, 179
Kasdorf, Hans, 111
Käsemann, E., 234, 261, 263, 358
Kearney, Michael, 7
Keay, E., 195
Keller, Charles R., 36
Kelly, J.M., 275
Kelly, J.N.D., 305, 311, 313, 335, 337, 347-348
Kennedy, George, 341

Kenny, Joseph, 188, 194
Kilmartin, Edward J., 336
King, P., 244
King, Roberta, 117
King, Theophilus, 61
Kipo Hill, 50
Klein, Martin, 21
Knight, William, 36, 58, 77
Knox, W.L., 241
Kopytoff, Igor, 21
Kouzes, James M., 371, 373
Kukah, Matthew Hassan, 175, 181-184, 187-189, 194-195, 200
Kumuyi, William F., 107, 142-143, 145-146, 156, 162-165, 169, 378
Küng, Hans, 280, 282, 293, 297-298, 322, 365,
Ladd, George E., 241, 244, 248
Laird, Macgregor, 41, 47
Lake, K., 244
Lang, R., 67-68, 94
Larbi, E. Kingsley, 379
LaRue, Cleophus J., 126
Lassman, Peter, 202-203
Latin, David, 167, 173, 194, 196, 227, 259, 348
Layton, Bentley, 308
Lehman, Chester K., 241, 249
Lewis, I.M., 28, 111-112, 240
Lightner, R.P., 233
Lindsay, Gordon, 142
Little, K.L., 7, 13, 17-18, 52, 67, 78-79, 87, 95, 116, 136, 150-151, 155, 164, 185, 249, 262, 294, 311, 316, 330, 335, 369, 381
Lokoja, 41, 49
Longenecker, Richard N., 375
Longman III, Tremper, 284
Lugard, Frederick, Lord, 153, 177

Macaulay, G.L., 109
Macaulay, T.B., 61
Macaulay, Zachary, 35
MacCormac, Earl R., 36
MacMullen, Ramsay, 330
Macquarrie, John, 293
MacQueen, James, 41
Manson, T.W., 258-259
Marcel, Simon, 253, 306, 332
Mare, W. Harold, 279
Marioghae, Michael, 79, 215, 224
Marshall-Fratani, Ruth, 148, 155, 157, 159, 163, 165
Marshall, I. Howard, 247, 277
Marshall, Ruth, 152, 158, 160, 169, 368, 374, 378, 384
Martin, James P., 21, 99, 147, 238-239, 267-268, 277, 280-281, 359, 391
Martin, Ralph P., 21, 99, 147, 238-239, 267-268, 277, 280-281, 359, 391
martyrdom, 319, 323, 325-328, 330
Martyr, Justin, 312, 327-330, 332-334, 336-340
martyrs, 325-328
Mathieson, W.L., 41
Maxwell, John C., 373
McFague, Sallie, 294
McGiffert, Arthur, 241, 249, 270
McKenzie, P.R., 84
Meade, D.G., 314
Medaiyese, J.A., 106
Meeks, Wayne, 264, 267, 271
Meillassoux, Claude, 21
Mensah, S.A., 109
Mersch, Emile, 298
Meyer, Harding, 228-229
Miers, Suzanne, 21
missiology, 74, 89, 124, 368

missional, xx, 2-3, 224, 287, 350, 353, 366-367, 370
missionary (ies), 3, 7, 9, 14-15, 17-18, 27-28, 32-55, 57-68, 71-78, 80-90, 94-95, 97-98, 100, 105, 110, 116, 123-125, 142, 178, 214-216, 218-220, 223, 226, 241, 243, 257, 267, 269, 287, 319, 328-331, 341, 353-354, 367-370, 374, 378-379, 387
mission churches, 93, 101, 104, 112, 119, 125
mission(s), xx, 1-2, 4, 7, 9-10, 14, 20, 29, 31-40, 42-55, 57-60, 63-75, 77-78, 80-81, 83-89, 93-97, 99-102, 104, 112, 119, 123-125, 133, 139-140, 142, 144, 146-147, 166-167, 175, 181, 212, 214-222, 227, 229-230, 235, 238, 241, 246-247, 251-252, 255, 260, 270, 274, 286-287, 289-291, 294-295, 301, 305-307, 312-313, 351, 353-358, 360-362, 367-368, 370-371, 374, 376-379, 386-391
Mitton, C. Leslie, 282, 292
Mobley, Harris, 85
Mockler-Ferryman, A.F., 41
Moffatt, James, 270
Mohammed, Murtala, 151
Moltmann, J‚rgen, 386
Moody, Dale, 289
Morris, Leon, 278
Morton-Williams, Peter, 14
Mueller, J.R., 314
Munck, J., 258
Murphy-O'Connor, J., 267, 277,
Myers, Bryant L., 387
Nair, Kannan, 13
nationalism, 66, 89, 93-98, 179, 308

native ministry, 57-60, 69
ndi oha, 10
Neill, Stephen, 59-60, 89, 95, 247, 267, 374
Nero, 260, 318
Newbigin, Leslie, 355, 363, 389
Nicholls, Bruce J., 387
Niger, the, 10, 14, 19-20, 22, 25, 39, 41-42, 47-52, 60, 64, 66-70, 80, 94-97, 100-101, 215-216, 220
Noel, Baptist, 75
Northern Christian Association (NCA), 183-185
Obadare, D.O., 107
Obasanjo, Olusegun, 151, 160, 204
O'Connor, Thomas, 55
Odubanjo, David, 103-104, 106, 109-110
Oduduwa, 11
Odunaike, Samuel Olusegun, 110, 140
Odunlami, Sophia, 103
Ofonagoro, W.I., 194
Ogbomosho, 46
Ogboni Fraternity, the, 14, 83
Ogundare, T.O., 55
Oha, 10
Ojo, John Odunayo, 106, 129
Ojo, Matthews, xx, 110, 141-143, 158, 166
Ojo, Tunde, 140
Ojukwu, Odumegu, 184
Oke, Francis Wale, 106, 158-159, 384
Okogie, Anthony Olubunmi, 187, 204, 386
Okorocha, Cyril, 132
Olagunju, T., 144
Olodumare (God), 117
Olojede, D., 199

Olorun (*Eleda*), 26
Olson, Roger E., 123, 343-344, 356
Olukayode, Akinsanya, 104, 110
Omoyajowo, J. Akinyele, 55, 102
Onasinwo, 104
O'Neill, J.C., 247, 267
Onishi, Norimitsu, 386
Ononyemu, Lugard, 153
Organization of Islamic Conference (OIC), 149, 160, 186, 188, 197, 199-200
Origen, 123, 311-312, 326-327, 330, 334-335, 341-349, 361
Oritsejafor, Ayo, 165, 204
Oroge, E.A., 80
Osborne, T.L., 142
Oshitelu, Josiah, 102, 107-108, 121
Oshokoya, Timothy Gbadebo, 139
Oshun, C.O., 102
Osuwa, Friday Chinyere, 140
Oyovbaire, S., 144
Paden, J.N., 180-182
Page, Jesse, 42, 49
Pagels, Elaine, 308
Parrinder, Geoffrey, 14, 83
Paul, St., 83, 258, 266-267, 273, 277
Peel, J.D.Y., 11, 22, 26, 83, 96, 102-103, 107, 109, 112, 116, 119, 121, 127-131
Pentecostal Fellowship of Nigeria (PFN), 160
Pentecostalism, 107, 109, 130, 133, 135-140, 142-143, 145, 148, 152, 155, 157, 159, 161, 163, 165, 167, 169, 212, 368, 374, 378, 384, 386
Pepple, King, 50
Perfect, George, 109, 345, 384
Perkins, Pheme, 313
Perrot, C., 336

persecutions, Christians, 315-316, 318, 321, 326, 328, 332
Phillips, Arthur, 16, 79
Pityana, N., 85
Plato, 310, 332, 343
Pliny, the governor, 317, 336
Polhill, John, 253, 257, 260, 274
polygamy, 16-17, 29, 76-79, 82, 85, 108
Porter, Andrew, 67
Posner, Barry Z., 371, 373
Praxeas, 348-349
pre-Christian, 3, 7, 9, 16, 19, 28-29
Precious Stone Society, 102-103, 110
Price, Thomas, 93, 384
prophetic Christianity, 100-101
Protestant Missions, 31, 33-34, 42, 52, 84-85, 88-89, 94, 175, 216, 220, 354
pseudepigrapha, 310, 314
Pythagoras, 332
Quadratus, 330, 333
Radamacher, E.D., 233
Rahner, Karl, 379
Rambo, Lewis R., 111-112
Rashid, S.K., 195
Ray, Benjamin C., 27, 118, 127-128, 131-132
Reasoner, Mark, 264, 318, 327
Redeemed Christian Church of God (RCCG), 3, 107, 139-140, 142, 144-146, 162
Reed, Larry, 387
Reid, Daniel G., 238-239, 267-268, 277, 280-281, 359
Richardson, Cyril C., 321
Richardson, S., 195
Roberts, J.W., 234, 236-237
Robinson, D.W.B., 233
Robinson, J.A., 68, 94

Robinson, James M., 308
Robinson, J.T., 229
Roelofs, Gerard, 163
Rommen, Edward, 252-253, 362
Rose, Susan D., 23, 100, 107, 153, 333-334, 368
Routh, Eugene, 39, 46, 71
Rusch, William, 347
Russell, Allan, 136-137, 294
Ryder, A.F.C., 34
Ryken, Leland, 284
Sadare, 130
Salifu, Samuel, 201
Sambo, Yusuf, 197
Sampley, J. Paul, 288
Sandlay, William, 256, 258-259
Sanneh, Lamin, 32, 52, 67, 70, 73, 87, 95-102, 104, 111, 122-125, 130, 175, 178, 189, 193
Saucy, R., 233, 240
Schacht, Joseph, 195
Schaff, Philip, 313-314, 320, 325, 328, 330, 339-340
Schillebeeckx, Edward, 230
Schlorff, Sam, 362
Schmithals, Walter, 296
Schnackenburg, Rudolf, 229, 240-241, 248, 282-283, 285-286, 288, 290, 294-296, 298
Schön, James Frederick (J.F.), Rev., 26, 41-42
Schultze, Quentin J., 161
Second Republic, 151, 184, 191-194, 196-197
Seeberg, Reinhold, 309
Setzer, Claudia, 306
Shagari, Shehu, Alhaji, 151, 153
Sharia, 175, 185-186, 188, 191-197, 199, 204

Index

Shenk, Wilbert R., 54, 58, 68, 75-76, 123, 213, 229-230, 351, 367-371, 379, 388
Shepperson, George, 93
Shonekan, Ernest, 151
Sider, Robert, 348
Sierra Leone, 13, 40-44. 47, 59-60, 62
Simon, Marcel, 253, 306, 332
Slavery, 20-24, 40, 76, 78, 80-81
Slave trade, 20, 24, 39-41, 215
Sodeke, Chief, 44-45
Somoye, 107
Southern Baptist, 27, 33, 36, 38-39, 45-47, 55, 70-72, 80, 97
Speirs, Ronald, 202
Srawley, J.H., 338
Stanley, Brian, 75, 88, 124, 136, 354, 356
Stark, Rodney, 326
Steed, Christopher, 184
Stendahl, Krister, 307, 362, 364-365
Stephen, James, 35, 59-60, 89, 95, 124, 374
Stewart, William, 234-235
Stock, Eugene, 35, 66, 77, 367
Stone, Moses Ladejo, 46, 68, 72-73, 94, 98, 102-105, 110
Strabo, 268
Student Christian Movement (SCM), 140-141
Sudan Interior Mission (SIM), 215, 217
Sudan United Mission (SUM), 168, 215, 222-223, 282
Sumitra, Bishop, 79-80, 222
Sundkler, Bengt, 93, 99, 121, 184
Synan, Vinson, 135
Tabor, J., 326
Tacitus, 317-318
Talbert, Charles H., 375-378
Tasie, G.O.M., 67
Tate, W. Randolph, 357
Taylor, J.C., 47-48, 72
Taylor, Nicholas, 273
Teignmouth, Lord, 35
Tertullian, 326-328, 330, 334-335, 342, 347-349
The Apostolic Church of Nigeria (TAC), 102, 106-111, 138, 140, 241, 248, 253, 271, 273
Theissen, Gerd, 267, 270, 273, 277
Third Republic, 194, 197-198
Tidball, Derek, 272
Townsend, Henry, 44-45, 61-63, 215
Trajan, Emperor, 317-318, 336
Trimingham, J. Spencer, 28-29, 175
Trypho, 329, 332-334, 339
Turaki, Yusufu, 88, 177
Turner, Harold W., 99, 102, 104, 108, 112, 119, 121, 126
umunna, 10-11
United Nations Development Programme, 387
United Native African Church, 69-70, 98, 100
Van Engen, Charles, 287, 371
Vaughan, Idris, 72, 109
Vaughn, J.C., 46
Venn, Henry, 23, 36, 42, 54-55, 57-65, 67-68, 70, 75-77, 79, 94, 125, 218
Venn, John, Rev., 35
Verkuyl, Johannes, 368
Vincent, David Brown, 96, 98
Volf, Miroslav, 291
Von Dobschütz, Ernst von, 250, 277,
Wach, Joachim, 25
Wagner, C. Peter, 372
Wainwright, G., 338-339

Walker, F. Deaville, 47
Walker, Williston, 324, 342-343, 347
Walls, Andrew F., 34-35, 50, 87, 100, 125, 131, 178, 351, 374, 389, 391
Warburton, J., 44-45
Ward, R. Bowen, 237-240
Warren, Max, 58, 65, 77
Watson, Francis, 265, 356-357, 360
Weber, Max, 202-203
Webster, J.B., 67, 72-74, 95-96, 98-99
Wedderburn, A.J.M., 260-261
Wesselschmidt, Quentin, 323-324
West, Martin, 11, 14, 16, 18-21, 24, 28-29, 32, 40-41, 49, 51-52, 61, 63-64, 67, 70, 73, 80, 84, 87, 93, 95-97, 99-102, 104, 111, 123, 130, 152, 162, 174-175, 178-179, 193, 215-216, 219-221, 223, 268, 335, 342, 348-349, 351, 391
Wheelwright, Philip, 294
Wiefel, Wolfgang, 257, 260-261
Wikenhauser, Alfred, 256
Wilberforce, William, 35, 44
Wiles, Maurice, 303-304
Wilhoit, James C., 284
Wilkie, Arthur, 216
Wilkinson, J., 244
Williams, Peter, 58, 60, 67, 316, 318, 324
Williams, Robert Lee, 58, 60, 67, 316, 318, 324
Wisse, Frederik, 308
Wobo, M. Sam, 107
Wood, A. Skevington, 282
Wood, Beulah R., 387
Wood, Jonathan (J.B.), 66-67
Wood, W.J., 213

Yamamori, Tetsunao, 387
Yates, Timothy E., 58, 60
Yoruba, 9, 11-12, 14-15, 19, 22, 24, 26-27, 42-46, 48, 50, 64-67, 72-73, 77-78, 80-84, 95-96, 98-99, 101-102, 104, 107, 111-114, 116-118, 125, 127-129, 131-132, 155, 179, 217, 220